I0021366

The Definitive Guide to Data Integration

Unlock the power of data integration to efficiently manage, transform, and analyze data

Pierre-Yves BONNEFOY

Emeric CHAIZE

Raphaël MANSUY

Mehdi TAZI

The Definitive Guide to Data Integration

Group Product Manager: Kaustubh Manglurkar
Publishing Product Manager: Apeksha Shetty
Book Project Manager: Kirti Pisat
Senior Editor: Nazia Shaikh
Technical Editor: Kavyashree K S
Copy Editor: Safis Editing
Proofreader: Safis Editing
Indexer: Rekha Nair
Production Designers: Jyoti Kadam and Gokul Raj S.T
Senior DevRel Marketing Executive: Nivedita Singh

First published: March 2024

Production reference: 1070324

Published by
Packt Publishing Ltd.
Grosvenor House
11 St Paul's Square
Birmingham
B3 1RB, UK

ISBN 978-1-83763-191-9

www.packtpub.com

To my incredible wife, Mélanie, whose unwavering support and encouragement have been my guiding star through every choice and challenge. And to my precious children, Ewann and Kléo, who bring boundless joy and purpose to every moment. Every moment with you is a treasure. With all my love.

– Pierre-Yves BONNEFOY

To my beloved wife, Laure, whose unwavering support and shared wisdom continually light my way. To my children, Henri, Hugo, and Timothée, who constantly refresh my perspective and bring joy to my days. And to my parents, whose profound wisdom and nurturing have sculpted the core of my being.

– Emeric CHAIZE

To the amazing women in my life: my mother, Khadija, whose love and sacrifices have shaped me into the person I am today; you have my eternal respect. To my irreplaceable wife, Hind, my anchor in the storm, who stands by me in every situation; life is better because we're going through it together. To my precious daughters, Ayah and Mayssa, the apples of my eye; you inspire me to be better every day. To my father, Mohamed, for all his life lessons, and to my in-laws for being so welcoming and kind.

– Mehdi TAZI

Foreword

My journey into the data integration world started in 1998 when the company where I served as a database consultant was acquired by an American software vendor specializing in this field. Back then, the idea of a graphical ETL solution seemed far-fetched; drawing lines with a mouse between sources and target components to craft data movement interfaces for analytical applications appeared unconventional. We were accustomed to developing code in C++, ensuring the robustness and performance of applications. Data warehouses were fed through batch-mode SQL processes, with orchestration and monitoring managed in shell scripts.

Little did we anticipate that this low-code, no-code ETL solution would evolve into a standard embraced by global companies, marking the onset of the data integration revolution. The pace was swift. Growing data volumes, expanding sources to profile, operational constraints, and tightening deadlines propelled changes in data tools, architectures, and practices. Real-time data integration, data storage, quality, metadata and master data management, enhanced collaboration between business and technical teams through governance programs, and the development of cloud-based applications became imperative challenges for data teams striving for operational excellence.

The past 25 years flashed by, and the revolution persists, keeping my passion for data ablaze. The rise of artificial intelligence, exemplified by the success of ChatGPT, necessitates vast data processing for model building. This, in turn, compels a deeper reliance on data engineering techniques. Authored by seasoned data professionals with extensive project deployments, this book offers a comprehensive overview of data integration. My sincere gratitude to them, Pierre-Yves, Emeric, Raphael, and Mehdi, for crafting this invaluable resource! Covering essential concepts, techniques, and tools, this book is a compass for every data professional seeking to create value and transform their business. May your reading journey be as enjoyable as mine!

In our data-driven era, the ability to seamlessly integrate, manage, and derive insights from diverse data sources is paramount. This book embarks on a journey through the intricate landscape of data integration, from its historical roots to the cutting-edge techniques shaping the modern data stack.

We begin by unraveling the essence of data integration, emphasizing its transformative impact on industries and decision-making processes. Navigating through the complexities of our contemporary data landscape, we explore the challenges and opportunities that beckon innovation.

This book is not just about theory; it's a practical guide. We delve into the nuts and bolts of data integration, from defining its core concepts to understanding the nuances of the modern data stack. We examine the tools, technologies, and architectures that form the backbone of effective integration, ensuring a technology-agnostic foundation for enduring relevance.

As we trace the evolution of data integration through history, we shine a spotlight on open source technologies, acknowledging their transformative role in democratizing data. The exploration extends to diverse data sources, types, and formats, preparing you to navigate the intricacies of real-world data integration scenarios.

The chapters unfold progressively, equipping you with skills to tackle the challenges posed by different data architectures and integration models. From workflow management to data transformation, data exposition to analytics, each section builds on the last, providing a comprehensive understanding of the intricacies involved.

The journey concludes with a forward-looking gaze into the future of data integration, exploring emerging trends, potential challenges, and avenues for continued learning.

We invite you to embark on this exploration, empowering yourself with the knowledge and skills to master the dynamic world of data integration.

Happy reading!

Stephane Heckel

Data Sommelier

DATANOSCO

https://www.linkedin.com/in/stephaneheckel/

Contributors

About the authors

Pierre-Yves BONNEFOY is a versatile data and cloud architect boasting over 20 years of experience across diverse technical and functional domains. With an extensive background in software development, systems and networks, data analytics, and data science, Pierre-Yves offers a comprehensive view of information systems. As the CEO of Olexya and CTO of Africa4Data, he dedicates his effort to delivering cutting-edge solutions for clients and promoting data-driven decision-making. As an active board member of French Tech Le Mans, Pierre-Yves enthusiastically supports the local tech ecosystem, fostering entrepreneurship and innovation while sharing his expertise with the next generation of tech leaders. You can contact him at pybonnefoy@olexya.com.

Emeric CHAIZE, with over 16 years of experience in data management and cloud technology, demonstrates a profound knowledge of data platforms and their architecture, further exemplified by his role as president of Olexya, a data architecture company. His background in computer science and engineering, combined with hands-on experience, has honed his skills in understanding complex data architectures and implementing efficient data integration solutions. His work at various small and large companies has demonstrated his proficiency in implementing cloud-based data platforms and overseeing data-driven projects, making him highly suited for roles involving data platforms and data integration challenges. You can contact him at echaize@olexya.com.

Raphaël MANSUY is a seasoned technology executive and entrepreneur with over 25 years of experience in software development, data engineering, and AI-driven solutions. As a founder of several companies, he has demonstrated success in designing and implementing mission-critical solutions for global enterprises, creating innovative technologies, and fostering business growth. Raphaël is highly skilled in AI, data engineering, DevOps, and cloud-native development, offering consultancy services to Fortune 500 companies and start-ups alike. He is passionate about enabling businesses to thrive using cutting-edge technologies and insights. You can contact him at raphael.mansuy@elitizon.com.

Mehdi TAZI is a data and cloud architect with over 12 years of experience and the CEO of an IT consulting and investment company. He specializes in distributed information systems and data architecture. He navigates through both platform and application facets. Mehdi designs information systems architectures that answer customers' needs by setting up technical, functional, and organizational solutions, as well as designing and coding in languages such as Java, Scala, or Python. You can contact him at mehdi@tazimehdi.com/tazimehdi.com.

About the reviewers

David Soyez, a seasoned senior data and cloud architect, boasts 25 years of diverse experience spanning numerous projects in service companies and direct client engagements. Renowned for his expertise in deploying, maintaining, and auditing complex decision-making platforms, particularly on IBM and AWS technologies, David excels at swiftly adapting to new or ongoing projects, ensuring seamless integration and process mastery. His broad technical and functional knowledge makes him an invaluable asset in the ever-evolving world of data and cloud architecture.

Sam Bessalah has been an Independent Architect, with more than 12 years of experience in building data platforms in multiple industries across Europe. From companies like Criteo, Algolia, Euronext, LeBonCoin (Adevinta), Deutsche Borse, Axa or Decathlon.Passionate about distributed systems, database architectures, data processing engines, and Data Engineering. An early user and developer on Big Data platforms like Hadoop or Spark, he helps his clients and partners build efficient data pipelines with modern data tools, focusing on aligning business value with data architecture.

John Thomas, a data analytics architect and dedicated book reviewer, combines his passion for data and technology in his work. He has successfully designed and implemented data warehouses, lakes, and meshes for organizations worldwide. With expertise in data integration, ETL processes, governance, and streaming, John's eloquent book reviews resonate with both tech enthusiasts and book lovers. His reviews offer insights into the evolving technological landscape shaping the publishing industry.

Table of Contents

3

Architecture and History of Data Integration   37

4

Data Sources and Types   71

5

Columnar Data Formats and Comparisons   101

6

Data Storage Technologies and Architectures   135

7

Data Ingestion and Storage Strategies   163

8

Data Integration Techniques   191

9

Data Transformation and Processing   235

10

Transformation Patterns, Cleansing, and Normalization   271

11

Data Exposition and APIs   287

14

15

16

Prospects and Challenges   421

Preface

The Definitive Guide to Data Integration is your go-to resource for navigating the complexities of modern data integration. With a focus on the latest tools, techniques, and best practices, this guide takes you on a journey to master data integration and unleash the full potential of your data. In this comprehensive guide, you will begin by examining the challenges and key concepts of data integration in the digital era, such as managing huge volumes of data and dealing with various data types. You will gain a deep understanding of the modern data stack and its architecture, as well as the role of open source technologies in shaping the data landscape. You will delve into the layers of the modern data stack, covering data sources, types, storage, integration techniques, transformation, and processing. You will learn about data exposition and APIs, ingestion and storage strategies, data preparation and analysis, workflow management, monitoring, data quality, and governance. Packed with practical use cases, real-world examples, and insights into the future of data integration, *The Definitive Guide to Data Integration* is an essential resourcefor data electics. By the end of this book, you will have the knowledge and skills needed to maximize your data's potential and excel in the ever-evolving world of data.

Who this book is for

This book is meticulously crafted for professionals and enthusiasts in the fields of data management, analytics, and information technology. It is especially valuable for data analysts, data engineers, and IT professionals involved in data integration, as well as business analysts seeking to deepen their understanding of data-driven strategies. As a reader, you ideally possess a basic understanding of database concepts and data processing and a keen interest in the evolving landscape of data integration technologies. Whether you are a seasoned expert looking to refine your skills or a newcomer eager to grasp the fundamentals, this book serves as a comprehensive guide through the intricate world of data integration.

What this book covers

Chapter 1, Introduction to Our Data Integration Journey, explores data integration's evolution and significance, discussing the proliferation of data sources and the evolving landscape. It tackles the complexities and opportunities in modern data integration and outlines the book's purpose and vision.

Chapter 2, Introducing Data Integration, covers the definition of data integration, the modern data stack, and strategies in data integration. It details the role of data in businesses and examines the techniques, tools, and technologies used in data integration processes.

Chapter 3, Architecture and History of Data Integration, traces the history of data integration, the impact of open source technologies, and various architectures. It discusses the future of data integration, highlighting trends such as real-time and AI-driven integrations.

Chapter 4, Data Sources and Types, discusses the variety of data sources including relational and NoSQL databases, flat files, and APIs. It also explores different data types and formats, emphasizing their importance and challenges in data integration processes.

Chapter 5, Columnar Data Formats and Comparisons, focuses on columnar data formats, contrasting them with traditional row-based methods, emphasizing their advantages in analytics. It explores the challenges of working with different data formats and the necessity of data format conversion.

Chapter 6, Data Storage Technologies and Architectures, delves into data storage technologies such as data warehouses, lakes, and object storage, discussing their strengths and weaknesses. It also covers various data architectures and their impact on data integration, including physical and logical layers, data modeling, and partitioning.

Chapter 7, Data Ingestion and Storage Strategies, covers the goals and strategies of data ingestion, outlining efficient, scalable, and adaptable methods for diverse data sources. It also discusses data storage and modeling techniques, and strategies for optimizing storage performance and defining adapted strategies.

Chapter 8, Data Integration Techniques, explores different data integration models and architectures, covering point-to-point integration, middleware, batch, micro-batching, and real-time approaches. It also discusses common data integration patterns such as ETL and ELT and organizational models for data management.

Chapter 9, Data Transformation and Processing, introduces various data transformation techniques including filters, aggregations, and joins. It delves into SQL's role in data transformation and massively parallel processing systems, discussing their applications and challenges in data processing.

Chapter 10, Transformation Patterns, Cleansing, and Normalization, explores transformation patterns such as lambda and kappa architectures, their pros and cons, and their applications in data pipelines. It delves into data cleansing and normalization, which are crucial for good data quality and consistency in integration.

Chapter 11, Data Exposition and APIs, covers strategic motives for data exposure in analytics, seamless data exchange, and the role of various data exposition technologies. It focuses on APIs and strategies for data exposure, and compares different data exposure solutions.

Chapter 12, Data Preparation and Analysis, discusses the importance of data preparation, strategies for selecting data transformations, and key concepts in reporting and self-analysis, all of which are crucial for effective decision-making and business insights.

Chapter 13, Workflow Management, Monitoring, and Data Quality, examines workflow and event management, monitoring in data stacks, the significance of data quality and observability, and data governance and compliance in managing data assets.

Chapter 14, Lineage, Governance, and Compliance, explores the significance of data lineage in decision-making and compliance, techniques for visualizing data journeys, and the importance of adhering to regulations with robust governance frameworks.

Chapter 15, Various Architecture Use Cases, discusses data integration in scenarios such as real-time data analysis, cloud-based, geospatial, and IoT data analysis, covering the specific challenges, tools, and techniques for each use case.

Chapter 16, Prospects and Challenges, focuses on the future of data integration within the modern data stack, highlighting emerging trends, challenges, and opportunities, and provides guidance for further learning in data integration.

To get the most out of this book

Before beginning, it's important to know that this book assumes you have a foundational understanding of data sources and types, including relational databases, NoSQL, flat files, and APIs. You should be familiar with basic data formats such as CSV, JSON, and XML. The book builds on these basics to explore data integration models, architectures, and patterns, with practical applications across various industries. Having prior experience with SQL and understanding its role in data transformation will be beneficial. Additionally, knowledge of data storage technologies and architectures will help you make the most of the content.

Software/hardware covered in the book	Operating system requirements
SQL and data transformation	Windows, macOS, or Linux
Massively parallel processing systems	Windows, macOS, or Linux
Spark for data transformation	Windows, macOS, or Linux
Data storage technologies (data warehouses, data lakes, and object storage)	Windows, macOS, or Linux
Data modeling techniques	Windows, macOS, or Linux
Data integration models (ETL and ELT)	Windows, macOS, or Linux
Data exposition technologies (Streams, REST APIs, and GraphQL)	Windows, macOS, or Linux

If you are using the digital version of this book, we advise you to type the code yourself or access the code from the book's GitHub repository (a link is available in the next section). Doing so will help you avoid any potential errors related to the copying and pasting of code.

The following are some additional installation instructions and information:

- You should have a stable internet connection to access the online resources and repositories mentioned in the book.

- Familiarize yourself with basic command-line operations as they are commonly used in setting up and managing data environments.

- Installation of a database system that supports SQL, such as MySQL, PostgreSQL, or a similar system, may be required to follow the practical examples.

- For massively parallel processing systems and Spark, ensure that Java is installed on your system as it is required for running Spark-based applications.

- It's recommended to have a code editor or an **Integrated Development Environment (IDE)** that supports database management and big data processing, such as PyCharm, Jupyter, or Visual Studio Code, to facilitate code writing and testing.

- The versions of software and examples provided are current as of the book's publication. You should always check for the latest versions to ensure compatibility and access to the latest features.

Download the example code files

You can find the images and flowcharts for this book on GitHub at `https://github.com/PacktPublishing/The-Definitive-Guide-to-Data-Integration`. If there's an update to the code, it will be updated in the GitHub repository.

We also have other code bundles from our rich catalog of books and videos available at `https://github.com/PacktPublishing/`. Check them out!

Conventions used

There are a number of text conventions used throughout this book.

`Code in text`: Indicates code words in text, database table names, folder names, filenames, file extensions, pathnames, dummy URLs, user input, and Twitter handles. Here is an example: "Data is then inserted into the tables using the INSERT INTO statement."

A block of code is set as follows:

```
# Filter employees with salary greater than $50,00
filtered_employees_df = employees_df.filter(employees_df.salary >
50000)
```

> **Tips or important notes**
> Appear like this.

Get in touch

Feedback from our readers is always welcome.

General feedback: If you have questions about any aspect of this book, email us at `customercare@packtpub.com` and mention the book title in the subject of your message.

Errata: Although we have taken every care to ensure the accuracy of our content, mistakes do happen. If you have found a mistake in this book, we would be grateful if you would report this to us. Please visit www.packtpub.com/support/errata and fill in the form.

Piracy: If you come across any illegal copies of our works in any form on the internet, we would be grateful if you would provide us with the location address or website name. Please contact us at copyright@packtpub.com with a link to the material.

If you are interested in becoming an author: If there is a topic that you have expertise in and you are interested in either writing or contributing to a book, please visit authors.packtpub.com.

Share Your Thoughts

Once you've read *The Definitive Guide to Data Integration*, we'd love to hear your thoughts! Scan the QR code below to go straight to the Amazon review page for this book and share your feedback.

https://packt.link/r/1-837-63191-3

Your review is important to us and the tech community and will help us make sure we're delivering excellent quality content.

Download a free PDF copy of this book

Thanks for purchasing this book!

Do you like to read on the go but are unable to carry your print books everywhere?

Is your eBook purchase not compatible with the device of your choice?

Don't worry, now with every Packt book you get a DRM-free PDF version of that book at no cost.

Read anywhere, any place, on any device. Search, copy, and paste code from your favorite technical books directly into your application.

The perks don't stop there, you can get exclusive access to discounts, newsletters, and great free content in your inbox daily

Follow these simple steps to get the benefits:

1. Scan the QR code or visit the link below

https://packt.link/free-ebook/9781837631919

2. Submit your proof of purchase
3. That's it! We'll send your free PDF and other benefits to your email directly

1

Introduction to Our Data Integration Journey

Data integration plays a pivotal role in the changing landscape of technology, serving to connect diverse data sources and facilitate the smooth transmission of information. This process is essential for ensuring that different systems and applications can work together effectively, enabling organizations to make well-informed decisions and derive valuable insights from their data. As we embark on this journey, *Chapter 1* serves as our starting point, offering a panoramic view of the significance, history, and present landscape of data integration. We'll uncover its foundational principles, explore the multifaceted challenges, and grasp the transformative opportunities that lie ahead. Additionally, this chapter sets the stage for our overarching goal: to present a technology-agnostic theory of data integration, ensuring the relevance and longevity of our discussions. By the end of this chapter, you'll be well equipped with a holistic understanding, setting the tone for the deeper explorations in subsequent chapters.

The following topics will be covered in this chapter:

- The essence of data integration
- The contemporary landscape
- Challenges and opportunities
- The purpose and vision of this book

The essence of data integration

In the age of digitization and rapid technological advancements, data stands as the lifeblood of modern organizations. From influencing strategic decisions to driving innovations, data has woven itself into the very fabric of business operations. Yet, as its importance grows, so does the challenge of harnessing its true potential. Here lies the essence of data integration.

Data integration is not just about combining data from different sources; it's about creating a cohesive, comprehensive view of information that drives insights and actions. This process, though seemingly straightforward, is riddled with complexities that have evolved over time, shaped by the ever-changing nature of data sources, formats, and business needs.

In this section, we'll delve into the pivotal role of data in our current era and trace the evolution of data integration. By understanding its essence, we set the foundation for the subsequent chapters, offering a lens through which we can better appreciate the nuances and intricacies of the broader landscape of data integration.

The pivotal role of data in the modern world

In today's digital age, data stands as the lifeblood of our interconnected world. It plays a quintessential role, permeating every facet of our daily lives, businesses, and even global economies. From smartphones capturing our preferences to businesses leveraging insights for innovation, data has become an indispensable asset.

It's not just the ubiquity of data that's noteworthy; it's the transformative power it holds. Data drives informed decision-making, fuels technological advancements and even shapes global narratives. Consider the expansive growth of social media platforms, e-commerce sites, or health informatics. At the heart of their success lies the adept use of data, synthesizing vast amounts of information to deliver personalized experiences, drive sales, or improve patient outcomes.

Furthermore, in sectors such as finance, healthcare, and logistics, data serves as the foundation for trust and reliability. Accurate data ensures transparent transactions, effective treatments, and efficient supply chains. Conversely, data inaccuracies can lead to financial discrepancies, medical errors, or logistical mishaps.

However, with great power comes great responsibility. The increasing reliance on data has raised pertinent questions about privacy, security, and ethical use. As we continue to weave data into our societal fabric, it's imperative to address these challenges, ensuring that the benefits of data are realized while minimizing the potential pitfalls.

In essence, data's pivotal role in the modern world is undeniable. As we delve deeper into the nuances of data integration, understanding this central importance of data will be key to appreciating the challenges and opportunities that lie ahead.

The evolution of data integration – a brief history

Data integration, as a concept, has deep historical roots, evolving alongside the very technological advancements that necessitated its existence.

In the earliest days of computing, data was largely siloed. Systems were standalone, and data sharing meant manual processes, often involving physical transfer mechanisms such as magnetic tapes. Integration, in this era, was more an exception than a rule, with interoperability challenges being the norm.

As the digital age advanced in the 1980s and 1990s, the development of databases and enterprise systems marked the era. Data began to be centralized, but with centralization came the challenge of integrating data from diverse sources, leading to the onset of **extract, transform, and load** (**ETL**) processes. These processes were pivotal in allowing businesses to consolidate data, albeit with manual and batch-oriented methods.

The dawn of the internet era in the late 1990s and early 2000s transformed data integration. Web services and **application programming interfaces** (**APIs**) began to emerge as the preferred mechanisms for data exchange. The concept of real-time data integration started to gain traction, and the move toward more modular and service-oriented architectures facilitated this.

Fast forward to the present day, and we find ourselves in a world dominated by cloud platforms, big data technologies, and **artificial intelligence** (**AI**). Data integration now isn't just about merging data from two systems; it's about aggregating vast streams of data from myriad sources in real time and making sense of it.

Over the years, the challenges have shifted from basic data transfer to real-time synchronization, schema matching, data quality, and more. The tools, methodologies, and platforms have evolved, but the core objective remains the same: making data accessible, reliable, and actionable.

In understanding the evolution of data integration, we not only appreciate the strides made but also gain insights into the trajectory it's set to take in the future.

Next, we'll discuss the contemporary landscape.

The contemporary landscape

As we transition from understanding the fundamental nature and historical context of data integration, it becomes imperative to position ourselves in the present. The contemporary landscape of data integration is a vivid tapestry marked by rapid technological advancements, proliferating data sources, and evolving business needs. This dynamic environment offers both challenges and opportunities, demanding a nuanced approach to harness the true power of integrated data.

In this section, we will explore the current state of affairs in the realm of data integration. We'll delve into the explosion of data sources and the implications they bring, shedding light on the challenges they present. Furthermore, we'll examine the paradigm shifts that are reshaping data integration strategies, highlighting the innovative methods and approaches that organizations are adopting to stay ahead in this ever-evolving field.

By grasping the intricacies of the contemporary landscape, readers will be better equipped to navigate the complexities of modern data integration, making informed decisions that align with the latest trends and best practices.

The surge in data sources and its implications

In the last few decades, the data landscape has witnessed a transformative explosion. From traditional relational databases to weblogs, social media feeds, **Internet of Things (IoT)** devices, and more, the variety and volume of data sources have grown exponentially. This surge isn't merely quantitative; it's qualitative, adding layers of complexity to the task of data integration.

Several factors have contributed to this upsurge:

- **Digital transformation**: As businesses and institutions have digitized their operations, every process, transaction, and interaction has begun to generate data. This transition has resulted in an array of structured and unstructured data sources.

- **Proliferation of devices**: With the rise of IoT, billions of devices, from smart thermostats to industrial sensors, continuously generate streams of data.

- **Social media and user-generated content**: Platforms such as Facebook, Twitter, and Instagram have given a voice to billions, with each post, like, share, and comment contributing to the data deluge.

However, with this surge comes profound implications:

- **Complexity**: The diversity in data sources means a wide array of formats, structures, and semantics. Integrating such heterogeneous data requires sophisticated methodologies and tools.

- **Volume**: The sheer amount of data generated poses challenges in storage, processing, and real-time integration.

- **Quality and consistency**: As data sources multiply, ensuring data quality and consistency across these sources becomes paramount. Dirty or inconsistent data can lead to flawed insights and decisions.

- **Security and privacy**: With more data comes greater responsibility. Ensuring data privacy, especially with personal and sensitive information, and securing it from breaches are crucial.

In essence, while the surge in data sources offers unprecedented opportunities for insights and innovation, it brings forth challenges that necessitate robust, scalable, and intelligent data integration strategies.

The paradigm shifts in data integration strategies

The world of data integration has never been static. As the landscape of data sources has evolved, so too have the strategies and methodologies employed to integrate this data. This section delves into the significant paradigm shifts that have marked the evolution of data integration strategies over the years.

Historically, data integration was primarily a linear, batch-driven process, businesses operated in relatively isolated IT environments, and data integration was a matter of moving data between a few well-defined systems, often on a scheduled basis. The primary tools of the trade were ETL processes, which were well suited for these environments.

However, the explosion of data sources, combined with the demand for real-time insights, has rendered this approach inadequate. The modern era, marked by cloud computing, big data, and a push toward real-time operations, has demanded a shift in strategy. Here are the key facets of this paradigm shift:

- **From batch to real time**: The emphasis has shifted from batch processes to real-time or near-real-time data integration. This change facilitates timely insights and decision-making, which are critical in today's fast-paced business environment.

- **Decentralization and federation**: Instead of centralizing data in one place, modern strategies often involve federated approaches, where data can reside in multiple locations but be accessed and integrated seamlessly as needed.

- **Data lakes and data warehouses**: With the influx of varied data, organizations are turning to data lakes to store raw data in their native format. This approach contrasts with traditional data warehouses, which store processed and structured data.

- **APIs and microservices**: The rise of APIs and microservices has provided a more modular, flexible, and scalable approach to data integration. Data can be accessed and integrated across platforms without the need for cumbersome ETL processes.

- **Self-service integration**: This involves empowering end users to integrate data as per their requirements, reducing dependency on IT teams and speeding up the integration process.

In essence, the strategies and tools of data integration have transformed, adapting to the changing nature and demands of the data landscape. This paradigm shift ensures that businesses can leverage their data effectively, driving insights, innovation, and competitive advantage.

Next, we'll discuss the challenges and opportunities regarding data integration.

Challenges and opportunities

The path of data integration is not always a straightforward one. As with any transformative process, it brings with it a unique set of challenges that organizations must navigate. However, within these challenges also lie immense opportunities—the chance to redefine processes, uncover novel insights, and drive unparalleled growth.

In this section, we venture into the dual realm of challenges and opportunities presented by modern data integration. We'll dissect the complexities that today's data-rich environment brings, from the intricacies of merging diverse data sources to ensuring data quality and integrity. While these challenges can appear daunting, understanding them is the first step toward harnessing the potential they conceal.

Simultaneously, we'll shine a light on the opportunities that await those willing to embrace these challenges. From fostering innovation to unlocking new avenues of growth, the rewards of effectively navigating the world of data integration are manifold.

By confronting these challenges head on and capitalizing on the inherent opportunities, organizations can set the stage for a future where data integration becomes a cornerstone of their success.

Embracing the complexity of modern data integration

The modern era of data is characterized by a dizzying array of sources, formats, and volumes. Each day, organizations grapple with vast streams of data from websites, IoT devices, social media, cloud platforms, and legacy systems, to name just a few. This multitude of data, while offering unparalleled opportunities, brings with it inherent complexities that challenge traditional integration methods.

Several dimensions of this complexity are worth highlighting:

- **Variety**: Unlike the past, where data was primarily structured and resided in relational databases, today's data takes myriad forms. Structured data now coexists with semi-structured data, such as JSON and XML, and unstructured data, such as images, video, and text.

- **Velocity**: The speed at which data is generated, processed, and made available has increased manifold. Real-time analytics, streaming data, and the need for instantaneous insights have added layers of complexity to integration processes.

- **Volume**: The sheer quantity of data being generated is staggering. From terabytes to petabytes, organizations are now dealing with volumes of data that were unimaginable just a decade ago.

- **Veracity**: With the influx of data comes the challenge of ensuring its accuracy and trustworthiness. Integrating data from disparate sources necessitates robust validation and cleansing mechanisms.

Embracing this complexity requires a shift in mindset and approach:

- **Holistic integration platforms**: Modern integration solutions go beyond just ETL. They offer capabilities such as data quality management, metadata management, and real-time processing, all under one umbrella.

- **Flexibility and scalability**: Given the dynamic nature of data sources and volumes, integration solutions must be agile. They should easily accommodate new sources and scale as data volumes grow.

- **Collaboration and governance**: As data become more democratized, with business users playing an active role in integration processes, it's vital to have robust governance mechanisms. This ensures that data remains consistent, accurate, and secure, even as multiple stakeholders engage with it.

In summary, the complexities of modern data integration are undeniable. However, by embracing these complexities, organizations can unlock the true potential of their data, driving insights, innovations, and strategic advantages in today's competitive landscape.

Prospects for future innovation and growth

The challenges presented by modern data integration, while daunting, also pave the way for unprecedented opportunities. As organizations around the globe recognize the value of seamless data integration, the future beckons with promises of innovative solutions and expansive growth in this domain. Let's explore some of these prospects:

- **Advanced integration architectures**: As the boundaries between data storage, processing, and analytics blur, we can expect more unified and holistic integration architectures. These will likely merge the capabilities of data lakes, warehouses, and processing engines, ensuring smoother data flows and more efficient analytics.

- **Integration with AI**: AI and machine learning have begun to play pivotal roles in data integration. From automating mundane data-mapping tasks to predicting data quality issues, AI is set to redefine the boundaries of what's possible in data integration.

- **Enhanced data governance and quality tools**: As the importance of data integrity grows, there will be increased investments in tools that ensure data accuracy, consistency, and security. These tools will likely harness machine learning to detect anomalies and ensure data quality proactively.

- **Federated and edge integration**: With data generation happening at the edge (thanks to devices such as IoT sensors), the need for edge integration will grow. Instead of sending all data to central repositories, processing and integration might happen closer to the data source, ensuring timeliness and reducing data transfer costs.

- **Self-service and citizen integrators**: The trend toward democratizing data will continue, with more user-friendly and intuitive tools allowing business users to perform integration tasks. This will speed up data availability and reduce the strain on IT departments.

- **Cloud-native integration platforms**: As businesses increasingly adopt cloud infrastructures, integration platforms will evolve to be cloud-native. This will offer better scalability, flexibility, and integration with other cloud services.

- **Global data marketplaces**: The future might see the emergence of global data marketplaces where organizations can buy, sell, and exchange data. Effective data integration will be at the core of these platforms, ensuring data from diverse sources can be seamlessly accessed and used.

In conclusion, the horizon of data integration is luminous with potential. While challenges persist, the prospects for innovation, driven by technological advancements and an ever-growing emphasis on data-driven strategies, ensure that data integration remains a dynamic and evolving field. The organizations that harness these innovations will be well poised to lead in the data-driven future.

Next, we'll discuss the purpose and vision of this book.

The purpose and vision of this book

Embarking on a journey through the world of data integration necessitates not just a map but a clear purpose and vision. It's essential to understand the "*why*" behind this expedition, the guiding principles that will light our way, and the ultimate goals we aspire to achieve.

In this section, we delve into the heart of this book's purpose and the broader vision it upholds. We aim to do more than merely impart knowledge; our goal is to provide a timeless foundation, one that remains relevant amid the ever-evolving technological landscape. By championing a technology-agnostic approach, we seek to transcend the fleeting nature of tools and platforms, focusing instead on the enduring principles of data integration.

Furthermore, we'll outline the journey ahead, setting expectations and providing a roadmap for the chapters to come. This will ensure that as readers navigate through the subsequent sections, they do so with a clear understanding of the broader context and the milestones we aim to achieve.

By grounding ourselves in a clear purpose and vision, we establish a strong foundation, ensuring that this exploration of data integration is both enlightening and impactful.

Laying a theoretical foundation

The world of data integration is vast and multifaceted, and navigating it requires more than just practical tools and techniques. It demands a solid theoretical foundation that provides clarity, direction, and an understanding of the underlying principles that drive effective integration. This foundation is not just about understanding the "*how*" but delving deep into the "*why*."

A robust theoretical framework offers several advantages:

- **Guiding principles**: It establishes the core principles that underpin effective data integration, ensuring that strategies and solutions are grounded in well-understood concepts rather than fleeting trends.

- **Unified understanding**: As data integration spans multiple domains, from IT to business analytics, a shared theoretical foundation ensures that all stakeholders have a common language and understanding. This unity is critical for collaborative efforts and reduces the risk of miscommunication or misalignment.

- **Flexibility in application**: A good theory transcends specific technologies or platforms. It offers a blueprint that can be applied across various tools, systems, and scenarios. As technologies evolve, the theoretical foundation remains consistent, ensuring continuity and relevance.

- **Basis for innovation**: With a clear understanding of the foundational principles, innovators and practitioners can push the boundaries, developing new techniques and solutions that are rooted in theory but are forward-looking in their application.

- **Educational value**: For newcomers to the field, a well-articulated theoretical foundation serves as an invaluable learning resource. It provides context, imparts essential knowledge, and paves the way for deeper exploration and mastery.

In this book, our aim is not just to provide practical insights but to build this theoretical foundation. We seek to lay down the bedrock upon which readers can construct their understanding, strategies, and solutions, ensuring that their endeavors in data integration are both effective and enduring.

Technology-agnostic approach – aiming for timelessness

In the ever-shifting sands of the technological landscape, tools, platforms, and methodologies frequently come and go. What's considered cutting-edge today might be obsolete tomorrow. However, the foundational principles and strategies of data integration remain relevant, transcending the ephemeral nature of specific technologies. It's with this perspective that we emphasize a technology-agnostic approach in this book.

Here's why such an approach is paramount:

- **Enduring relevance**: By focusing on core principles rather than specific tools or platforms, the content remains relevant and applicable over time. This longevity ensures that readers can return to this book as a resource, irrespective of the technological shifts in the industry.

- **Broad applicability**: A technology-agnostic framework can be applied across a range of tools and platforms. Whether an organization uses a legacy system or the latest cloud-based solution, the foundational strategies and insights presented here can guide its integration efforts.

- **Encouraging innovation**: By not being tied to a specific technology, readers are encouraged to think innovatively. They can apply the principles learned here to new tools or methodologies that emerge, fostering a spirit of innovation and adaptability.

- **Avoiding vendor lock-in**: A focus on underlying principles over specific solutions ensures that organizations don't become overly reliant on a single vendor or platform. This independence allows for flexibility and choice, which is critical for long-term strategic planning.

- **Facilitating cross-functional collaboration**: A technology-agnostic approach is more inclusive, allowing professionals from various backgrounds—whether they're IT specialists, data scientists, or business analysts—to collaborate effectively. A shared foundational understanding bridges the knowledge gaps that might exist between these groups.

In essence, our aim is to present a timeless guide to data integration. By adopting a technology-agnostic stance, we hope to provide readers with insights and strategies that remain pertinent and valuable, no matter how the technological winds may shift in the future.

Charting the journey ahead – what to expect

As we embark on this exploration of data integration, it's essential to set the stage for what lies ahead. This journey, rich in insights and knowledge, will weave through the intricate tapestry of data integration, from its foundational principles to its advanced applications.

Here's a glimpse of the path we'll tread:

- **Deep dives into core concepts**: Beyond just scratching the surface, we'll delve into the heart of data integration, unpacking complex concepts, methodologies, and strategies to provide a comprehensive understanding.

- **Practical insights and case studies**: The theory, while essential, will be complemented by real-world applications. Through case studies and practical examples, we'll demonstrate how theoretical knowledge translates into tangible results in diverse scenarios.

- **Evolving trends and innovations**: Data integration is not a static field. As we move through the chapters, we'll shed light on the latest trends, technologies, and innovations that are shaping the future of data integration.

- **Ethical considerations and best practices**: In today's data-driven world, ethics and best practices are paramount. We'll address the responsibilities that come with handling data, ensuring that readers are equipped to navigate the ethical complexities of the domain.

- **A holistic perspective**: Beyond just the technicalities, we aim to provide a holistic view of data integration, considering its business implications, strategic importance, and the human elements involved.

In essence, this book aims to be more than just a guide, it aspires to provide an understanding of the *"why"* behind data integration in a timeless and technology-agnostic approach by offering a blend of theoretical insights and practical applications, aiming to guide both newcomers and seasoned professionals through the evolving landscape of data integration.

Summary

Throughout this chapter, we delved into the ever-evolving realm of data integration, highlighting its pivotal role in connecting disparate data sources and facilitating seamless information flow. The significance, history, and current landscape of data integration were thoroughly explored. We also shed light on the multifaceted challenges faced in this domain, while recognizing the transformative opportunities ahead.

Data integration stands as a cornerstone of modern technology, and this chapter laid the foundation for our understanding by offering a panoramic view of its essential aspects. Traversing its history, challenges, and current relevance, we are now better equipped to delve deeper into the intricacies of this domain.

The journey is just beginning. In the next chapter, we will dive deeper into the very concept of data integration.

2

Introducing Data Integration

Data integration is important because it creates the groundwork for obtaining insightful conclusions in the field of data management and analysis. In today's data-driven world, the capacity to quickly collect and harmonize data, which is constantly expanding in volume, diversity, and complexity, from diverse sources is critical.

This chapter will go into the concept of data integration, delving into its principles, importance, and implications for your day-to-day work in our increasingly data-centric world.

We will go through the following topics:

- Defining data integration
- Introducing the modern data stack
- Data culture and strategy
- Data integration techniques, tools, and technologies

Defining data integration

Data integration is the process of combining data from multiple sources to assist businesses in gaining insights and making educated decisions. In the age of big data, businesses generate vast volumes of structured and unstructured data regularly. To properly appreciate the value of this information, it must be incorporated in a format that enables efficient analysis and interpretation.

Take the example of **extract, transform, and load** (ETL) processing, which consists of multiple stages, including data extraction, transformation, and loading. Extraction entails gathering data from various sources, such as databases, data lakes, APIs, or flat files. Transformation involves cleaning, enriching, and transforming the extracted data into a standardized format, making it easier to combine and analyze. Finally, loading refers to transferring the transformed data into a target system, such as a data warehouse, where it can be stored, accessed, and analyzed by relevant stakeholders.

The data integration process not only involves handling different data types, formats, and sources, but also requires addressing challenges such as data quality, consistency, and security. Moreover, data integration must be scalable and flexible to accommodate the constantly changing data landscape. The following figure depicts the scope for data integration.

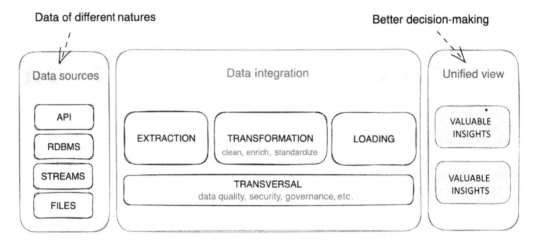

Figure 2.1 – Scope for data integration

Understanding data integration as a process is critical for businesses to harness the power of their data effectively.

> **Warning**
>
> Data integration should not be confused with data ingestion, which is the process of moving and replicating data from various sources and loading it into the first step of the data layer with minimal transformation. Data ingestion is a necessary but not sufficient step for data integration, which involves additional tasks such as data cleansing, enrichment, and transformation.

A well-designed and well-executed data integration strategy can help organizations break down data silos, streamline data management, and derive valuable insights for better decision-making.

The importance of data integration in modern data-driven businesses

Data integration is critical in today's data-driven enterprises and cannot be understated. As organizations rely more on data to guide their decisions, operations, and goals, the ability to connect disparate data sources becomes increasingly important. The following principles emphasize the importance of data integration in today's data-driven enterprises.

Organization and resources

Data integration is critical in today's competitive business market for firms trying to leverage the power of their data and make educated decisions. Breaking down data silos is an important part of this process since disconnected and unavailable data can prevent cooperation, productivity, and the capacity to derive valuable insights. Data silos often arise when different departments or teams within an organization store their data separately, leading to a lack of cohesive understanding and analysis of the available information. Data integration tackles this issue by bringing data from several sources together in a centralized area, allowing for smooth access and analysis across the enterprise. This not only encourages greater team communication and collaboration but also builds a data-driven culture, which has the potential to greatly improve overall business performance.

Another aspect of data integration is streamlining data management, which simplifies data handling processes and eliminates the need to manually merge data from multiple sources. By automating these processes, data integration reduces the risk of errors, inconsistencies, and duplication, ensuring that stakeholders have access to accurate and up-to-date information, which allows organizations to make more informed decisions and allocate resources more effectively.

One additional benefit of data integration is the ability to acquire useful insights in real time from streaming sources such as **Internet of Things (IoT)** devices and social media platforms. As a result, organizations may react more quickly and efficiently to changing market conditions, consumer wants, and operational issues. Real-time data can also assist firms in identifying trends and patterns, allowing them to make proactive decisions and remain competitive.

For a world of trustworthy data

Taking into consideration the importance of a good decision for the company, it is important to enhance customer experiences by integrating data from various customer touchpoints. In this way, businesses can gain a 360-degree view of their customers, allowing them to deliver personalized experiences and targeted marketing campaigns. This can lead to increased customer satisfaction, revenue, and loyalty.

In the same way, quality improvement involves cleaning, enriching, and standardizing data, which can significantly improve its quality. High-quality data is essential for accurate and reliable analysis, leading to better business outcomes.

Finally, it is necessary to take into consideration the aspects of governance and compliance with the laws. Data integration helps organizations maintain compliance with data protection regulations, such as the **General Data Protection Regulation (GDPR)** and **California Consumer Privacy Act (CCPA)**. By consolidating data in a centralized location, businesses can more effectively track, monitor, and control access to sensitive information.

Strategic decision-making solutions

Effective data integration enables businesses to gain a comprehensive view of their data, which is needed for informed decision-making. By combining data from various sources, organizations can uncover hidden patterns, trends, and insights that would have been difficult to identify otherwise.

Furthermore, with data integration, you allow organizations to combine data from different sources, enabling the discovery of new insights and fostering innovation.

The following figure depicts the position of data integration in modern business.

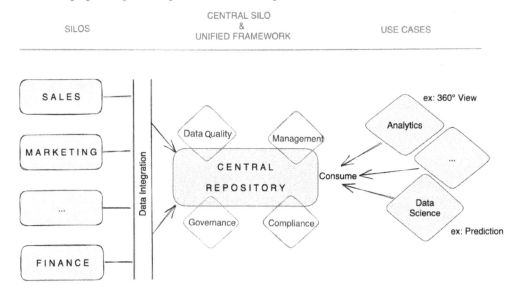

Figure 2.2 – The position of data integration in modern business

Companies can leverage these insights to develop new products, services, and business models, driving growth and competitive advantage.

Differentiating data integration from other data management practices

The topics surrounding data are quite vast, and it is very easy to get lost in this ecosystem. We will attempt to clarify some of the terms currently used that may or may not be a part of data integration for you:

- **Data warehousing**: Data warehousing refers to the process of collecting, storing, and managing large volumes of data from various sources in a centralized repository. Although data integration is a critical component of building a data warehouse, the latter involves additional tasks such as data modeling, indexing, and query optimization to enable efficient data retrieval and analysis.

- **Data migration**: Data migration is the process of transferring data from one system or storage location to another, usually during system upgrades or consolidation. While data integration may involve some data migration tasks, such as data transformation and cleansing, the primary goal of data migration is to move data without altering its structure or content fundamentally.

- **Data virtualization**: Data virtualization is an approach to data management that allows organizations to access, aggregate, and manipulate data from different sources without the need for physical data movement or storage. This method provides a unified, real-time view of data, enabling users to make better-informed decisions without the complexities of traditional data integration techniques.

- **Data federation**: Data federation, a subset of data virtualization, is a technique that offers a unified view of data from multiple sources without the need to physically move or store the data in a central repository. Primarily, it involves the virtualization of autonomous data stores into a larger singular data store, with a frequent focus on relational data stores. This contrasts with data virtualization, which is more versatile, as it can work with various types of data ranging from RDBMS to **NoSQL**.

- **Data synchronization**: Data synchronization is the process of maintaining consistency and accuracy across multiple copies of data stored in different locations or systems. Data synchronization ensures that changes made to one data source are automatically reflected in all other copies. While data integration may involve some synchronization tasks, its primary focus is on combining data from multiple sources to create a unified view.

- **Data quality management**: Data quality management is the practice of maintaining and improving the accuracy, consistency, and reliability of data throughout its life cycle. Data quality management involves data cleansing, deduplication, validation, and enrichment. Although data quality is a crucial aspect of data integration, it is a broader concept that encompasses several other data management practices.

- **Data vault**: Data vault modeling is an approach to designing enterprise data warehouses, introduced by Dan Linstedt. It is a detail-oriented hybrid data modeling technique that combines the best aspects of **third normal form** (**3NF**), which we will cover in *Chapter 4*, *Data Sources and Type*s, dimensional modeling, and other design principles. The primary focus of data vault modeling is to create a flexible, scalable, and adaptable data architecture that can accommodate rapidly changing business requirements and easily integrate new data sources.

By differentiating data integration from these related data management practices, we can better understand its unique role in the modern data stack. Data integration is vital for businesses to derive valuable insights from diverse data sources, ensuring that information is accurate, up to date, and readily accessible for decision-making.

Challenges faced in data integration

Data integration is a complex process that requires enterprises and data services to tackle various challenges to effectively combine data from multiple sources and create a unified view.

Technical challenges

As an organization's size increases, so does the variety and volume of data, resulting in greater technical complexity. Addressing this challenge requires a comprehensive approach to ensure seamless integration across all data types:

- **Data heterogeneity**: Data comes in various formats, structures, and types, which can make integrating it difficult. Combining structured data, such as that from relational databases, with unstructured data, such as text documents or social media posts, requires advanced data transformation techniques to create a unified view.

- **Data volume**: The sheer volume of data that enterprises and data services deal with today can be overwhelming. Large-scale data integration projects involving terabytes or petabytes of data require scalable and efficient data integration techniques and tools to handle such volumes without compromising performance.

- **Data latency**: For businesses to make timely choices, real-time or near-real-time data integration is becoming essential. Integrating data from numerous sources with low latency, on the other hand, can be difficult, especially when dealing with enormous amounts of data. To reduce latency and provide quick access to integrated data, data services must use real-time data integration methodologies and technologies.

> **Industry good practice**
>
> To overcome technical challenges such as data heterogeneity, volume, and latency, organizations can leverage cloud-based technologies that offer scalability, flexibility, and speed. Cloud-based solutions can also reduce infrastructure costs and maintenance efforts, allowing organizations to focus on their core business processes.

Integrity challenges

Once data capture is implemented, preferably during the setup process, maintaining data integrity becomes important to ensure accurate decision-making based on reliable indicators. Additionally, it's essential to guarantee that the right individuals have access to the appropriate data:

- **Data quality**: Ensuring data quality is a significant challenge during data integration. Poor data quality, such as missing, duplicate, or inconsistent data, can negatively impact the insights derived from the integrated dataset. Enterprises must implement data cleansing, validation, and enrichment techniques to maintain and improve data quality throughout the integration process.

- **Data security and privacy**: Ensuring data security and privacy is a critical concern during data integration. Enterprises must comply with data protection regulations, such as GDPR or the **Health Insurance Portability and Accountability Act (HIPAA)**, while integrating sensitive information. This challenge requires implementing data encryption, access control mechanisms, and data anonymization techniques to protect sensitive data during the integration process.

- **Master data management (MDM)**: Implementing MDM is crucial to ensure consistency, accuracy, and accountability in non-transactional data entities such as customers, products, and vendors. MDM helps in creating a single source of truth, reducing data duplication, and ensuring data accuracy across different systems and databases during data integration. MDM strategies also aid in aligning various data models from different sources, ensuring that all integrated systems use a consistent set of master data, which is vital for effective data analysis and decision-making.

- **Referential integrity**: Maintaining referential integrity involves ensuring that relationships among data in different databases are preserved and remain consistent during and after integration. This includes making sure that foreign keys accurately and reliably point to primary keys in related tables. Implementing referential integrity controls is essential to avoid data anomalies and integrity issues, such as orphaned records or inconsistent data references, which can lead to inaccurate data analytics and business intelligence outcomes.

> **Note**
>
> Data quality is a crucial aspect of data integration, as poor data quality can negatively impact the insights derived from the integrated dataset. Organizations should implement data quality tools and techniques to ensure that their data is accurate, complete, and consistent throughout the integration process.

Knowledge challenges

Implementing and sustaining a comprehensive data integration platform requires the establishment, accumulation, and preservation of knowledge and skills over time:

- **Integration complexity**: Integrating data from various sources, systems, and technologies can be a substantial task. To streamline and decrease complexity, businesses must use strong data integration tools and platforms that handle multiple data sources and integration protocols.

- **Resource constraints**: Data integration initiatives frequently necessitate the use of expert data engineers and architects, as well as specific tools and infrastructure. Enterprises may have resource restrictions, such as a shortage of experienced staff, budget limits, or insufficient infrastructure, which can hinder data integration initiatives.

Enterprises may establish effective data integration strategies and realize the full potential of their data assets by understanding and tackling these problems. Implementing strong data integration processes will allow firms to gain useful insights and make better decisions.

> **Tip**
>
> To address knowledge challenges such as integration complexity and resource constraints, organizations can use user-friendly and collaborative tools that simplify the design and execution of data integration workflows. These tools can also help reduce the dependency on expert staff and enable non-technical users to access and use data as needed.

Introducing the modern data stack

The modern data stack is a combination of tools, technologies, and platforms that are designed to simplify the process of extracting, converting, and loading data from several sources into a centralized storage system. The stack components are generally chosen to fit the company's needs exactly, hence promoting simplicity in addition to being cost effective. This stack enables businesses to manage, analyze, and gain insights from their data to make educated decisions. The current data stack's components can be broadly classified in the following figure.

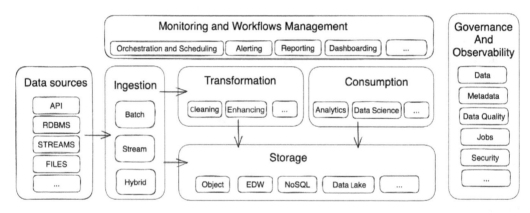

Figure 2.3 – Overview of the modern data stack

Initially, it is essential to identify the components encompassing the recognition, capturing, and measurement of data integrity for the information being integrated into the data platform. The modern data stack, with its multitude of components, provides organizations with a flexible and scalable framework for managing and deriving value from their data. By adopting the right tools, technologies, and platforms, organizations can create a powerful data ecosystem that supports their data-driven decision-making and business objectives.

Data sources

The data stack starts with the data sources, which can include relational databases, NoSQL databases, flat files, APIs, or data streams generated by sensors or devices. These sources are responsible for producing the raw data that will be ingested, processed, and stored within the modern data stack.

> **Tip**
>
> Data sources are the starting point of the modern data stack, providing the raw data that will be ingested, processed, and stored within the stack. Organizations should identify and evaluate their existing and potential data sources to determine their relevance, quality, and availability for their business objectives.

Data ingestion

Data ingestion refers to the process of moving and replicating data from various sources and loading it into the first step of the data layer with minimal transformation. Data ingestion can be used with real-time streaming, change data capture, APIs, or batching. Ingestion is the first step to ensure a smooth and efficient data transfer process. Tools such as Airbyte or Fivetran can help build this layer.

Storage

The modern data stack includes various storage technologies for managing and storing data. Various storage options exist, ranging from solutions that primarily provide efficient storage in terms of performance and non-specialized redundancy in the analytical aspect but are capable of adapting to different situations, to more specialized solutions offering high performance during data intersections required for various layers such as a data warehouse. The choice of data storage depends on the organization's specific requirements and the type of data being managed. Technologies such as MinIO, Ceph, or Scality, which are distributed object storage systems compliant with S3 API, can be a good foundation for the storage layer.

Transformation

Data transformation is the process of combining data from different sources and creating a unified view. This process involves data cleansing, validation, enrichment, and transformation (filter, mapping, lookup, aggregate, and so on) to ensure data consistency and quality. At this stage, data transformation plays a crucial role. It facilitates the transfer and synchronization of various data types and formats between systems and applications. This step is commonly called data integration. Compute engines such as dbt or Spark can help process your data.

> **Note**
>
> Transformation is a key component of the modern data stack, as it ensures that the ingested data is consistent and standardized for analysis and consumption. Organizations should define their transformation logic and rules based on their business requirements and target system specifications.

Consumption

Data consumption can take various forms, with different methods employed to analyze and visualize information for distinct purposes. Three common approaches to data consumption include reporting/dashboarding, data science, and **enterprise performance management (EPM)**.

Reporting and dashboarding are essential tools for organizations to effectively monitor their performance and make data-driven decisions. Reports provide structured and detailed information on various aspects of a business, while dashboards offer a visual representation of **key performance indicators (KPIs)** and metrics, allowing stakeholders to quickly grasp the overall health of the organization. The usage of technologies such as Tableau software combined with Presto-based solutions can help achieve that.

EPM is a comprehensive approach to company planning, consolidation, and reporting. EPM entails combining several management procedures, such as budgeting, forecasting, and financial analysis, to improve an organization's overall performance. EPM assists businesses in achieving their goals and maintaining a competitive edge in the market by connecting business strategies with operational procedures.

Data science is an interdisciplinary field that combines cutting-edge tools and algorithms to extract insights from huge and complicated databases. Data scientists use techniques such as machine learning, statistical modeling, and artificial intelligence to forecast future trends, uncover patterns, and optimize business processes, allowing firms to make more informed strategic decisions.

> Tip
> Consumption is the ultimate goal of the modern data stack, as it enables organizations to analyze and visualize their integrated data for various purposes. Organizations should choose the appropriate tools and methods for data consumption based on their analytical needs and capabilities.

Management and monitoring

Workflow management and monitoring ensure a seamless execution of processes and timely delivery of accurate information. Workflow management focuses on designing, automating, and coordinating the various tasks, streamlining the process, and minimizing the risk of errors. On the other hand, monitoring upholds the effectiveness and dependability of data integration workflows. By continuously tracking the progress of data integration tasks, monitoring helps identify potential bottlenecks, performance issues, and data discrepancies. This real-time oversight allows organizations to proactively address problems and ensure data quality.

Data governance and observability

The set of policies, methods, and practices that regulate data collection, storage, and use is known as **data governance**. It tackles issues such as data quality, security, privacy, and compliance in order to ensure that data is accurate, consistent, and accessible to authorized users. A well-executed data governance structure can assist firms in maintaining data trust, reducing risks, and improving decision-making capabilities.

Observability, on the other hand, refers to the ability to monitor and comprehend the many components of a data ecosystem. It is necessary to monitor and visualize metrics, logs, and traces in order to get insight into the performance, dependability, and functionality of data pipelines, systems, and applications. Effective observability enables organizations to proactively identify and fix issues, maximize resource utilization, and ensure continuous data flow across their infrastructure. Observability, as opposed to monitoring, is concerned with the quality and consumption of data within the organization rather than technological factors. In many cases, tools such as DataHub can be very helpful in implementing observability.

The role of cloud-based technologies in the modern data stack

Cloud-based technologies have played a significant role in shaping the modern data stack, providing organizations with greater flexibility, scalability, and cost effectiveness compared to traditional on-premises solutions. Nonetheless, the cloud strategy is not limited to the public cloud but can also be implemented through various solutions within the private cloud. The following points highlight the importance of cloud-based technologies in the modern data stack:

- **Scalability**: Cloud-based services provide nearly limitless scalability, allowing businesses to quickly and easily modify their computing, storage, and processing capabilities to meet their needs. This adaptability assists businesses in avoiding overprovisioning and ensuring that they only pay for the resources they use.

- **Cost effectiveness**: Organizations can decrease capital costs on hardware, software, and maintenance by embracing cloud-based infrastructure and services. Cloud providers' pay-as-you-go pricing model helps enterprises to better manage their operational costs while benefiting from cutting-edge technologies and functionalities.

- **Speed and agility**: Cloud-based solutions enable enterprises to swiftly provision and deploy new data stack components, allowing them to respond to changing business requirements more quickly. Businesses can experiment with new tools and technologies using cloud-based services without making large upfront infrastructure costs.

- **Global availability**: Cloud companies have data centers in multiple regions throughout the world, guaranteeing users have minimal latency and high availability. With a worldwide presence, businesses can store and process data closer to their customers, boosting performance and user experience.

- **Integration and interoperability**: Cloud-based data stack components are designed to interact smoothly with other cloud services, making it easier to connect and coordinate data activities across many platforms. This compatibility makes data handling more streamlined and efficient.

- **Managed services**: Cloud service providers provide managed services for various data stack components such as data integration, transformation, storage, and analytics. These managed services handle the underlying infrastructure, maintenance, and updates, allowing businesses to focus on essential business processes and gain value from their data.

- **Security and compliance**: Cloud companies invest heavily in security and compliance to ensure that their services fulfill industry standards and regulations. Organizations can benefit from advanced security features such as encryption, identity and access control, and network security by employing cloud-based services to protect their data and maintain compliance with data protection requirements.

- **Tools and services ecosystem**: The cloud ecosystem is home to a wide range of tools and services designed to meet the needs of the modern data stack. This diverse ecosystem enables enterprises to choose the finest tools and solutions for their individual use cases and objectives, fostering innovation and driving growth.

The paradigm has clearly shifted, as cloud-based technologies have transformed the modern data stack, offering businesses the flexibility, scalability, and cost effectiveness required to manage their data assets effectively. Organizations may build a robust, agile, and secure data stack that supports data-driven decision-making and business goals by implementing cloud-based solutions.

The evaluation of the data stack from traditional to cloud-based solutions

Over the years, the data stack has evolved significantly, shifting from traditional on-premises solutions to cloud-based technology. The necessity to manage rapidly growing volumes of data, as well as the growing need for real-time data processing and analytics, has fueled this change.

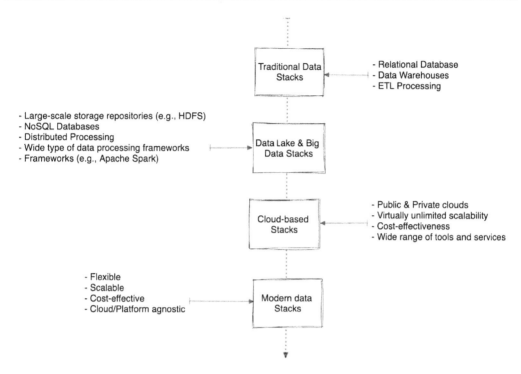

Figure 2.4 – Evolution of data stack

Traditional data stack

In the early days of data management, organizations primarily relied on monolithic, on-premises solutions such as relational databases and data warehouses. These systems were designed to handle structured data and were often limited in terms of scalability, flexibility, and integration capabilities. Data integration and processing tasks were typically performed using ETL processes, which were often time consuming and resource intensive.

The emergence of big data technologies and data lake architecture

The advent of big data technologies, such as **Hadoop** and NoSQL databases, marked a significant shift in the data stack landscape. These technologies were designed to handle large volumes of unstructured and semi-structured data, providing organizations with the ability to process and analyze diverse data sources. The implementation of distributed processing systems has significantly enhanced the handling and examination of large-scale data collections.

With the growing need to store and process various types of data, data lakes emerged as a popular alternative to traditional data warehouses. Data lakes are large-scale storage repositories that can store raw, unprocessed data in its native format, offering greater flexibility and scalability. Organizations began adopting data lake architectures to accommodate the diverse data types and sources they were working with, enabling them to perform more advanced analytics and derive deeper insights.

Cloud-based solutions

As cloud computing gained popularity, businesses began to use cloud-based services to construct and manage their data stacks. The cloud had various advantages over traditional options, including nearly limitless scalability, cost effectiveness, and access to a diverse set of tools and services. Cloud-based data storage solutions grew in popularity as a means of storing data on the cloud, while managed services offered scalable data warehousing and analytics capabilities.

Modern data stack

The modern data stack draws upon the cumulative advancements of previous iterations, harnessing the best aspects of each stack to deliver an optimized solution. This modern approach to data management is highly versatile, assuring its relevance and adaptability in today's fast-changing technological scene. The introduction of IoT is a crucial development that has altered the modern data stack. With billions of connected devices across the world continuously producing large volumes of data, IoT has spurred the demand for efficient and scalable streaming solutions. These systems are specifically intended to handle real-time data processing, allowing enterprises to make more educated decisions based on current facts. The modern data stack also stresses data quality, governance, and security, ensuring that enterprises can trust and successfully manage their data.

The benefits of adopting a modern data stack approach

Adopting a modern data stack approach brings numerous benefits to organizations, allowing them to leverage the latest technologies and best practices in data management, integration, and analytics. Some of the key benefits of embracing a modern data stack include the following:

- **Scalability**: Modern data stacks are built on cloud-based technologies that offer virtually unlimited scalability, enabling organizations to handle growing volumes of data without worrying about infrastructure limitations. As data needs grow or fluctuate, the modern data stack can easily scale up or down to accommodate these changes, ensuring optimal performance and cost efficiency.

- **Flexibility**: The modern data stack is designed to accommodate diverse data sources and types, providing organizations with the ability to integrate and process data from various systems and formats. This flexibility allows organizations to derive insights from a wide range of data, supporting more comprehensive and informed decision-making.

- **Agility**: By leveraging modern data stack tools and services, organizations can accelerate their data integration, transformation, and analytics processes, enabling them to quickly respond to changing business requirements and market conditions. This agility helps organizations to stay competitive and adapt to the rapidly evolving business landscape.

- **Cost efficiency**: The adoption of a modern data stack built on cloud-based technologies enables organizations to take advantage of pay-as-you-go pricing models and eliminate the need for costly on-premises infrastructure investments. This cost efficiency allows organizations to optimize their data management expenses and allocate resources more effectively.

- **Improved data quality and governance**: A modern data stack emphasizes the importance of data quality, governance, and security. By adopting best practices and leveraging advanced data quality tools, organizations can ensure that their data is accurate, complete, and consistent, which in turn leads to more reliable insights and decision-making.

- **Real-time data processing and analytics**: The modern data stack enables organizations to process and analyze data in real time, allowing them to react to events and trends as they happen. This capability is particularly valuable for businesses that need to make timely decisions based on the latest data, such as those in finance, marketing, and operations.

- **Ease of use and collaboration**: Modern data stack tools and services are often designed with user friendliness and collaboration in mind, making it easier for teams to work together and access the data they need. This ease of use and collaboration helps organizations break down data silos and foster a more data-driven culture.

Adopting a modern data stack approach offers organizations numerous benefits, including scalability, flexibility, agility, cost efficiency, improved data quality, real-time analytics, and ease of use. By embracing the modern data stack, organizations can build a robust and agile data infrastructure that supports their data-driven decision making and business objectives.

Next, we'll discuss culture and strategy.

Data culture and strategy

In today's corporate environment, data has become a critical tool for firms seeking to obtain insights, make educated decisions, and maintain a competitive edge. Companies must understand their existing and future data cultures, as well as develop a well-defined data strategy, in order to properly harness the power of their data. There are different techniques for data management, each with advantages and disadvantages. This section will look at several data management strategies, the concept of data-centricity, and how businesses might use data as a service, product, or mesh.

Data cultures

As you embark on efforts concerning a company's data platform or systems, a crucial first step involves evaluating the existing and desired state of the organization's data culture mindset. Here are some of the various data-centric cultures.

Data anarchy

Data anarchy refers to a situation where business operations professionals, dissatisfied with their IT department's support, create and manage their own unofficial databases or "shadow IT." In this approach, data is scattered across various systems, departments, and individuals without any centralized control or governance. While data anarchy provides flexibility and autonomy to individual teams, it can lead to inconsistency, duplication, and data silos, making it difficult to obtain a comprehensive view of the organization's data landscape.

Data monarchy

Data monarchy centralizes data management under a single authority, often the IT department or a dedicated data team. This approach ensures data consistency and standardization but can hinder agility and slow down data access for business users, who often have to rely on the central authority for data requests.

Data aristocracy

In a **data aristocracy**, multiple data stewards from different departments share the responsibility of managing data. This approach balances centralization and decentralization, allowing for better collaboration and data sharing across the organization while maintaining some level of control and governance.

Data democracy

Data democracy empowers all employees to access and use data as needed for their job functions. This approach fosters a data-driven culture, encourages innovation, and improves decision-making across the organization. However, it requires robust data governance policies and practices to ensure data quality, security, and compliance.

Data management strategies

Data currently exists in your organization, and your objective is to foster increased commitment and enhanced structuring. Under these circumstances, it is advantageous to establish the approach or approaches related to data administration:

- **Data centric**: A data-centric approach places data at the center of the enterprise. Data is viewed as a valuable asset in this approach, and its quality, accessibility, and security are of the utmost significance. Companies may accelerate innovation, improve operational efficiency, and improve customer experiences by implementing a data-centric strategy.

- **Data as a service** (**DaaS**): DaaS is a concept in which data is delivered to customers on demand via a cloud-based platform. This strategy enables enterprises to instantly access and combine data from several sources without the need for infrastructure setup or maintenance. DaaS provides faster decision-making, better collaboration, and lower costs by charging enterprises just for the data they consume.

- **Data as a product** (**DaaP**): Treating data as a product involves packaging and selling data to customers or partners. Companies can monetize their data by providing valuable insights, analytics, or datasets to external parties. This approach can create new revenue streams and increase the organization's market value. However, it also requires strong data governance and security measures to protect sensitive information and ensure compliance with data protection regulations.

- **Data mesh**: A data mesh is a decentralized data architecture that distributes data ownership and management across different domains or teams within an organization. This approach breaks down data silos and promotes collaboration, while still maintaining data governance and security. A data mesh enables organizations to scale their data infrastructure efficiently and leverage data as a strategic asset for innovation and growth.

Organizations must carefully assess their data management needs, internal capabilities, and strategic goals to determine the best approach for their data company strategy depending on their current and future data cultures. By adopting a data-centric mindset and leveraging innovative data models such as DaaS, DaaP, and data mesh, companies can harness the full potential of their data to drive growth, innovation, and success in today's competitive business environment.

Next, we'll discuss data integration techniques, tools, and technologies.

Data integration techniques, tools, and technologies

Data integration is a complex process that necessitates the use of numerous tools and technologies to **extract**, **transform**, and **load** data from diverse sources into a centralized location. In this chapter, we will go over some of the most important data integration tools and technologies, including open source and commercial solutions, as well as criteria to consider when choosing the correct tools and technologies for your data integration project.

Data integration techniques

Data integration is an essential process for organizations that need to consolidate data from disparate sources to gain insights and make informed decisions. However, the process can be heterogeneous, especially when dealing with large volumes of data from different sources. Data integration involves extracting data from multiple sources, transforming it into a consistent format, and loading it into a central location. To achieve this, organizations need to use various tools and technologies that can help them streamline the process and ensure data quality, ranging from open source solutions to commercial tools.

Data integration architectures outline the diverse approaches to processing and transferring data from source to target systems. These methods can be mixed and matched according to specific requirements, considering that the slowest transformation method will impact the overall processing time.

Batch processing, for example, which involves gathering and processing data in big batches at regular intervals, is appropriate for large-scale projects when data latency is not an issue. Micro-batching is a batch processing variation that works with smaller batches at shorter intervals and is suited for applications that require minimal latency but not real-time processing. Real-time processing, on the other hand, is perfect for projects that require low latency and data to be processed and evaluated quickly. Incremental processing is appropriate for cases in which enormous amounts of data are generated but only a small fraction of the data changes over time, hence lowering processing time and coherence.

Data integration patterns, such as **extract, load, and transform** (ELT), refer to the different ways data is transformed and loaded into the target system. ETL is a traditional approach that is batch oriented and suitable for projects where data quality and transformations are complex. In contrast, ELT is a modern method that leverages the processing power of the target system and is appropriate for projects where data transformations are relatively simple.

Overview of key tools and technologies

There are various tools and technologies available for data integration, each with its own advantages and limitations. Here are some of the key tools and technologies used for data integration.

ETL tools

ETL tools are software applications that automate the ETL process; they can be code-based or **graphical user interface** (GUI) based. The tools help design and execute ETL workflows, map data elements between sources, and transform the data. ETL tools can be on-premises or cloud-based, and they may be commercial or open source.

The following screenshot shows the ETL steps:

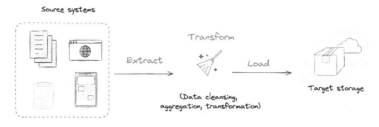

Figure 2.5 – ETL steps

The first step involves extracting data from source systems. The ETL tool connects to these sources using connectors or APIs. During extraction, the tool reads the data. The second step is the most complex one; it is the step where data is transformed into a suitable format/model for analysis. This step includes operations such as cleaning, normalization, enrichment, and filtering. The third and last step is loading into the target storage system, such as a data lake or data warehouse.

Data integration middleware

Data integration middleware is software that provides a standardized interface for data exchange between different applications, databases, and platforms. Data integration middleware can handle complex data transformations, and it can also provide advanced features such as data quality, data governance, and data security. Middleware can take many forms, the most common being an **enterprise service bus** (**ESB**). It can be used to integrate different applications, such as **customer relationship management** (**CRM**) and **enterprise resource planning** (**ERP**) systems, to enable interoperability and facilitate data exchange.

The following screenshot shows the data integration middleware:

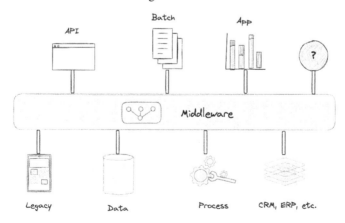

Figure 2.6 – Data integration middleware

Data integration middleware can be used to move data between source systems and a central data repository.

Cloud-based integration platforms

Cloud-based integration platforms provide a cloud-based infrastructure for data integration, enabling organizations to access and integrate data from different sources and applications. Cloud-based integration platforms can be more cost effective than on-premises solutions, and they can also provide scalability and flexibility.

The following screenshot shows cloud-based integration platforms:

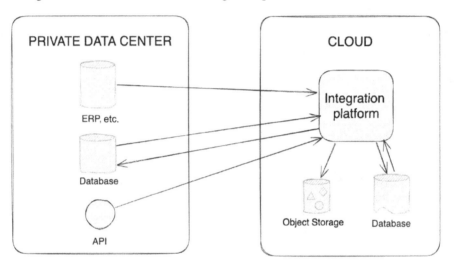

Figure 2.7 – Cloud-based integration platforms

Here's an overview of how these platforms typically operate:

- **Data collection**: The platform gathers data from various sources, including on-premises databases, cloud storage, or SaaS applications, using connectors or APIs from diverse environments such as private data centers, cloud platforms, or public domains.

- **Data processing**: Once collected, the data is transformed, cleaned, and normalized to ensure it's in the correct format and quality for analysis directly into the cloud inside the integration platform. This can involve filtering, aggregation, or merging data from different sources.

- **Data delivery**: The processed data is then pushed to its destination, which could be a database, data warehouse, or another business application for further analysis, reporting, or real-time decision-making.

Data virtualization tools

Data virtualization tools represent a modern approach to data management; they enable organizations to access and integrate data from different sources and applications without physically moving or replicating the data. Data virtualization tools can provide real-time access to data, and they can also reduce data replication and storage costs. These tools stand out for their ability to provide real-time data access and reduce costs related to data replication and storage. The operation of data virtualization tools involves several key steps. The following screenshot shows data virtualization tools:

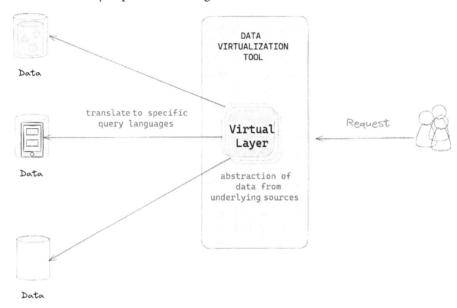

Figure 2.8 – Data virtualization tools

Here's an overview of how these platforms typically operate:

- **Data source connectivity**: The platform establishes connections using connectors or APIs to diverse sources such as traditional databases, cloud storage solutions, big data systems, and real-time data streams

- **Virtual data layer creation**: The platform forms a virtual layer that abstracts data from its sources, allowing seamless interaction as if it's from a unified database, despite it being scattered across various locations

- **Query translation and integration**: The platform translates queries into each source's language, and retrieves and integrates data, presenting it in a unified format without needing physical data replication, reducing storage costs and complexity

This real-time process eliminates the need for data replication or physical movement, leading to significant reductions in storage costs and complexities associated with maintaining data consistency. Consequently, data virtualization tools offer a flexible, efficient, and cost effective means for data integration, empowering organizations to utilize their data assets more effectively for analytics and informed decision-making.

They can be implemented in different types:

- **Query engine-based tools**: These are designed with powerful query engines that can retrieve and integrate data from diverse sources in real time. They are particularly useful in situations where immediate access to data across varied data environments is crucial.

- **Middleware-oriented tools**: Acting as a middleware layer, these tools facilitate a seamless connection between data sources and applications. They play a crucial role in enabling data access and manipulation without the complexities of dealing with various data structures and formats.

- **Data federation tools**: Specializing in creating a virtual database, these tools provide a unified view of data from multiple sources. They are invaluable for aggregating data from different databases and filesystems, presenting it as a cohesive dataset.

Data quality tools

Data quality tools improve the accuracy, consistency, completeness, and integrity of data during integration processes and work by offering a suite of functionalities. Here's a succinct overview of the main steps in maintaining and enhancing the quality of data:

- **Data profiling**: Analyze existing data to understand the structure, quality, and issues by identifying patterns, outliers, and inconsistencies.

- **Data cleansing**: Correct or remove incorrect, corrupted, improperly formatted, duplicate, or incomplete data. It includes error correction, data normalization, and deduplication.

- **Data enrichment**: Enhance data quality by appending related information from external sources, providing a richer, more comprehensive dataset.

- **Data validation**: Check data accuracy and consistency against predefined rules and constraints to ensure it meets quality standards and business requirements.

These tools automate many aspects of the data quality process, significantly reducing manual effort and the likelihood of human error, and they are integral in ensuring that the data used for analysis and decision-making is reliable and valuable. These tools can be coding-based tools, configuration-based tools, and/or UI-based tools.

Open source and commercial tools

Data integration tools and technologies can be commercial or open source. Commercial tools require the acquisition of a usage right to have unrestricted access, including current and future features, and to ensure vendor-based support. Open source solutions are supported by the community and sometimes by service companies. Therefore, the associated cost is directly related to the need for services within the scope of using these solutions.

Factors to consider when selecting tools and technologies

When selecting the right data integration tools and technologies for your data integration project, you need to consider several factors, including the size and complexity of the data sources, the target system's processing power, the data integration project's requirements, and the organization's budget and IT expertise. Here are some factors to consider when selecting tools and technologies.

The following table lists the factors to consider when selecting tools and technologies.

Category	Criteria	Description
Adaptive architecture	Scalability	Tools should manage current data volumes and expand for future growth.
	Flexibility	Solutions must support various data formats, structures, and diverse transformations.
	Integration capabilities	Ensure tools integrate with various sources and platforms, providing standardized interfaces.
	Support and maintenance	Choose tools backed by reliable vendors with strong support and maintenance.
Governance and compliance	Data governance features	Tools should include data lineage, stewardship, and cataloging for consistent, compliant management.
	Security features	Prioritize tools with robust security measures such as encryption, access controls, and auditing.
	Data quality features	Look for tools ensuring data quality through profiling, cleansing, and enrichment.
Company strategy	Company cultures	Consider tools aligning with the organization's values and practices.
	Team expertise	Select tools matching team skills or those with manageable learning curves to reduce training costs.
	Ease of use	Prefer tools with user-friendly interfaces for all users.
	Cost	Tools should be affordable, considering license fees, implementation, and maintenance costs against the budget.

Table 2.1 – Factors to consider when selecting tools and technologies

When selecting the most suitable data integration tools and technologies for your endeavor, it's vital to take into account a range of aspects, such as data source size and intricacy, the target system's processing capabilities, project necessities, and the organization's financial resources and technical know-how. Moreover, assessing adaptive architecture, governance and compliance, and corporate strategy is essential. By carefully examining these elements, you can make sure that the chosen tools and technologies correspond to your organization's cultural environment, team expertise, and financial limitations, ultimately resulting in a successful data integration project tailored to your specific needs and objectives.

Summary

Data integration tools and technologies are required for enterprises to maximize the value of their data assets. Organizations may choose the best approach for their data integration project and achieve their data integration goals effectively and efficiently by understanding the various tools and technologies available for data integration. The amount and complexity of the data sources, the target system's processing power, the requirements of the data integration project, and the organization's budget and IT competence all influence the choice of data integration tools and technologies. Organizations can guarantee that their data is integrated accurately, efficiently, and securely by adopting the right data integration tools and technologies, allowing them to make data-driven decisions and achieve a competitive advantage in the data-driven business landscape.

In the next chapter, we'll delve into the evolution of data integration and investigate the diverse structures established to cater to requirements at every phase.

3

Architecture and History of Data Integration

In this chapter, we'll go back in time to review the history of data integration and explore diverse architectures, which are crucial for comprehending the trajectory of this rapidly progressing subject matter. *To know where we are going, we must first understand where we have been*, as the adage goes. With this in mind, we'll look at the beginnings, milestones, and key technologies that have formed the field of data integration, offering context for its current condition and possibilities.

Understanding the historical context and evolution of data integration architectures enables organizations to make more informed decisions as they adapt to new trends and technologies. We can get vital insights into the aspects that will define data integration's future development by evaluating its origins, major milestones, and underlying motives that have driven its progress.

This comprehensive review will prepare you and your business abilities to traverse the complicated and ever-changing world of data-driven solutions. So, let's journey through the rich history of data integration and study the key architectures that have brought us to where we are today.

The following topics will be covered in this chapter:

- History of data integration
- Influential open source data technologies
- The impact of open source on data integration and analytics
- Data integration architectures
- The future of data integration

History of data integration

The biography of data integration is long, but we want to focus on a few key events to explain both current and future advancements in data integration, starting with mainframes up to the modern data stack.

Early data processing and mainframes

Before open source data platform software emerged, mainframes were the foundation for data processing in big organizations. These powerful computers managed huge amounts of data and completed complex calculations quickly. IBM's System/360, introduced in 1964, was among the first influential mainframe computers and laid the groundwork for many business computing systems.

Mainframe technologies, such as COBOL and IMS, provided early solutions for data storage, management, and processing. Despite their high costs and proprietary nature, mainframes were widely adopted by organizations due to their reliability, security, and performance.

> **Expert advice**
>
> Mainframes are still used today by some large organizations that need high reliability and security for their data processing. However, they are often integrated with other technologies, such as cloud computing and open source software, to enhance their capabilities and reduce costs.

The relational database revolution – Codd's model and early RDBMSs

The relational database revolution started in 1970 when Edgar F. Codd, an IBM researcher, published a paper called *A Relational Model of Data for Large Shared Data Banks*. This paper introduced the idea of relational databases, a novel method for organizing and structuring data. Codd's work formed the basis for modern **relational database management systems** (**RDBMS**) and transformed the data storage and management field.

Codd's relational model enabled data representation in tables, which consist of rows and columns. This model simplified data understanding and manipulation while preserving consistency and integrity. The main advantage of this representation was the ability to create relationships between tables using keys, enabling efficient data retrieval and updating.

The relational model led to the development of **Structured Query Language** (**SQL**), designed for relational databases. SQL simplified user interaction with relational databases and allowed complex queries and updates.

The 1970s and 1980s saw early relational database management systems such as System R, Ingres (database), Oracle, and IBM's DB2. These systems implemented the relational model, offering users powerful data storage and retrieval capabilities. As businesses recognized the importance of structured data storage and management, demand for RDBMSs grew, ushering in a new data technology era.

During this time, other companies developed their relational database systems. Microsoft launched SQL Server, Sybase created Adaptive Server Enterprise, and Informix developed Informix Dynamic Server. This rapid innovation and competition phase led to significant advancements in relational database technology, making it the leading data storage approach for years.

The following figure shows the key features and structure of an RDBMS:

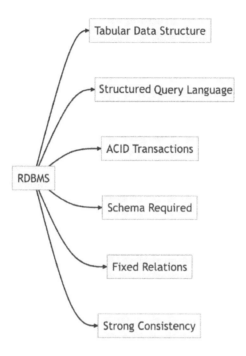

Figure 3.1 – RDBMS structure and key features

RDBMSs offer numerous benefits and features. These include a defined structure for data storage, an accessible and standardized query language, as well as interaction protocols that ensure data integrity. Among these protocols, the principles of **Atomicity, Consistency, Isolation, and Durability (ACID)** stand out, fostering reliable and secure data management. For instance, in a banking system, when transferring money from Account A to Account B, atomicity ensures the entire transaction either succeeds fully or is aborted entirely. Consistency maintains the system's correctness, upholding predefined rules such as total balance across accounts. Isolation ensures that concurrent transactions don't impact each other's execution, and durability guarantees that once a transaction is committed, it remains so, even in the event of a system failure.

The data warehouse pioneers – Kimball, Inmon, and Codd

In the early 1990s, pioneers such as Ralph Kimball and Bill Inmon led the charge in creating the concept of data warehousing as a mechanism for storing, analyzing, and reporting on large-scale, integrated data. Their work set the groundwork for the modern data warehouse, which has since become an indispensable part of the data management environment.

Ralph Kimball, a data warehousing expert, introduced the concept of a dimensional data model that focused on simplicity and ease of understanding for end users. Kimball's approach, known as the star schema, used denormalized data structures with a central fact table containing quantitative data, surrounded by dimension tables that provided descriptive context. This model made it easy for business users to navigate and understand data, enabling them to perform complex analyses and generate reports with minimal technical expertise.

Bill Inmon, on the other hand, advocated for a more structured, normalized approach to data warehousing, emphasizing the importance of a single, unified data model for the entire organization. Inmon's approach, often referred to as the top-down methodology or the **Corporate Information Factory** (**CIF**), called for the creation of a centralized, enterprise-wide data warehouse that served as the primary source of truth for all analytical applications. This approach promoted data consistency and integrity across the organization but required more upfront design work and a longer implementation timeline.

In parallel with the development of data warehouse methodologies, multidimensional cubes emerged as a popular data storage and analysis technique. Pioneered by Edgar F. Codd, the father of the relational model, multidimensional cubes allowed for the efficient storage and querying of data across multiple dimensions. This approach, known as **online analytical processing** (**OLAP**), enabled users to explore data in a flexible, interactive manner, facilitating complex analyses and decision-making such as the analytical breakdown of accounting accounts used by management controllers.

The contributions of Kimball and Inmon and the development of multidimensional cubes played a crucial role in shaping the future of data warehousing and the broader data management landscape. Their work paved the way for the evolution of modern data warehousing technologies, which now incorporate elements of both Kimball's and Inmon's methodologies, as well as advanced analytical capabilities enabled by OLAP and other innovations. In addition to these foundational concepts, it's important to acknowledge the role of datamarts in this framework. Datamarts, which are subsets of data warehouses tailored to the specific needs of a department or business unit, provide more focused, subject-oriented data for targeted analysis. They facilitate quicker access to relevant data, enabling departments to make more efficient and informed decisions without the need to query the entire data warehouse.

> ### Industry good practice
> When designing a data warehouse, it is important to consider the trade-offs between Kimball's and Inmon's methodologies. Kimball's approach is more suitable for agile development and user-friendly analysis, while Inmon's approach is more suitable for consistent and comprehensive data modeling. A hybrid approach that combines elements of both methodologies can also be used to balance the advantages and disadvantages of each.

The following figure shows the relationship between a fact table and dimension tables:

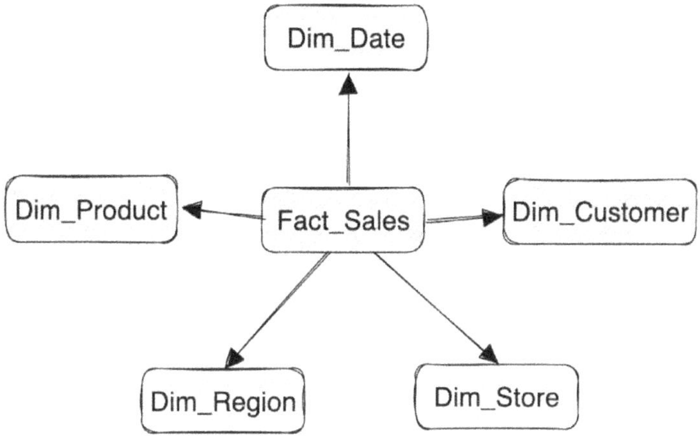

Figure 3.2 – Kimball's star schema concept

In this example, we have a fact table called `Fact_Sales` and five dimension tables called `Dim_Date`, `Dim_Product`, `Dim_Customer`, and `Dim_Store`. The arrows indicate the relationships between the fact table and the dimension tables.

The emergence of open source databases – MySQL, PostgreSQL, and SQLite

In the mid-1990s, open source databases such as MySQL, PostgreSQL, and SQLite emerged, indicating a substantial move away from proprietary systems and making database technology more accessible. This shift sparked the innovation of data management.

MySQL, which was first released in 1995, soon gained popularity as an easy-to-use, efficient, open source RDBMS. Its ability to manage massive volumes of data, as well as its compatibility with a variety of programming languages, makes it a popular choice for online applications. The acquisition of MySQL by Sun Microsystems, and then by Oracle, added resources to the project, solidifying its status as the top open source database solution.

Another open source RDBMS is PostgreSQL, which grew out of the Ingres project at the University of California, Berkeley. It was released in 1996 with an emphasis on extensibility and respect to SQL standards, allowing support for sophisticated features such as user-defined data types and stored procedures. PostgreSQL has developed a reputation for dependability and performance, making it suited for enterprise applications.

SQLite, first released in 2000, is an open source, serverless SQL database engine that provides developers with a lightweight and portable solution. SQLite was created to be incorporated directly into programs, eliminating the need for a separate server, thus making it perfect for mobile and desktop applications. Its tiny size, ease of use, and cross-platform compatibility resulted in widespread acceptance across a wide range of sectors.

The rise of open source databases such as MySQL, PostgreSQL, and SQLite revolutionized data management. By making powerful data storage and manipulation features available to a wider audience, these databases spurred industry growth and innovation. As a result, open source databases have become essential components of the modern data stack, laying the foundation for future advances in data management and storage technologies.

The advent of big data – Hadoop and MapReduce

The rise of big data brought about significant changes in the data environment by introducing new technology and processes capable of dealing with the increasing volume, diversity, and speed of data. Among the most notable inventions during this period were Hadoop, an open source framework for distributed data storage and processing, and MapReduce, a programming model for processing big datasets in parallel over several nodes.

Doug Cutting and Mike Cafarella created Hadoop in 2006, motivated by Google's research papers on their distributed filesystem and data processing approach. The **Hadoop Distributed File System (HDFS)** for scalable and dependable data storage and the Hadoop MapReduce engine for parallel data processing are the key components of Hadoop. Hadoop's architecture and scalability make it an attractive choice for businesses dealing with large-scale, unstructured data volumes that older systems couldn't handle.

MapReduce, developed by Google researchers Jeffrey Dean and Sanjay Ghemawat, revolutionized data processing by offering a simple yet effective programming approach for large-scale data. The MapReduce model consists of two primary functions: the `Map` function, which converts incoming data into key-value pairs, and the `Reduce` function, which processes the `Map` function's output by aggregating or summarizing the key-value pairs. This method allowed for parallel processing over numerous nodes, allowing for the efficient examination of massive amounts of data.

The launch of Hadoop and MapReduce signaled the beginning of the big data age and cleared the way for various other open source technologies and platforms, such as Apache Spark, to build on their foundations. These developments have had a long-term impact on the data environment, driving the constant growth of data management systems and influencing how businesses approach data integration, transformation, and storage.

> **Warning**
> Hadoop and MapReduce are powerful tools for processing large-scale data, but they also have some limitations – for example, they are not very efficient for iterative algorithms that require multiple passes over the same data, such as machine learning or graph processing. They also have high latency for interactive queries as they rely on batch processing. To overcome these limitations, other technologies, such as Apache Spark and Apache Flink, have been developed to provide faster and more flexible data processing.

The following figure shows an example of a MapReduce process:

Figure 3.3 – Example of a MapReduce process

The preceding diagram illustrates a simple MapReduce process. Input data is split into chunks and processed by multiple mapper nodes (**Mapper 1**, **Mapper 2**, and **Mapper 3**). The mappers generate key-value pairs, which are then shuffled and sorted before being sent to reducer nodes (**Reducer 1** and **Reducer 2**). The reducer nodes aggregate or summarize the grouped key-value pairs, and the final output data is produced as a result.

The rise of NoSQL databases – MongoDB, Cassandra, and Couchbase

The appearance of NoSQL databases brought about a notable change in data management as companies looked for ways to manage the varied and ever-changing nature of today's data. NoSQL, meaning **not only SQL**, includes a range of databases created to overcome the challenges that traditional relational databases face when dealing with large amounts of unstructured, semi-structured, or schemaless data. MongoDB, Apache Cassandra, and Couchbase are some examples of NoSQL databases that have arisen to meet these needs.

MongoDB, released in 2009 by Dwight Merriman and Eliot Horowitz, is a document-oriented database that stores data in a flexible, JSON-like format called **BSON**. Its schemaless design enables developers to store complex and hierarchical data structures, making it well-suited for handling diverse data types and frequent schema changes. MongoDB offers horizontal scaling through sharding, which involves splitting the data across multiple servers and provides high availability with automatic failover and replication.

Apache Cassandra, developed at Facebook by Avinash Lakshman and Prashant Malik in 2008, is a highly scalable and distributed wide-column store designed for handling large volumes of data across many commodity servers. Cassandra combines the benefits of both systems to offer a highly available, fault-tolerant, and partition-tolerant database. It is particularly well-suited for use cases that require high write and read throughput, such as time series data or event logging.

Couchbase, first launched in 2010 as Membase, is a distributed, document-based NoSQL database with a flexible data model, high performance, and easy scalability. It combines the strengths of an in-memory caching system, Memcached, with a persistent storage layer, creating an efficient data management solution for web, mobile, and IoT applications. Couchbase also supports N1QL, a SQL-like query language, making querying and data manipulation in a NoSQL environment more straightforward.

The emergence of NoSQL databases such as MongoDB, Cassandra, and Couchbase has broadened the capabilities of the modern data stack, giving organizations increased flexibility and adaptability in handling their data. These databases, together with other open source technologies mentioned in this chapter, have been instrumental in shaping today's data landscape and will continue to impact the development of data management systems in the future.

The following figure shows the key features of a NoSQL structure:

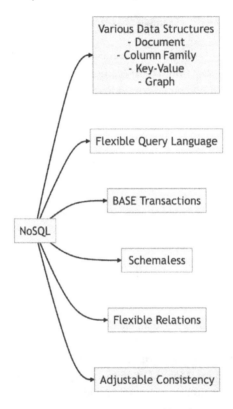

Figure 3.4 – NoSQL structure and key features

The new features provided by these NoSQL storage solutions make it possible to set up new storage and query solutions.

The growing open source ecosystem and its impact on data technologies

The open source movement significantly influences the creation and adoption of new data technologies. It encourages collaboration and innovation among developers, leading to a variety of tools, platforms, and solutions that change how organizations handle data.

Open source communities have driven innovation and standardization in many aspects of the data stack. From databases to data integration tools, open source technologies have been crucial in shaping today's data landscape. Some of the key benefits of the expanding open source ecosystem in data technologies are as follows:

- **Rapid innovation**: Open source development allows a large community of developers to contribute and improve the code base, leading to quick advancements and continuous new features. This collaboration has let open source data technologies evolve at an impressive pace, often surpassing proprietary solutions in innovation and adaptability.

- **Affordability**: Open source data technologies are often free or have low licensing fees, making them accessible to organizations of all sizes. This democratizes access to advanced data management tools and analytics capabilities, enabling even small businesses to benefit from data-driven decision-making.

- **Customization and adaptability**: Open source technologies offer extensive customization, allowing organizations to tailor solutions to their needs. This flexibility helps businesses adapt and evolve their data infrastructure as requirements change or new use cases arise.

- **Interoperability and standardization**: The open source ecosystem has helped develop common standards and protocols that promote interoperability between different data technologies. This simplifies how various systems and platforms can be integrated into the data stack, streamlining data management processes and reducing complexity.

- **Knowledge sharing and skill growth**: Open source communities thrive on knowledge sharing and collaboration, enabling developers and data professionals to learn from one another and develop their skills. This has led to the widespread adoption of best practices and cutting-edge techniques across the data management field.

The expanding open source ecosystem profoundly affects data technologies, driving innovation and making advanced data management tools more accessible. As the open source community continues to grow and evolve, it will play a crucial role in shaping the future of data management and analytics.

The emergence of data science

Data science is an expanding field that changes how we gather, handle, and examine data, fundamentally transforming traditional methods of data interaction, establishing more efficient protocols, and leveraging technology to uncover deeper insights. It combines skills from statistics, computer science, and math to gain insights from data. In this section, we'll look at data science's definition, range, history, and how it has influenced data integration and analytics.

The definition and scope of data science

Data science is the process of using scientific methods, algorithms, and systems to get knowledge and insights out of data. Statistics, machine learning, and data mining are among the approaches used to analyze, process, and visualize data. Data science has numerous uses in business, healthcare, social sciences, and engineering.

Data gathering, data preparation, data analysis, and data visualization are all important phases in data science. Data is collected during the data collecting phase from sources such as databases, sensors, and social media platforms. The data is cleaned, structured, and converted during the data preparation step to make it ready for analysis. Statistical and machine learning technologies are employed in the data analysis phase to gain insights and knowledge from the data. Finally, the data visualization phase provides the results in a way that they are simple to grasp and interpret.

The historical origins of data science

Data science has its roots in subjects such as statistics, computer science, and mathematics. In the early 2000s, the term **data science** was coined to reflect the expanding discipline of data analysis, which was becoming increasingly essential in business and industry. However, data science concepts and procedures have been around for a long time.

Statistics has long been a valuable tool in data analysis. Statistical pioneers such as Ronald Fisher and Jerzy Neyman established the foundations of modern statistics in the early twentieth century, including hypothesis testing, regression analysis, and experimental design. These techniques are still commonly utilized in data science today.

Data science has benefited greatly from advances in computer science. Computer scientists began developing algorithms for data analysis and machine learning in the 1950s and 1960s. These approaches were originally employed in picture and speech recognition but were later repurposed for data science.

Mathematics has also had an important influence on the development of data science. Linear algebra, calculus, and probability theory have all played important roles in the development of mathematical models and algorithms for data analysis.

The impact of data science on the evolution of data integration and analytics

Data science has greatly influenced the development of data integration and analytics. Previously, data integration mainly dealt with gathering and processing data from sources such as databases and flat files. However, with the advent of big data and data science, data integration has become more intricate.

Now, data integration encompasses collecting and processing data from various sources, such as social media, sensors, and mobile devices. This data is often unstructured, necessitating sophisticated algorithms and methods for processing and analysis.

Similarly, data science has influenced the progression of analytics. In the past, analytics mainly focused on descriptive and diagnostic analysis, which entailed examining historical data to detect patterns and trends. However, with the rise of data science, analytics has become more advanced.

At the time of writing, analytics includes predictive and prescriptive analysis, which employs statistical and machine learning methods to make data-based predictions and suggestions. This has allowed organizations to make better-informed decisions and achieve a competitive edge in their industries.

Next, we'll discuss influential open source data technologies.

Influential open source data technologies

Several solutions must be studied at the level of data integration and open source solutions. We can consider solutions such as Hadoop, Spark, and Kafka, or even solutions such as Presto. These different solutions make it possible to support large volumes and thus meet the challenges of today's companies.

Hadoop and the Hadoop ecosystem

Hadoop leverages the principles of distributed file systems, allowing storage capacity and computing power to be scaled by distributing data and processing across multiple nodes in a cluster.

The Hadoop ecosystem comprises numerous tools and components that enhance and extend its capabilities. These components assist in data ingestion, storage, processing, and analysis. Some of the key components in the Hadoop ecosystem are as follows:

- **HDFS**: This is Hadoop's primary storage layer and offers a fault-tolerant, distributed storage system designed for large datasets. It splits files into blocks and stores them across multiple nodes in a cluster, ensuring high availability and reliability.

- **MapReduce**: MapReduce is a programming model and execution framework that enables parallel processing of large datasets in Hadoop.

- **Yet Another Resource Negotiator** (**YARN**): YARN manages cluster resources and allocates them to applications running on the system as Hadoop's resource management and job scheduling component.

- **HBase**: HBase is a dispersed, column-based NoSQL database that functions on the HDFS framework, enabling users to access sizeable datasets on a row-by-row basis for both reading and writing operations instantly. It demonstrates particular proficiency when dealing with extensive tables that consist of millions of columns and have data that is distributed sparsely.

- **Hive**: Hive is a data warehousing solution built on Hadoop that offers a SQL-like interface for querying and analyzing large datasets typically stored in HDFS. It converts SQL queries into MapReduce jobs, allowing users familiar with SQL to work with Hadoop.

- **Sqoop**: Sqoop is a tool for transferring data between Hadoop and relational databases, enabling data ingestion into HDFS from external sources.

- **Flume**: Flume is a distributed, reliable, and highly available service that was created to efficiently collect, aggregate, and transfer vast amounts of log data to HDFS.

The Hadoop ecosystem has been crucial in the big data revolution, allowing organizations to process and analyze enormous datasets cost-effectively. It has served as the foundation for various modern data processing frameworks and tools, promoting innovation and collaboration within the data community.

> **Expert advice**
>
> NoSQL databases offer many benefits for handling diverse and complex data sources, but they also have some drawbacks. For example, they often sacrifice some aspects of data consistency and integrity in favor of availability and scalability. They also have less support for complex queries and transactions than relational databases. Therefore, it is important to choose the right type of database for your data integration needs, depending on the characteristics and requirements of your data sources.

Apache Spark – flexible data processing and analytics

Apache Spark is an open source, distributed computing system developed to address the limitations of Hadoop's MapReduce programming model. Spark was created in 2009 at UC Berkeley's AMPLab. In 2013, it was donated to the Apache Software Foundation. This versatile data processing platform handles various workloads efficiently. These include batch processing, interactive queries, streaming, and machine learning.

One notable advantage of Spark over MapReduce is its in-memory data processing, enabling it to cache intermediate results in memory and greatly improving the performance of iterative algorithms. This feature makes Spark ideal for machine learning and graph processing tasks that often require multiple iterations over the same dataset.

Spark provides APIs in multiple programming languages, such as Scala, Python, Java, and R, allowing developers to write applications in their preferred language. It also offers a high-level set of libraries, including the following:

- **Spark SQL**: An API library for querying structured data that uses SQL or the Dataset/DataFrame APIs. It supports various data sources, such as Hive, Avro, Parquet, ORC, JSON, and JDBC.

- **Spark Streaming**: A library for processing real-time data streams, enabling developers to build scalable and fault-tolerant streaming applications.

- **Spark Structured Streaming**: A library for processing real-time data streams in a batch-like manner, treating streaming data as a series of small, continuously appended micro-batches. It supports various data sources, such as Kafka, Azure Event Hubs, and Amazon Kinesis, making it a popular choice for real-time data processing in modern data architectures.

- **MLlib**: A machine learning library with algorithms for regression, classification, clustering, and recommendation, as well as model evaluation and hyperparameter tuning tools.

- **GraphX**: A graph processing library that offers a flexible graph computation API and a set of built-in graph algorithms.

Apache Spark has gained popularity for large-scale data processing and analytics due to its flexibility, performance, and ease of use. Its integration with the Hadoop ecosystem and support for diverse workloads make it a valuable tool for data-driven organizations.

> Industry good practice
>
> Apache Spark is widely used in the industry for various data processing and analytics tasks, such as **extract, transform, and load** (ETL), batch processing, streaming processing, machine learning, graph processing, and interactive queries. Some examples of companies that use Spark include Netflix, Uber, Airbnb, LinkedIn, Facebook, Amazon, and Microsoft.

The following figure shows the key features of the Spark ecosystem:

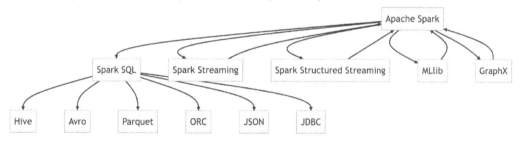

Figure 3.5 – Spark ecosystem and key features

The fact that the Spark solution integrates many features allows it to remain relevant over time facilitating its incorporation into complex and varied architectural environments.

Apache Kafka – a distributed streaming platform

Apache Kafka is a platform for creating real-time data pipelines and streaming applications. Developed by LinkedIn in 2010 and later given to the Apache Software Foundation in 2011, Kafka has become popular for its high performance, reliability, and ability to scale. It allows organizations to handle and examine data streams instantly, which helps them put event-based architectures and microservices into practice.

Kafka's architecture consists of producers, consumers, and brokers. Producers write data to Kafka topics, while consumers read data from these topics. Brokers are the intermediary nodes that store and manage the messages in a distributed, partitioned, and replicated fashion. This architecture allows Kafka to handle millions of events per second with low latency.

Here are some of the key features of Apache Kafka:

- **Distributed and fault-tolerant**: Kafka's distributed nature enables it to scale horizontally and provide high availability, ensuring no single point of failure
- **Durability**: Kafka stores messages on disk, ensuring data durability in the event of node failures
- **Stream processing**: Kafka Streams, a lightweight library for building stream processing applications, allows developers to process and analyze real-time data within their Kafka applications
- **Connectors**: Kafka Connect, a framework for connecting Kafka with external systems, simplifies the integration process with various data sources and sinks

> Warning
>
> Apache Kafka is a powerful platform for creating real-time data pipelines and streaming applications, but it also requires careful configuration and monitoring to ensure optimal performance and reliability. Some common challenges that Kafka users face include data loss or duplication, broker failures or unavailability, consumer lag or offset management, security issues, schema evolution or compatibility, and resource utilization or optimization.

The following figure shows the Kafka ecosystem:

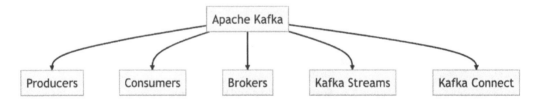

Figure 3.6 – Kafka ecosystem

The various connectors that are put in place allow unlimited interconnection as well as a capacity to evolve to meet the most complex needs. This is why the Kafka solution is widely acclaimed within companies.

Foundational MPP technologies

Massively parallel processing (**MPP**) refers to the use of many processors (or computers) to perform coordinated computations simultaneously by communicating with each other as needed. It plays a crucial role in handling large-scale data workloads, as well as powering real-time data access and analytics, by leveraging distributed systems principles.

MPP technologies encompass databases and query engines designed to handle large-scale data processing across many independent nodes. Traditional MPP databases, such as HP Vertica and Teradata, are self-contained systems that manage data storage, processing, and optimization internally. They are engineered for high performance on dedicated hardware and are optimized for complex analytics on structured data.

In contrast, modern MPP query engines such as Athena, Presto, and Impala decouple the compute and storage aspects of data processing. These engines are designed to work with data stored in distributed filesystems such as Hadoop (HDFS) or object storage such as Amazon S3 and Azure ADLS. They are inherently more flexible, allowing users to query data where it lies without the need to import it into a proprietary system. You only need to describe the data to read, which is generally done on technical data catalogs/metadata layers.

The role of a technical catalog, also known as a metadata layer (for example, AWS Glue or Hive Metastore), is critical in modern MPP technologies. It stores metadata about the data sources, including the location of the files, the format, and the structure of the data. This metadata is used by the query engines to understand where and how to access the data, enabling them to perform queries efficiently without needing to manage the storage layer. It acts as a map of data, allowing MPP engines to optimize query execution by distributing workloads and retrieving only relevant data.

The architecture of MPP technologies

As illustrated in the following schema, modern MPP engines utilize the technical catalog to understand the data in the storage system.

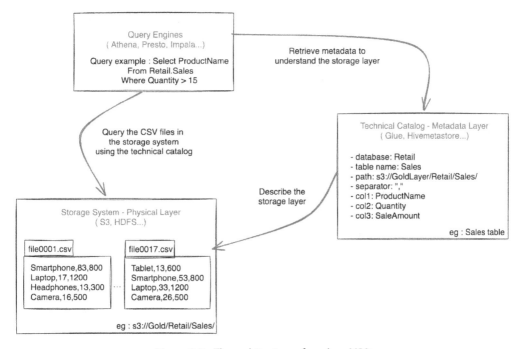

Figure 3.7 – The architecture of modern MPP

Here, S3 represents the storage system, and Glue Data Catalog represents the technical catalog. The SQL-like queries are translated into actions that interact with the storage layer. For example, when a query is executed to select products with a quantity greater than 15, the engine uses the catalog to understand the query, where it can find the data on S3 and how to extract **ProductName** for projection and **Quantity** for filtering. Then, it ensures that the engines are querying the correct datasets and interpreting the file contents accurately, which is vital for returning correct and fast query results.

Trino (formerly known as PrestoSQL)

Trino, an open source distributed SQL query engine, enables high-performance full-scan SQL queries across different data sources. Originally created by Facebook, Trino is adaptable to a broad range of data sources, spanning from Hive and Cassandra to relational databases, and even proprietary data storage systems. Its standout feature is its capability to amalgamate data from diverse sources, which makes it a perfect fit for data federation scenarios.

Trino's architecture is designed for high-speed analytical processing, with in-memory and pipelined execution of queries, support for a variety of data formats, and extensibility to query other data sources. Its strong support for ANSI SQL, including complex queries, joins, and window functions, makes it user-friendly and versatile.

PrestoDB

PrestoDB, which was initially engineered by Facebook, is a freely available SQL query engine that operates in a distributed manner. At the time of writing, it is under the stewardship of the Presto Foundation. Similar to Trino, PrestoDB can perform queries directly on various data sources.

The key distinguishing feature of PrestoDB is its extensible architecture. PrestoDB's architecture is pluggable, meaning it's easy to connect new data sources and build functions, data types, or even control structures. This has driven its adoption in various organizations as it can integrate with many existing data infrastructures.

Starburst

Starburst is an enterprise-ready distribution of Presto that provides additional features, such as security, connectivity, and manageability, on top of what the open source PrestoDB offers. It provides a unified analytics platform, allowing users to analyze data across various sources without requiring data movement.

Starburst's enhancements include added security features such as data encryption, role-based access control, and integration with existing security tools. It also offers connectors to various data sources, performance enhancements, and enterprise-level support.

Amazon Athena

Amazon Athena, as a SaaS platform, functions as a dynamic query service, enabling straightforward data analysis directly within **Amazon Simple Storage Service (Amazon S3)** through the use of conventional SQL. As a serverless service, it's particularly appealing for its ease of management and scalable performance.

Athena is designed to handle complex analysis, including large-scale join, window, and array functions. Utilizing Athena eliminates the requirement for intricate ETL tasks to ready your data for examination. You simply establish the schema or use an existing one and initiate inquiries using conventional SQL.

One of the key features of Athena is its integration with AWS Glue. AWS Glue is a fully administered service that's designed to facilitate the ETL process for data for easy analytics preparation and data loading. Leveraging AWS Glue Data Catalog, Athena can effectively manage data in unstructured, semi-structured, and structured formats.

Moreover, Athena leverages a distributed architecture to execute queries, allowing it to deliver fast performance, even for large datasets and complex queries. Athena also supports both manual and automatic partitioning of datasets to improve query performance.

In terms of security, Athena integrates with AWS Lake Formation to provide fine-grained access control policies for databases, tables, and columns. It also supports encryption of data in transit and at rest.

As an integral part of the AWS ecosystem, Athena brings a powerful SQL querying capability directly to the vast store of data in S3, making it an important player in the open source and cloud-based data integration landscape.

Ahana

Initiated in 2020, Ahana has a core focus on enhancing user interactions with Presto, an open source SQL query engine designed for executing analytic queries on a wide range of data sources, irrespective of their scale. Ahana Cloud, Ahana's managed service for Presto, streamlines the process of utilizing Presto in cloud environments.

Ahana Cloud for Presto is a fully integrated, cloud-native managed service that's designed to simplify the deployment, management, and integration of Presto. It enables users to execute SQL queries across multiple data sources, including Amazon S3, Apache Hadoop, and relational and NoSQL databases.

Ahana's key advantage is its commitment to the open source nature of Presto, ensuring users have complete transparency and control over their workloads. Ahana's managed Presto offering is designed to provide easy scalability, allowing businesses to grow their operations with their data workloads.

In 2023, IBM successfully took over Ahana, a burgeoning company specializing in the provisioning of commercial and managed variants of Presto, an open source distributed query engine. This acquisition has led to IBM's induction into the Presto Foundation, a non-profit entity launched in 2019 by leading tech companies including Facebook, Uber, Twitter, and Alibaba, all under the purview of the Linux Foundation. IBM's partnership with Ahana is rooted in the latter's significant contributions to Presto, boasting four committers and two representatives on the Technical Steering Committee. Ahana views IBM as the perfect partner for both the firm and the Presto community, given IBM's track record of open source contributions and its extensive market penetration.

History of MPP databases

These MPP technologies have had a significant impact on data integration, especially in hybrid data environments. They provide the ability to access and analyze data across different sources, enhancing flexibility, reducing data movement, and enabling real-time insights. These are invaluable capabilities in today's data-driven business landscape.

The following figure shows the ecosystem of the MPP Presto/Trino ecosystem:

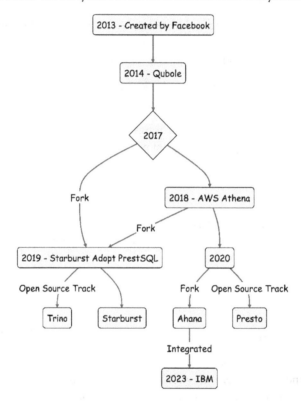

Figure 3.8 – The MPP Presto/Trino ecosystem

This schema illustrates how MPP technologies interact with different data sources and their role in the broader data integration landscape. These technologies, with their ability to federate queries across multiple data sources, serve as a crucial bridge in any data architecture.

Expert advice

MPP technologies are essential for handling large-scale data workloads that require high performance and concurrency. They enable parallel execution of queries across multiple nodes in a cluster while leveraging distributed systems principles. Some examples of MPP technologies include Trino (formerly PrestoSQL), PrestoDB, Starburst, Amazon Athena, and Ahana Cloud for Presto.

These MPP technologies have had a significant impact on data integration, especially in hybrid data environments. They provide the ability to access and analyze data across different sources, enhancing flexibility, reducing data movement, and enabling real-time insights. These are invaluable capabilities in today's data-driven business landscape. Next, we will discuss other influential open source data technologies that have made significant contributions to data integration and analytics.

Other influential open source data technologies

In addition to Hadoop, Spark, and Kafka, several other open source data technologies have significantly impacted the data integration landscape. Some notable examples are as follows:

- **Apache Flink**: A streaming data processing framework that supports both batch and real-time processing, it excels in event-driven applications and stateful computations.

- **Apache NiFi**: A data integration tool that provides a web-based interface for designing, controlling, and monitoring data flows.

- **Apache Cassandra**: This is a widely adaptable, distributed NoSQL database system that's designed to manage and distribute substantial amounts of data across numerous standard servers. Its peer-to-peer structure ensures superior availability and prevents any single point of failure.

These technologies, along with many others, contribute to the rich and evolving open source ecosystem, enabling organizations to build efficient and scalable data integration solutions.

Tip

Many other open source data technologies have made significant contributions to data integration and analytics. Some notable examples include Apache Flink (a streaming data processing framework), Apache NiFi (a data integration tool), and Apache Cassandra (a distributed NoSQL database system). You can learn more about these technologies by visiting their official websites or reading their documentation.

Next, we'll discuss the impact of open source on data integration and analytics.

The impact of open source on data integration and analytics

The widespread accessibility of data processing and analysis has been largely driven by the growth of open source technologies. As more powerful tools and platforms become available to a broader user base, data-driven decision-making has transformed various sectors. The open source movement allows individuals and organizations to utilize sophisticated data processing and analytics techniques without requiring substantial financial or technical resources.

This widespread accessibility has created a level playing field for businesses of all sizes, enabling them to tap into the full potential of their data. With access to cutting-edge tools and technologies, organizations can now make well-informed decisions, spot patterns and trends, and extract valuable insights from their data. The availability of open source resources has ultimately contributed to the increased adoption of data integration and analytics solutions, as well as the overall expansion of data-driven approaches in diverse industries.

Lowering barriers to entry

The expansion of open source alternatives has considerably decreased the barriers to data integration and analysis. Traditionally, powerful data processing technologies necessitated a significant financial investment in proprietary software and hardware, limiting their application to major organizations.

Open source technology has now enabled small and medium-sized organizations to gain access to strong capabilities without incurring large upfront fees. Open source software can be freely downloaded, modified, and used, eliminating licensing fees that may have previously stifled usage. Furthermore, the open source community promotes knowledge exchange through extensive documentation, tutorials, and forums, making it easier for beginners to learn.

Open source solutions have increased the availability of data integration and analytics by lowering these barriers, allowing more companies to benefit from data-driven decision-making and innovation.

Fostering innovation and collaboration

Open source data integration and analytics technologies have promoted innovation and cooperation worldwide. By sharing the source code, open source initiatives invite developers and researchers to contribute their thoughts, enhancements, and bug fixes. This teamwork accelerates new feature development and enables quick issue identification and resolution, ensuring the technology adapts to users' changing needs.

Moreover, the open source community fosters interdisciplinary collaboration, uniting people with various skills and expertise. This knowledge and idea exchange often results in unique solutions that might not have been possible within a single organization. Consequently, open source projects often serve as hubs for advanced technologies and best practices in data integration and analytics.

By encouraging a collaborative atmosphere, open source projects have driven the rapid progress of data integration and analytics technologies, equipping organizations with increasingly advanced tools to extract value from their data.

However, this model also comes with challenges, such as ensuring continuous support, managing the life cycle of the product effectively, addressing skill-sourcing issues, and maintaining the sustainability of the project. Organizations adopting these technologies must consider these factors to leverage the collaborative and innovative nature of open source projects effectively while mitigating potential risks. For example, the security aspects are not often taken into account and need further manual implementation to be compatible with your company. There are also many cases where the product was initially open source and subsequently became paid for. To illustrate that, we can, for example, compare open source Cassandra with its enterprise variant provided by DataStax. Open source Cassandra offers the flexibility and customization that are hallmarks of open source projects. Users have full control over their deployments, integration, and configurations for specific needs. However, this comes with the responsibility of handling updates, security patches, and intricate administration tasks.

In contrast, Cassandra Enterprise simplifies these processes. It automates many of the maintenance tasks, such as patching and updates, reducing the administrative burden on users. It often includes security features and streamlined integration with other enterprise tools. However, this ease of use and added features in the enterprise version come at a cost.

Promoting the adoption of best practices and cutting-edge techniques

The open source approach to data integration and analytics tools has significantly contributed to the adoption of best practices and state-of-the-art techniques. By making advanced technologies available to more people, open source projects have encouraged knowledge and expertise sharing, allowing users to learn from each other and build on existing solutions.

The open source community often leads innovation in data integration and analytics, pushing the limits of what's possible. As a result, these communities play a key role in creating and sharing best practices applicable across different industries and use cases. This ongoing improvement ensures that organizations using open source tools stay current with the latest techniques and methods to maximize their data's value.

Additionally, the open source ecosystem's extensive documentation, tutorials, and forums help users keep up with new developments and best practices, promoting the widespread adoption of advanced data integration and analytics techniques.

Having discussed the influence of open source technologies on data processing and analysis democratization and innovation, we will now explore various data integration architectures. This will lay the groundwork for understanding how these architectures have developed to tackle the intricate challenges organizations face when managing and integrating their data assets.

Next, we'll discuss data integration architectures.

Data integration architectures

At first, the need for distinct data architectures didn't seem crucial. However, over time, specialized and centralized architectures started to take shape. As needs diversified and grew, the demand for decentralized or microservice architectures also emerged, highlighting new requirements that had previously been overlooked.

Traditional data warehouses and ETL processes

Data warehouses have been at the core of data integration for decades. Traditional data warehouses are centralized repositories that are designed to store and manage large volumes of structured data from various sources. They enable organizations to consolidate their data, perform analytical queries, and generate valuable insights for informed decision-making.

One of the key aspects of traditional data warehouses is the ETL process. This process involves three main steps:

- **Extract**: Data is extracted from various sources, such as relational databases, flat files, or APIs.

- **Transform**: The extracted data is cleaned, transformed, and enriched according to predefined business rules and requirements. This step is crucial for ensuring data quality and consistency across the data warehouse.

- **Load**: The transformed data is loaded into the data warehouse, where it can be stored, managed, and accessed by analytical applications.

The following figure shows the steps involved in the ETL process:

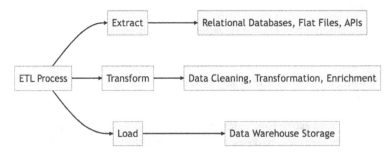

Figure 3.9 – The ETL process

The ETL process is usually carried out in batch mode, where large amounts of data are processed at scheduled times – for example, daily or weekly. This method has its drawbacks, including data availability delays and possible data pipeline bottlenecks. However, it is widely used because of its simplicity, scalability, and compatibility with various data sources and warehouse technologies.

Traditional data warehouses often use relational databases and SQL for data querying and management. Well-known examples include Teradata, Oracle, and IBM DB2. These systems are valued for their performance, reliability, and support for complex analytical queries. However, they have limitations, such as inflexible data modeling, difficulties handling unstructured or semi-structured data, and high costs for licensing and infrastructure.

With changes in the data landscape, organizations need to process and analyze increasingly diverse and complex data sources. This shift led to new data integration architectures, such as data lakes and data meshes, which address traditional data warehouse limitations and offer more flexibility, scalability, and cost-efficiency.

Traditional data warehouses and ETL processes are still relevant in many cases, especially for organizations with clear data integration needs, established data governance practices, and a focus on structured data. By understanding the pros and cons of traditional data warehouses and ETL processes, organizations can make informed decisions about the best data integration architecture for their specific requirements.

Optimizing data transformation processes outside of databases is crucial, especially when dealing with extensive datasets. It helps circumvent bottlenecks caused by database infrastructure limitations or concurrency issues. Implementing efficient sorting, aggregation, and other transformation operations in the data pipeline can significantly improve performance. This approach not only speeds up processing but also ensures that the database load is manageable, leading to a smoother, more efficient data handling experience.

The following figure shows the detailed steps of the ETL process in data warehousing transformation:

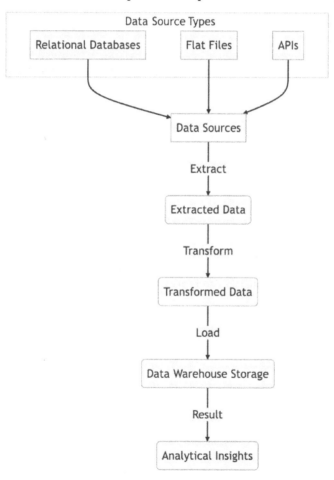

Figure 3.10 – Data warehouse ETL steps

In this section, we explored traditional data warehouses and the ETL process, two critical components of traditional data integration architectures. Traditional data warehouses, acting as centralized repositories, have been instrumental in storing and managing structured data from various sources, providing consolidated data for analytical queries and insightful decision-making.

The ETL process, a key feature of traditional data warehouses, involves extracting data from diverse sources, transforming it for consistency, and loading it into the data warehouse for storage and access. Despite certain drawbacks, such as data availability delays and potential pipeline bottlenecks, this method remains prevalent due to its simplicity, scalability, and compatibility with a range of data sources and warehouse technologies.

However, as data landscapes evolve, traditional data warehouses and ETL processes are encountering limitations, particularly in handling unstructured or semi-structured data, along with the high costs associated with licensing and infrastructure. The emergence of new data integration architectures, such as data lakes and data meshes, is addressing these limitations and offering increased flexibility, scalability, and cost-efficiency.

In conclusion, while the data integration landscape is evolving, traditional data warehouses and ETL processes continue to play a significant role, particularly for organizations with established data governance practices and a focus on structured data. Understanding the advantages and challenges associated with these traditional methods will empower organizations to make informed decisions about the most suitable data integration architecture for their specific needs.

Data lakes and the emergence of ELT processes

Data lakes were developed to address the increasing demand for adaptable and scalable data integration frameworks. They are centralized storage systems that hold and manage large amounts of raw data in its original format, whether structured, semi-structured, or unstructured. Data lakes help organizations gather and store various data sources in an affordable and expandable way, with minimal initial data transformation.

The following screenshot shows data lakes and **extract, load, transform** (**ELT**) processes:

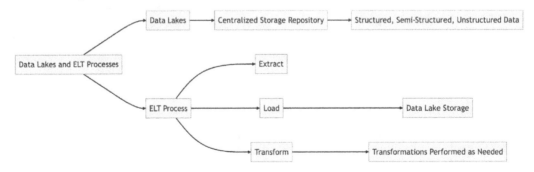

Figure 3.11 – Data lakes and ELT processes

The rise of data lakes has led to the emergence of the ELT process, which is a paradigm shift from the traditional ETL process. In ELT, data is first loaded into the data lake in its raw form, and transformations are performed later, as needed, by analytical applications or during data consumption. This approach offers several advantages over the traditional ETL process:

- **Flexibility**: Data lakes support a wide variety of data formats and structures, allowing organizations to integrate diverse data sources more easily. This flexibility enables organizations to adapt to changing data requirements and explore new data-driven use cases without extensive upfront investment in data transformation.

- **Scalability**: Data lakes are designed to scale horizontally, making it easier to accommodate growing data volumes and workloads. By leveraging distributed storage and processing technologies, such as Hadoop and Apache Spark, data lakes can provide high levels of performance and fault tolerance, even with massive amounts of data.

- **Agility**: The ELT process allows organizations to perform data transformations on an as-needed basis, enabling them to iterate and experiment with different data models and analytics approaches more quickly. This agility is particularly valuable in fast-paced, data-driven environments, where business requirements and analytical needs can evolve rapidly.

- **Cost-efficiency**: Data lakes often rely on open source technologies and commodity hardware, which can significantly reduce infrastructure and licensing costs compared to traditional data warehouses. Additionally, the ELT process reduces the need for expensive data transformation tools and resources, further contributing to cost savings.

Although data lakes have benefits, they also bring some issues, such as data governance, data quality, and data security. Companies must create strong data management methods and use the right tools and technology to tackle these problems successfully.

The emergence of ELT processes and data lakes has expanded the range of options available for data integration, providing organizations with more flexibility and choice. By understanding the benefits and drawbacks of data lakes and the ELT process, organizations can determine whether this architecture is suitable for their specific data integration needs.

The following figure shows the ELT steps involved in a data lake:

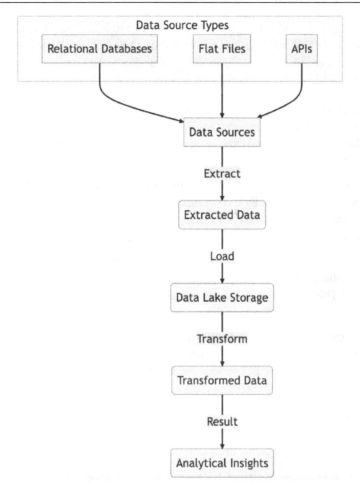

Figure 3.12 – Data lake ELT steps

In summary, data lakes and ELT processes offer an alternative to traditional data warehouses and ETL processes, particularly for organizations dealing with diverse and complex data sources. By carefully considering the advantages and challenges of data lakes and ELT processes, organizations can make informed decisions about the most appropriate data integration architecture for their specific requirements.

Data as a Service and Data as a Product

Data as a Service (DaaS) and **Data as a Product (DaaP)** are emerging ideas in data integration that stress the significance of treating data as a valuable and accessible resource. Both methods aim to simplify data access, enhance data quality, and enable faster decision-making by streamlining data acquisition and use.

DaaS is a cloud-based approach that delivers data on demand, usually through APIs or web services. Providers manage data storage, processing, and management so that organizations can access and use data without in-house infrastructure or resources. This model offers cost savings, scalability, and flexibility, making it easy to access and integrate data from multiple sources without extensive data management expertise or infrastructure investment.

DaaP focuses on treating data as an asset that can be packaged, marketed, and potentially sold, just like any other product. Organizations must invest in data quality, governance, and usability to ensure that their data products are reliable, accurate, and user-friendly. DaaP promotes a culture of data ownership and accountability as teams responsible for creating and maintaining data products must ensure their data meets user needs and complies with relevant regulations and standards.

Both DaaS and DaaP share common principles, such as data quality, SLA, accessibility, and usability, but differ in implementation and focus.

DaaS provides data as a service, often through APIs or data platforms, allowing both internal and external users to access and use data without the need to manage the underlying infrastructure. Data services can be monetized and sold to external users while also being used internally for business processes and decisions.

DaaP emphasizes creating and maintaining high-quality, accessible, and usable data assets designed to meet the needs of a wide range of end users, both internal and external. This approach encourages teams to take ownership of their data and treat it as a valuable product, maximizing its potential to generate insights and drive decisions and innovation. For example, in the banking sector, DaaP could involve developing a centralized data platform where every piece of customer data – transactions, account details, interaction history, and so on – is treated as a product. Banks could refine this data to provide personalized financial advice, tailored loan offers, or improved fraud detection services. For example, a bank might analyze transaction patterns to create a product that predicts and alerts customers to potential unauthorized transactions, adding value to the customer experience and enhancing trust and loyalty.

The following figure provides a summary of DaaS and DaaP:

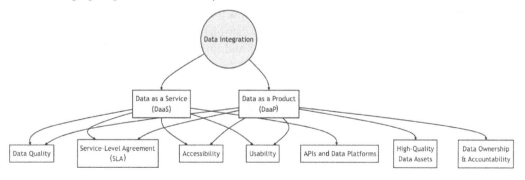

Figure 3.13 – Summary of DaaS and DaaP

In summary, both concepts share common principles but differ in their implementation and focus. DaaS centers on delivering data as a service, while DaaP highlights creating high-quality data assets for a broad array of users. Adopting these models can help organizations streamline data access, improve data quality, and enable better data-driven decisions.

Data mesh and decentralized data integration

Data mesh is a modern approach to data integration that focuses on decentralization, domain-oriented ownership, and self-serve data infrastructure. It was developed in response to the limitations of centralized data integration approaches, such as data lakes and data warehouses, which can struggle to scale efficiently and accommodate the increasingly diverse and complex data needs of large organizations.

The core principles of data mesh are as follows:

- **Domain-oriented ownership**: Data mesh promotes the idea that data should be owned and managed by the teams responsible for the specific business domains they serve. This approach encourages cross-functional collaboration, ensures that data is treated as a first-class product, and fosters accountability for data quality and governance.

  The following figure shows domain-oriented ownership in data mesh:

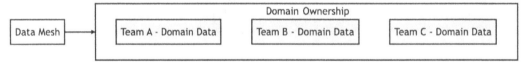

Figure 3.14 – Data mesh – domain-oriented ownership

- **Decentralized architecture**: Data mesh relies on a distributed and decentralized architecture that allows multiple teams to work independently while still maintaining interoperability and consistency. This architecture enables organizations to scale their data integration efforts more effectively and respond more quickly to changing business requirements.

- **Self-serve data infrastructure**: Self-serve data infrastructure is important in a data mesh as it allows domain teams to find, access, and handle data on their own without needing help from central data teams. This method reduces delays and speeds up data-based decision-making throughout the company.

The following figure shows the decentralized architecture in data mesh:

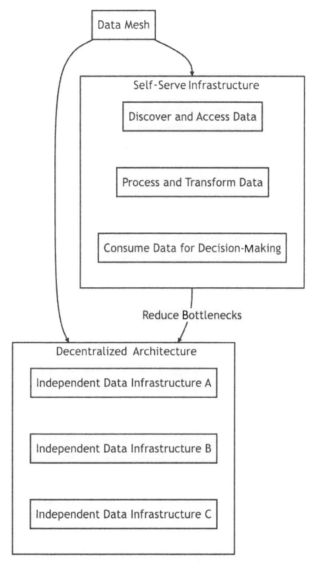

Figure 3.15 – Data mesh – decentralized architecture

- **Standardized data exchange and governance**: To enable effective data sharing and collaboration across different teams and domains, data mesh requires the adoption of standardized data exchange formats, APIs, and metadata. These standards ensure that data is easily discoverable, accessible, and interoperable across the organization while also supporting consistent data governance and security practices.

The following figure shows standardized data exchange and governance in data mesh:

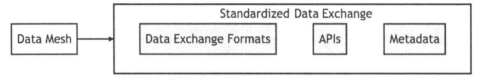

Figure 3.16 – Data mesh – standardized data exchange and governance

- **DaaP**: Data mesh recognizes the importance of treating data as a valuable asset with a product-centric mindset. In this approach, data products are designed, built, and maintained while considering the end users' needs and requirements. Treating data as a product ensures that data assets are reliable, usable, and of high quality, thus maximizing their potential for generating insights and driving business decisions. This perspective also encourages domain teams to take greater responsibility for their data and fosters a culture of data-driven decision-making across the organization.

The following figure shows the strategy of DaaP in data mesh:

Figure 3.17 – Data mesh – DaaP

Data mesh offers several benefits, such as improved scalability, agility, and collaboration, but it also presents challenges, including the need for a cultural shift toward domain-oriented data ownership and the requirement for robust and standardized data infrastructure. Implementing a data mesh architecture requires careful planning, investment in the right tools and technologies, and a strong commitment to fostering a data-driven culture across the organization.

In conclusion, data mesh is a promising approach to data integration that addresses some of the limitations of traditional centralized architectures. By embracing domain-oriented ownership, decentralized architecture, and self-serve data infrastructure, organizations can harness the potential of data mesh to drive more efficient, scalable, and agile data integration efforts.

The role of cloud computing in modern data integration architectures

Cloud computing has had a significant impact on modern data integration architectures by providing scalable, adaptive, and cost-effective solutions for data storage, processing, and analysis. As organizations generate and use massive volumes of data, cloud-based data integration platforms have emerged as a popular solution for managing this data and supporting effective data-driven decision-making:

- **Scalability**: Scalability is a significant advantage of cloud computing in data integration. As data volume and complexity increase, cloud-based platforms may easily expand storage and computational capabilities to meet these rising needs. This elasticity enables firms to tackle large-scale data integration problems without significant upfront infrastructure or maintenance costs.

- **Flexibility**: Cloud computing provides a diverse set of data integration tools and services to meet a variety of use cases and requirements. Organizations can pick between managed services such as AWS Glue or Google Cloud Data Fusion and open source options such as Apache Nifi or Airflow. This adaptability enables enterprises to choose the solutions that best fit their needs and integrate them into their existing data architecture.

- **Cost-effectiveness**: Cloud-based data integration systems typically offer a pay-as-you-go pricing approach, allowing enterprises to pay only for the services they use. This methodology eliminates the need for significant capital investments in hardware and software, minimizing the overall cost of ownership associated with data integration chores.

- **Improved collaboration and real-time access**: Cloud-based data integration systems enable enterprises to centralize their data and make it easily accessible to teams across the organization. This centralization promotes team collaboration and provides users with real-time access to the most recent and accurate information for decision-making.

- **Security and compliance:** Cloud companies provide strong security measures and compliance certifications, assuring data protection and compliance with industry standards and legislation. This relieves enterprises of the burden of managing security and compliance internally, allowing them to focus on key business tasks.

Finally, cloud computing is critical in modern data integration architectures because it provides scalable, adaptive, and cost-effective options for processing enormous amounts of data. Organizations may successfully manage data integration chores by employing cloud-based platforms and services and fostering greater collaboration, real-time access, and data-driven decision-making.

Next, we'll discuss the future of data integration.

The future of data integration

In our opinion, there has been a significant movement in technology and architecture in recent years, with the goal of providing to entities of all sizes, from fledgling start-ups to global business titans. Despite these developments, a plethora of requirements remain unsatisfied or unaddressed, particularly when it comes to functionality and integration within a sophisticated ecosystem, virtually overlapping with operational systems.

Open source-driven standardization and unteroperability

Open source has greatly contributed to standardization and compatibility in the data integration field. The cooperative nature of open source projects supports the creation of shared data formats, protocols, and interfaces, which helps various tools and technologies work together effortlessly.

A primary benefit of open source-driven standardization is the decrease in vendor lock-in, allowing organizations to select the most suitable tools and technologies for their needs without having to worry about compatibility issues. Furthermore, the widespread use of open source solutions fosters consistency across the industry, making it easier for developers to apply their skills to different platforms.

Another essential factor of open source's impact on data integration is interoperability. The ability of different systems to work effectively together enables organizations to integrate data from multiple sources, regardless of the underlying technologies. This adaptability and versatility have become critical for modern data-driven businesses, ensuring that data integration efforts can keep up with the industry's ever-changing demands.

The role of open source in driving the innovation and adoption of emerging data technologies

Open source has been essential in propelling the innovation and acceptance of developing data technologies. Open source helps with sharing ideas and expertise among developers, academics, and organizations by establishing a collaborative atmosphere. This speeds up the creation and refinement of novel data integration, processing, and analytics approaches.

The open source methodology enables rapid iteration and testing, allowing creative solutions to gain support within the community quickly. As these solutions demonstrate their worth, the industry will be increasingly willing to adopt them. Open source also lowers the entrance barrier, making cutting-edge technologies available to a broader range of organizations, including small firms and start-ups.

Furthermore, open source has a democratizing influence on the data environment, enabling the development of solutions tailored to individual demands. Because open source initiatives are flexible and extensible, organizations may adapt and improve on current technology, ensuring that they remain at the forefront of data integration breakthroughs.

Potential future trends in data integration

In terms of potential future trends, we can see that data integration is becoming more complex and larger in scale, while there is also an increasing demand for real-time insights. Some of the key trends that we can identify in this context are as follows:

- **Real-time data integration**: As the need for timely decision-making becomes more critical, organizations will increasingly prioritize real-time data integration. This will drive the development of tools and techniques that enable the seamless integration of streaming data sources.

- **Machine learning and AI-driven integration**: Advanced algorithms and machine learning models will play a more significant role in automating data integration tasks, such as data cleansing, transformation, and schema mapping. This will streamline the integration process and improve overall data quality.

- **Data privacy and security**: As data privacy regulations become more stringent, ensuring secure data integration will be of paramount importance. Future data integration solutions will focus on providing robust security features and maintaining compliance with data protection laws.

- **Hybrid and multi-cloud integration**: As organizations continue to adopt hybrid and multi-cloud strategies, seamless data integration across diverse environments will become increasingly important. This will lead to the development of more flexible and scalable data integration solutions that can effectively handle data movement between on-premises and cloud systems.

- **Metadata-driven integration**: Metadata management will play a more significant role in the future of data integration. Leveraging metadata to automate data discovery, lineage, and cataloging will streamline the integration process and ensure data consistency across different systems.

The following figure encapsulates the potential future trends in data integration, outlining the primary areas of focus and the burgeoning technologies that will shape the landscape of data integration in the coming years:

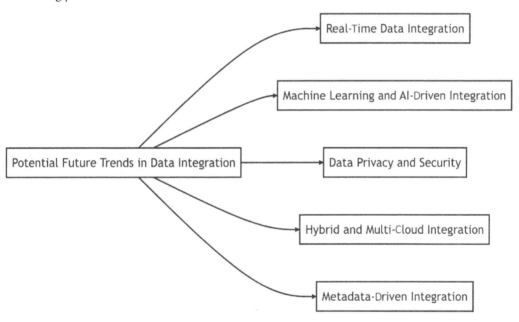

Figure 3.18 – Potential future trends in data integration

Open source solutions are now thoroughly incorporated into the data landscape, addressing a wide range of needs. Yet, functional coverage concerning data quality and governance is still nascent in terms of implementation, as are the escalating needs surrounding the hybridization of architectures. Hence, it is essential to actively monitor all existing and upcoming solutions related to data platforms.

Summary

As we complete this chapter, let's pause to reflect on our journey through the unique architecture and rich history of data integration. We've disassembled the inner workings of data integration, beginning with its fundamental architecture and tracing its evolution over time. We've seen the evolution of data integration from its humble beginnings as a simple tool for integrating data to its current position as a crucial component in practically all commercial, research, and social data ecosystems. We've also discovered how it interacts with other data infrastructure components and supports critical activities such as data transformation, quality control, and metadata management.

The examination of different integration styles allowed us to see the versatility and adaptability of data integration techniques. All of these diverse concepts are invaluable as we proceed on our data journey, shedding light on the crucial role of data integration in making information accessible, usable, and meaningful.

As we step into the next chapter, we'll shift our focus to the origin of all data processes: data sources and types. Here, we will dive into the myriad kinds of data sources that feed into the data integration architecture. This exploration will equip us with the necessary tools to understand and navigate the vast and varied landscape of data, thereby enabling us to better comprehend how different data types can be harnessed and integrated to drive meaningful insights.

4

Data Sources and Types

Data sources are the starting points for data that organizations use in operations or analysis. They can be structured or unstructured, in various formats, and located in separate places. In modern data integration, data sources are essential for providing accurate, timely, and reliable information to the right individuals when needed.

We will start by identifying different data sources – the wellsprings of information that fuel our data systems. Ranging from relational databases and NoSQL databases to flat files and APIs, we will decipher the characteristics that distinguish these sources and the contexts where they shine the brightest.

Moving on, we will delve into the rich array of data types and structures. Understanding the variety and nuances of these constructs will empower you to handle data more proficiently, tailoring your approaches to best fit the nature of the data you are working with.

Finally, we will acquaint you with common data formats, such as **comma-separated values** (**CSV**), **JavaScript Object Notation** (**JSON**), and **Extensible Markup Language** (**XML**). Each of these formats offers a unique way of representing data, bringing along its advantages and challenges. A deeper understanding of these formats will equip you to make informed choices on which to use in specific scenarios.

The following topics will be covered in this chapter:

- **Understanding the data sources**: Relational databases, NoSQL, flat files, APIs, and more
- Working with data types and structures
- **Going through data formats**: CSV, JSON, XML, and more
- **Data sources**: relational databases, NoSQL, flat files, and APIs

Integrating data from diverse sources is becoming increasingly critical as organizations aim to fully utilize their data's potential. Data integration helps break down data silos, offers a comprehensive view of operations, and supports informed decision making. It is an essential component of today's data stack design, which includes data ingestion, transformation, storage, and analysis.

Understanding the data sources: Relational databases, NoSQL, flat files, APIs, and more

Understanding multiple data sources and their properties is essential for integrating data from many sources. Relational databases, NoSQL databases, flat files, streams, and APIs are all common data sources. Each data source has unique features and use cases, and knowing their differences is essential for successful data integration.

In this section, we will go through various data sources, their function in data integration, and their benefits and drawbacks. We will also explore the importance of data sources in today's data stack architecture, as well as the influence of data integration on data quality, governance, and compliance. By the end of this part, readers should have a thorough understanding of the value of data sources in data integration and how to use them for improved insights and decisions.

In today's data landscape, a variety of data sources are used to store and manage information. Each type of data source has unique features and serves distinct purposes. In this section, we will discuss the main characteristics and differences between major data sources, along with popular examples of each.

Relational databases use the relational model to organize data in tables made up of rows and columns. They employ **structured query language** (**SQL**) to define, manipulate, and retrieve data. Common relational databases include MySQL, PostgreSQL, Oracle, and Microsoft SQL Server. They are suitable for managing structured data and maintaining relationships between data entities with primary and foreign keys.

NoSQL (**not only SQL**) databases were developed to overcome the limitations of relational databases in terms of scalability, flexibility, high availability, and performance. NoSQL databases handle unstructured, semi-structured, or structured data and are ideal for managing large data volumes with high write loads. Types of NoSQL databases include document-based (e.g., MongoDB), column-based (e.g., Cassandra), key-value (e.g., Redis), and graph databases (e.g., Neo4j). We will study these different databases in more detail in the *NoSQL databases* section.

Flat files are straightforward data storage formats that store data in plain text or binary formats such as CSV, JSON, XML, or Excel. They can be read and written in various programming languages and tools. Flat files are appropriate for small-scale data storage and exchange but may become unmanageable for large-scale data processing due to limited scalability and the absence of built-in indexing or querying features.

Application Programming Interfaces (**APIs**) act as intermediaries, enabling different software applications to communicate and share data. APIs facilitate data retrieval from diverse sources, including web services, social media platforms, and **Software-as-a-Service** (**SaaS**) applications. RESTful and GraphQL APIs are typical web APIs that enable data exchange over the internet using standard protocols such as HTTP and JSON.

> **Note**
>
> When choosing a data source for your application, consider factors such as data structure, scalability, performance, and specific use cases. There is no one-size-fits-all solution, and you may need to use a combination of data sources to meet your data integration needs.

In conclusion, the selection of data sources depends on factors such as data structure, scale, performance needs, and the specific use case. Comprehending the main characteristics and differences between data sources can help organizations choose the most suitable solutions for their data integration requirements.

Relational databases

Relational databases serve as the bedrock of data management in various enterprise applications, prized for their robustness, ease of use, and reliability. They're designed to handle structured data, with information meticulously organized into tables made up of rows and columns. This data arrangement, along with SQL as the standard language for interaction, enables seamless data manipulation and retrieval. This section provides an overview of the key features that make relational databases indispensable for data management. We will explore how SQL operates within these databases, how data is modeled and normalized, and what considerations are involved in managing and using these systems.

History of relational databases

The relational database model was introduced by Dr. Edgar F. Codd, an IBM researcher, in his 1970 paper, *A Relational Model of Data for Large Shared Data Banks*. This model revolutionized data management by organizing data into tables with rows and columns, allowing easy manipulation and retrieval of information. Over the years, SQL was developed as a standard language for interacting with relational databases.

Popular relational databases, such as MySQL, PostgreSQL, Microsoft SQL Server, and Oracle, have emerged over time, each with unique features and capabilities. These databases have become the backbone of many enterprise applications and continue to be widely used for their robustness, reliability, and ease of use.

Key features of relational databases

Relational databases offer several key features that make them ideal for storing and managing structured data:

- **Structure and organization of data**: Data in a relational database is organized into tables, which consist of **rows (records)** and **columns (attributes)**. This structure allows efficient storage and easy querying of data.

- **Data integrity and consistency**: Relational databases enforce **atomicity**, **consistency**, **isolation**, and **durability** (**ACID**) properties, ensuring data integrity and consistency, even in the face of hardware failures or crashes.

- **Indexing and query optimization**: Relational databases support various indexing techniques, such as B-trees, bitmap indexes, and hash indexes, which can significantly speed up query performance. Query optimizers analyze and choose the most efficient execution plan for a given SQL query.

- **Support for transactions and concurrent users**: Transactions enable multiple users to access and modify the database concurrently without conflicts or inconsistencies. This is crucial for applications requiring simultaneous access by multiple users, such as banking systems or e-commerce platforms.

- **Security features**: Relational databases provide robust security mechanisms, including authentication, authorization, and encryption, ensuring that only authorized users can access or modify data.

SQL – the language of relational databases

SQL serves as the standard language for communication with relational databases.

It allows users to define, manipulate, and retrieve data using a set of predefined operations:

- **SQL syntax and operations**: SQL operations include `SELECT` (to retrieve data), `INSERT` (to add new records), `UPDATE` (to modify existing records), and `DELETE` (to remove records).

- **Data definition and manipulation**: SQL supports **data definition language (DDL)** operations for creating, altering, and deleting database objects such as tables, indexes, and constraints. **Data manipulation language (DML)** operations allow the insertion, modification, and retrieval of data within those objects.

- **Complex query capabilities**: SQL provides advanced querying features, such as `JOIN` (to combine data from multiple tables), `GROUP BY` (to aggregate data), `HAVING` (to filter aggregated data), subqueries (to nest queries within other queries), and importantly, window functions (using `OVER (PARTITION BY ...)` syntax), which enable more sophisticated analytical operations over a set of rows related to the current row. Window functions are crucial for tasks such as running totals, moving averages, and rank assignments within specific partitions of the data.

- **Stored procedures, triggers, and views**: Stored procedures are sections of precompiled SQL code that can be called to perform complex operations, offering a programmability feature that greatly depends on the database vendor. While they can significantly enhance efficiency and reusability for complex operations, their use can also introduce governance challenges and potentially generate performance bottlenecks within the database infrastructure, particularly concerning concurrency and resource management. Triggers, on the other hand, are actions automatically executed in response to specific events in the database, enabling automated data integrity and business rule enforcement. However, like stored procedures, they must be used judiciously to prevent unintended performance impacts. Views are virtual tables created by querying one or more existing tables, providing a simplified or customized representation of the data, which can improve data accessibility and security by abstracting the underlying table structures.

The following screenshot shows the different types of queries in SQL:

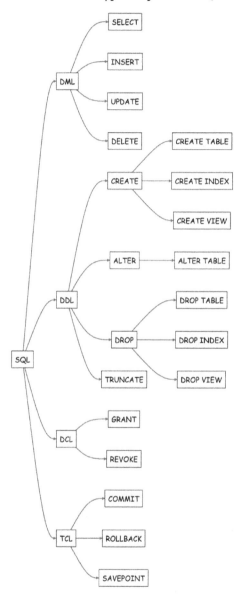

Figure 4.1 – Different types of queries in SQL

The primary features of SQL facilitate operations on data structures, and subsequently on the data itself, while also considering elements related to access control. This balance between structural manipulation and direct data operation emphasizes SQL's robust capabilities for data management.

Here is an example of an SQL structure to represent the same user data:

```sql
CREATE TABLE user (
    id INT,
    lastName VARCHAR(50),
    firstName VARCHAR(50),
    age INT,
    email VARCHAR(100),
    street VARCHAR(100),
    city VARCHAR(50),
    country VARCHAR(50)
);
CREATE TABLE phone (
    user_id INT,
    type VARCHAR(50),
    number VARCHAR(20)
);

INSERT INTO user (id, lastName, firstName, age, email, street, city,
country)
VALUES (123456, 'Doe', 'John', 30, 'johndoe@example.com', '123 Main
Street', 'City', 'Country');

INSERT INTO phone (user_id, type, number)
VALUES (123456, 'mobile', '1234567890');

INSERT INTO phone (user_id, type, number)
VALUES (123456, 'work', '0987654321');
```

In this example, we are creating two tables: `user` to store the user information and `phone` to store the user's phone numbers. The columns in the `user` table correspond to the user's attributes, while the columns in the `phone` table correspond to the attributes of the phone numbers.

Data is then inserted into the tables using the `INSERT INTO` statement.

This represents a simple structure of a relational database to store user data with a relationship between the `user` and `phone` table based on the foreign key `user_id`.

It should be noted that this example represents the structure and data in the form of SQL queries, but in practice, you would need a DBMS such as MySQL, PostgreSQL, or SQLite to execute these queries and manage the data persistently.

Data modeling and normalization in relational databases

Data modeling in relational databases involves creating an **entity-relationship** (**ER**) model that represents the structure of the data and its relationships. The ER model consists of entities (tables), attributes (columns), and relationships (foreign key constraints).

The process of organizing data in a database to reduce redundancy and improve data integrity is called **normalization**.

Normalization involves decomposing tables into smaller, more manageable tables without losing any information.

The process follows several **normal forms** (**NF**), each with specific rules, which are represented in the following table:

Normal Form	Definition	Criteria
1NF	First NF	A table is in 1NF if it has a primary key. All its columns contain atomic values (no repeating groups or nested data structures).
2NF	Second NF	A table is in 2NF if it is in 1NF. All its non-primary key columns depend on the whole primary key, not just a part of it (no partial dependencies).
3NF	Third NF	A table is in 3NF if it is in 2NF. All its non-primary key columns depend only on the primary key, not on other non-primary key columns (no transitive dependencies).
BCNF 4NF 5NF	Boyce-Codd NF Fourth NF Fifth NF	A table is in these forms if it is in 3NF. More advanced normal forms that address specific issues and further improve data integrity and consistency.

Table 4.1 – Comparison of the various NFs

We will develop these different forms further in *Chapter 7, Data Ingestion and Storage Strategies*.

Use cases for relational databases

Relational databases are well-suited for a variety of use cases due to their robustness, flexibility, and support for complex queries. Some common use cases include the following:

- **Enterprise applications**: Many business applications, such as **customer relationship management (CRM)** systems, **human resource management systems (HRMS)**, and **enterprise resource planning (ERP)** systems, rely on relational databases to store and manage large amounts of structured data

- **E-commerce platforms**: Relational databases can efficiently manage inventory, customer data, order processing, and payment information for online stores

- **Financial systems**: Banking, insurance, and investment applications benefit from the strong data integrity and security features of relational databases

- **Healthcare systems**: Patient records, medical history, and treatment plans can be securely stored and easily accessed in relational databases

- **Content management systems (CMS)**: Websites and blogs can use relational databases to store and manage articles, pages, and user data

While relational databases have proven effective in many use cases, they may not be the best choice for every application. For instance, they may not be ideal for handling very large datasets, unstructured data, or real-time data processing. In such cases, alternative data storage solutions, such as NoSQL databases, columnar data formats, or data streaming platforms, might be more appropriate.

Limitations of relational databases

Despite their widespread use and numerous advantages, relational databases also have some limitations:

- **Scalability**: As the volume of data and the number of users increase, relational databases can struggle to maintain performance. While vertical scaling (adding more resources to a single server) can help, horizontal scaling (distributing data across multiple servers) can be challenging due to the relational model's reliance on joins and transactions.

- **Handling unstructured data**: Relational databases are designed for structured data, making it difficult to store and manage unstructured data, such as text, images, and videos, efficiently.

- **Flexibility**: The rigid schema of relational databases can be a disadvantage when dealing with constantly changing data requirements. Modifying the schema can be time consuming and may require downtime.

- **Complex queries**: Some types of queries, such as hierarchical or graph-based queries, can be difficult to express and execute efficiently using SQL.

Conclusion

Relational databases have been a mainstay in the world of data storage and management for decades. They offer a powerful and flexible way to organize structured data, maintain data integrity, and support complex queries. However, they are not without their limitations, particularly when it comes to scalability and handling unstructured data.

> **Tip**
>
> SQL is a powerful and widely used language for interacting with relational databases. However, it can also be challenging to write and optimize complex queries. To improve your SQL skills, you can use online resources such as SQLZoo, W3Schools, or Khan Academy. As the volume, variety, and velocity of data continue to grow, new data storage and management solutions have emerged to address the shortcomings of relational databases. These include NoSQL databases, columnar data formats, and data streaming platforms, which offer different trade-offs and are better suited for specific use cases. Understanding the strengths and weaknesses of each approach is crucial for choosing the right data storage solution for your application.

NoSQL databases

We will now turn our attention to a significant milestone in the evolution of data management – NoSQL databases. This section presents a crucial shift from traditional databases and the relational model to more flexible, scalable, and diverse data management solutions.

NoSQL databases emerged as a response to the need for handling vast amounts of unstructured and semi-structured data. These databases are designed to handle requirements that are difficult to meet with conventional relational databases, such as scalability, speed, and varied data types.

History of NoSQL databases

The term **NoSQL** was first used in 1998 by Carlo Strozzi to describe his lightweight, open source relational database that did not use SQL. However, the modern interpretation of NoSQL emerged in the late 2000s as the need for more scalable and flexible data storage solutions grew. The rise of big data, social media platforms, and cloud computing further emphasized the limitations of traditional relational databases, leading to the development of various NoSQL databases.

Types of NoSQL databases

There are four primary types of NoSQL databases and each one has its own unique features and use cases:

- **Document-based**: These databases store data as documents, often in JSON or BSON format. They offer flexible schema, allowing for varying fields and data types within the same collection. Examples include MongoDB and Couchbase.

- **Column-based**: These databases store data as columns rather than rows, enabling efficient querying and storage of sparse data. They are designed for high write and read throughput and are well suited for distributed systems. Examples include Apache Cassandra and HBase.

- **Key-value**: These databases store data as key-value pairs, enabling fast and straightforward lookups. They are suitable for caching, session management, and real-time analytics. Examples include Redis and Amazon DynamoDB.

- **Graph databases**: These databases store data as nodes and edges in a graph, enabling efficient querying of relationships between entities. They are well-suited for social networks, recommendation engines, and fraud detection. Examples include Neo4j and Amazon Neptune.

- **Hybrid SQL/NoSQL**: Some databases combine the benefits of relational databases with the flexibility of NoSQL databases, offering support for both structured data and unstructured data. PostgreSQL, for example, is a popular open source relational database system that also supports NoSQL features such as JSON data storage and full-text search. This hybrid approach allows developers to leverage the advantages of both SQL and NoSQL databases within a single system, making it suitable for a wide range of applications that require both relational and non-relational data storage.

- **Time series database** (**TSDB**): A TSDB is a specialized type of database designed specifically for handling time series data, which consists of data points indexed by time. Time series data can be found in various domains, such as finance, the **Internet of Things** (**IoT**), monitoring systems, and more. These databases are optimized for the efficient storage, querying, and analysis of time series data.

The following screenshot shows the various NoSQL types and software classifications:

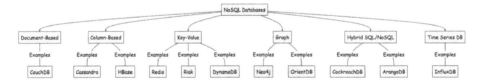

Figure 4.2 – Various NoSQL types and software classification

Here is a representation using a NoSQL database, specifically a document-oriented database such as MongoDB:

```
{
    "_id": "123456",
    "lastName": "Doe",
    "firstName": "John",
    "age": 30,
    "email": "johndoe@example.com",
    "address": {
```

```
    "street": "123 Main Street",
    "city": "Cityville",
    "country": "Countryville"
  },
  "phones": [
    { "type": "mobile", "number": "1234567890" },
    { "type": "work", "number": "0987654321" }
  ]
}
```

In a document-oriented NoSQL database, such as MongoDB, data is stored as JSON documents. Each document represents an independent record that can have a flexible structure.

> **Note**
>
> NoSQL databases offer greater flexibility and scalability than relational databases, but they also come with trade-offs. One of the most important trade-offs is the CAP theorem, which states that a distributed system can only guarantee two out of three properties: consistency, availability, and partition tolerance. Depending on the type of NoSQL database you choose, you may have to sacrifice one of these properties for the others.

In this example, we have a document representing a user with different attributes:

- `"_id"`: The unique identifier of the user.
- `"lastName"`: The user's last name.
- `"firstName"`: The user's first name.
- `"age"`: The user's age.
- `"email"`: The user's email address.
- `"address"`: A sub-document representing the user's address with additional attributes (`"street"`, `"city"`, and `"country"`).
- `"phones"`: An array of sub-documents representing the user's phone numbers. Each sub-document has `type` and `number` attributes.

The flexibility of the document structure allows for easy addition or removal of fields as per the needs of the application without requiring a rigid schema. This offers great adaptability for use cases that may have varying or evolving data.

Key features of NoSQL databases

NoSQL databases offer several key features that differentiate them from relational databases:

- **Schema flexibility**: NoSQL databases often support dynamic or schema-less data models, allowing for easy adaptation to changing data requirements

- **Horizontal scalability**: NoSQL databases are designed to scale out by distributing data across multiple servers, enabling them to handle large volumes of data and high write loads

- **High performance**: By optimizing for specific data models and use cases, NoSQL databases can provide better performance than relational databases for certain workloads

- **Support for diverse data types**: NoSQL databases can handle unstructured, semi-structured, and structured data, making them suitable for a wide range of applications

Use cases for NoSQL databases

NoSQL databases are well suited for a variety of use cases, including the following:

- **Big data processing**: NoSQL databases can handle large volumes of data with high write loads, making them ideal for big data applications, such as log and event data processing

- **Content management and delivery**: The flexibility and performance of NoSQL databases make them suitable for managing and delivering diverse content types, such as web pages, multimedia, and metadata

- **Real-time analytics**: The fast read and write capabilities of key-value and column-based NoSQL databases are ideal for real-time analytics and monitoring applications

- **Social networks and recommendation engines**: Graph databases can efficiently model and query complex relationships between users, content, and products, making them well suited for social networks and recommendation engines

Conclusion

NoSQL databases have emerged as a powerful alternative to relational databases, offering greater scalability, flexibility, and performance for specific use cases.

> **Note**
>
> Some databases combine the benefits of relational databases with the flexibility of NoSQL databases, offering support for both structured and unstructured data. PostgreSQL is a popular open source relational database system that also supports NoSQL features such as JSON data storage and full-text search. This hybrid approach allows developers to leverage the advantages of both SQL and NoSQL databases within a single system, making it suitable for a wide range of applications that require both relational and non-relational data storage.

By understanding the strengths and weaknesses of each type of NoSQL database, developers can make informed decisions about the best data storage solution for their applications.

Understanding the differences between these sources and their respective use cases in data integration

To effectively integrate data from various sources, it is crucial to understand the strengths and weaknesses of each data source type and determine the most suitable option for a specific use case. This section compares data sources and provides examples of real-world use cases for each data source type.

Here is a comparison of data sources based on their strengths and weaknesses:

Data Source	Strengths	Weaknesses	Use Cases
Relational databases	Data consistency, integrity, well-defined schema, and support for complex relationships.	Limited scalability, inflexibility in handling unstructured data, and complex query optimization.	Financial systems, inventory management, and CRM.
NoSQL databases	High scalability flexibility of the schemas and in handling various data types, support for high write loads.	Trade-offs between consistency, availability, and partition tolerance (CAP theorem), and varying query languages and capabilities.	Big data analytics, social media applications, and real-time data processing.
TSDBs	Performance, data compression, time-based data retention, scalability, and built-in time series functions.	Limited data model, learning curve, complexity, integration issues, maturity, and support.	Real-time monitoring and analysis, IoT data processing, and metrics collection.
Flat files	Simplicity, ease of use, and compatibility with multiple programming languages and tools.	Limited scalability, lack of built-in indexing or querying capabilities, and limited support for data consistency and integrity.	Data exchange, configuration files, and small-scale data storage.
APIs	Standardized data exchange, real-time data access, and support for external data sources.	Dependency on third-party services and potential performance bottlenecks.	Real-time data integration, web and mobile applications, and data aggregation from multiple services.

Table 4.2 – A comparison of various data sources

In conclusion, each data source comes with its unique strengths and weaknesses, underlining the importance of choosing the appropriate one based on the specific use case, scalability requirements, and data model. This highlights the importance of understanding the data landscape and tailoring the data strategy accordingly to harness maximum benefits. Ultimately, the right combination of these data sources can enable effective data management and facilitate informed decision making.

Data source choices and use cases

After considering all the previous elements, it is necessary to take a step back in order to select the right solution for the right reasons.

Choosing the right data source

Selecting the right data source depends on factors such as data structure, scalability requirements, performance demands, and specific use cases. Consider the following questions when choosing a data source:

- What type of data do you have (structured, semi-structured, or unstructured)?
- What are your scalability requirements (small scale or large scale)?
- What are your performance requirements (read heavy, write heavy, or balanced)?
- Are there any specific features or functionalities needed (e.g., complex relationships, real-time data access, support for external data sources, etc.)?

Example of use cases

Here is a set of examples to understand the scenarios adapted for each solution.

Here are some examples of this for relational databases:

- Financial institutions use relational databases to maintain customer records, transactions, and account details, ensuring data consistency and integrity
- E-commerce platforms utilize relational databases for inventory management and order processing, where maintaining relationships between products, orders, and customers is vital

Here are some examples of this for NoSQL databases:

- Social media applications often use NoSQL databases to store user profiles, friend lists, and activity feeds, benefiting from the flexibility and scalability provided by these databases
- Streaming platforms implement NoSQL databases for real-time data processing and analytics, enabling personalized content recommendations and user experience enhancements
- NoSQL databases are generally a more suitable solution for implementing time series use cases than **Relational Database Management Systems** (**RDBMSs**) thanks to their schema flexibility and performances in high-speed data retrieval

Here are some examples of this for TSDBs:

- **Financial market analysis**: A TSDB can be used to store and analyze stock prices, currency exchange rates, and other financial data for trend analysis and forecasting

- **IoT and sensor data management**: TSDBs are commonly used for storing and analyzing data generated by IoT devices and sensors, such as temperature, humidity, and energy usage

- **IT infrastructure monitoring**: TSDB can help store and analyze metrics such as CPU usage, memory consumption, and network bandwidth in real time for monitoring the performance and health of IT systems

- **Environmental monitoring**: A TSDB can be used to store and analyze data collected from weather stations, such as temperature, rainfall, and air quality measurements

Here are some examples of this for flat files:

- Businesses exchange data in CSV or Excel format for reporting, analysis, and data migration purposes

- Software applications store configuration data in JSON or XML files, which can be easily parsed and modified

Here are some examples of this for APIs:

- Mobile applications rely on APIs to access real-time weather data, location services, and other external data sources

- Data integration platforms use APIs to aggregate data from multiple SaaS applications, such as CRM, marketing automation, and project management tools, enabling comprehensive data analysis and business intelligence

Next, we'll discuss data types and structures.

Working with data types and structures

Now, our attention shifts to an integral component of our data journey: data types and structures. Understanding these elements is not just a theoretical exercise. It is akin to learning the grammar of a new language, the very language of data.

Data types define the nature of information that we store and manipulate. They are the fundamental building blocks that help us to shape and understand our data. On the other hand, data structures refer to the ways we organize and store these types of data to optimize efficiency and accessibility, thereby maximizing the value we can extract from our data.

In this section, we will explore a variety of data types, from simple, scalar types such as integers and Booleans, to complex, structured types such as lists and dictionaries. We'll also venture into the realm of semi-structured data types, such as XML and JSON, which offer a bridge between the rigid structure of tabular data and the more flexible world of unstructured data.

Introduction to data types and structures and their importance in data integration

Data types and structures are foundational elements that define how data is organized, represented, and processed within a computer system. Understanding these components is essential for effectively integrating data from various sources, as they affect how data is stored, retrieved, and transformed.

Let's first define data types and structures:

- **Data types**: Data types define the nature of data, such as integers, floating-point numbers, strings, and Booleans. They determine the operations that can be performed on the data, how much memory is allocated for storage, and the format in which the data is stored.

- **Data structures**: Data structures are specialized formats for organizing, storing, and managing data, such as arrays, linked lists, trees, and graphs. They enable efficient data manipulation, retrieval, and search operations, allowing the implementation of various algorithms and data processing techniques.

Let's see why understanding data types and structures is important for effective data integration:

- **Data consistency**: Ensuring data consistency across different sources requires a clear understanding of the data types and structures used. This allows the correct handling and mapping of data during the integration process, preventing issues such as data corruption or loss of information.

- **Data transformation**: Data types and structures play a significant role in data transformation processes, as they dictate the operations that can be performed on the data. Knowledge of these components helps in designing effective data transformation workflows, enabling the conversion of data from one format or structure to another as needed.

- **Performance optimization**: Different data types and structures have varying performance characteristics, affecting the efficiency of data integration processes. By understanding these characteristics, it is possible to optimize data storage, retrieval, and processing, leading to improved performance and reduced resource usage.

- **Data quality**: A thorough understanding of data types and structures helps maintain data quality during the integration process. This ensures that data remains accurate, consistent, and reliable, enabling better decision making and insights.

In summary, a solid understanding of data types and structures is crucial for effective data integration. It allows the proper handling and transformation of data, optimization of performance, and maintenance of data quality, ensuring a seamless and efficient integration process.

Overview of different types of data structures

Data structures refer to the various ways data is organized, stored, and managed. Understanding different data structures is crucial for efficient data analysis, as the choice of the appropriate structure can significantly impact the efficiency and accuracy of data processing. This section provides an in-depth overview of three primary data structures -structured, semi-structured, and unstructured data -along with their key characteristics, differences, and examples of data sources for each type.

Structured data

Structured data is a highly organized format where data is stored in rows and columns, following a specific schema or structure. This type of data is easily searchable, as its organization allows efficient querying and processing. Structured data is typically stored in relational databases, which use tables to represent relationships between various data entities.

Here are the key characteristics of structured data:

- Highly organized format with a predefined schema
- Data is stored in rows and columns, often in tables
- Easily searchable and processable

Structured data is ideal for situations where the relationships between data entities are well defined and need to be maintained consistently. This type of data can be queried and processed using SQL, which allows for powerful and efficient data manipulation. In addition, structured data can be optimized for storage and retrieval through indexing, which helps improve the performance of database operations.

Here are some examples of data sources of structured data:

- Relational databases (e.g., MySQL, PostgreSQL, Oracle, etc.)
- Spreadsheets (e.g., Microsoft Excel, Google Sheets, etc.)
- **Customer relationship management** (**CRM**) systems
- Semi-structured data

Semi-structured data

Semi-structured data lies between structured and unstructured data, as it contains elements of both. While semi-structured data does not follow a rigid schema, it does have some level of organization or structure, often represented using tags or markers. Common formats for semi-structured data include JSON, XML, and CSV files, which can be more flexible than structured data formats while still maintaining a level of organization.

Here are the key characteristics of semi-structured data:

- A mix of structured and unstructured elements

- Contains some level of organization or structure, often using tags or markers

- More flexible than structured data, but not as easily searchable

Semi-structured data is particularly useful when data sources need to be integrated, and the data structure might evolve over time. This data format allows for more flexibility in handling data, as it can accommodate changes in data structure more easily than rigid, structured data formats. However, this flexibility can come at the cost of increased complexity in data processing, as semi-structured data may require additional parsing and processing to extract the relevant information.

Here are some examples of data sources of semi-structured data:

- JSON and XML files (e.g., API responses, configuration files, etc.)

- CSV files (e.g., exported data from databases, spreadsheets, etc.)

- Log files (e.g., example server logs, application logs, etc.)

Unstructured data

Unstructured data is the least organized data structure, often consisting of text, images, videos, or other multimedia content. This type of data does not follow a predefined schema and can be challenging to analyze and process. Unstructured data is prevalent in various sources, and its analysis often requires **natural language processing** (**NLP**) techniques, computer vision, or other advanced algorithms to extract valuable insights.

Here are the key characteristics of unstructured data:

- Lacks a predefined schema or structure

- Can consist of text, images, videos, or other multimedia content

- Challenging to analyze and process

Unstructured data accounts for a significant portion of the data generated today, particularly with the rise of social media and other web-based content. This type of data can provide valuable insights, but it often requires more advanced techniques to process and analyze.

As organizations increasingly recognize the value of unstructured data, there has been a growing interest in developing new methodologies and tools to analyze and process it. Machine learning algorithms, NLP, and computer vision techniques have emerged as essential tools in this context, helping businesses unlock the hidden potential of unstructured data.

Here are some examples of data sources of unstructured data:

- Text documents (e.g., Word files, PDFs, emails, etc.)

- Social media content (e.g., Tweets, Facebook posts, Instagram captions, etc.)

- Images and videos (e.g., photographs, YouTube videos, multimedia presentations, etc.)

- Audio files (e.g., podcasts, voice recordings, music files, etc.)

Choosing the right data structure types

Here is a recap of the key differences between the three data structure types:

Data Structure Type	Key Characteristics	Examples of Data Sources
Structured	Highly organized, predefined schema, and easily searchable.	Relational databases, spreadsheets, and CRMs.
Semi-structured	A mix of structured and unstructured, and some organization.	JSON, XML, CSV files, and log files.
Unstructured	No predefined schema; diverse content types.	Text documents, social media, and multimedia.

Table 4.3 – Comparison of data structure types

In summary, understanding the differences between structured, semi-structured, and unstructured data is vital in determining the appropriate methods and tools for data processing and analysis. Each data structure type has its own set of characteristics, benefits, and challenges, and organizations need to consider these factors when choosing how to store, manage, and analyze their data. By selecting the right data structure and using appropriate techniques, businesses can unlock valuable insights and drive data-driven decision making.

Organizations should carefully consider their data sources and requirements when choosing the appropriate data structure type. By doing so, they can ensure that their data management strategies are efficient, effective, and capable of delivering valuable insights to support decision-making processes.

Examples of data types

We will now explore various data types that form the backbone of data analytics and data science. These types each bring a unique dimension to the data landscape. By understanding their distinct features and potential applications, you will garner a comprehensive understanding of how these diverse data types contribute to effective data analysis and decision making.

Textual data

Also known as unstructured data, it consists of written or typed language, representing human communication in the form of text. This type of data is prevalent in various sources, including emails, social media posts, news articles, and books. Textual data is often challenging to analyze, as it requires NLP techniques to extract insights and understand patterns, sentiments, or topics.

Numerical data

Numerical data represents data in the form of numbers, typically used to quantify or measure various aspects. Numerical data is further classified into two types: **discrete** and **continuous data**. Discrete data refers to whole numbers or integers, such as the number of employees in a company or the number of products sold. Continuous data, on the other hand, includes real numbers with decimal values, such as temperature, weight, or distance. Numerical data lends itself to mathematical and statistical analysis, enabling a better understanding of trends and relationships between variables.

Categorical data

Categorical data, also known as **qualitative or nominal data**, represents data points classified into distinct categories or groups. These categories are often non-numeric and represent characteristics, such as gender, ethnicity, or product types. Categorical data can be further subdivided into ordinal data, where the categories have a natural order or ranking, such as education levels or customer satisfaction ratings. Categorical data analysis often involves techniques such as frequency distribution, cross-tabulation, or chi-square tests to identify patterns or associations among categories.

Time series data

Time series data is a collection of data points recorded or observed over time at regular intervals. This type of data is prevalent in fields such as finance, economics, and meteorology, where the data points represent stock prices, GDP growth, or temperature readings over time. Time series data analysis aims to understand the underlying structure and patterns in the data, such as trends, seasonality, or cycles. Techniques for time series analysis include moving averages, exponential smoothing, and **autoregressive integrated moving average (ARIMA)** models.

Geospatial data

Geospatial data, or spatial data, is data associated with geographic locations or coordinates. This data type is essential in fields such as geography, urban planning, and environmental studies, where understanding the spatial distribution of phenomena is crucial. Geospatial data can be represented in various formats, such as points, lines, or polygons, and can be visualized using maps or other **geographic information system (GIS)** tools. Analysis of geospatial data involves techniques such as spatial autocorrelation, spatial interpolation, and geo statistics to identify spatial patterns, relationships, and trends.

The following screenshot shows the various examples of data types:

Figure 4.3 – Examples of data types

As we wrap up this section on various data types, we've established the significant role each plays in the wider realm of data analytics. This understanding is instrumental in deriving varied insights and making well-informed decisions. However, as we transition into the next section, we'll delve deeper into the structures of this data – structured, semi-structured, and unstructured – and their implications for data integration. We'll evaluate their strengths and weaknesses, examine how to handle different data structures during integration, and look at practical examples of their use. By doing so, we can further refine our approach to data handling and maximization.

Understanding the differences between these structures and their implications for data integration

In today's data-driven world, it's important to understand the differences between structured, semi-structured, and unstructured data, as well as their implications for data integration. Each data structure has its own unique strengths and weaknesses, which can influence the choice of data integration techniques and strategies. In this section, we'll compare these data structures and provide insights on handling them in data integration scenarios. We'll also discuss some real-world use cases for each data structure type to give you a better understanding of their practical applications.

The following table shows the strengths and weaknesses of data structures:

Data Structure Type	Strengths	Weaknesses
Structured	It is easier to query and analyze, has a well-defined schema, and is efficient.	It's inflexible; it can't handle diverse data types and its schema maintenance is costly.
Semi-structured	It is more flexible than structured data and it supports diverse data types.	It is less efficient than structured data, harder to query, and lacks strict schema.
Unstructured	It is highly versatile and it accommodates various content types.	It is difficult to analyze, requires advanced tools, and lacks organization.

Table 4.4 – Strengths and weaknesses of data structure types

Let's look at some guidelines on how to handle data structures in data integration.

Handling different data structures in data integration

When integrating data from various sources, it's crucial to consider the types of data structures involved. Here are some guidelines on how to handle each data structure type during data integration:

- **Structured data**: Since structured data is well organized and easily searchable, you can use traditional **Extract, Transform, and Load** (**ETL**) processes to integrate it. This involves extracting data from sources, transforming it into the desired format, and loading it into a target data warehouse or system. However, be mindful of schema maintenance, as any changes to the schema can be costly and time consuming.

- **Semi-structured data**: With semi-structured data, you may need to use a combination of traditional ETL and **Extract, Load, and Transform** (**ELT**) processes. This is because semi-structured data can be more diverse and complex than structured data. You might need to extract the data, load it into a suitable storage system (e.g., a data lake), and then transform it as needed for analysis. Tools such as Apache NiFi and Apache Kafka can help with managing semi-structured data integration.

- **Unstructured data**: Unstructured data requires more advanced tools and techniques for integration, such as machine learning algorithms, NLP, or computer vision. You'll need to preprocess the data, extracting valuable information and converting it into a more structured format before integrating it with other data sources. Tools such as Apache Tika, OpenCV, and TensorFlow can be helpful for handling unstructured data.

Here are some real-world use cases for each data structure type:

- **Structured data**: An e-commerce company might store customer purchase data in a relational database, making it easier to analyze and generate insights for targeted marketing campaigns and product recommendations.

- **Semi-structured data**: A healthcare organization may collect patient data from various sources, such as **electronic health records** (**EHRs**) and medical devices. They can use semi-structured data formats such as JSON or XML to store this diverse information in a data lake for further analysis.

- **Unstructured data**: A media company might analyze social media posts, articles, and multimedia content to identify trends and sentiments related to their products or services. They would need advanced techniques to extract valuable insights from this unstructured data.

In conclusion, understanding the differences between structured, semi-structured, and unstructured data and their implications for data integration is essential for organizations looking to harness the power of their data. By choosing the right data integration strategies and tools based on the data structures involved, you can ensure that your organization is well equipped to make data-driven decisions and unlock valuable insights.

Next, we'll discuss data formats.

Going through data formats: CSV, JSON, XML, and more

Data formats are important in the realm of data integration since they govern the way data is stored, transferred, and processed. Grasping the significance of data formats is critical for successful data integration, as it facilitates smooth interaction between various systems and applications. In this section, we will examine prevalent flat data formats, including CSV, JSON, and XML. Comprehending the importance of data formats and their respective advantages and disadvantages will help you to have efficient data integration. Choosing the proper format tailored to your requirements can guarantee uninterrupted communication between systems and applications, leading to precise and streamlined data exchange. To allow comparison between different files formats, we will use an example of a dataset based on the details of a user's information.

CSV

CSV is a simple and widely used file format for storing and exchanging tabular data. It originated in the early days of computing, with its first documented use dating back to 1972 when it was implemented in the Fortran 66 programming language. Since then, CSV has become a popular choice for exchanging data between applications, databases, and programming languages due to its simplicity, human readability, and broad support across platforms.

CSV files are often used for storing and exchanging data in a table format, where each row represents a record and each column corresponds to a field or attribute. CSV files are plain text files, making them easily readable by humans and easily generated and processed by software. They are commonly used in data export and import scenarios, such as moving data between databases, spreadsheet applications, or data analysis tools.

Although there is no official standard for the CSV format, several organizations have published guidelines and specifications for CSV files. In 2005, the **Internet Engineering Task Force** (**IETF**) published RFC 4180, which provides a common definition of the CSV format. Additionally, ISO/IEC 27025:2019 is an international standard that specifies best practices for using CSV and other delimiter-separated formats in the exchange of data.

The following are lists of the strengths and weaknesses of CSV compared to JSON and XML.

Here are CSV's strengths:

- **Simplicity**: CSV files are simple, easy to read, and easy to create, making them ideal for storing and exchanging structured data

- **Compatibility**: CSV files are supported by virtually all spreadsheet applications, databases, and programming languages, ensuring seamless data exchange across platforms

- **Compactness**: CSV files are generally smaller than equivalent JSON or XML files, making them more efficient in terms of storage and transmission

Here are CSV's weaknesses:

- **Lack of support for complex data structures**: CSV files are limited to tabular data and cannot represent hierarchical or nested data structures such as JSON and XML

- **No standardized schema**: CSV files do not have a standardized way to define the structure, data types, or relationships between fields, making it challenging to validate and interpret the data accurately

- **Limited character encoding support**: CSV files do not natively support Unicode, which can lead to issues when working with non-ASCII characters or international data

Compared to JSON and XML, CSV files are well-suited for simple tabular data storage and exchange due to their simplicity, compatibility, and compactness. However, they are less suitable for complex data structures, lack a standardized schema, and have limited character encoding support, making JSON or XML a better choice for such use cases.

Here's an example of a CSV structure representing a user's details:

```
id,lastName,firstName,age,email,street,city,country,type,number

123456,Doe,John,30,johndoe@example.com,123 Main
Street,Cityville,Countryville,mobile,1234567890

123456,Doe,John,30,johndoe@example.com,123 Main
Street,Cityville,Countryville,work,0987654321
```

In this example, each line in the CSV file represents a user with their attributes separated by commas. The attributes are the same as those in the previous JSON example:

- `id`, `lastName`, `firstName`, `age`, and `email`: These columns represent the user's attributes

- `street`, `city`, and `country`: These columns represent the address attributes

- `type` and `number`: These columns represent the phone number attributes

The CSV format is commonly used to store and exchange tabular data, notably in spreadsheets and databases. Each line of the CSV file represents a distinct record, and each column contains a specific value of that record.

JSON: A versatile data interchange format

JSON is a lightweight data-interchange format that has gained widespread adoption in the software industry due to its simplicity, readability, and ease of use. JSON was introduced by Douglas Crockford in the early 2000s as a more human-readable alternative to XML. It is a language-independent text format, but it uses conventions that are familiar to programmers of the C family of languages. This includes C, C++, C#, Java, JavaScript, Perl, Python, and many others.

JSON is used for a wide range of applications, such as data storage, data interchange between client and server applications, and configuration files. It has become the de facto standard for data exchange in web services and APIs due to its compact size and compatibility with JavaScript, the most widely used programming language for web development.

The JSON format is regulated by several standards, including the IETF RFC 8259, ECMA-404 and ISO/IEC 21778:2017. These standards define the JSON syntax and ensure interoperability between different programming languages and platforms.

The following is a list of JSON's strengths:

- **Human readable**: JSON is easy to read and write, making it more accessible for developers
- **Lightweight**: JSON has a smaller footprint compared to XML, making it faster to transmit and parse
- **Language-independent**: JSON is supported by almost all modern programming languages, allowing for seamless data exchange between diverse systems
- **Native JavaScript support**: JSON is easily manipulated in JavaScript, making it the go-to format for web applications and APIs

The following is a list of JSON's weaknesses:

- **Limited data types**: JSON only supports a limited set of data types, such as strings, numbers, Booleans, objects, and arrays
- **Lack of schema support**: Unlike XML, JSON does not natively support schema validation, which can lead to issues when validating data structures
- **Limited support for metadata**: JSON does not support metadata or namespaces, unlike XML, which may require additional processing for specific use cases

This is how JSON compares to CSV:

- **Hierarchical data**: JSON can represent complex, nested data structures, whereas CSV is limited to tabular data
- **Self-describing**: JSON is self-describing, as it includes the field names, making it easier to understand the structure of the data without additional documentation

This is how JSON compares to XML:

- **Simplicity**: JSON has a more straightforward syntax than XML, making it easier to read and write
- **Performance**: JSON is generally more compact and faster to parse than XML, leading to better performance in data exchange

Here is an example of a JSON structure to represent a user's details:

```json
{
  "id": 123456,
  "lastName": "Doe",
  "firstName": "John",
  "age": 30,
  "email": "johndoe@example.com",
  "address": {
    "street": "123 Main Street",
    "city": "Cityville",
    "country": "Countryville"
  },
  "phones": [
    { "type": "mobile", "number": "1234567890" },
    { "type": "work", "number": "0987654321" }
  ]
}
```

In this example, we have a JSON object representing a user with several attributes:

- `"id"`: The unique identifier of the user (an integer)

- `"lastName"`: The user's last name (a string)

- `"firstName"`: The user's first name (a string)

- `"age"`: The user's age (an integer)

- `"email"`: The user's email address (a string)

- `"address"`: A nested JSON object representing the user's address with additional attributes (`"street"`, `"city"`, and `"country"`)

- `"phones"`: A JSON array representing the user's phone numbers

Each phone number is a JSON object with the `"type"` attributes (the type of phone; for example, `"mobile"` or `"work"`) and `"number"` (the phone number itself). This JSON format is commonly used to exchange structured data between applications, as it is easy for machines to read and parse.

In conclusion, JSON is a versatile and widely adopted data interchange format with a simple, human-readable syntax. It has become the preferred choice for web services and APIs due to its compatibility with JavaScript and its lightweight nature compared to XML. While JSON has some limitations, such as a lack of schema validation and support for metadata, its strengths make it an excellent choice for many use cases in modern software development.

XML

XML is a flexible and versatile markup language designed to store and transport data. It was developed by the **World Wide Web Consortium** (**W3C**) in 1996 as a more advanced and flexible alternative to HTML, which was primarily used for displaying data at the time. XML allows users to define their own tags and structures to represent complex data, making it a powerful tool for various applications.

- **History**: XML was created as an evolution of the **Standard Generalized Markup Language** (**SGML**), a widely used markup language for representing complex documents. XML aimed to simplify the complexity of SGML while retaining its flexibility and extensibility. Over the years, XML has become a popular format for data exchange between applications and platforms due to its ability to represent diverse data structures.

- **Usage**: XML is used in a variety of contexts, including web services, document storage, configuration files, and data exchange between applications. It is a popular choice for representing hierarchical data, such as nested objects and arrays, as well as more complex data models. XML's flexibility allows users to create custom schemas to define the structure and semantics of their data, enabling efficient and accurate data exchange.

- **Regulation**: XML is governed by a set of international standards developed by the W3C, such as the XML 0 and XML 1 specifications. These standards define the syntax, parsing rules, and validation mechanisms for XML documents. Additionally, other ISO standards, such as ISO/IEC 19510:2013, have been developed to provide guidelines for using XML in specific industries or applications.

Let's discuss its strengths and weaknesses compared to CSV and JSON.

Here are the strengths:

- **Flexibility**: XML allows users to define custom tags and attributes, enabling the representation of complex data structures and relationships

- **Extensibility**: XML can be easily extended to incorporate new elements or attributes, making it suitable for evolving data models

- **Standardization**: XML is supported by a wide range of international standards and tools, ensuring consistent handling and processing across different platforms and applications

- **Human readable**: XML is a text-based format, making it easy to read and understand by humans

These are the weaknesses:

- **Verbosity**: XML's syntax is more verbose compared to CSV and JSON, resulting in larger file sizes and increased processing times

- **Complexity**: The flexibility and extensibility of XML can make it more challenging to learn and work with compared to simpler formats such as CSV and JSON

- **Performance**: Parsing and processing XML data can be slower than CSV or JSON due to its verbose syntax and complex structure

Here is an example of an XML structure to represent a user's details:

```xml
<user>
  <id>123456</id>
  <lastName>Doe</lastName>
  <firstName>John</firstName>
  <age>30</age>
  <email>johndoe@example.com</email>
  <address>
    <street>123 Main Street</street>
    <city>Cityville</city>
    <country>Countryville</country>
  </address>
  <phones>
    <phone>
      <type>mobile</type>
      <number>1234567890</number>
    </phone>
    <phone>
      <type>work</type>
      <number>0987654321</number>
    </phone>
  </phones>
</user>
```

In this example, we use XML tags to represent the user's attributes:

- `<user>`: The root tag that encapsulates all the user information
- `<id>`, `<lastName>`, `<firstName>`, `<age>`, `<email>`: The simple tags that represent the different user attributes
- `<address>`: The tag that encapsulates the user's address details
- `<street>`, `<city>`, `<country>`: The tags that represent the address attributes
- `<phones>`: The tag that encapsulates the user's phone number details
- `<phone>`: The tags representing each phone number
- `<type>`, `<number>`: The tags representing the phone number attributes

XML is a format commonly used to exchange structured data between applications, notably in older systems or in specific protocols that use XML as an exchange format.

In conclusion, XML is a powerful and flexible markup language that has found widespread adoption for representing complex data structures and exchanging data between applications. While it may have certain drawbacks compared to simpler formats such as CSV and JSON, XML's extensibility and standardization make it an essential tool for many use cases.

Others

There are several other data formats available besides CSV, JSON, and XML, each with its unique strengths and weaknesses. Some popular alternatives are as follows:

- **YAML (YAML Ain't Markup Language)**: YAML is a human-readable data serialization format that is often used for configuration files and data exchange between languages with different data structures. It is like JSON but uses indentation and simpler punctuation marks to denote structure, making it more visually appealing and easier to read and write.

- **Protocol Buffers**: Developed by Google, **Protocol Buffers (Protobuf)** is a binary serialization format that focuses on small message sizes and fast parsing. It requires a predefined schema for data structures, enabling efficient encoding and decoding of messages. It is particularly suitable for communication between services and storage of structured data.

- **MessagePack**: MessagePack is a binary serialization format that is more compact than JSON and faster to encode and decode. It is designed to be both human readable and machine efficient, making it a suitable choice for high-performance applications that need to process large amounts of data.

- **Avro**: Developed by Apache, Avro is a binary serialization format that supports schema evolution and is widely used in big data and streaming applications. It allows for efficient data encoding and decoding while maintaining compatibility between different versions of the schema.

- **Thrift**: Developed by Apache, Thrift is a binary communication and serialization protocol that supports multiple programming languages. It allows developers to define data structures and services in a single language-agnostic file, which can then be used to generate code for various languages. It is particularly useful for building and integrating large-scale, cross-language systems.

Each of these data formats has its unique advantages and use cases, and the best choice depends on the specific requirements of your application, such as performance, readability, flexibility, and compatibility.

Here is an example of a YAML structure to represent the same user details:

```
id: 123456
lastName: Doe
firstName: John
age: 30
email: johndoe@example.com
address:
 street: 123 Main Street
 city: City
 country: Country
 phones:
```

```
-type: mobile
  number: "1234567890"
-type: work
  number: "0987654321"
```

In this example, we use the YAML syntax to represent the user's attributes:

- `id`, `lastName`, `firstName`, `age`, `email`: The keys representing the various user attributes
- `address`: The key encapsulating the details of the user's address
- `street`, `city`, `country`: The keys representing the address attributes
- `phones`: The key encapsulating the details of the user's phone numbers
- `-`: An indicator to represent an item in a list
- `type`, `number`: The keys representing the phone number attributes

The YAML format is often used for configuration and data exchange, as it is easy for humans to read and write. It is also used in automation and configuration management tools.

Summary

In this chapter, we delved into the critical role data sources play in operations and analysis, providing valuable, timely, and reliable information to the right individuals when required. Different data sources, including relational databases, NoSQL databases, flat files, and APIs, were highlighted, with each being evaluated for its unique characteristics and best use cases.

The chapter then explored various data types and structures, aiming to enhance the reader's capability to handle data more effectively and adjust their strategies according to the nature of the data. Following this, we examined common data formats, such as CSV, JSON, and XML, discussing their unique representation of data, along with their respective advantages and challenges. This knowledge equips you to make informed decisions about which format to use in specific scenarios.

In addition, we briefly touched upon the domain of columnar data formats, highlighting their advantages, particularly for analytical workloads, and the accompanying challenges. The chapter concluded with a comparison of different data formats, illustrating the impact of format choice on performance, compatibility, and complexity, and assisting the reader in selecting the right format for their specific data integration tasks.

This comprehensive overview prepares the reader for the subsequent chapter. The upcoming chapter deepens our exploration of columnar data formats, elaborating on their benefits and challenges, particularly for analytical workloads. It will further illustrate the implications of choosing specific data formats on performance, compatibility, and complexity, thus aiding in the decision-making process for particular data integration tasks.

5

Columnar Data Formats and Comparisons

We will continue our exploration of data sources in this chapter, specifically by going into the domain of columnar data formats. As you'll learn, these formats offer compelling advantages, particularly for analytical workloads. However, they also come with challenges that necessitate thoughtful consideration.

Then, we will compare the advantages and challenges of different data formats. Here, we will illustrate how the choice of format impacts performance, compatibility, and complexity. This will aid you in weighing the pros and cons and selecting the right format for your specific data integration tasks.

The following topics will be covered in this chapter:

- Exploring columnar data formats
- Understanding the advantages and challenges of working with different data formats

Exploring columnar data formats

This section goes into the world of data formats, highlighting the significance of understanding each's benefits. We will explore four widely used columnar data formats, namely **Apache Parquet**, **Apache ORC**, **Apache Iceberg**, and **Delta Lake**.

Grasping the nuances of these formats is crucial, as their performance and specific use cases vary. For instance, Apache Parquet shines in big data processing frameworks, while Apache ORC excels in high-performance analytics. Similarly, Apache Iceberg is tailored for large-scale data lakes with frequent schema modifications and high concurrency, whereas Delta Lake is optimized for Apache Spark-based applications.

> **Important note**
>
> Columnar data formats are not a new concept. They have been around since the 1970s when they were first proposed by Michael Stonebraker and his colleagues at UC Berkeley. However, they have gained popularity in recent years due to the emergence of big data and analytical workloads that require fast and efficient data processing.

Understanding the advantages of each format allows you to select the most appropriate solution for your needs, leading to more efficient and accurate data management.

Introduction to columnar data formats

Columnar data formats are a type of data storage format designed for efficiently storing and processing large-scale datasets, particularly those involving analytical workloads. Unlike traditional row-based formats, which store data in a row-wise manner, columnar formats organize data by columns. Each column is stored independently, enabling improved compression ratios and faster query performance, especially for analytical queries that involve a subset of the columns in the dataset.

Benefits of columnar data formats

There are several key advantages to using columnar data formats:

- **Improved compression**: Columnar storage allows for better compression since the data within a column are often homogeneous, making it easier to compress. This leads to reduced storage costs and faster query performance as less data needs to be read from disk.

- **Flexible schema evolution**: Columnar formats often support schema evolution, which allows for changes to the schema without having to rewrite the entire dataset. This makes it easier to accommodate evolving business requirements and data structures.

- **Faster query performance**: In analytical workloads, queries typically involve a small number of columns.

- **Columns filtering**: With columnar storage, only the required columns need to be read from disk, reducing the amount of I/O and speeding up query execution. Additionally, modern analytical engines can take advantage of vectorized processing, which further improves query performance for columnar data.

- **Enhanced data skipping**: Columnar formats can enable data skipping through techniques such as predicate pushdown and min/max statistics. This allows analytical engines to skip over irrelevant data, further speeding up query performance.

- **Metadata**: Columnar data formats provide faster query performance and more efficient use of storage by storing metadata on the column level, such as maximum, minimum, and count values. This metadata is computed during the writing process, eliminating the need for costly and time-consuming computation during query execution.

Common use cases for columnar data formats

Columnar data formats are well-suited for various scenarios, particularly those involving large-scale analytical processing:

- **Data warehousing**: Columnar formats are ideal for storing large amounts of historical data, enabling efficient analytical queries and reporting

- **Big data analytics**: As organizations increasingly rely on big data for insights, columnar formats help improve query performance and reduce storage costs for massive datasets

- **Real-time analytics**: By using columnar formats in combination with streaming data platforms, organizations can perform real-time analytics on large-scale datasets with low latency

- **Machine learning**: Columnar formats can speed up the feature extraction process and reduce the amount of data that needs to be loaded into memory, making it easier to train machine learning models on large datasets

Overall, columnar data formats offer significant benefits for a wide range of analytical workloads, making them an essential component of modern data architectures.

Representation of differences between row and columnar storage

To understand the fundamental differences between the two forms, we'll start with a visual representation of a dataset's logical representation. This image aims to provide a clear understanding of the order of the data and organization within the collection. By learning this logical representation, you will become more effective at handling data, scrutinizing it skillfully, and drawing meaningful conclusions from it.

The following screenshot shows a logical representation of a dataset:

	Name	Country	Age
row 1	a1	b1	c1
row 2	a2	b2	c2
row 3	a3	b3	c3

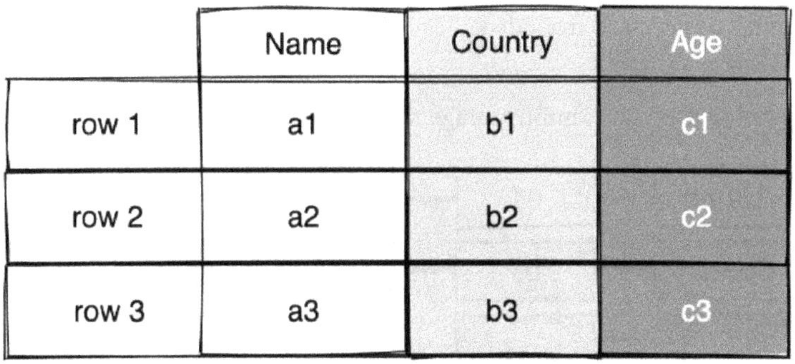

Figure 5.1 – Logical representation of a dataset

Important note

Row storage is a data storage technique that organizes and preserves data records in sequential rows. This methodology is well-suited for **online transaction processing (OLTP)** and transactional tasks because it promotes effective data aggregation and precise column selection. Records are maintained consecutively, promoting swift recovery of singular records and expedited handling of transactional workloads. This configuration benefits analytics by enabling users to concentrate on specific columns, simplifying the aggregation and examination of data according to distinct attributes or standards.

The following screenshot shows a row storage representation:

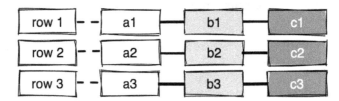

Figure 5.2 – Row storage

Important note

Columnar storage has risen to prominence as a preferred option for managing precomputed metrics such as minimum, maximum, and average values. This storage structure presents multiple benefits, making it apt for such operations. Storing metadata with column data allows for better-informed decisions during query execution, resulting in performance enhancements and helping to exhibit superior compression rates in comparison to row-based storage. The improved compression not only diminishes storage needs but also bolsters query performance since less data must be accessed from disk.

The following screenshot shows a column storage representation:

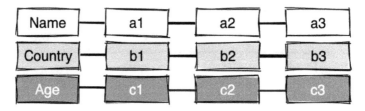

Figure 5.3 – Column storage

We've concluded our examination of the two distinct storage methodologies in data management—row and columnar storage. These techniques, each with their unique advantages, dictate how data is stored, accessed, and utilized within a database system.

Row storage, with its sequential arrangement of data records, is particularly useful in OLAP and analytical tasks where data aggregation and precise column selection are paramount. On the other hand, columnar storage shines in managing precomputed metrics due to its improved performance, superior compression rates, and potential for better-informed decision-making during query execution.

The key to effective data management lies in understanding the nature of your data, the type of queries most frequently executed, and the balance between read and write operations. Such insights will guide you in choosing the right storage format, ensuring optimal performance, storage efficiency, and, overall, a successful data handling operation.

As we continue our exploration into different data sources and types, let's keep in mind these fundamental storage methodologies, as they underpin many of the systems we'll examine. The journey to effective data management is paved with informed decisions, and the choice between row and columnar storage is indeed one of them.

Apache Parquet

Apache Parquet is an open-source columnar storage format designed specifically for the needs of large-scale, distributed data processing systems, such as Apache Spark, Apache Hive, and Apache Impala. Developed by Cloudera and Twitter, Parquet is optimized for performance, storage efficiency, and compatibility with a wide range of data processing frameworks. As a result, it has become the de facto standard for columnar storage in the Hadoop ecosystem.

> **Important note**
>
> Parquet is one of the most widely used columnar data formats in the Hadoop ecosystem. It is compatible with many data processing frameworks, such as Spark, Hive, and Impala, and supports various compression and encoding techniques. Parquet is also integrated with popular cloud data warehouse solutions, such as Snowflake, Amazon Redshift, Databricks, and Google BigQuery.

Key features and benefits of Parquet

Parquet offers several key features and benefits that make it well-suited for large-scale data processing tasks:

- **Columnar storage**: By organizing data in a columnar format, Parquet enables better compression and more efficient query execution, particularly for analytical workloads.

- **Schema evolution**: Parquet supports schema evolution, allowing users to modify the schema of a dataset without needing to rewrite the entire dataset.

- **Compression and encoding**: Parquet supports a variety of compression algorithms and encoding techniques, enabling users to optimize storage efficiency and query performance based on the specific characteristics of their data.

- **Integration with data processing frameworks**: Parquet is widely supported by popular data processing frameworks such as Apache Spark, Apache Hive, and Apache Impala, making it easy to integrate into existing data processing pipelines.

- **Vectorized processing**: By storing data in a columnar format, Parquet enables modern analytical engines to leverage vectorized processing, further improving query performance.

Parquet schema design and data types

Parquet uses a hierarchical schema representation, such as JSON or Avro, which allows for complex and nested data structures. The schema is defined using a combination of **basic** data types (for example, int, long, float, double, Boolean, and binary) and **complex** data types (for example, arrays, maps, and structs).

When designing a Parquet schema, it is important to consider the specific requirements of the data and the intended analytical workloads. Factors such as data types, nullability, and column ordering can impact storage efficiency and query performance. For example, placing frequently accessed columns together can help reduce the amount of I/O required for analytical queries.

Compression and encoding techniques in Parquet

Parquet supports a variety of compression algorithms, including Snappy, LZO, Gzip, and LZ4, allowing users to choose the best compression method based on their data characteristics and performance requirements. In addition to compression, Parquet also supports several encoding techniques, such as dictionary encoding, run-length encoding, and delta encoding, which can further improve storage efficiency and query performance.

Choosing the right combination of compression and encoding techniques depends on the specific characteristics of the data, as well as the requirements of the analytical workloads. In general, it is recommended to test different compression and encoding options to determine the optimal configuration for a given dataset.

Reading and writing Parquet files with popular data processing frameworks

Parquet's wide support across various data processing frameworks makes it easy to read and write Parquet files in a variety of programming languages and environments. For example, Apache Spark, Apache Hive, and Apache Impala all provide native support for reading and writing Parquet data, allowing users to seamlessly integrate Parquet into their existing data processing pipelines.

In addition to these data processing frameworks, there are also numerous libraries and tools available for working with Parquet data in languages such as Python, Java, and Scala. These libraries and tools can simplify the process of reading and writing Parquet files, as well as performing schema evolution and other data management tasks.

Performance considerations and best practices

When working with Parquet, it is essential to consider various performance factors to ensure optimal storage efficiency and query performance. Here are some best practices and performance considerations to keep in mind:

- **Choose the right compression and encoding techniques**: As mentioned earlier, selecting the appropriate compression algorithm and encoding technique can significantly impact storage efficiency and query performance. Test different options to find the best combination for your specific data and workload:

- **Partitioning**: Partitioning your data can dramatically improve query performance by reducing the amount of data that needs to be read for a given query. Use partition columns that are commonly used in filter conditions to achieve the most significant performance gains.

- **Column ordering**: Place frequently accessed columns together in the schema to minimize I/O during analytical queries. This can help improve query performance by reducing the amount of data that needs to be read from the disk.

- **Row group size**: Parquet organizes data into row groups, which are the unit of parallelism during query execution. Choosing the right row group size can impact query performance, as smaller row groups may lead to increased parallelism, while larger row groups can result in better compression. The optimal row group size depends on the specific data and workload, so it's essential to experiment with different row group sizes to determine the best configuration.

- **Use vectorized processing**: Modern analytical engines can leverage vectorized processing to improve query performance further. Ensure that your data processing framework supports vectorized processing with Parquet and enables it when possible.

By following these best practices and performance considerations, you can optimize your use of Apache Parquet to achieve maximum storage efficiency and query performance in your data processing pipelines.

The following screenshot shows an Apache Parquet design:

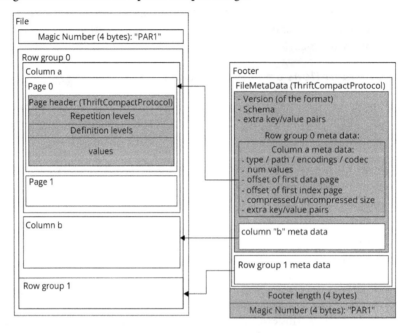

Figure 5.4 – Apache Parquet design

Here is an example of how one might write and read data with the Parquet format using the `PyArrow` library in Python:

```
import pyarrow.parquet as pq
import pyarrow as pa
import pandas as pd
# Creating a pandas DataFrame
data = pd.DataFrame({
    'id': [123456, 123457],
    'lastName': ['Doe', 'Smith'],
    'firstName': ['John', 'Jane'],
    'age': [30, 25],
    'email': ['johndoe@example.com', 'janesmith@example.com'],
    'address': ['123 Main Street', '456 Oak Avenue'],
    'city': ['City', 'Oak'],
    'country': ['Country', 'Tree'],
    'phoneType': ['mobile', 'work'],
    'phoneNumber': ['1234567890', '0987654321']
})
# Convert the DataFrame into an Arrow Table
table = pa.Table.from_pandas(data)
```

```
# Write the Table to a Parquet file
pq.write_table(table, 'user.parquet')

# Reading the Parquet file
table2 = pq.read_table('user.parquet')

# Convert the Table back into a DataFrame
data2 = table2.to_pandas()
print(data2)
```

Please note that this code requires the `pyarrow` and `pandas` libraries, which can be installed with pip install `pyarrow` pandas.

In this example, we create a `pandas` DataFrame with user data, convert the DataFrame into an arrow table, and then write the table to a Parquet file. Then, we read the Parquet file into another table, which we then convert back into a DataFrame to print it. You can also utilize alternative libraries, such as `pola.rs`, to perform similar actions effectively.

Apache ORC

Apache **optimized row columnar** (**ORC**) is a highly efficient columnar storage format designed for Hadoop-based big data processing systems such as Hive, Spark, and Presto. ORC was created to address the limitations of other columnar formats, such as Parquet and Avro, and it offers substantial improvements in terms of compression, query performance, and overall efficiency.

> **Important note**
>
> ORC is optimized for Hive's vectorized query engine, which can significantly improve query performance for columnar data. However, not all data processing frameworks support vectorized processing, and some may even perform worse with ORC than with other columnar formats. Therefore, it is important to test your queries with different formats and frameworks to find the optimal configuration for your use case.

Key features and benefits of ORC

The ORC (Optimized Row Columnar) format stands out for its distinctive blend of efficiency and performance, including:

- **High compression**: ORC offers better compression than other columnar formats, which results in reduced storage costs and improved query performance

- **Light-weight compression algorithms**: ORC uses Zlib or Snappy for compression, offering a good balance between storage efficiency and query performance

- **Predicate pushdown**: ORC supports predicate pushdown, which helps reduce the amount of data read from disk during queries, thus improving query performance

- **Built-in support for complex data types**: ORC natively supports complex data types such as structs, lists, and maps

- **ACID support**: ORC provides support for ACID transactions in Hive, allowing users to perform update and delete operations

ORC schema design and data types

ORC uses a schema to define the structure of the stored data. The schema consists of columns, each with a specific data type. ORC supports various data types, including the following:

- **Primitive data types**: integer, long, float, double, Boolean, string, date, and timestamp

- **Complex data types**: struct, list, and map

Compression and encoding techniques in ORC

ORC uses lightweight compression algorithms such as Zlib and Snappy to achieve high compression rates while maintaining good query performance. Additionally, ORC uses various encoding techniques, such as run length encoding, dictionary encoding, and lightweight compression, to reduce the storage footprint further.

Reading and writing ORC files with popular data processing frameworks

Many data processing frameworks, such as Hive, Spark, and Presto, have built-in support for reading and writing ORC files. This support makes it easy to integrate ORC into your data processing pipelines without the need for additional libraries or tools.

Performance considerations and best practices

Choose the right compression algorithm: Test different compression algorithms (Zlib or Snappy) to find the best balance between storage efficiency and query performance for your use case.

- **Use predicate pushdown**: Leverage ORC's predicate pushdown feature to reduce I/O and improve query performance.

- **Optimize schema design**: Place frequently accessed columns together and use appropriate data types to minimize I/O and improve query performance.

- **Use vectorized processing**: Modern data processing engines can leverage vectorized processing to improve query performance. Ensure that your data processing framework supports vectorized processing with ORC and enables it when possible.

- **Partitioning**: Partition your data based on frequently used filter conditions to minimize the amount of data read during queries and improve performance.

Like the Parquet example, we can use the `pyarrow` library in Python to read and write ORC files. Here is an example:

```
import pyarrow.orc as orc
import pyarrow as pa
import pandas as pd

# Creating a pandas DataFrame
data = pd.DataFrame({
    'id': [123456, 123457],
    'lastName': ['Doe', 'Smith'],
    'firstName': ['John', 'Jane'],
    'age': [30, 25],
    'email': ['johndoe@example.com', 'janesmith@example.com'],
    'address': ['123 Main Street', '456 Oak Avenue'],
    'city': ['City', 'Oak'],
    'country': ['Country', 'Tree'],
    'phoneType': ['mobile', 'work'],
    'phoneNumber': ['1234567890', '0987654321']
})

# Convert the DataFrame into an Arrow Table
table = pa.Table.from_pandas(data)

# Write the Table to an ORC file
with open('user.orc', 'wb') as f:
    orc.write_table(table, f)

# Reading the ORC file
with open('user.orc', 'rb') as f:
    table2 = orc.ORCFile(f).read()

# Convert the Table back into a DataFrame
data2 = table2.to_pandas()
print(data2)
```

Please note that this code requires the `pyarrow` and `pandas` libraries, which can be installed with `pip install pyarrow pandas`.

This code creates a `pandas` DataFrame with user data, converts the DataFrame into an arrow table, then writes the table to an ORC file. Then, it reads the ORC file into another Table, which it then converts back into a DataFrame to print it.

Delta Lake

Delta Lake is an open-source storage layer designed to provide reliability, performance, and flexibility for data processing systems. Built on top of Apache Spark, Delta Lake brings ACID transactions and scalable metadata handling and unifies streaming and batch data processing, making it a popular choice for big data applications. Delta Lake adds a transaction log to Parquet data lakes, enabling concurrent reads and writes while maintaining consistency.

The primary motivation behind Delta Lake is to address the limitations of existing data lakes, which struggle to provide consistent and reliable access to data, especially when dealing with concurrent writes and updates. Delta Lake was created by Databricks, a company that offers a unified analytics platform built around Apache Spark. Since its release, Delta Lake has gained significant traction in the big data ecosystem due to its robust features and seamless integration with existing data processing tools.

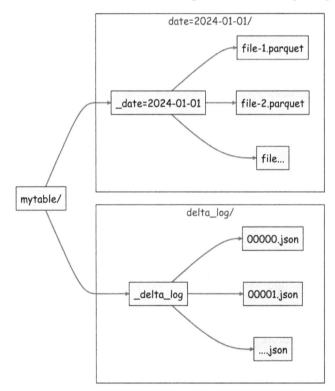

Figure 5.5 – Example of Delta Lake folder hierarchy

In this section, we will delve into the various aspects of Delta Lake, including its key features, benefits, schema design, data types, versioning, transactions, time travel, and integration with popular data processing frameworks. We will also discuss performance considerations and best practices when working with Delta Lake.

> **Important note**
>
> Delta Lake is a popular choice for building reliable and scalable data lake solutions. It provides ACID transactions, schema evolution, data versioning, and time travel features that enhance the functionality and performance of data lakes. Delta Lake is also well-integrated with Spark, which is one of the most powerful and versatile data processing engines in the market.

Key features and benefits of Delta Lake

Delta Lake offers numerous features that contribute to its growing popularity:

- **ACID transactions**: Ensures data consistency and reliability in big data environments by providing atomic, consistent, isolated, and durable transactions. This is a crucial feature in preventing data corruption and ensuring that concurrent write operations do not interfere with one another.

- **Schema enforcement and schema evolution**: Provides flexibility in adapting to changing data requirements. Schema enforcement prevents the ingestion of data that does not conform to the expected schema, while schema evolution allows for the seamless addition and modification of columns in the schema over time.

- **Time travel**: Allows access to previous versions of data for audit and historical analysis. This feature enables users to query and analyze data as they existed at a specific point in time, making it easier to identify changes, perform root-cause analysis, and meet regulatory requirements.

- **Unified batch and streaming data processing**: Simplifies data processing workflows by providing a single API for both batch and streaming operations. This allows users to build complex data pipelines without the need to manage separate systems for batch and streaming data.

- **Support for data versioning**: Facilitates managing data changes over time by maintaining multiple versions of the data in the Delta Lake. This feature enables data rollback, time travel, and auditing capabilities.

- **Scalable metadata handling**: As datasets grow, traditional data lakes often struggle with metadata management. Delta Lake addresses this issue by providing a scalable metadata management system that can handle large volumes of data without sacrificing performance.

- **Integration with popular data processing frameworks**: Delta Lake's compatibility with Apache Spark makes it easy to integrate with existing big data ecosystems. Furthermore, Delta Lake can work seamlessly with other popular big data tools such as Apache Hive and Presto, expanding its reach and utility in the data processing landscape.

- **Optimized storage format**: Delta Lake is compatible with the columnar storage format, Parquet, which offers significant performance benefits. Parquet stores data in a columnar format, allowing for efficient compression and encoding techniques that can greatly improve query performance.

Delta Lake schema design and data types

When designing a Delta Lake schema, consider the following best practices:

- **Use a hierarchical, nested data structure for complex data types**: This allows you to store and query data more efficiently, as it reduces the need for complex join operations.

- **Choose appropriate data types based on the nature of the data**: Selecting the right data type for each column is crucial for optimizing storage, query performance, and data consistency. Delta Lake supports a wide range of data types, including numeric, string, binary, date, and complex types such as arrays, maps, and structs.

- **Normalize the schema to reduce redundancy**: Normalizing the schema ensures that data is stored in a consistent and efficient manner. This helps in reducing data redundancy, improving query performance, and simplifying data management.

- **Leverage partitioning and bucketing for improved query performance**: Partitioning divides your dataset into smaller, more manageable pieces based on one or more columns. This enables faster querying, as only relevant partitions need to be scanned. Bucketing organizes data in a way that enables efficient joins, reducing the need for shuffling data during query execution.

Versioning, transactions, and time travel in Delta Lake

In order to implement the Delta Lake format, here are the three essential points to take into account:

- **Versioning**: Delta Lake maintains a transaction log, which records every change made to the data in the form of versions. This enables users to access and analyze historical versions of the data, making it easier to track changes, perform root-cause analysis, and meet regulatory requirements.

- **Transactions**: Delta Lake's ACID transaction support ensures that concurrent write operations do not interfere with one another, preventing data corruption and maintaining consistency. This is particularly important when dealing with multiple writers and complex data pipelines.

- **Time travel**: Time travel enables users to query and analyze data as they existed at a specific point in time. This feature is particularly useful for auditing, debugging, and recovering from errors. To use time travel in Delta Lake, you can simply specify the desired version or timestamp when querying the data.

Integrating Delta Lake with popular data processing frameworks

Delta Lake is built on top of Apache Spark and is designed to be compatible with existing data processing tools and frameworks. Some popular integrations include the following:

- **Apache Spark**: Delta Lake's seamless integration with Apache Spark allows users to take advantage of Spark's powerful data processing capabilities, such as distributed computing and advanced analytics while benefiting from Delta Lake's reliability and performance features.

- **Apache Hive**: Delta Lake can be accessed from Apache Hive, a popular data warehouse framework, using the Hive connector for Delta Lake. This enables users to perform queries and transformations using Hive's SQL-like query language, HiveQL.

- **Presto**: Presto is a high-performance, distributed SQL query engine designed for big data processing. By using the Presto connector for Delta Lake, users can efficiently query and analyze data stored in Delta Lake.

- **Databricks**: Delta Lake is natively supported in the Databricks platform, which offers a unified analytics platform built around Apache Spark. Databricks users can easily work with Delta Lake data using Databricks notebooks and APIs.

- **Apache Flink**: With the Delta Lake connector for Apache Flink, users can read and write data from Delta Lake using Flink's DataStream API, which supports both batch and streaming data processing.

Performance considerations and best practices

To optimize performance when working with Delta Lake, consider the following best practices:

- **Choose appropriate data types and schema designs**: Designing a well-structured schema with appropriate data types is crucial for optimizing storage and query performance.

- **Leverage partitioning and bucketing**: Partitioning and bucketing can significantly improve query performance by reducing the amount of data that need to be scanned and enabling more efficient join operations.

- **Use columnar data formats**: Delta Lake is compatible with columnar data formats such as Parquet, which offer significant performance benefits due to efficient compression and encoding techniques.

- **Optimize file sizes**: To minimize I/O overhead, ensure that your Delta Lake files are of an optimal size. Large files can cause unnecessary I/O and memory overhead, while small files can lead to excessive metadata management overhead. Aim for a file size between 128 MB and 1 GB, depending on your specific use case and query patterns.

- **Compact small files**: In some cases, you may end up with many small files, which can negatively impact performance. Periodically run the "OPTIMIZE" command in Delta Lake to compact small files into larger ones and improve query performance.

- **Use Z-Ordering for multi-dimensional clustering**: Z-Ordering is a technique that allows you to cluster your data in multiple columns, which can significantly improve query performance for specific access patterns. Use the ZORDER BY clause in the OPTIMIZE command to take advantage of this feature.

- **Incremental updates and upserts**: Delta Lake supports merge operations, which allow you to efficiently update and upsert data in your Delta Lake tables. Use the MERGE INTO statement to perform these operations while maintaining ACID transaction guarantees.

- **Monitor and tune performance**: Regularly monitor the performance of your Delta Lake queries and operations to identify bottlenecks and areas for improvement. Adjust your schema design, partitioning strategy, and other configuration settings as needed to optimize performance.

By following these best practices and performance considerations, you can ensure that your Delta Lake deployment is optimized for your specific use case and provides the reliability, performance, and flexibility needed for your data processing workflows.

Delta Lake does not support native operations with `pandas`, a Python library used for data manipulation and analysis. The recommended way to work with Delta Lake in Python is to use delta-rs or PySpark. This last is Apache Spark's Python API since Delta Lake is built on top of Apache Spark.

However, if you are interested in working with the data stored in Delta Lake using `pandas`, you would need to convert the Spark DataFrame into a `pandas` DataFrame. Here is an example of how you might do that:

```
from pyspark.sql import SparkSession
# Initialising Spark
spark = SparkSession.builder \
  .appName("example") \
  .getOrCreate()


# Enabling SQL commands and Delta Lake operations
spark.sql("SET spark.sql.extensions=com.databricks.spark.sql.
DeltaSparkSessionExtension")
spark.sql("SET spark.sql.catalog.spark_catalog=org.apache.spark.sql.
delta.catalog.DeltaCatalog")


# Reading a Delta Lake table into a Spark DataFrame
df = spark.read.format("delta").load("/path/to/delta_table")


# Converting the Spark DataFrame to a pandas DataFrame
pandas_df = df.toPandas()


# Now you can use pandas operations on the pandas_df object
```

In this example, we're reading data from a Delta Lake table into a Spark DataFrame, then converting that Spark DataFrame into a `pandas` DataFrame.

> **Important note**
>
> It is recommended to work with Delta Lake files mainly in Spark Session. Please note that converting a Spark DataFrame into a `pandas` DataFrame can be expensive because it collects all the dataset's partitions to the driver node. This can cause an out-of-memory error if the dataset is too large to fit in the driver node's memory. You can even use the `deltalake` library to work directly with the files on S3 storage.

Apache Iceberg

Apache Iceberg is an open-source table format designed for high-performance data lake tables. It provides a robust and flexible foundation for managing large datasets in distributed storage systems such as Hadoop and cloud object stores. Iceberg was initially developed by Netflix and is now a part of the Apache Software Foundation. It is built to address some of the limitations and challenges associated with managing data lakes, including schema evolution, hidden partitions, atomic updates, and more.

> **Important note**
> Iceberg is a relatively new columnar data format that aims to address some of the limitations and challenges of existing data lake solutions. It provides scalable metadata handling, partition evolution, atomic updates, and data-skipping features that improve data lake efficiency and reliability. Iceberg is also compatible with various data processing engines, such as Spark, Flink, and Hive.

Key features and benefits of Iceberg

Some of the key features and benefits of Apache Iceberg include the following:

- **Schema evolution**: Iceberg allows for schema evolution, enabling you to add, delete, or modify columns without affecting the underlying data

- **Partition evolution**: Iceberg supports partition evolution, allowing you to change the partitioning strategy without needing to rewrite the entire dataset

- **Atomic updates**: Iceberg provides ACID transaction guarantees, ensuring that updates and deletes are atomic and consistent

- **Scalability**: Iceberg is designed to scale horizontally, allowing you to manage very large datasets in a distributed storage system efficiently

- **Data skipping and predicate pushdown**: Iceberg leverages metadata to enable data skipping and predicate pushdown, significantly improving query performance

- **Extensibility**: Iceberg's modular architecture allows you to integrate with various data processing engines, such as Apache Spark, Apache Flink, and Apache Hive

Iceberg schema design and data types

When designing your Iceberg schema, you need to consider the data types, structure, and partitioning strategy. Iceberg supports a wide range of data types, including primitives such as integers, floating-point numbers, and strings, and more complex types such as arrays, maps, and structs. Iceberg also supports nested data types, allowing you to store hierarchical data within your tables.

When defining your schema, you should consider how your data will be queried and accessed. Organizing your data in a hierarchical structure and selecting the appropriate partitioning strategy can significantly impact query performance.

Partitioning strategies and configuration

Iceberg supports several partitioning strategies, including identity, range, and bucketing. When selecting a partitioning strategy, consider your query patterns and access requirements. For example, if your queries often filter on specific columns, you may benefit from partitioning your data on those columns using an identity or range strategy. If your queries are more focused on evenly distributing data across partitions, you may consider using bucketing.

When configuring partitioning, consider the granularity of your partitions. Too many small partitions can lead to excessive metadata overhead, while too few large partitions can limit parallelism and query performance.

Integrating Iceberg with popular data processing frameworks

Apache Iceberg can be integrated with various data processing frameworks, such as Apache Spark, Apache Flink, and Apache Hive. This integration allows you to leverage Iceberg's advanced features and performance optimizations within your existing data processing pipelines and workflows.

When integrating Iceberg with these frameworks, you'll need to configure the appropriate connector or library for your chosen engine. For example, when using Iceberg with Apache Spark, you'll need to include the Iceberg-Spark runtime library and configure your Spark session to use the Iceberg catalog.

Performance considerations and best practices

To optimize the performance of your Apache Iceberg deployment, consider the following best practices:

- Choose the appropriate partitioning strategy based on your query patterns and access requirements
- Optimize the size of your partitions to balance metadata overhead and query parallelism
- Leverage Iceberg's built-in support for data skipping and predicate pushdown to improve query performance
- Regularly compact small files and remove deleted data using Iceberg's maintenance procedures, such as file compaction and garbage collection
- Monitor and tune the performance of your Iceberg tables by collecting and analyzing metrics from your data processing engines and storage systems
- Consider using Iceberg's Time Travel feature to enable point-in-time queries, allowing you to access historical data snapshots for analytics and debugging purposes
- Ensure your data processing frameworks are configured correctly to take full advantage of Iceberg's features and performance optimizations

- When integrating Iceberg with other data processing engines, use the latest version of the Iceberg libraries and connectors to benefit from ongoing improvements and bug fixes

By following these best practices, you can optimize the performance of your Apache Iceberg deployment and ensure that your data lake tables are scalable, efficient, and easy to manage.

Apache Iceberg does not support native Python bindings, so you cannot directly read or write Iceberg tables with `pandas`. However, you can use PySpark (the Python API for Apache Spark) to work with Iceberg tables. Here is an example of how to read data from an Iceberg table into a Spark DataFrame, and then convert that to a `pandas` DataFrame:

```
from pyspark.sql import SparkSession
# Initialising Spark
spark = SparkSession.builder \
    .appName("example") \
    .getOrCreate()
# Configure the Iceberg source
spark.conf.set("spark.sql.catalog.catalog-name", "org.apache.iceberg.
spark.SparkCatalog")
spark.conf.set("spark.sql.catalog.catalog-name.type", "hadoop")
spark.conf.set("spark.sql.catalog.catalog-name.warehouse", "/path/to/
warehouse")
# Reading an Iceberg table into a Spark DataFrame
df = spark.sql("SELECT * FROM catalog-name.database.table-name")
# Converting the Spark DataFrame to a pandas DataFrame
pandas_df = df.toPandas()
# Now you can use pandas operations on the pandas_df object
```

In this example, replace `catalog-name`, `database`, and `table-name` with your Iceberg catalog name, database name, and table name, respectively. Additionally, replace `"/path/to/warehouse"` with the path to your Hadoop warehouse.

> **Important note**
>
> As for Delta Lake files, it is recommended to work with Iceberg files mainly in Spark Session or to use an interpreter such as Trino, Dremio, or any other interface that will manage the ACID transactions. You can even use the `pyiceberg` library to work directly with the files on S3 storage.

Columnar data formats in cloud data warehouses

Cloud data warehouse solutions have gained significant traction in recent years due to their scalability, ease of use, and cost-effectiveness. These solutions enable organizations to store and analyze massive amounts of data without having to manage complex on-premises infrastructure. Three of the most popular cloud data warehouse solutions are Snowflake, Amazon Redshift, and Google BigQuery.

Snowflake is a fully managed, multi-cloud data warehouse designed for high performance, concurrency, and ease of use. It supports a wide range of data formats, including columnar formats, and provides advanced features such as automatic scaling, data sharing, and data versioning.

Amazon Redshift is a fully managed, petabyte-scale data warehouse service by **Amazon Web Services** (**AWS**). It uses a columnar storage format to optimize query performance and supports a broad set of data processing and analytics tools.

Google BigQuery is a serverless, multi-cloud data warehouse offered by **Google Cloud Platform** (**GCP**). It enables super-fast SQL queries by using a columnar storage format and provides features such as automatic scaling, data encryption, and integration with various data processing tools.

How columnar data formats are used in cloud data warehouses

Cloud data warehouses leverage columnar data formats to optimize query performance and reduce storage costs. In a columnar format, data is stored in a column-wise fashion, allowing for efficient compression and encoding techniques. This format enables cloud data warehouses to read only the required columns during query execution, minimizing I/O operations and improving query performance. Moreover, columnar formats provide better data compression, reducing storage costs and network latency.

Snowflake, Amazon Redshift, and Google BigQuery all use columnar data formats internally to store and process data. While these solutions may use different underlying formats and technologies, they all take advantage of the benefits provided by columnar storage.

Performance and cost optimization strategies

When working with columnar data formats in cloud data warehouses, several performance and cost optimization strategies can be employed to achieve the best results:

- **Use an appropriate data format**: Choose a suitable columnar data format, such as Parquet or ORC, when ingesting data into your cloud data warehouse. This will enable the warehouse to take full advantage of the performance benefits provided by columnar storage.

- **Optimize data partitioning and clustering**: Organize your data in a way that minimizes the amount of data scanned during query execution. This can be achieved by partitioning data on frequently used filter columns and clustering data on columns with high cardinality or that are frequently used in join operations.

- **Use materialized views and caching**: Materialized views and caching can help improve query performance by pre-computing and storing query results. This allows the data warehouse to serve subsequent queries faster, reducing compute costs.

- **Monitor and optimize query performance**: Regularly monitor the performance of your queries and identify bottlenecks. Use query optimization techniques, such as rewriting queries, creating appropriate indexes, or adjusting the data warehouse's configuration settings to improve performance.

- **Optimize data storage and compression**: Choose the appropriate compression and encoding techniques for your columnar data to minimize storage costs and improve query performance. Some cloud data warehouses, such as Amazon Redshift and Google BigQuery, automatically handle this for you.

By implementing these strategies, you can maximize the benefits of using columnar data formats in your cloud data warehouse, resulting in improved query performance and reduced costs.

Choosing the right columnar data format for your application

This table provides guidance on selecting the appropriate columnar data format for your application, with a focus on on-premises data frameworks. It remains applicable to cloud services depending on the underlying data technology they use. For instance, AWS Athena utilizes Presto, while AWS EMR supports Spark, Trino, or Presto:

Factors to Consider	Apache Parquet	Apache ORC	Apache Iceberg	Delta Lake
Data Processing Frameworks	Hadoop, Spark, Impala	Hive	Hadoop, Spark	Spark
Main usage	Versatile, good performance	High-performance analytics	ACID transactions, large-scale data	ACID transactions, technical versioning
Integration and Optimization	Widely supported, well-optimized	Optimized for Hive's vectorized engine, good integration with Cloudera, Hadoop distribution	Well-supported, good optimization	Well-integrated with Spark, Databricks, and some cloud providers
Compression Techniques	Snappy, Gzip, LZO, Brotli	Zlib, Zstd, Snappy, LZO	Snappy, Gzip	Snappy, Gzip
Encoding Techniques	Dictionary, RLE, Bit Packing	RLE, light-weight compression	RLE, Dictionary	RLE, Dictionary
Schema Evolution	Supported	Supported	Supported	Supported
ACID Transactions	Not supported	Not supported	Supported	Supported

Factors to Consider	Apache Parquet	Apache ORC	Apache Iceberg	Delta Lake
Time Travel	Not supported	Not supported, but supported with Hive 3	Supported	Supported
File Size	Good for large files	Good for large files	Good for large files	Good for large files
Metadata Handling	Standard	Standard	Improved metadata performance	Standard
Indexing Support	Not built-in, can use external tools	Not built-in, can use external tools	Not built-in, can use external tools	Not built-in, can use external tools

Table 5.1 – Comparing columnar data formats

By considering these factors and testing different columnar data formats with your data, you can make an informed decision and select the most suitable format for your application. In summary, choosing the right columnar data format for your application involves considering the specific requirements of your use case, the data processing frameworks and tools you plan to use, and your performance and storage needs. By carefully evaluating these factors and testing different columnar data formats with your data, you can make an informed decision and select the most suitable format for your application.

By considering these factors and testing different columnar data formats with your data, you can make an informed decision and select the most suitable format for your application. In summary, choosing the right columnar data format for your application involves considering the specific requirements of your use case, the data processing frameworks and tools you plan to use, and your performance and storage needs. By carefully evaluating these factors and testing different columnar data formats with your data, you can make an informed decision and select the most suitable format for your application.

In addition to the factors outlined in the table, it's crucial to consider performance and volume management benchmarks when selecting a columnar data format for your application. Benchmarks that measure read/write speeds, compression efficiency, and the ability to handle large-scale datasets can provide invaluable insights into how a data format might perform under different workloads. For instance, Apache Parquet and ORC have been widely recognized for their efficient compression and fast processing capabilities, making them suitable for high-performance analytics. Meanwhile, Apache Iceberg and Delta Lake offer advanced features such as ACID transactions and time travel, which can be pivotal for applications requiring data integrity and historical data analysis. By conducting or consulting benchmarks that simulate your specific use cases and data volumes, you can gain a clearer understanding of which format will best meet your application's needs in terms of performance, scalability, and maintenance overhead.

Evaluating these benchmarks allows you to make a more informed decision, balancing between operational efficiency and advanced features to find the format that not only fits your current requirements but also scales effectively with your data growth. It's advisable to review recent benchmark studies or conduct your own tests to ensure the chosen format aligns with your performance objectives and the unique characteristics of your data.

In addition to performance and volume management benchmarks, it's essential to weigh the cost (technical and human) and benefits of implementing ACID transactions in your columnar data storage. While formats such as Apache Iceberg and Delta Lake offer robust ACID transaction capabilities, when enabling precise data integrity and historical data analysis, it's crucial to consider whether your specific use case necessitates such features. In scenarios where the complete rewrite of a table is not cost-prohibitive, and the volume of data or the frequency of updates does not justify the overhead of ACID transactions, adopting these features might be counterproductive. The development and maintenance costs associated with implementing ACID transactions might surpass the benefits, especially if a daily or periodic table refresh could suffice for your application's needs.

Therefore, when selecting a columnar data format, evaluate if the advanced data integrity features align with your operational requirements and cost constraints. For some applications, the simplicity and lower overhead of non-ACID formats could result in a more efficient and cost-effective solution. This underscores the importance of a holistic approach to selecting a data format, considering not only performance benchmarks but also the operational context and the cost-benefit ratio of data integrity features. Conducting thorough evaluations or consulting case studies can help you determine the most practical and economical choice for your data architecture, ensuring that you do not incur unnecessary development costs for features that may not provide proportional value to your operations.

Conclusion and future trends in columnar data formats

Throughout this chapter, we have explored the importance of columnar data formats and their applications in various domains. Columnar data formats, including Apache Parquet, Apache ORC, Delta Lake, and Apache Iceberg, provide numerous advantages, such as improved query performance, data compression, and efficient storage.

These formats have found their place in diverse use cases, ranging from big data processing to cloud-based data warehouses such as Snowflake, Amazon Redshift, and Google BigQuery. By understanding the unique features of each columnar format and choosing the right one for specific applications, organizations can optimize their data storage and processing capabilities.

Emerging trends and technologies in columnar data formats

As technology advances, new trends and technologies are emerging in the realm of columnar data formats:

- **Integration with machine learning frameworks**: As machine learning and artificial intelligence become increasingly important, columnar data formats will play a crucial role in efficiently storing and processing the large volumes of data required for ML models. The integration of columnar formats with popular ML frameworks such as TensorFlow and PyTorch is expected to grow.

- **Improved data lake solutions**: Data lakes are becoming central to modern data architectures. Columnar data formats such as Delta Lake and Apache Iceberg are evolving to provide better support for data lake solutions, offering features such as schema evolution, data versioning, and time travel.

- **Enhanced data security and privacy**: With the rise of data privacy regulations, data security and privacy are becoming critical aspects of data management. Future developments in columnar data formats may include advanced encryption and access control mechanisms to ensure data confidentiality and compliance.

- **Real-time processing capabilities**: As real-time data processing gains importance, columnar data formats are expected to adapt to support low-latency, high-throughput scenarios, enabling organizations to derive insights from their data in real time.

Next, we'll discuss the advantages and challenges of working with different data formats.

Understanding the advantages and challenges of working with different data formats

The world of data is vast and diverse, with organizations handling data in various formats for different purposes. Two primary categories of data formats are flat files (CSV, JSON, and XML) and columnar data formats (Parquet, ORC, Delta Lake, and Iceberg). Understanding the advantages and challenges of working with these different data formats is crucial for effective data integration, which is essential for organizations to unlock insights and make data-driven decisions. This chapter will delve into the structural differences between flat files and columnar data formats, explore their advantages and challenges, and explain how to handle them in data integration. Furthermore, we will discuss real-world use cases that favor each data format and the factors to consider when choosing the most suitable data format for a specific scenario. The goal is to provide a comprehensive understanding of these data formats and their implications, helping you make informed decisions in your data integration projects.

Flat files versus columnar data formats

The journey of data integration is akin to piecing together a puzzle. Various types of data formats represent the diverse pieces, and comprehending their distinct shapes, strengths, and weaknesses is vital to creating a cohesive data picture. Now, we turn our attention to the comparison and contrast of two unique data formats: **flat files** and **columnar data formats**.

Flat files, such as CSV, JSON, and XML, are the simple, row-based structures that many of us are familiar with. Each record or data point forms a row with the fields divided into columns, creating an easily readable, widely compatible structure. Columnar data formats, including Parquet, ORC, Delta Lake, and Iceberg, differ by organizing data into columns, a structure that brings its own benefits and challenges.

Our exploration of these formats will dive into the structural differences between them, the advantages and challenges each format presents, and the specific instances where one might be preferred over the other. We'll look at how to handle these formats in data integration, shedding light on the appropriate libraries, tools, and best practices that make the process smoother.

By engaging with diverse data formats, we'll expand our data handling repertoire and take another step towards mastering data integration. Whether you are choosing between a flat file and a columnar format for a specific data integration project or seeking to broaden your understanding of the data landscape, this section will guide you along the way. Let's unravel the intricacies of these data formats together.

Structural differences between flat files and columnar data formats

Flat files and columnar data formats represent two distinct approaches to organizing and storing data. Flat files, such as CSV, JSON, and XML, store data in a row-based format. In a flat file, each record is represented as a row, and the fields within a record are organized in columns. This row-based organization allows easy human readability and is suitable for applications that require frequent record updates.

> **Important note**
>
> Flat files are easy to create and read, especially with random or unitary access data, but they can become cumbersome when dealing with large datasets, especially in analytics use cases. Columnar data formats are more efficient for storing, optimizing, and processing large datasets, especially for analytical workloads. However, they may require more complex tools and libraries to work with them. Therefore, it is important to consider the nature of your data and the type of queries you need to perform when choosing between flat files and columnar formats.

Columnar data formats, such as Parquet, ORC, Delta Lake, and Iceberg, store data in a columnar fashion. Instead of organizing data by rows, columnar formats group data by columns. Each column is stored separately, allowing for efficient compression and encoding techniques. This arrangement is particularly advantageous for analytical workloads that involve querying large datasets, as it enables faster query execution and more efficient use of resources.

Advantages and challenges of flat files

Flat files have several advantages:

- **Simplicity**: Flat files are easy to create, read, and modify. They have a simple structure, and their row-based organization allows for easy human readability. This makes them a popular choice for exchanging data between applications and systems.

- **Portability**: Flat files are platform-independent and can be read by any software that supports the file format. This makes them an ideal choice for data exchange between different systems.

- **Compatibility**: Flat files are widely supported by various data processing tools and programming languages, making it easy to work with them in most applications.

However, flat files also have some challenges:

- **Scalability**: Flat files can become cumbersome when dealing with large datasets. As the volume of data grows, the time and resources required to process and manipulate flat files can become significant, especially for analytical workloads.

- **Lack of data compression**: Flat files do not inherently support data compression, which can lead to increased storage costs and slower data processing times when working with large datasets.

- **Limited support for complex data types**: Flat files may not natively support complex data types or hierarchical structures, making it challenging to represent complex relationships in data.

Advantages and challenges of columnar data formats

Columnar data formats offer several advantages:

- **Performance**: Columnar data formats enable faster query execution and more efficient use of resources, particularly for analytical workloads. By storing data column-wise, they allow more efficient data compression and encoding techniques, reducing the storage footprint and speeding up query execution.

- **Compression**: Columnar data formats can achieve better compression ratios than flat files due to the homogeneity of data within each column. This results in reduced storage costs and faster data processing times.

- **Support for complex data types**: Columnar data formats often support complex data types and hierarchical structures, making it easier to represent intricate relationships in data.

However, columnar data formats also come with challenges:

- **Complexity**: Columnar data formats can be more complex than flat files, making them harder to work with for developers and data engineers who are new to the technology

- **Record updates**: Columnar data formats are not well-suited for scenarios requiring frequent updates to individual records, as updating a single record involves modifications to multiple columns

- **Tooling support**: While support for columnar data formats is growing, some tools and platforms may not yet fully support them, requiring additional effort to integrate columnar formats into existing workflows

In summary, flat files and columnar data formats each have their advantages and challenges. Flat files are simple, portable, and widely supported, making them suitable for data exchange and applications requiring frequent record updates. Columnar data formats, on the other hand, offer better performance and compression for analytical workloads but may be more complex to work with and less suitable for scenarios involving frequent record updates. Understanding the differences between these data formats is crucial for making informed decisions about the best data format for a given data integration project.

Handling different data formats in data integration

When working with various data formats in data integration projects, it's essential to understand the specific tools, libraries, and approaches that can facilitate the process. Each data format may require different methods for reading, writing, and transforming data. Here are some recommendations for handling different data formats in data integration:

- **Use the appropriate libraries and tools**: Many programming languages and data processing frameworks provide libraries and tools for working with different data formats. Ensure that you choose the right libraries and tools for your specific use case and data format.

- **Leverage data format conversion tools**: Data format conversion tools can help you convert data between different formats. For example, you might need to convert a CSV file to Parquet or JSON to XML. These tools can simplify the process and help maintain data consistency across different formats.

- **Apply best practices for each data format**: Different data formats have unique best practices for performance, storage, and query optimization. Familiarize yourself with these best practices and apply them to ensure efficient data integration.

Examples of use cases for each data format

Selecting the optimal data format is pivotal for the success of any data integration project, as each format comes with its unique set of features designed to cater to specific use cases. Here, we explore examples of use cases for each data format, highlighting their strengths and how they can best serve your project needs.

- **CSV**: CSV files are commonly used for data exchange between applications and systems due to their simplicity and wide support. They are often used to store structured data, such as customer information or product catalogs, which can be easily imported into databases or data processing tools for further analysis.

- **JSON**: JSON is a popular format for representing semi-structured data, such as configuration files or data from APIs. It is widely used in web applications and mobile apps for data exchange between client and server. JSON is also commonly used to store NoSQL data in document-based databases such as MongoDB.

- **XML**: XML is a versatile format for representing hierarchical data structures and is often used in industries that require complex data interchange, such as finance, healthcare, and telecommunications. XML is also commonly used to store configuration data for applications and to represent data in web services.

- **Avro**: Avro is a data serialization system designed for efficient data encoding and decoding. It's often used in distributed data systems and big data platforms, such as Kafka, due to its compactness and speed. Avro is schema-based, meaning the schema is defined once and can be used to read and write data without specifying the schema each time. This makes it ideal for storing large volumes of data and for data exchange in systems where forward and backward compatibility is crucial. Avro is also well-suited for complex, evolving data structures, often found in real-time data processing scenarios

- **Parquet, ORC, Delta Lake, and Iceberg**: Columnar data formats are primarily used in big data and analytics workloads to improve query performance and reduce storage costs. They are commonly used with data processing frameworks, such as Apache Spark, Apache Hive, and Databricks, as well as cloud-based data warehouses, such as Snowflake, Amazon Redshift, and Google Big Query.

Understanding the advantages and challenges of working with different data formats is essential for making informed decisions about the best data format for your data integration project. By considering the specific use case, performance requirements, and tooling support, you can select the most appropriate data format to meet your needs.

Handling different data formats in data integration

When dealing with data integration projects, it's essential to understand how to handle different data formats efficiently. The strategies for working with flat files and columnar data formats may differ due to their unique characteristics and use cases. In this section, we'll discuss strategies for handling flat files and columnar data formats in data integration projects.

Here are some strategies for working with flat files in data integration:

- **Use appropriate parsers and serializers**: When working with flat files such as CSV, JSON, or XML, use the appropriate parsers and serializers to read and write data efficiently. Many programming languages and data processing frameworks provide built-in support or libraries for handling various flat file formats. For example, in Hive-based technologies, Serialization and deserialization libraries, often called SerDes, are provided.

- **Leverage schema inference or define schemas explicitly**: Flat files may not always have a well-defined schema. In such cases, you can use schema inference techniques to determine the schema automatically based on the data. Alternatively, you can define the schema explicitly to ensure consistency and avoid errors during data processing.

- **Handle missing, malformed, or inconsistent data**: Flat files can contain missing, malformed, or inconsistent data. Implement error handling and data validation strategies to deal with such issues during data integration. You may need to clean, transform, or discard problematic data depending on the requirements of your project.

- **Optimize storage and compression**: Flat files can be large and consume significant storage resources. To minimize storage costs and improve performance, consider using compression algorithms and storage optimization techniques that are compatible with your chosen data format.

- **Parallelize data processing**: When working with large flat files, you can parallelize data processing to improve performance. Split the files into smaller chunks and process them concurrently using multiple threads or distributed computing frameworks such as Apache Spark or Hadoop.

Here are some strategies for working with columnar data formats in data integration:

- **Choose the right columnar format**: When working with columnar data formats, select the most suitable format based on your specific use case, performance requirements, and tooling support. Consider factors such as compression, encoding, and support for advanced features such as schema evolution and transactional consistency.

- **Define appropriate partitioning and clustering strategies**: Columnar data formats benefit from efficient partitioning and clustering strategies to improve query performance. Determine the best partitioning and clustering keys based on your data access patterns and query requirements.

- **Use vectorized processing**: Columnar data formats enable vectorized processing, which can significantly improve query performance. Ensure that your data processing framework supports vectorized processing and is configured to take advantage of this feature.

- **Optimize for analytical workloads**: Columnar data formats are primarily designed for analytical workloads. Optimize your data integration pipeline to take advantage of features such as predicate pushdown, column pruning, and filter pushdown to improve query performance.

- **Handle schema evolution and schema enforcement**: Columnar data formats often support schema evolution, allowing you to add, remove, or modify columns without rewriting the entire dataset. Use the schema evolution and schema enforcement features to maintain data consistency and integrity throughout the data integration process.

By implementing these strategies for handling flat files and columnar data formats in data integration, you can improve the efficiency, performance, and reliability of your data integration pipeline.

Real-world use cases – Flat files vs. columnar data formats

Different data formats are suitable for different use cases depending on the specific requirements and constraints of the project. In this section, we'll explore some real-world use cases that favor flat files and columnar data formats, along with the benefits they offer in each scenario.

Use cases that favor flat files and their benefits include the following:

- **Data exchange and interoperability**: Flat files such as CSV, JSON, and XML are widely used for data exchange and interoperability between systems due to their simplicity and human-readability. They are supported by most programming languages and platforms, making it easy to share and consume data across different systems.

- **Small-scale data processing**: Flat files are suitable for small-scale data processing tasks, such as data cleaning, filtering, and simple aggregations. They are easy to process using standard programming languages and libraries, which makes them a convenient choice for quick data analysis and manipulation.

- **Data storage and archiving**: Flat files can be an appropriate choice for storing and archiving historical data that don't require frequent access or complex querying. Flat files can be easily compressed and stored in low-cost storage solutions such as object storage or tape archives for long-term retention.

- **Log file processing**: Log files generated by applications, servers, or network devices are often stored in plain-text formats such as CSV or JSON. Flat files are suitable for log file processing, as they allow for the easy parsing, filtering, and analysis of log data using standard tools and libraries.

Use cases that favor columnar data formats and their benefits include the following:

- **Large-scale analytics**: Columnar data formats such as Parquet, ORC, Delta Lake, and Iceberg are designed for large-scale analytical workloads. They offer superior query performance, compression, and encoding compared to flat files, making them ideal for big data processing and complex analytics tasks.

- **Data warehousing and business intelligence**: Columnar data formats are widely used in data warehousing and business intelligence applications, where the fast and efficient querying of large datasets is crucial. They enable efficient data storage, retrieval, and analysis, allowing users to gain insights from vast amounts of data quickly.

- **Machine learning and data mining**: Columnar data formats are well-suited for machine learning and data mining applications, as they enable efficient data access and processing for large-scale feature extraction, model training, and evaluation tasks. They can significantly improve the performance and scalability of machine learning pipelines.

- **Real-time and streaming data processing**: Columnar data formats such as Delta Lake and Iceberg support real-time and streaming data processing with low-latency query capabilities and transactional consistency. They are ideal for use cases that require real-time insights and decision-making based on large volumes of continuously generated data.

In summary, flat files are well-suited for simple, small-scale data processing tasks, data exchange, and interoperability, while columnar data formats excel in large-scale analytics, data warehousing, and real-time data processing scenarios. Choosing the right data format for your use case can significantly improve the efficiency, performance, and overall success of your data integration project.

Factors to consider when choosing data formats

When selecting the appropriate data format for your project, it's crucial to consider various factors that can impact the efficiency, performance, and cost of your data integration process. Here are some key factors to keep in mind:

- **Data size and complexity**: Consider the volume and complexity of the data you're working with. Flat files are more suitable for smaller datasets and simple processing tasks, while columnar formats are better for large-scale analytics and complex data manipulation.

- **Query performance and data processing requirements**: Evaluate the query performance and processing needs of your project. Columnar formats offer superior query performance for analytical workloads, whereas flat files might be sufficient for simpler data processing tasks.

- **Compatibility with existing tools and infrastructure**: Ensure that the chosen data format is compatible with the tools, frameworks, and infrastructure you're using. This includes programming languages, data processing platforms, and storage systems.

- **Data storage and cost considerations**: Assess the storage and cost implications of using different data formats. Columnar formats typically offer better compression rates and storage efficiency, while flat files can be more suitable for archiving and low-cost storage solutions.

- **Team skills and expertise**: The expertise of your team members plays a significant role in choosing a data format. If your team is already familiar with a particular data format and its associated tools, it may be more efficient to leverage their existing knowledge.

Taking these factors into account will help you make an informed decision when choosing the most suitable data format for your data integration project, ultimately leading to better performance, efficiency, and cost savings.

Conclusion

Throughout this chapter, we have explored the advantages and challenges of working with different data formats, including flat files and columnar data formats. The choice between these formats largely depends on the specific use cases and requirements of your data integration project. Flat files, such as CSV, JSON, and XML, offer simplicity and ease of use, while columnar formats, such as Parquet, ORC, Delta Lake, and Iceberg, provide improved performance and storage efficiency for analytical workloads.

Selecting the right data format is a crucial aspect of a successful data integration process, as it can significantly impact query performance, storage costs, and compatibility with existing tools and infrastructure. It is essential to carefully consider the factors discussed in this chapter to make an informed decision based on your project's unique needs.

We encourage you to explore the world of data formats and data integration techniques further to deepen your understanding and make more informed decisions in your future projects. By continuously learning and adapting, you'll be better equipped to tackle the challenges that come with handling diverse and complex data sources.

Importance of data format conversion in data integration

The conversion of data format plays a pivotal role in data integration, as it facilitates the seamless flow of information between different data sources and systems. Organizations handle data from various sources, such as relational databases, NoSQL databases, APIs, and flat files, which often come in different data formats, including CSV, JSON, XML, and columnar formats, such as Parquet and ORC. Converting these diverse data formats into a consistent format is essential for several reasons:

- **Compatibility**: Data integration demands compatibility between different data formats to enable smooth data processing and analysis. Data format conversion ensures that all data sources can be ingested and processed by the target system or data warehouse, allowing efficient data consolidation and accessibility.

- **Performance**: Different data formats have unique performance characteristics. Converting data into an optimized format can significantly improve query performance and reduce processing time, empowering organizations to make data-driven decisions more quickly.

- **Data quality**: Data format conversion also helps maintain data quality by ensuring consistency and standardization across data sources. This process reduces the risk of data corruption, missing values, and other data quality issues that could undermine the reliability of analytics and insights.

When converting data formats, organizations must consider several key factors, including the following:

- **Data loss and precision**: Ensuring that no data is lost or compromised during the conversion process is critical. Organizations should pay close attention to data types, precision, and encoding to preserve data integrity.

- **Scalability**: As data volumes increase, the chosen conversion method should be scalable and efficient, capable of handling larger datasets without significant performance degradation.

- **Tooling and infrastructure**: Organizations should evaluate the available tools and infrastructure to support the data format conversion process. This assessment includes selecting appropriate ETL or ELT tools, data processing frameworks, and data storage solutions that align with the organization's needs and goals.

- **Team expertise**: The team's skills and expertise are essential for the proper conversion of data types. Organizations should ensure that team members are familiar with the appropriate tools and processes and are capable of efficiently dealing with any issues that arise during the conversion process.

By understanding the importance of data format conversion and carefully considering these crucial factors, organizations can ensure successful data integration, enabling them to unlock the full potential of their data assets and drive informed decision-making.

Summary

In this chapter, we provided an in-depth exploration of columnar data formats. The focus was on their potential advantages and challenges, particularly for analytical workloads. The chapter highlighted the unique aspects of these formats, discussing how their architecture and data storage mechanism set them apart and make them ideal for certain data use cases.

Furthermore, the chapter delved into a detailed comparison of various data formats, reflecting upon how the choice of a format impacts performance, compatibility, and complexity. This analysis was aimed at helping you weigh the pros and cons of different formats and select the most appropriate one for your specific data integration tasks.

After gaining a solid understanding of data formats, we have prepared for the upcoming chapter, The following section will look at the critical process of data ingestion and how it fits into a company's data management strategy. It will cover the fundamentals of efficient data handling, from collection and processing to storage, with an emphasis on optimizing data formats and compression techniques for improved performance.

6

Data Storage Technologies and Architectures

To obtain a competitive advantage in today's fast-paced, data-driven world, firms must manage and analyze their data assets. This data takes many forms, ranging from structured data such as commercial transactions to unstructured data such as social media posts or emails. The capacity to store and process these many types of data quickly is critical for any business looking to profit from the insights concealed inside its data.

Data storage systems are critical in the journey from raw data to actionable insights. With so many data storage systems on the market, it is critical for you, as a data professional, to grasp the distinctions between them and choose the one that best meets your organization's specific needs.

In this chapter, we will walk you through the important central analytics data storage systems, including data warehouses, data lakes, and object storage. We will go over the features, benefits, and drawbacks of each option, allowing you to make an informed decision about which solution is best for your company. By the end of this chapter, you will have the expertise to confidently select the best storage solution for your organization's specific needs.

We invite you to examine your organization's goals, the types of data you must deal with, and data processing demands as we delve into each of these storage solutions. Remember that the best answer for one organization may not be the best solution for another. There is no such thing as a one-size-fits-all strategy for data storage, but with the information in this chapter, you will be well on your way to determining the optimal solution for your organization's unique data landscape.

It is critical to consider data kinds, data processing requirements, scalability, cost, and security while assessing various storage solutions. Each storage solution has its own set of benefits and drawbacks, and recognizing these distinctions can help you make the best option for your firm. Keep in mind that the perfect data storage solution should not only suit your current demands but should also be adaptive and expandable to handle future growth and developing data requirements.

This chapter will delve deeper into each of these key analytics data storage solutions. We will discuss their essential characteristics, applications, and benefits, as well as their limitations and drawbacks. This in-depth examination will enable you to make an informed decision when selecting the best data storage option for your firm.

In addition, we will guide you through the process of comparing and selecting the best storage solution for your organization's specific needs. We will go over the elements to consider, trade-offs, and the decision-making process involved in deciding on the appropriate storage technology for your company.

As you navigate the complex landscape of data storage technologies, it's crucial to understand that there isn't a one-size-fits-all solution that meets the needs of every organization or use case perfectly. The most effective strategy often involves integrating a variety of storage systems, each with its distinct advantages, to build a resilient and flexible data infrastructure. For example, you might leverage a data warehouse for processing and analyzing structured data, while a data lake could be ideal for storing and processing unstructured data. Object storage, on the other hand, might be your go-to solution for large-scale, long-term data storage requirements. Each of these components, working in harmony, can ensure a comprehensive data management strategy that aligns with your specific needs.

To summarize, any data professional looking to make informed judgments regarding their organization's data architecture must first grasp the various data storage technologies and their features, benefits, and constraints. You will be well-prepared to choose the optimal storage solution for your organization's needs and make the most of the valuable insights hidden inside your data if you have a thorough understanding of data warehouses, data lakes, and object storage. So, let's dive in and learn more about these critical data storage technologies.

This chapter will delve into the following subjects:

- Central analytics data storage technologies
- Data architectures
- Positions and roles in data management

Central analytics data storage technologies

To help you grasp the differences between different storage systems, first, we will go over the evolution of data storage options. In the early days of computing, data storage was limited to tangible media such as tapes and hard drives. As businesses expanded and data volumes grew, the need for more efficient and scalable storage solutions became evident. This resulted in the creation of relational databases, which enabled structured storing of data, as well as the capacity to query it using SQL.

However, as the variety and volume of data increased at an exponential rate, corporations confronted new issues in data storage and processing. The rise of big data, as defined by the three **Vs** – **volume**, **variety**, and **velocity** – necessitated the development of new storage solutions capable of handling the massive volumes of data generated by modern enterprises. As a result, data warehouses, data lakes, and object storage emerged as viable alternatives for organizing and storing data at scale.

Data warehouses are built to store structured data in an ordered fashion, allowing for efficient searching and analysis. They describe the structure of the data using a schema, which allows for improved data consistency and integrity. Data warehouses are commonly used for business intelligence and reporting, where quick access to aggregated data is required.

Data lakes, on the other hand, offer a more versatile storage solution that can handle organized, structured, semi-structured, and unstructured data. They can store data in its raw format, without the need for a predetermined schema, enabling data input from a wide range of sources more easily. Data lakes are ideal for enterprises that require massive amounts of different data storage, as well as complex analytics or machine learning operations.

Object storage is a scalable and cost-effective storage solution in which data is stored as objects, each with a unique identifier. This method of data storage is appropriate for dealing with unstructured or semi-structured data such as photos, videos, and documents. Object storage is a popular choice for storing vast amounts of data in the cloud since it is a durable and available solution.

Data warehouses

Data warehouses have played an important role in helping firms manage and derive value from their data in the realm of data storage and analysis. As we discussed in *Chapter 3*, the origins of data warehouses can be traced back to the pioneering work of industry pioneers such as Ralph Kimball, Bill Inmon, and Edgar Codd. Data warehouses have grown over time to meet increasingly complicated data storage and analytics needs, but they also have their own set of issues and constraints. In this section, we will look at data warehouses' essential characteristics, use cases, benefits, and downsides, as well as how their evolution has influenced their current capabilities and limitations.

Overview and key features

A data warehouse is a large, centralized repository for storing and managing structured data from many organizational sources. Data warehouses are built to facilitate the efficient querying and analysis of massive amounts of data, allowing businesses to obtain valuable insights and make data-driven choices.

Data warehouses have the following key features:

- **Mandatory schema design**: A schema design, such as the star or snowflake schema, is commonly used in data warehouses to organize and structure data for efficient querying and reporting. These schemas aid in query performance optimization and facilitate data analysis for end users. (We will cover this in the *Schema-on-write* section.)

- **Data integration**: Data warehouses are designed to incorporate data from a variety of sources, including transactional databases, flat files, and external data streams. To ensure consistency and reliability, this integration procedure frequently includes data cleaning, transformation, and aggregation.

- **Scalability**: Data warehouses are built to manage vast amounts of data and to grow in size as an organization's data requirements grow. This scalability means that data warehouses can handle growing data quantities and complicated analytical tasks without sacrificing performance.

- **Data history**: Historical data is frequently stored in data warehouses, allowing organizations to track patterns and changes over time. This historical viewpoint is useful for comprehending how an organization has evolved and making educated judgments regarding future strategies and activities. Reports and dashboards can be built based on this data to showcase both current and past perspectives, with the current view often referred to as the "as-is" view and the past perspective frequently termed referred to as the "as-of" view.

Use cases and benefits

Data warehouses are well-suited for a variety of use cases, including the following:

- **Business intelligence (BI) and reporting**: Data warehouses excel at supporting BI and reporting tasks, such as generating financial reports, analyzing customer behavior, and monitoring **key performance indicators** (**KPIs**). These insights help organizations make informed decisions and drive business growth.

- **Advanced analytics**: Data warehouses can also support advanced analytics tasks such as predictive modeling, machine learning, and data mining. By leveraging the wealth of data stored in a data warehouse, organizations can uncover hidden patterns and trends, enabling more accurate forecasting and decision-making.

- **Data consolidation**: Data warehouses provide a single, unified platform for consolidating and managing data from various sources across an organization. This consolidation simplifies data management, improves data quality, and enables more accurate and consistent reporting and analysis.

Data warehouses bring many benefits, including the following:

- **Improved data quality**: Data warehouses promote data quality through data integration, transformation, and validation processes. These processes help ensure that data is consistent, well-formatted and typed, accurate, and reliable, resulting in more trustworthy insights and better decision-making.

- **Enhanced performance**: Data warehouses are optimized for query performance, enabling fast and efficient data analysis. This performance optimization allows organizations to generate insights more quickly and make timely, data-driven decisions.

- **Scalability and flexibility**: Data warehouses can scale to accommodate growing data volumes and analytical workloads, ensuring that organizations can continue to derive value from their data as their needs evolve.

Limitations and drawbacks

Despite their many benefits, data warehouses also have some limitations and drawbacks:

- **Limited support for unstructured data**: Data warehouses are designed primarily for structured data and may struggle to accommodate unstructured data such as text, images, or video. This limitation can make it challenging for organizations with diverse data needs to fully leverage the power of a data warehouse.

- **Complexity and cost**: Implementing and maintaining a data warehouse can be complex and costly, particularly for smaller organizations with limited resources. This complexity can make it challenging for organizations to fully realize the benefits of a data warehouse, especially if they lack the necessary expertise and infrastructure.

- **Data latency**: Data warehouses often rely on batch processing to load data, which can result in data latency. This latency means that real-time or near-real-time analysis may not be possible, limiting the usefulness of data warehouses for some use cases.

- **Rigidity**: Data warehouses typically require a predefined schema, which can make it challenging to accommodate changes in data sources or business requirements. This rigidity can lead to time-consuming and costly schema modifications when changes arise.

In summary, data warehouses have long been a data storage industry standard that provides enterprises with a centralized, scalable platform for organizing and analyzing massive amounts of structured data. Because of their skills in enabling business intelligence, reporting, and advanced analytics, they are a useful asset to many firms looking to leverage data for strategic decision-making and growth.

However, they also have constraints and drawbacks, such as limited support for unstructured data, complexity and cost, data latency, and rigidity. When contemplating a data warehouse for your firm, it is critical to balance these considerations with your specific goals and resources. You can make an informed choice about whether data warehouses are the perfect fit for your organization's data storage and analysis needs by carefully assessing their use cases, benefits, and constraints.

Data lakes

Now that we've discussed the benefits and limitations of data warehouses, let's delve into another popular data storage technology: data lakes. Emerging as an alternative to traditional data warehouses, data lakes offer a more flexible and scalable solution for storing and processing diverse types of data, including unstructured and semi-structured data.

Overview and key features

A data lake is a centralized repository designed to store vast amounts of raw data in its native format until it is needed for analysis. (We will cover this in more detail in the *Schema-on-read* section.) Unlike data warehouses, which rely on structured and organized data, data lakes accommodate data in any form, including structured, semi-structured, and unstructured data. This flexibility allows organizations to store data from multiple sources, such as social media, **Internet of Things** (**IoT**) devices, log files, and more, without the need for time-consuming data transformation processes upfront. Here is an overview of the key features of the data lake architecture:

- **Schema-on-read**: Data lakes store data in its raw format, only applying schema and structure when the data is ready for analysis. This approach enables more flexibility in data storage and usage as analysts can decide on the structure and format at the time of analysis.

- **Scalability**: Data lakes can handle large volumes of data with ease, making them suitable for organizations dealing with big data and rapid data growth.

- **Cost-effectiveness**: Data lakes often leverage inexpensive storage solutions, such as cloud-based object storage, which can lower the overall storage cost compared to traditional data warehouses.

- **Support for diverse data types**: Data lakes can store structured, semi-structured, and unstructured data, allowing organizations to leverage a wide variety of data sources for analysis.

- **Data processing capabilities**: Many data lakes are built on top of distributed computing frameworks such as Apache Hadoop or Apache Spark, providing powerful processing capabilities for large-scale data analysis.

- **Metadata**: Files within data lake storage systems contain not only the data itself but also metadata describing the files. This metadata may include information such as the file creation date, size, and access permissions. Customizable metadata allows users to add relevant information for their use case, which is helpful when searching and managing objects.

- **Data durability and redundancy**: A data lake is mainly implemented in a form of distributed information storage such as **Hadoop Distributed File System** (**HDFS**). Those storage systems are designed to provide high levels of data durability and redundancy by automatically distributing data across multiple storage nodes. This ensures data remains accessible, even if one or more nodes fail. Data replication and erasure coding techniques are commonly employed to achieve this level of durability and redundancy.

Use cases and benefits

Data lakes are an ideal solution for organizations with diverse data types and large data volumes. Here are some common use cases and benefits of data lakes:

- **Big data analytics**: Data lakes are well-suited for storing and processing vast amounts of data, enabling organizations to perform advanced analytics and extract valuable insights

- **Real-time data processing**: Data lakes can support real-time data ingestion and processing, allowing organizations to gain immediate insights from their data

- **Data exploration and discovery**: Data lakes provide a flexible environment for data scientists and analysts to explore raw data, discover new patterns, and test hypotheses without the constraints of predefined schemas

- **Machine learning and artificial intelligence**: Data lakes can store the large volumes of data required for training machine learning models, enabling organizations to leverage AI for data-driven decision-making

- **Enabling data democratization**: Data lakes can help democratize access to data, allowing various stakeholders within an organization to easily access and analyze data to support decision-making

Limitations and drawbacks

While data lakes offer many advantages, they also come with their own set of challenges and limitations:

- **Data governance and security**: The flexible nature of data lakes can make it challenging to establish and enforce data governance and security policies. This may lead to issues with data quality, consistency, and compliance.

- **Skills and expertise**: Working with data lakes often requires specialized knowledge and skills in big data technologies such as Hadoop and Spark. Organizations may need to invest in training or hire skilled professionals to effectively leverage their datalake.

- **Data swamp risk**: Without proper data management and governance, a data lake can quickly become a "data swamp," where unorganized and unused data accumulates, making it difficult to extract meaningful insights.

- **Integration with existing systems**: Integrating data lakes with existing data storage solutions, such as data warehouses or operational databases, can be challenging and may require additional resources and expertise.

In summary, data lakes provide a versatile and scalable substitute for conventional data warehouses, especially for businesses working with a wide variety of data kinds and substantial volumes of data. Organizations must be aware of the difficulties and restrictions posed by data governance, security, and integration to fully realize the promise of data lakes.

We'll continue to look at various data storage technologies in this chapter, such as object storage, and provide you with the knowledge you need to choose the best storage option for your organization's particular requirements. The focus of the following section will be object storage. There, you will be provided details on its main characteristics, applications, and advantages, as well as any potential downsides and restrictions. You'll be better able to choose the best option for your organization's data storage and analytics needs if you are aware of the many storage alternatives you can use.

Object storage

Now, let's dive into object storage, an increasingly popular data storage technology, particularly for handling unstructured data such as images, videos, and documents. Object storage offers a highly scalable, cost-effective solution that differs from traditional file storage systems, which organize data hierarchically. Object storage uses a flat address space that simplifies management and scalability.

Overview and key features

Here are some of the key features of object storage:

- **Flat address space**: Unlike traditional filesystems, object storage doesn't rely on a hierarchical directory structure. It uses a flat address space in which each object receives a unique identifier, making data management simpler and offering virtually unlimited scalability. However, to simplify data identification, most object storage systems employ a naming convention similar to the hierarchical one. For example, an object key often contains the / symbol, which is visually represented in the user interface as folders.

- **Metadata**: Just like data lake files, objects within object storage systems contain not only the data itself but also metadata describing the object. This metadata may include information such as the object's creation date, size, and access permissions. Customizable metadata allows users to add relevant information for their use case, which is helpful when searching for and managing objects.

- **Data durability and redundancy**: Object storage systems are also designed on top of distributed systems to provide high levels of data durability and redundancy, in addition to data distribution across the cluster nodes. The data is mainly replicated in other data centers. In terms of cloud-based object storage such as S3, depending on the chosen storage class, objects can be replicated within different nodes, different regions, and different availability zones.

- **Simple and scalable access**: Object storage systems utilize RESTful APIs for easy integration with applications and services. This enables developers to effortlessly access, store, and retrieve objects using familiar HTTP methods, such as GET, PUT, and DELETE.

Use cases and benefits

Object storage is a desirable alternative for businesses wishing to store and handle massive amounts of unstructured data since it has a variety of use cases and advantages. Let's look at some typical use case scenarios:

- **Backup and archiving**: Because of its scalability, dependability, and affordability, object storage is a great option for backup and archiving needs. Large volumes of data can be kept by organizations for long periods, assuring data security and accessibility.

- **Delivering and storing media material**: Object storage is excellent for delivering and storing media content, including pictures, videos, and audio files. It is simple to manage and serve content to people all around the world thanks to its scalability and support for custom metadata.

- **Big data analytics**: Object storage can be a great option for storing and processing significant amounts of unstructured data. Organizations can store, retrieve, and analyze enormous volumes of data rapidly and affordably thanks to its scalable and accessible nature.

Limitations and drawbacks

While object storage offers numerous advantages, it is essential to be aware of its limitations and drawbacks:

- **High performance with low latency**: Object storage might not be the best choice for very high-performance, low-latency workloads due to its eventual consistency model and potential for the overhead associated with RESTful API calls. For workloads requiring high-performance and real-time data access, block or file storage solutions may be more appropriate.

- **Complexity**: Object storage can be more complex to set up and manage compared to traditional file storage systems.

To summarize, object storage is a flexible and scalable option for businesses dealing with substantial amounts of unstructured data. Next, you will discover how to compare and select the best storage solution, including the variables to consider and the trade-offs involved. Following that, we'll investigate data lakes and their advantages, which, depending on your organization's needs, could either complement or replace object storage.

Comparing and choosing the right storage solution

Now that we've explored data warehouses, data lakes, and object storage, it's time to discuss how to choose the best storage solution for your organization. Selecting the right technology depends on several factors, trade-offs, and the decision-making process that suits your specific needs. When choosing the right solution, you must consider the following distinct aspects:

- **Data type and structure**: Consider the types of data your organization deals with – that is, whether it's structured, semi-structured, or unstructured. Data warehouses are more suited for structured data, while data lakes can accommodate all types of data, and object storage is excellent for handling unstructured data.

- **Scalability**: Evaluate your organization's data storage needs in terms of size, growth rate, and accessibility. Data lakes and object storage offer virtually unlimited scalability, whereas data warehouses may have limitations.

- **Performance**: Determine the performance requirements of your organization, such as query speed, data processing, and real-time analytics. Data warehouses typically offer high performance for structured data, while data lakes may require additional optimization.

- **Data integration and transformation**: Assess the level of integration and transformation your data requires. Data warehouses typically involve more upfront data processing, while data lakes store raw data and enable processing at the time of analysis.

- **Cost**: Evaluate the total cost of ownership, including acquisition, maintenance, and scaling expenses. Data warehouses can be expensive to set up and maintain, while data lakes and object storage can offer lower costs, particularly for large-scale storage.

Trade-offs and the decision-making process

Choosing the right storage solution often involves making trade-offs based on your organization's priorities. Here are some aspects to consider in the decision-making process:

- **Flexibility versus performance**: Data lakes offer flexibility in handling various data types, but performance may be compromised if they're not optimized. Data warehouses, on the other hand, provide high performance for structured data but may not be as flexible.

- **Data processing**: Consider whether you wish to preprocess data before storage or store raw data for processing during analysis. Data warehouses typically involve preprocessing, while data lakes allow for raw data storage and processing as needed.

- **Long-term versus short-term needs**: Evaluate your organization's long-term data storage needs and whether your chosen solution can grow and evolve with your requirements. Data lakes and object storage offer significant scalability, while data warehouses might be more suitable for organizations with stable, structured data needs.

- **Security and governance**: Assess the security and governance requirements of your organization. Data warehouses generally have well-established security measures, while data lakes may require additional effort to ensure proper data governance and security.

- **Cost consideration**: Assess the financial implications of your storage choice. Data warehouses can incur high licensing and infrastructure costs, while data lakes and object storage might offer more cost-effective solutions, especially for large-scale data needs.

- **Lifecycle management**: Evaluate the ease of managing the data life cycle within the storage solution. Data lakes provide flexibility in storing raw data but may require rigorous management to maintain data quality over time, whereas data warehouses offer structured, well-governed environments, simplifying data life cycle management.

As you venture into the world of data storage, it is essential to understand that not all storage solutions are created equal. Performance, scalability, and functionality can vary significantly across object storage systems such as Amazon S3, distributed filesystems such as HDFS, and data warehouses such as Redshift.

Object storage systems such as S3 excel at handling vast amounts of unstructured data, allowing you to store and retrieve files in a highly scalable and cost-effective manner. However, certain operations, such as renaming objects, are not natively supported. Instead, you will have to perform a copy and delete operation, which can introduce performance bottlenecks, especially when using frameworks such as Spark, which rely on file manipulation.

On the other hand, distributed filesystems such as HDFS are designed to handle large datasets across multiple nodes, making them a popular choice for big data processing. HDFS provides a hierarchical file structure and supports operations such as renaming, but it may not be as cost-effective or scalable as object storage systems such as S3.

Data warehouses, built for heavy-duty analytics and complex querying, prioritize performance and data consistency. These specialized solutions store and process structured data, delivering high-speed querying and real-time insights. However, they may not be as well-suited for storing unstructured data or handling high write loads.

This is why it is common for businesses to combine multiple storage solutions by adopting a hybrid storage systems strategy to tailor to their unique needs, especially when the company must handle a diverse range of data types and use cases. Such a strategy provides the best of both worlds. By using different data storage solutions, companies can optimize performance, security, and scalability by targeting the right storage system for each specific type of use case.

This strategy is based on the concept of **polyglot persistence**, which is an approach that embraces the idea of employing different data storage technologies to best suit the requirements of each use case. Rather than relying on a one-size-fits-all storage solution, polyglot persistence empowers you to cherry-pick the right technology for each task at hand. This may involve using relational databases for structured data, NoSQL databases for handling big data or semi-structured information, and data warehouses for advanced analytics.

Polyglot persistence encourages you to think beyond the constraints of a single storage system and harness the strengths of various technologies to unlock the full potential of your data. By adopting this flexible and pragmatic approach, your business can ensure it is equipped to handle the ever-evolving data landscape and stay ahead of the competition.

Lakehouse

In the context of data management, lakehouse represents a transformative shift that brings together the best characteristics of data warehouses and data lakes to handle the volume and diversity of data that a data lake can manage, while also providing the reliability, performance, and transactional capabilities where data warehouses excel.

The lakehouse architecture implements a storage layer that can handle diverse data types (similar to a data lake), and a query/management layer that provides transactional consistency, schema enforcement, and high performance (similar to a data warehouse).

Open file formats such as Parquet and Delta play central roles in achieving the lakehouse architecture because they are open file formats that ease querying and integration while offering advanced metadata features:

- **Ease of querying**: Both Parquet and Delta optimize data for queries. Parquet's columnar storage format is designed for efficient querying, particularly for analytical processing and large-scale data operations. Delta, on the other hand, maintains a transaction log, enabling quick access to older versions of data and facilitating complex operations.

- **Open file format**: Being open source, both Parquet and Delta foster interoperability and ease of integration with various data processing frameworks. They can be used across different platforms and technologies, thus eliminating vendor lock-in issues and encouraging the use of diverse, best-of-breed data tools.

- **Ease of integration**: Both formats are designed to work seamlessly with popular big data processing tools such as Apache Hadoop, Apache Spark, and others. This simplifies the implementation of a lakehouse architecture. In a nutshell, open file formats such as Parquet and Delta provide the flexibility and efficiency needed to handle the vast volumes and diverse types of data within a lakehouse while also ensuring that this data can be reliably managed, queried, and integrated with other systems.

- **Metadata management**: Managing metadata is a crucial part of any data infrastructure. Delta particularly excels in this area by offering scalable metadata handling. It allows you to track the history of the data and how it has been processed, as well as how it has changed over time.

One practical and prevalent model of implementing a lakehouse is the medallion architecture. This architecture represents the data journey through different stages of refinement – staging, bronze, silver, gold, and insight.

Overview and key features

The medallion architecture provides a structured methodology for managing and refining data within a lakehouse through bronze, silver, and gold layers. The process begins with ingesting raw data into the bronze layer, followed by progressive refinement through the silver and gold layers, with the outcome being insightful and actionable data. After years of implementing it, we found that two optional layers could be added to enhance this architecture and make it work in almost all scenarios. Let's look at the steps that are involved:

- **Staging**: This optional layer serves as the initial entry point for certain types of data requiring consolidation before being sent to the raw layer, such as streaming data on brokers or using CDC. Acting as a buffer, it primarily focuses on ingesting data from various sources, especially those that arrive continuously, effectively managing the flow before it reaches the raw layer.

- **Bronze**: Also known as the "raw" layer, data from external systems is received exactly as it was in the source system, with additional metadata columns capturing data such as load date and time, process ID, and more. The bronze layer focuses on capturing modification data and serves multiple functions: providing a historical archive for source data (cold storage), data lineage, auditability, and reprocessing without the need to reread data from the source system if necessary. When dealing with continuous flows such as CDC or streaming, it's common to first store the data in the staging, and then consolidate it on the bronze layer.

- **Silver**: In this layer, data is identified and strictly processed to keep it light to prioritize speed and agility. This layer focuses on technical aspects, including operations such as data deduplication, normalization, cleaning, and removing cross-references and null values. Processing also combines data from various sources to deliver the enterprise's business entities with a set of rules that ensure they're compliant with the enterprise's minimal data quality rules (for example, stock, transactions without duplicates, and cross-referenced tables). Those entities and views help unleash self-service analytics, ad hoc reporting, and in some cases advanced analytics and machine learning use cases.

- **Gold**: This layer typically focuses on creating business-level aggregates, KPIs, and other derived datasets that are essential for business intelligence, reporting, and machine learning. Here, final business transformations and quality rules are applied. The data is generally denormalized and optimized for read access with minimal joins, often stored in a columnar format. It's modeled using BI-oriented schemas such as data marts or star schemas. Finally, data organization follows a chosen model based on enterprise needs, such as core data products or data domains. This organization varies across companies: some replicate data from the silver layer with specific business transformations and quality rules, while others organize it around specific, ready-to-use projects with tailored transformations and quality rules.

- **Insight**: Some companies have evolved their data architecture to include a split in the gold layer, creating two distinct areas: the traditional gold area, which focuses on delivering business entities and aggregates for ad hoc BI and machine learning use cases, and the insight area, which is tailored for specific use cases. In the optional insight layer, data is meticulously modeled, filtered, and organized for optimal consumption for targeted needs. The filtering process is designed to select only the data that's essential for the specific use case. While utilizing patterns such as "design by query," the data is modeled to align closely with consumption queries, facilitating straightforward usage and minimizing the need for additional transformations, such as filtering or ETL. This layer typically offers a ready-to-use model that can be directly integrated into dashboards, reports, and other decision-making tools, enhancing efficiency and clarity in data-driven insights.

The following figure represents the medallion layers:

Figure 6.1 – Medallion layers

All these steps can be performed to store the data of the company, depending on the size of the data and the needs of preparation. For example, if there is only one data representing tools, the insight layer can be avoided.

Use cases and benefits

The medallion architecture, with its structured approach, caters to diverse analytics needs, from real-time processing to machine learning models. By progressively refining data, it ensures that users at different stages have access to the appropriate level of data detail and quality.

Limitations and drawbacks

While the medallion architecture offers a structured approach to data management, it also has some challenges. Data being divided into multiple stages might lead to increased complexity in data governance and management. Additionally, the decision of when and what data should be promoted to the next layer requires careful consideration to avoid unnecessary data duplication and storage costs.

In summary, the lakehouse concept, coupled with the medallion architecture, provides a comprehensive and structured approach to data management. It combines the flexibility of data lakes with the structured querying capabilities of data warehouses, thereby catering to diverse data workloads. As with any architecture, organizations should thoroughly evaluate their specific needs, capabilities, and data strategies before implementing this model.

To help you visualize the differences between the storage options, here's a comparison table:

Factor	Data Warehouse	Data Lake	Object Storage	Lakehouse
Data Type	Structured	All types	All types	All types
Performance	High	Moderate	Moderate	Moderate
Scalability	Moderate	High	High	High
Data Accessibility	SQL, BI tools	APIs, BI tools, SQL	APIs, BI tools if using FS abstraction interfaces or APIs	SQL, BI tools, APIs
Cost	Higher	Moderate	Low	Moderate
Security	High	Moderate	Moderate	Moderate
Integration	Moderate	Moderate	Moderate	Moderate

Table 6.1 – Storage comparison table

That's why, when it comes to choosing the best storage option for your business, you must carefully analyze several variables, trade-offs, and decision-making procedures, and it's crucial to evaluate each storage solution in the context of your specific use case. By understanding the strengths and weaknesses of object storage, distributed filesystems, and data warehouses, you can make informed decisions to optimize performance, scalability, and cost for your business's data needs and assist you in achieving your data-driven goals. The effectiveness of your selected storage option will be improved as we examine data architectures in the next section.

> **Expert advice**
>
> The lakehouse concept is a promising new paradigm that combines the best features of data lakes and data warehouses, enabling you to store and process diverse types of data with high performance and reliability. However, implementing a lakehouse architecture requires careful planning and design, as well as choosing the right technologies and tools that support this vision.

Next, we'll discuss data architectures.

Data architectures

It's critical to comprehend the significance of data architectures as we go further into the field of data storage. The designs for organizing, storing, and managing data within a company are known as data architectures. They assist in ensuring that data is effectively kept, readily available, and well-integrated across numerous systems. We will introduce data architectures in this section and go through the significance of logical and physical layer separation, as well as the value of data modeling.

Let's start by defining the distinction between data architectures and data storage technologies. The foundational technologies that are used to store and manage data include data lakes, data warehouses, and object storage. However, the structure, organization, distribution, and design principles that control how data is stored, retrieved, and modified within those systems are provided by data architectures.

Here are some of the advantages of a well-designed data architecture for an organization:

- **Strong data architecture**: This ensures that data is acquired, processed, and stored reliably, which improves data quality and yields more trustworthy insights

- **Enhanced data integration**: Data architectures make it simpler for companies to combine and analyze data from diverse systems by facilitating the consumption of data from numerous sources

- **Data management**: Data architectures simplify data management and aid organizations in making better use of their data assets by offering a clear framework and organization for data storage and access

- **Greater scalability**: Organizations may scale their data storage and processing capacities as their demands change thanks to a flexible and adaptable data architecture

- **Better performance**: Efficient data architectures can accelerate organizations' abilities to gain insights by enhancing the performance of data storage and retrieval procedures

The distinction between physical and logical layers will be a major topic of discussion as we look at data architectures. The actual hardware and storage infrastructure needed to hold data, such as servers, disks, and network components, are referred to as physical layer components. The data model, schema, and indexing techniques are all represented in the logical layer, which is where the data is organized and structured within the storage system.

Data modeling is yet another essential element of data structures. The structure, connections, and limitations of the data within a storage system are defined by data modeling. It aids businesses in better understanding and managing their data assets, resulting in accurate representation and accessibility of data.

Multiple advantages, including greater flexibility, better performance, and better data management, result from separating these levels. Next, we'll cover the benefits of separating physical and logical layers, along with best practices for constructing data layers.

Separation between the physical and logical layers

A fundamental idea in data structures that has a significant impact on the effectiveness, adaptability, and performance of your data storage systems is the division of physical and logical levels. This section will cover the advantages of this separation, best practices for creating data layers, and case studies and examples to show how these ideas work in practice.

Overview and benefits

The physical layer of a data architecture, as was indicated in the preceding section, refers to the actual hardware and infrastructure used for storage, including servers, disks, and network components. The data model, schema, and indexing techniques are all represented in the logical layer, which is where the data is organized and structured within the storage system.

Separating these layers provides several benefits:

- **Flexibility**: By decoupling physical storage infrastructure from logical data organization, you may more readily change your storage solutions as your organization grows and evolves. You may, for example, transfer your data to a new storage technology or increase storage capacity without having to redo the entire data architecture.

- **Performance gains**: By separating the physical and logical layers, you may optimize each layer independently. For example, you can improve data query performance by fine-tuning data logical organization, such as the indexing method, without changing the underlying storage technology.

- **Easier management and maintenance**: By separating the physical and logical levels, you can diagnose and maintain each layer individually, making it easier to discover and handle faults in your data architecture.

- **Better data security and privacy**: By separating the layers, you may apply more granular security features at both the physical and logical levels, such as access limits and encryption. This aids in protecting sensitive data and compliance with data privacy requirements.

Best practices for designing data layers

Here are some best practices to consider when designing the physical and logical layers of your data architecture:

- **Choose the correct storage technology**: Select a storage technology that meets your organization's needs and requirements while considering criteria such as scalability, performance, affordability, and compatibility with existing systems.

- **Optimize data organization**: Organize your data so that it is easy to access, query, and change. This may entail creating an efficient data model, schema, and indexing approach tailored to your use cases and query patterns.

- **Implement data splitting and sharding**: Partitioning and sharding can help you distribute data over many storage devices or nodes, boosting performance and scalability. Select the partitioning or sharding method that best fits your data and query patterns.

- **Monitor and improve performance**: Regularly monitor the performance of your data architecture and make changes as needed. This may require improving the physical storage infrastructure, such as adding additional storage capacity or upgrading hardware, or refining data logical organization, such as modifying the indexing strategy.

- **Plan for development and change**: Design your data architecture with flexibility and scalability in mind, expecting that your organization's data storage demands and requirements may vary over time. This will help ensure that your data architecture can adapt to changing demands.

Case studies and examples

Let's look at some real-world examples of how organizations have benefited from separating the physical and logical layers of their data architectures:

- **E-commerce company**: The performance of a large e-commerce company's data warehouse needed to be improved since it was finding it difficult to manage the volume of client data and sales transactions that were growing. The business was able to optimize its data model, schema, and indexing approach without needing to replace the current storage hardware by dividing the physical and logical layers. This led to improved query performance and a data warehouse that was better equipped to handle the expanding amount of data.

- **Healthcare provider**: Strict data privacy laws that demanded the security of private patient data had to be followed by a healthcare provider. The company put strong security measures in place at both levels of its data architecture by separating the physical and logical layers. They used encryption at the physical storage layer and access controls at the logical layer to maintain the security and regulatory compliance of sensitive patient data.

- **Financial services firm**: To support its risk management and investment decision-making processes, a financial services organization was required to handle and analyze huge volumes of trading data. The firm was able to improve its data architecture for high-performance analytics by separating the physical and logical layers, guaranteeing that data queries and analyses were conducted rapidly and efficiently. This enabled the company to make more informed judgments and adapt to changing market conditions more quickly.

- **Manufacturing company**: A global manufacturing firm sought to consolidate data from several sources, such as ERP systems, IoT devices, and production equipment, to gain better visibility into its operations and improve productivity. By separating the physical and logical levels of its data architecture, the organization was able to create a flexible and scalable data model that could support multiple data kinds and sources. As a result, the business was able to create a unified view of its operations, which resulted in better decision-making and more efficient processes.

These examples highlight the importance of separating a data architecture's physical and logical levels. Organizations can design more flexible, efficient, and secure data storage systems that support their needs and requirements by following best practices and harnessing the benefits of this separation.

Schema management

In today's information-based society, the capacity to effectively manage and manipulate data is crucial. Schema management is a crucial element of data administration as it involves preparing, implementing, and creating data structures. The two most fundamental schema management systems, schema-on-read and schema-on-write, will be compared and contrasted here.

> **Warning**
>
> Schema-on-read and schema-on-write are two fundamental approaches to managing schemas in your data architecture. They have different advantages and disadvantages depending on your data type, performance, flexibility, and consistency requirements. Be careful not to mix up these approaches or apply them inconsistently as this can lead to data errors or inefficiencies.

Schema-on-read

The schema-on-read technique defines and applies the data schema during the data retrieval process. This means that the schema is enforced when data is read and processed rather than when it is ingested or stored. This type of schema pattern is used in data lake technologies.

Here are the advantages:

- **Flexibility**: Schema-on-read offers greater flexibility in handling data from various sources and formats as it can apply the schema to the read process. This feature is very useful, especially when the same data is consumed by different job versions that require using different schema versions.

- **Agility**: Since schema changes do not require modifications to the stored data, schema-on-read can be more agile and adapt more quickly to changing data requirements.

- **Faster data ingestion (performance on write)**: Without the need to enforce a schema during the writing process, ingestion is faster and more streamlined, making it easier to store diverse datasets without the need for extensive data transformation.

Now, let's look at the disadvantages:

- **Performance of read**: Applying the schema during data retrieval can lead to slower query performance, especially for complex or large datasets

- **Lack of data consistency**: Schema-on-read may result in data inconsistency as data validation and enforcement occur at the time of reading, not during ingestion

The following figure represents schema-on-read:

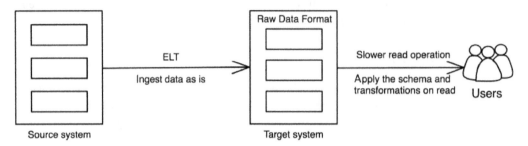

Figure 6.2 – Schema-on-read

Schema-on-write

Schema-on-write, as opposed to schema-on-read, enforces the data schema during the ingestion process. This means that before data is stored, it must conform to the standard.

Here are its advantages:

- **Data consistency**: Since the schema is enforced during data ingestion, schema-on-write ensures a higher level of data consistency as data is converted and processed to respect the column type of the target schema

- **Improved query performance on read**: As the schema is already applied when data is stored, query performance on consumption is faster

- **Easier data validation**: Enforcing the schema during the ingestion process allows for easier and more efficient data validation

Here are its disadvantages:

- **Reduced flexibility:** Schema-on-write requires data to adhere to a specific schema before ingestion, which can limit flexibility and complicate the process of incorporating diverse data sources. In some cases, reducing flexibility leads to the necessity of data duplication for many data storage technologies to answer the different needs of reads.

- **Slower data ingestion**: Data ingestion can be slower due to the need for schema enforcement and data validation.

The following figure represents schema-on-write:

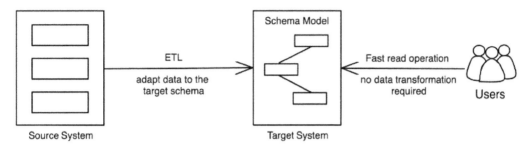

Figure 6.3 – Schema-on-write

Next, we'll discuss when to use schema-on-read and schema-on-write.

When to use schema-on-read versus schema-on-write

The need for consistency, flexibility, and performance can all play a part in deciding between schema-on-read and schema-on-write.

Consider the following table to help you make your decision:

Aspect	Schema-on-Read	Schema-on-Write
Flexibility	**High**: Adapts easily to diverse data sources	**Low**: Requires data to conform to a schema
Agility	**High**: Allows for quick adaptation to schema changes	**Low**: Schema changes may require data modifications, duplication, or schema improvement.
Data Ingestion Speed	**Fast**: No schema enforcement during ingestion	**Slower**: Schema enforcement during ingestion
Data Consistency	**Low**: Data validation occurs at read time	**High**: Enforced during data ingestion
Query Performance	**Slower**: Schema applied during data retrieval	**Faster**: Schema applied during data storage
Data Validation	Occurs during data retrieval	Occurs during data ingestion

Table 6.2 – Comparison of schema-on-read and schema-on-write

There is no definitive answer to whether schema-on-read or schema-on-write is better for your organization. The best practice is to use the appropriate approach for each use case, depending on your data needs and goals. For example, you may use schema-on-read for exploratory analysis or machine learning tasks that require flexibility and agility, while you may use schema-on-write for BI or reporting tasks that require performance and consistency.

In conclusion, managing schemas is a crucial part of any reliable data warehouse. By comparing and contrasting schema-on-read versus schema-on-write, you can determine which method offers the optimal combination of features for your company.

Version management

The capacity to monitor and control data and schema evolution is crucial in the field of data management. Data and schema versioning, two crucial facets of version management, will be discussed in this section. We will delve into their intended outcomes, actual case studies, and recommended procedures for putting them into action.

Data versioning management

Data versioning is a game-changer for businesses as it allows you to track and manage changes in your data over time. By maintaining a history of your data, you will always have a way to recover critical information and protect against data loss. Think of data versioning as a safety net for your company's most important asset (its data). Implementing data versioning is simple and can be integrated into your existing data management processes or underlying storage technology. Start by capturing and storing multiple versions of your datasets, ensuring you have a complete historical record at your fingertips. This practice not only safeguards your data but also empowers your team to analyze trends and make better decisions by accessing different versions of the data as needed. This is crucial for several reasons:

- **Protection against involuntary data changes**: Accidental updates or deletions of records can have significant consequences. Data versioning provides a safety net by allowing you to revert to a previous version if necessary.

- **Audit trails and compliance:** In industries with strict regulatory requirements, data versioning helps maintain an audit trail and ensures compliance by keeping a record of all changes made to the data.

- **Collaboration**: When multiple users work on the same dataset, data versioning enables them to track changes and avoid conflicts.

- **Disaster recovery**: In the event of a system failure or data corruption, data versioning allows you to quickly restore the most recent stable version of the data.

Data versioning can be useful for a financial institution that wishes to implement data versioning to track changes in customer account balances. By maintaining a historical record of account transactions, the institution can quickly identify and resolve discrepancies or investigate fraudulent activities.

> **Tip**
>
> Data versioning is a powerful technique that allows you to track and manage changes in your data over time. It can help you protect against accidental data loss, ensure compliance, enable collaboration, and support disaster recovery. To implement data versioning effectively, you need to choose a storage technology that supports versioning features, such as Delta Lake or Apache Hudi.

Schema versioning management

Schema versioning is the process of tracking and managing changes to the schema or structure of your data. It is essential for several reasons:

- **Legacy job compatibility**: As your data schema evolves, you need to ensure that legacy jobs and applications continue to run smoothly. Schema versioning allows these jobs to operate on the data with the appropriate schema model, minimizing disruption.

- **Consistency in schema evolution**: Schema versioning guarantees that schema changes are both forward- and backward-compatible, ensuring that data remains accessible and usable throughout its life cycle.

- **Temporal data consumption**: Schema versioning enables users to access and consume data from different periods accurately and consistently.

As an example, an e-commerce company may frequently update its product catalog schema to accommodate new features or attributes. By implementing schema versioning, the company can ensure that older analytical jobs and reporting tools can still access and process the data correctly, even as the schema evolves.

Best practices for schema versioning

Maintaining data integrity and ensuring seamless data access becomes increasingly important. A good schema versioning strategy not only preserves historical data but also encourages adaptability to future changes. Here are some critical schema versioning best practices:

- **Use schema evolution techniques**: Implement schema evolution techniques that allow you to add, remove, or modify schema elements without causing disruptions. This can be done using techniques such as schema-on-read or schema registry tools, which can help you manage schema changes more effectively.

- **Maintain backward and forward compatibility**: Ensure that your schema changes are both backward and forward-compatible. This will enable legacy applications to continue functioning and new applications to access historical data without issues. It can also be implemented using schema registry tools.

- **Document schema changes**: Don't forget to record the reasoning behind any schema updates you make. The more your team knows about how the data schema has changed over time, the more effectively they can troubleshoot problems and answer inquiries about the data's structure.

- **Automate schema migration**: When necessary, implement automated schema migration processes to reduce the risk of errors and minimize downtime during schema updates.

- **Test schema changes thoroughly**: Test schema changes extensively before deploying them to production environments. This includes testing for compatibility with existing applications, as well as ensuring that the changes do not introduce performance or scalability issues.

- **Monitor schema usage**: Regularly monitor how your schema is being used across different applications and services. This can help you identify potential issues or areas for improvement and ensure that your schema remains optimized for your data needs.

Expert advice

Schema versioning is the process of tracking and managing changes to the schema or structure of your data. It can help you maintain legacy job compatibility, ensure consistency in schema evolution, support temporal data consumption, and avoid conflicts or errors. To implement schema versioning effectively, you need to follow a schema evolution strategy that defines how to handle schema changes in a forward- and backward-compatible way.

In conclusion, both data and schema versioning play critical roles in ensuring the integrity, accessibility, and usability of your data throughout its life cycle. The risk of disruptions and data corruption can be reduced by using best practices and the appropriate tools to control the evolution of your data and schema. Because of this, you will be able to better adapt to the evolving requirements of your business and provide actionable insights based on your data.

Next, we'll discuss the different positions and roles in data management.

Positions and roles in data management

Translating theoretical concepts into practical implementations is where the real challenge lies, especially in complex fields such as data management. In this section, we aim to bridge this gap between theory and practice. We'll delve into the roles and responsibilities within teams, discuss solutions that are appropriate for each stage of the lakehouse architecture, and identify the key actors involved at each step. The intention is to provide a practical roadmap to help you navigate the implementation of the lakehouse architecture in your organization. We believe that understanding these practical aspects is just as important as understanding the theoretical framework, and we hope that this section will equip you with the tools you need to successfully implement the lakehouse architecture in your data management operations.

Roles and responsibilities at the team level

In the landscape of data management, the implementation of the lakehouse architecture, particularly the medallion architecture, requires a diverse set of skills, roles, and responsibilities at the team level. This approach, which combines the best of both worlds – data lakes and data warehouses – requires a clear definition in terms of who does what and at which stage of the process.

Before we delve into the specifics, it's crucial to note that the roles we'll discuss here are not exhaustive. Every organization is unique, with its own set of challenges and requirements. Depending on the complexity of your data operations and the size of your organization, there may be additional roles, or some of the roles we mention may be combined or split in different ways. Our aim here is to provide a broad overview of the typical roles involved in implementing the lakehouse architecture:

- **Data engineers**: Data engineers are the architects of the data pipeline. Their primary responsibility revolves around building and maintaining this pipeline, which forms the backbone of the lakehouse architecture. They are involved in ingesting raw data into the staging layer, ensuring that data from various sources is correctly and efficiently ingested into the system. Their role doesn't stop here, though; they apply preliminary transformations that are necessary to promote this raw data to the bronze layer. It involves data cleaning and structuring, ensuring that the data in the bronze layer is of acceptable quality and format. But their job extends even further as they participate in refining and enriching data for the silver layer, where more specific transformations are applied, and derived columns or features may be added to the datasets.

- **Data analysts**: Data analysts typically operate at the silver, gold, and insight layers. They are responsible for transforming data into a business-friendly format, creating derived datasets, KPIs, and other business-level aggregates that populate the gold layer. Their role is critical in bridging the gap between raw data and business insights as they translate technical data into actionable insights that can influence business strategies and decisions.

- **Data scientists**: Data scientists are the primary operators at the gold and insight layers. They work with refined and enriched data, applying their skills in statistics, machine learning, and predictive modeling to create predictive models, run simulations, and generate insights. They leverage the data in the gold layer to drive value, spot trends, identify patterns, and provide actionable insights to the business.

- **Data stewards**: Data stewards play a critical role in data governance. Their responsibilities span across all layers of the architecture, ensuring data quality, integrity, compliance, and accessibility. They are responsible for setting data standards, managing metadata, ensuring data privacy and security, and maintaining data dictionaries to help other team members understand the data.

- **Data consumers**: Lastly, there are data consumers, which include business users, decision-makers, and sometimes even clients. They usually interact with the gold and insight layers, leveraging the processed and refined data for business insights, reporting, decision-making, and other analytics tasks.

- **Data architects**: Data architects are pivotal in designing and managing the entire data infrastructure, including the lakehouse architecture. They work across all layers, making critical decisions about the overall design, choice of tools and technologies, data modeling, and schema design. The efficient data flow from the staging layer to the insight layer depends significantly on their design decisions. They also play a crucial role in ensuring data security, data privacy, and compliance with data governance policies.

- **Machine learning engineers**: Machine learning engineers typically operate at the gold and insight layers using the bronze and silver layers. They work closely with data scientists but primarily focus on the design, development, and deployment of machine learning models and algorithms. They take the data-driven insights and predictive models created by data scientists and translate them into production-level code. They often need to optimize the models for performance and scalability, making sure they can handle the volume and velocity of data in real-world scenarios. Their work forms the basis for advanced analytics and predictive capabilities in the Insight layer.

The following figure represents the interaction between the different roles:

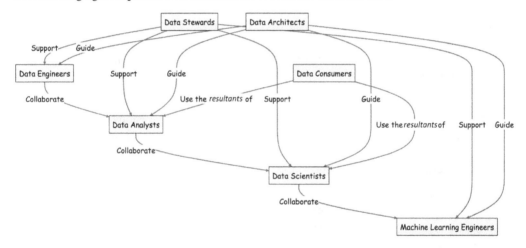

Figure 6.4 – Interaction between roles

Interactions among diverse roles can significantly fluctuate depending on the distinct cultural context of individual corporations.

Solutions adapted to each stage

With the variety of tasks and responsibilities at each layer of the medallion architecture, it's important to have the right solutions in place to facilitate these tasks:

- **Data ingestion tools**: At the staging and bronze layers, the focus is on data ingestion and preliminary processing. Tools such as Apache Kafka, Apache NiFi, or Logstash are often used to handle data being ingested from various sources.

- **Data processing and transformation tools**: The transition from bronze to silver involves more specific transformations and is where data processing and transformation tools come into play. Tools such as Apache Spark, Apache Beam, and Apache Flink are often used for data processing, while data-wrangling tools such as Trifacta or OpenRefine are used for data cleaning and transformation.

- **Data warehouse and BI tools**: At the gold and insight layers, data has been refined and is ready for analysis. This is where data warehouse solutions such as Google BigQuery, Amazon Redshift, or Snowflake come into play.

The right actors for each stage

Given the diversity of tasks involved in the medallion architecture, it's essential to have the right team with a broad range of skills. The roles mentioned in the preceding section should work in synergy to ensure the smooth functioning of the lakehouse architecture:

- Data engineers play a crucial role in the staging and bronze layers. Their strong technical skills are needed to handle the data ingestion process and apply the necessary transformations to prepare the data for the next stage.

- Data analysts shine in the silver and gold layers. Their understanding of the business and analytical skills are invaluable for transforming raw data into business-friendly information.

- Data scientists work primarily with the gold and insight layers. Their expertise in statistics, machine learning, and predictive analytics allows them to create valuable insights from the processed data.

- Data stewards are needed at all stages. They ensure the overall data quality, compliance, and accessibility, making it easier for everyone else to do their jobs.

- Data architects are vital at all stages. Their vision and expertise in managing complex data infrastructures help shape the lakehouse architecture from the ground up, ensuring its success.

- Machine learning engineers are most active in the gold and insight layers. Their skill in translating data insights into scalable, performant models helps drive the advanced analytics and predictive capabilities of the lakehouse architecture.

- Lastly, data consumers are the end users who interact mainly with the insight layer. Their feedback is invaluable for continuous improvement and alignment of the data strategy with business goals.

This team dynamic is a simplified view, and in reality, there might be overlapping responsibilities and more specialized roles depending on the organization's size and complexity. However, the principle remains the same: having the right actors at each stage is crucial for a successful implementation of the lakehouse architecture in real life.

Summary

As we conclude our exploration of data storage technologies and architectures in this chapter, we hope you now have a firm understanding of the intricacies of various data storage options, their respective advantages, and their potential drawbacks. We also delved into the concept of the lakehouse architecture and its various stages and discussed how this can be implemented practically in a real-life scenario.

We believe that this foundation in data storage technologies and architecture is critical for any data professional to make informed decisions about how to structure, manage, and optimize their data assets. The effective use of data storage technologies is not just about storing data efficiently; it's about making the data accessible, usable, and meaningful.

Looking ahead, we will be transitioning into a new yet interconnected topic in *Chapter 7, Data Ingestion and Storage Strategies*. Now that we have a solid understanding of the "where" in terms of data – where it resides and where it is stored – our next focus will be on "how" – how the data gets there in the first place, and how we can strategize this process for maximum efficiency and effectiveness.

In the next chapter, we'll delve into the various methods and strategies for data ingestion, with a focus on the diverse types of storage that can be leveraged for various use cases. We'll also discuss the significance of aligning your data ingestion and storage strategies with your overall business objectives and the unique requirements of your data ecosystem.

As we navigate the vast landscape of data management, the journey from storage to ingestion will reinforce the notion that every aspect of this field is interrelated and each choice impacts others. Stay with us as we continue to unravel these complex interconnections and guide you toward building a robust, efficient, and scalable data infrastructure.

7

Data Ingestion and Storage Strategies

Data ingestion stands as the critical starting point in handling and analyzing data. This is where it all kicks off, and as you're aware, a firm foundation is vital for the success of any project. In this chapter, we will venture into the captivating domain of data ingestion and uncover its significance, complexities, and advantages.

Picture yourself in charge of managing the data for a burgeoning company, where you work with a diverse range of data sources such as customer transactions, product evaluations, and social media interactions. Now, envision the task of gathering, processing, and storing all this information in a manner that renders it both accessible and usable for your organization. This is the moment when data ingestion takes center stage.

Furthermore, choosing the appropriate data formats and compression is another vital aspect of optimizing data ingestion. Selecting formats that support partitioning (chunking) and offer strong compression can significantly improve the efficiency of data processing.

The following topics will be covered in this chapter:

- The goal of ingestion
- Data storage and modeling techniques
- Optimizing storage performance
- Defining the adapted strategy

The goal of ingestion

The process of data ingestion entails obtaining data from a variety of sources, converting it into a uniform format, and loading it into an appropriate storage system. It's akin to a well-coordinated ballet, ensuring data is effectively transferred from its origin to its ultimate destination, primed for additional processing and analysis. In a nutshell, data ingestion serves as the cornerstone of any data-centric organization, laying the foundation for valuable insights and informed decision-making.

As we delve further into the realm of data ingestion, we'll explore the various facets that render it an integral component of contemporary data management. We will touch on the significance of efficiency, scalability, and adaptability in this process and how they contribute to a sturdy and dependable data ingestion framework.

But there's more – we will also investigate the array of storage options available for diverse use cases, guiding you in selecting the ideal solution for your organization. From data warehouses and data lakes to object storage, we will discuss the characteristics, advantages, and disadvantages of each, empowering you to make well-informed choices.

Lastly, we will assist you in crafting a customized data ingestion and storage strategy that aligns with your organization's distinct needs and limitations. You will learn best practices for establishing a sound strategy and techniques for assessing and refining it over time.

Efficiency in data ingestion

Diving deeper into the nuances of data handling, the importance of streamlining data ingestion is paramount. It encompasses efficient data transfer and optimal data movement techniques that ensure a more productive data handling process. This chapter dives into the details of how to optimize these aspects, from leveraging data compression algorithms to making use of data caching and exploring high-performance data ingestion technologies. Then, we'll segue into the concepts of parallelism and concurrency in data processing, elaborating on how they can vastly improve the rate and efficiency of data ingestion. The discussion also touches upon various tools and frameworks that can aid in parallel and concurrent data processing. Ultimately, the goal is to create a data management strategy that is both quick and resource-efficient.

Optimizing data transfer

Streamlining data ingestion is essential, and a significant aspect of this process involves optimizing data movement. The faster and more effectively you can transport data from its origin to your storage system, the better your entire data handling process will be.

Various techniques and tools can be employed to optimize data movement. One prevalent approach is using data compression algorithms, which reduce data size before transfer. This strategy lessens the bandwidth needed and shortens the time it takes for data to travel from the source to the destination. It's important to note that reducing data size before transfer is preferable. Therefore, you might consider converting data into more efficient formats such as ORC or Parquet at the source, which offer better compression and improved performance for analytical queries.

Caching is another method for refining data movement. Storing frequently accessed data in a cache reduces the latency associated with data retrieval. This accelerates the data ingestion process and lessens the load on your data sources and storage systems.

Additionally, high-performance data ingestion technologies such as Apache Kafka or Amazon Kinesis can be employed. These technologies are designed to handle large data volumes and ensure reliable and efficient data transfer. By considering these techniques and adopting suitable approaches, you can significantly enhance your data ingestion efficiency and overall data management process.

These optimizations reduce latency and processing time, as well as decrease infrastructure costs, particularly for cloud-based solutions with a pay-as-you-go billing model.

> **Tip**
>
> Data compression can reduce data size and transfer time, but it can also increase CPU usage and processing time. Choose a compression algorithm that balances compression ratio and speed, such as Snappy or Zstandard.

Parallelism and concurrency

Other crucial features of efficient data ingestion include processing and execution in parallel. The term **parallelism** refers to the practice of dividing a large task into several smaller tasks that can be run in parallel. The capacity of a system to handle multiple tasks simultaneously is known as **concurrency** or **simultaneous execution**.

The rate and efficiency of your data ingestion process can be greatly improved using parallelism and concurrency. You can process multiple data streams simultaneously by breaking your data ingestion tasks into smaller, parallel tasks. This improves your data ingestion system's overall throughput and makes more efficient use of resources such as CPU, memory, and network bandwidth.

> **Information**
>
> Parallelism and multithreading are two different concepts that are often mistakenly used interchangeably. Multi-threading creates an illusion of concurrency by rapidly switching between threads, allowing for prioritized and interactive tasks, while parallelism achieves real concurrency by running multiple tasks at once across different CPU cores or on different machines, making it ideal for intensive, long-running computations where the goal is to complete tasks more swiftly by distributing the workload.

As we explained previously, when working with large datasets in Parquet format, which is a popular columnar storage format, it is often used in combination with various compression algorithms, such as Snappy and Gzip. Even if Gzip often achieves better compression rates than Snappy, the latter can provide better overall performance because, in addition to Snappy's compression and decompression, which is faster than Gzip Parquet on Snappy is a splittable format that's designed to enable the parallel reading of chunks within a file before decompression as each chunk is compressed independently.

The following figure shows the splittability of Parquet compression:

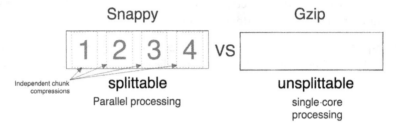

Figure 7.1 – Parquet compression's splittability

Partitioning and bucketing enable more manageable data processing and reduce the amount of data to be read and processed (we will cover this in the next section, *Optimizing storage performance*), while strong compression reduces the storage space and transfer time needed. You can use tools and frameworks made specifically for this purpose to add parallelism and concurrency to your data ingestion procedure. Popular open source frameworks that enable parallel and concurrent processing of data streams include Apache Flink and Apache Beam. Another option is to use a distributed computing platform such as Apache Spark, which is made for the simultaneous processing of massive amounts of data across a network of computers. Data ingestion can be scaled to handle even the largest workloads since it takes advantage of distributed computing.

> **Warning**
> Parallelism and concurrency can improve data ingestion throughput, but they can also introduce challenges such as synchronization, coordination, and error handling. Use tools and frameworks that simplify parallel and concurrent processing, such as Apache Spark or Apache Flink.

In summary, refining data movement and incorporating parallelism and concurrency are two essential strategies for streamlining data ingestion. By employing these techniques, you can ensure that your data ingestion process is both rapid and resource-efficient, laying the groundwork for a successful data management strategy.

Scalability in data ingestion

Scaling your data ingestion process is becoming increasingly important for efficient data management as the volume and variety of data sources rise. In the following subsections, we'll go over two of the most crucial aspects of scalable data ingestion: managing massive data volumes and adjusting to a growing data source.

Handling large data volumes

Many businesses now face the problem of having to deal with massive data explosions. Making timely decisions and gaining useful insights requires effectively consuming and processing these massive data volumes. Here are some methods that can help you deal with massive amounts of data:

- **Incremental data ingestion**: Instead of ingesting all data at once, focus on processing smaller batches or increments of data. This approach reduces the overall pressure on your data ingestion system, making it more manageable and resource-efficient.

- **Data partitioning**: Split your data into smaller, logical partitions based on specific attributes or criteria. This allows for parallel processing and more efficient data ingestion as each partition can be ingested independently.

- **Compression and encoding**: Reduce the size of your data by compressing and encoding it. This not only speeds up data transfer and processing but also reduces the amount of data that needs to be taken in.

- **Caching**: Implement caching mechanisms to temporarily store frequently accessed data in memory. This reduces the need for repeated data retrieval and ingestion, improving overall efficiency.

> **Industry good practice**
>
> Incremental data ingestion is a common practice for handling large data volumes. It involves ingesting only new or changed data, reducing the overall data volume and resource utilization. Tools such as Apache Kafka or Amazon Kinesis can help implement incremental data ingestion.

Scaling with data source growth

As your organization grows and your data sources expand, your data ingestion system must be able to adapt and scale accordingly. Here are some strategies for scaling your data ingestion process in line with data source growth:

- **Distributed processing**: Data can be processed in parallel across multiple nodes using distributed computing platforms such as Apache Spark, Hadoop, or Flink. The more data sources your data ingestion process can handle, the more processing power and resource efficiency you'll need.

- **Load balancing**: Implement load balancing techniques to distribute the workload across multiple data ingestion nodes evenly. This ensures that no single node becomes overwhelmed, thus maintaining high availability and performance even as the number of data sources increases.

- **Elasticity**: Create a data ingestion system that can expand or contract in response to fluctuating demands. Using containerization technologies such as Kubernetes or a cloud-based infrastructure that permits dynamic scaling can accomplish this.

- **Monitoring and automation**: Data ingestion bottlenecks, resource constraints, and other performance issues can be detected and fixed with the help of automation tools, which should be monitored constantly. This preventative measure ensures that your system can handle more data without sacrificing efficiency or scalability.

Expert advice

Distributed processing is a key strategy for scaling with data source growth. It allows you to process data in parallel across multiple nodes, increasing processing power and resource efficiency. Cloud-based infrastructure can provide dynamic scaling and elasticity for distributed processing.

In summary, addressing scalability in data ingestion involves implementing strategies to handle large data volumes and accommodate data source growth. By considering these aspects of scalability, you can build a robust and adaptable data ingestion system that effectively serves your organization's needs.

Adaptability in data ingestion

Adaptability is a critical aspect of data ingestion that ensures your system can handle the ever-changing data landscape. In this section, we will discuss three key elements of adaptability: supporting diverse data sources, embracing different data ingestion patterns, and evolving with the changing data landscape.

Supporting diverse data sources

As your organization grows, you will encounter a multitude of data sources, each with its unique characteristics and formats. It's essential to design your data ingestion system to accommodate this diversity. Here's how you can achieve this:

- **Plug-and-play architecture**: Develop or use a modular data ingestion framework that can easily integrate new data sources with minimal effort. This can be achieved by implementing standard interfaces, connectors, or APIs such as Kafka Connect and Airbyte.

- **Data normalization**: Ensure your system can convert and normalize data from various sources into a consistent format, thereby enabling seamless processing and analysis across the board.

- **Metadata management**: Implement a robust metadata management system to capture and maintain information about each data source, such as data types, schema, and lineage. This helps streamline data processing and provides better traceability.

> **Tip**
>
> Plug-and-play architecture can help you support diverse data sources with minimal effort. It involves using standard interfaces, connectors, or APIs to integrate new data sources into your data ingestion system. Tools such as Kafka Connect or Airbyte can provide plug-and-play architecture for data ingestion.

Supporting diverse patterns

Different data ingestion patterns serve different use cases. Some common patterns include **change data capture (CDC)**, delta ingestion, and full ingestion. It's important to support these patterns in your data ingestion system as they cater to varying needs and provide flexibility. Let's take a closer look at them:

- **CDC**: This pattern captures and processes only the changes in the data source, reducing the overall data volume to be ingested. The CDC technique achieves this thanks to the database transaction logs, which store all changes that have transpired within the database, including modifications, additions, and deletions.

- **Delta ingestion**: This approach involves ingesting only new data or data that has changed since the last ingestion, which is useful for incremental updates.

- **Full ingestion**: This pattern involves ingesting the entire dataset, which can be useful for initial data loads or when changes in the data source are too complex to track incrementally.

The following table provides a comparison of these ingestion patterns:

Data Ingestion Pattern	Ease of Implementation	Data Freshness	Resource Utilization
CDC	Moderate to high: CDC requires interaction with the source system's transaction logs, which can be complex to handle. However, it can be easy thanks to tools such as Debezium or AWS DMS.	High: CDC operates in near real time, capturing and ingesting changes as they occur.	CDC only processes changes, minimizing data volume and reducing resource usage. However, a high change rate can introduce significant overhead. It requires resources for monitoring database logs continuously and capturing changes, potentially necessitating dedicated tools and infrastructure.

Data Ingestion Pattern	Ease of Implementation	Data Freshness	Resource Utilization
Delta Ingestion	Moderate: Implementing delta ingestion doesn't require interaction with transaction logs but it does need a mechanism to identify new or changed data.	Moderate: Delta ingestion isn't real-time but it can be near real-time if it's executed frequently.	Delta ingestion only processes new or changed data, thereby reducing resource utilization. However, it may need more resources than CDC if changes are frequent and large. It requires resources to track changes and conduct frequent ingestions, depending on the frequency of updates.
Full Ingestion	Easy to high: Full ingestion can be straightforward for small data volumes but becomes complex and resource-intensive for larger datasets.	Low: Full ingestion is performed on a schedule, so data freshness is lower compared to other methods.	Full ingestion requires processing the entire dataset each time, leading to high resource utilization. It requires substantial resources for every ingestion process, especially for larger datasets. It can involve significant data transfer and processing costs.

Table 7.1: Comparison between ingestion patterns

To wrap up, ensuring adaptability in data ingestion is pivotal for managing the diverse and ever-evolving data landscape. This includes developing a system that can easily integrate new data sources, implementing robust metadata management, and supporting a range of data ingestion patterns to meet varying needs. We've discussed several techniques, such as CDC, delta ingestion, and full ingestion, each of which has its merits and trade-offs. By striking a balance between these methods and tailoring your data ingestion process to your specific needs, you can build a resilient and effective data management strategy. Finally, leveraging modern tools and frameworks can greatly assist in easing the complexity of these tasks, ultimately leading to a robust and adaptable data ingestion system.

Evolving with the changing data landscape

As data sources and technologies evolve, your data ingestion system must adapt accordingly. To ensure your system remains adaptable, consider the following:

- **Continuous learning**: Stay informed about emerging data technologies, formats, and best practices. Encourage your team to do the same, fostering a culture of learning and innovation.

- **Regular reviews and updates**: Periodically review and update your data ingestion system to address any inefficiencies, bottlenecks, or outdated technologies.

- **Experimentation**: Test new data ingestion techniques, tools, and technologies to identify potential improvements and keep your system up to date.

By focusing on adaptability, you can create a data ingestion system that thrives in the dynamic world of data management, allowing you to harness the full potential of your organization's data assets.

Next, we'll discuss data storage and modeling techniques.

Data storage and modeling techniques

The act of developing a visual representation of an organization's data and its relationships is known as data modeling. This representation, or model, assists developers and data architects in designing databases and systems that fit the needs of the organization. In data architecture, several data modeling strategies are routinely employed, and selecting the proper one might be important to the success of your analytics project. In this section, we will go through several data modeling strategies, their benefits and drawbacks, and how they can be used in various contexts.

Normalization and denormalization

Before diving into various modeling techniques, it is crucial to grasp the concepts of normalization and denormalization since they provide the foundation for understanding the **entity-relationship model** (**ERM**) and the star schema.

Normalization is a critical practice in database design that aims to eliminate redundancy and enhance data integrity. Primarily used in RDBMSs, normalization organizes data into entities and defines relationships between them. This process involves breaking down data into multiple connected tables, each holding a single type of data. A set of rules or normal forms guides the organization of data in these tables. While normalization reduces data redundancy and boosts integrity, it can also lead to more complex queries as additional joins might be necessary to retrieve related data.

By understanding these fundamental concepts, you will be better equipped to navigate the world of data modeling and make informed choices when designing efficient, well-structured databases.

The normalization process is guided by three basic normal forms:

- **First normal form (1NF)**: In 1NF, a table must have a primary key, and each column must contain atomic values, meaning that each value in a column is indivisible. This ensures that the data is meticulously organized and unique.

- **Second normal form (2NF)**: In 2NF, a table must meet the requirements of 1NF and have no partial dependencies. When a non-key attribute is dependent on a portion of the primary key, this is referred to as partial reliance. By ensuring that all non-key attributes are fully dependent on the primary key, 2NF helps maintain data consistency.

- **Third normal form (3NF)**: In 3NF, a table must meet the requirements of 2NF and have no transitive dependencies. When a non-key attribute depends on another non-key attribute, which, in turn, depends on the main key, this is referred to as transitive dependency. By eliminating transitive dependencies, 3NF ensures that each non-key attribute depends only on the primary key.

Consider the following basic example to illustrate the concepts of 1NF, 2NF, and 3NF. Take a look at the following table, which contains information about students and their courses:

Student ID	StudentName	CourseID	CourseName	CourseInstructor
1	Alice	101	Math	Prof. Johnson
1	Allice	102	Chemistry	Prof. Smith
2	Bob	101	Math	Prof. Johnson
3	Charlie	102	Chemistry	Prof. Smith
3	Charlie	103	Biology	Prof. Brown

Table 7.2: Student_Course_Info

1NF

To achieve 1NF, we must ensure that each column contains atomic values and that the table has a primary key. In our example, the table is already in 1NF as each column contains atomic values (indivisible values), and we have a composite primary key consisting of `StudentID` and `CourseID`, which uniquely identifies each row.

2NF

To achieve 2NF, we must ensure that there are no partial dependencies. In our example, we can see that `CourseName` and `CourseInstructor` are only dependent on `CourseID`, and `StudentName` is only dependent on `StudentID`. This creates partial dependencies as these attributes do not depend on the entire primary key (`StudentID`, `CourseID`).

To resolve this, we can break the table into two separate tables.

The following table shows the student dataset:

StudentID	StudentName
1	Allice
2	Bob
3	Charlie

Table 7.3: Student

The following table shows the course dataset:

CourseID	CourseName	CourseInstructor
101	Math	Prof. Johnson
102	Chemistry	Prof. Smith
103	Biology	Prof. Brown

Table 7.4: Course

The following table shows the `student_course` dataset:

StudentID	CourseID
1	101
1	102
2	101
3	102
3	103

Table 7.5: student_course

Now, the tables are in 2NF, with no partial dependencies, and contain only foreign index data.

3NF

To achieve 3NF, we must ensure that there are no transitive dependencies. In our example, all the tables are already in 3NF because there are no transitive dependencies present. Each non-key attribute depends solely on the primary key of its respective table.

Denormalization, on the other hand, is the process of combining data from several tables into a single table to reduce query complexity and improve query efficiency. Denormalization can cause data redundancy and poor data integrity, although it is commonly used to improve productivity in data warehouses and analytics systems.

> **Warning**
>
> Normalization and denormalization are two opposite approaches to data modeling that have different implications for performance and integrity. Normalization reduces redundancy and improves integrity, but it can also increase query complexity and latency. Denormalization simplifies queries and improves performance, but it can also increase storage needs and compromise integrity. Choose the appropriate level of normalization or denormalization based on your data characteristics and usage patterns.

ERM

The ERM is a widely used method for designing and structuring databases, making it easier for you to represent and understand complex data relationships. This user-friendly approach allows you to map out entities, which are the real-world objects in your system, along with the relationships that connect them. It's like creating a blueprint for your database! There are several advantages to using the ERM. Firstly, it's highly visual, enabling you to gain a clear overview of the database structure immediately. This can improve communication and collaboration among team members as everyone works from a shared understanding. Secondly, it promotes logical organization and consistency, ensuring a solid foundation for your database. Finally, it eliminates unnecessary data duplication and creates a leaner, more efficient database design.

However, there are some drawbacks to consider as well. The ERM can become increasingly complex as the number of entities and relationships grows, which might make it harder to maintain and understand. Additionally, the model may not always capture every nuance of your data or cater to specific database management system requirements. So, while the ERM offers a handy way to plan and design databases, it's essential to be aware of its limitations and adapt accordingly to ensure you're building a robust, efficient system that meets your needs.

Star schema and snowflake schema

The star schema is a widely used approach in data warehousing that makes querying and reporting more efficient by reducing the number of table joins required. It consists of a central fact table, which contains quantitative data, surrounded by one or more dimension tables that store descriptive information. The fact table and dimension tables are connected through foreign key relationships. Let's dive deeper into the structure and functioning of the star schema:

- **Fact table**: The fact table is the heart of the star schema. It contains quantitative or measurable data and is designed to support the analysis of **key performance indicators** (**KPIs**). The fact table usually contains many rows as it stores the granular data needed for analysis. The columns in the fact table consist of foreign keys (which reference the primary keys in dimension tables) and numerical measures. These measures are typically aggregated data, such as sums, counts, or averages, which provide insights into business performance.

- **Dimension tables**: Dimension tables contain descriptive information that helps provide context to the data in the fact table. These tables store the attributes or characteristics of the data, such as product details, customer information, and location data. Dimension tables are typically smaller than fact tables and are denormalized, meaning that they contain redundant data to minimize the number of table joins required for querying. This makes queries run faster as fewer joins lead to better performance. Denormalization is used in dimension tables in the star schema to reduce the number of table joins and enhance query efficiency. While greater storage requirements may come from data redundancy, the benefits of speedier querying frequently exceed the downsides.

The following figure shows the star and snowflake schema:

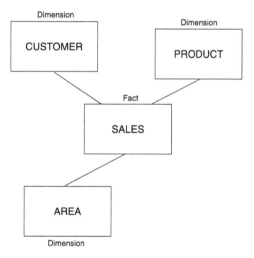

Figure 7.2: Star and snowflake schema

In summary, the star schema is a popular data modeling approach that provides an efficient and effective way to organize data for querying and reporting in data warehouses. By denormalizing dimension tables and connecting them to a central fact table, the star schema reduces the complexity of queries, leading to better performance and more accessible insights.

Hierarchical, network, and relational models

The hierarchical model organizes data in a tree-like form, with a single parent and zero or more children for each entry. This format is ideal for managing and displaying data with distinct parent-child relationships, such as organizational charts or filesystems. However, it is less adaptable and can be difficult to maintain when the relationships between data items are complicated or change frequently.

The network model is a hierarchical model modification that allows each record to have numerous parent and child records. This paradigm is more adaptable than the hierarchical model, but it is also more difficult to create, implement, and maintain.

The relational model, on the other hand, organizes data into tables with rows and columns, where each row represents a unique record and each column represents a record attribute. Primary and foreign keys are used to define associations between tables, making data architecture more flexible and scalable. The relational model has become the most used data model for database management systems due to its simplicity, versatility, and ease of use.

When choosing a data model for your company, consider the complexity of the interactions between data items, the need for flexibility and scalability, and the ease of use for both developers and end users. The relational model is typically the best answer for most enterprises due to its combination of simplicity, flexibility, and scalability. However, depending on your data architecture's specific requirements, the hierarchical or network model may be better suited in some circumstances.

Understanding and executing these many parts of data modeling will assist you in designing a data architecture that matches the demands of your organization and enables efficient and effective analytics. You may develop a data model that balances performance, maintainability, and scalability while ensuring that your analytics system delivers accurate and reliable insights to your users by carefully analyzing the trade-offs between different modeling techniques and approaches.

Object modeling

Object modeling stands out as an effective method in the varied field of data modeling because it is so in line with the tenets of object-oriented programming. The world is modeled as a collection of "objects," each of which possesses its own set of characteristics and interacts with others in specific ways. When working with complex data structures, the paradigm's elevated level of abstraction and encapsulation can be invaluable.

The concept of object modeling

Objects, attributes, and methods are the cornerstones of **object-oriented design** (**OOD**). An object is a representation of a real-world entity and has unique traits or attributes. A customer object, for instance, could have details such as "name," "address," and "purchase history" as attributes. Methods stand in for the actions and behaviors that an object is capable of.

The significance of the connections between objects is not overlooked in object modeling. In a retail **point of sale** (**POS**) system's database, for instance, a "purchase" object might have connections to "customer" and "product" objects. One-to-one, one-to-many, and many-to-many associations are all types of relationships between objects.

Object modeling in data management

When it comes to managing data, object modeling has many advantages. First, it has a natural fit with object-oriented languages, making the data model more accessible to programmers. Data and its associated behaviors are encapsulated in this way, making for more reliable and consistent information.

Modeling objects can be done either on top of object/document databases or relational databases. When modeling on the first type of databases, the modeling is natural and fits well; NoSQL databases such as MongoDB or CouchDB can answer this need. On the other hand, when modeling objects on top of conventional RDBMS, it may lack in-built support for object-oriented modeling. To bridge the gap between the object-oriented model and the relational database, **object-relational mapping** (**ORM**) tools were created.

In conclusion, object modeling is an effective method for visualizing interconnected data structures. Object-oriented programming paradigms and complex entity relationships are two areas where it can be useful, but it is not appropriate for every use case.

Data Vault

The modern data ecosystem is dynamic, fluid, and evolving at an unprecedented pace. Businesses require data modeling techniques that can accommodate the increasing complexity, volume, and diversity of data. This is where Data Vault modeling comes into play, serving as a resilient and adaptive data architecture for enterprise-level data warehousing.

The fundamentals of Data Vault

Dan Linstedt's Data Vault modeling is a methodology for long-term historical storage of data coming in from multiple operational systems to a unique database. It's also a way of looking at historical data that addresses issues such as auditing, data tracing, and loading speed. Its main components are hubs, links, and satellites.

Hubs are dedicated to storing unique business keys along with their descriptions. Each hub represents a unique business concept or object, such as a customer or product.

Links, as the name suggests, are about connections. They store the associations or relationships between business keys, effectively capturing the many-to-many relationships between business objects.

Satellites store all contextual or descriptive data. They hold the attributes related to the business keys (in hubs) or their relationships (in links). Importantly, satellites also capture the time-variant nature of this descriptive data, thereby providing a temporal perspective.

The relevance of Data Vault in today's data landscape

Data Vault modeling thrives in environments that demand agility, scalability, and robustness. Its flexible and modular architecture allows businesses to adapt to changing business rules and requirements without disrupting the existing data model. It also caters to the need for historical tracking and auditability, a crucial requirement in today's data-driven business world.

Nevertheless, implementing Data Vault modeling is not without its challenges. It requires a deep understanding of the methodology and its principles. The model's complexity can also pose issues when it comes to data extraction and usage, often necessitating an additional semantic or presentation layer for users.

In summary, Data Vault modeling is a potent data modeling technique for large-scale, enterprise-level data warehousing. It shines in scenarios that demand agility, historical traceability, and the ability to integrate diverse data sources. Despite its complexity, the benefits it offers in terms of scalability, adaptability, and resilience make it a worthy contender in the data modeling toolbox.

This exploration of Data Vault modeling adds another dimension to the wide spectrum of data modeling techniques available. The choice of modeling methodology should align with the characteristics of your data, the business requirements, and the nature of the use cases at hand. Different techniques will offer different benefits, and the optimal choice may depend on a combination of factors unique to your project.

Comparing data modeling techniques

Different data modeling techniques have their strengths and are suited to different situations.

The following comparison table provides a high-level overview of each technique:

Data Modeling Technique	Primary Use	Strengths	Weaknesses
Entity Relationship Mode	Used in operational/transactional database design to represent real-world entities and their relationships.	A simple and intuitive way to organize data that's useful for communication and planning. When using normalization, it ensures data consistency, reduces redundancy, simplifies data update processes, and improves data integrity.	Can be too abstract for complex databases and does not show data manipulation and control processes. When using normalization, it can lead to complex relational structures and slower query performance due to the need for multiple table joins.
Star Schema and Snowflake Schema	Used in data warehouse design for efficient querying and reporting.	Simplifies queries, improves query performance, and is easy for users to understand.	Redundancy can lead to increased storage needs, not suitable for transactional systems.
Hierarchical, Network, and Relational Models	Hierarchical and network models are used for legacy systems, while relational models are used in most modern applications.	Hierarchical and network models offer fast data access and navigational control. Relational models offer flexibility, data integrity, and ease of use.	Hierarchical and network models lack flexibility. Relational models can suffer from performance issues for complex queries.
Object Modeling	Used in object-oriented databases and software development.	Aligns with object-oriented programming paradigms and supports complex data types.	Not as widely supported or standardized as relational models and can be difficult to design and maintain.

Data Modeling Technique	Primary Use	Strengths	Weaknesses
Data Vault	Used for enterprise data warehousing to handle diverse, historical data from multiple sources.	Highly adaptable and resilient to change, supports auditing and traceability, and is good for historical storage.	Complexity can lead to difficult implementation and data usage and may require an additional semantic layer for user accessibility.

Table 7.6: Comparision table of data modeling techniques

These are widespread characteristics and considerations. The optimal choice of data modeling technique will depend on your specific use case, the nature of your data, and your operational requirements.

To summarize, data modeling is a critical component of developing a robust and efficient data architecture. Understanding and implementing appropriate data modeling techniques, such as the star schema or snowflake schema using normalization or denormalization, and the appropriate data model (hierarchical, network, or relational), can have a significant impact on your analytics system's performance and maintainability. Evaluating your organization's specific requirements, as well as the characteristics of your data, will enable you to make an informed decision about which data modeling technique to use.

Next, we'll discuss optimizing storage performance.

Optimizing storage performance

As we continue our discussion of data modeling techniques, we will look at some advanced techniques that can help you further optimize your data architecture for analytics and reporting. Partitioning, bucketing, and Z-ordering are all techniques that can improve query performance and data organization in your system.

Indexing

Indexing is a strategy for improving database query performance by establishing and maintaining a data structure (an index) that allows for faster data retrieval. Indexes on one or more columns of a table can be defined and can improve query performance. Indexes, on the other hand, have a cost in that they demand additional storage and might slow down data modification activities such as inserts, updates, and deletes. As a result, striking a balance between generating indexes for query efficiency and controlling the related overhead is critical.

Partitioning

Unlike indexing, partitioning does not require additional costs to improve queries. Partitioning divides a large table into smaller, easier-to-manage units/parts called partitions during the partitioning process. Better query performance and more effective data management can be achieved because each partition is stored separately and is accessible and maintainable separately.

Partitioning is especially useful when working with huge datasets since it allows you to conduct actions on a specified partition rather than having to scan the full table. Because less data must be read, queries can be executed more quickly.

The following figure shows various partitioning techniques:

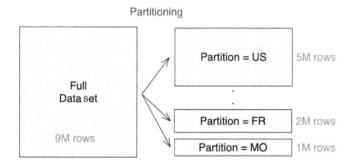

Figure 7.3: Partitioning techniques

In the preceding figure, the dataset is split into partitions based on the country, which is one row of the dataset.

Your unique use case and data characteristics determine the partitioning strategy you employ. Typical partitioning techniques include the following:

- **Range partitioning**: Data is divided according to a predetermined range of values for a particular column. Data that has a natural order, such as dates or numbers, responds well to this approach.

- **List partitioning**: A predefined list of values for a specific column is used to divide the data into diverse groups. For categorical data with a small number of distinct values, this method works best.

Depending on the underlying technology, partitioning is implemented in diverse ways and algorithmics. In some technologies, data partitions divide data using a function applied to a particular column or a set of columns. For example, when using hash partitioning in technologies such as Cassandra, data is distributed in a more even way across the nodes, improving load balancing and query performance on read.

In other technologies, partitioning divides data into partitions using a predictable pattern such as *DD/MM/YYYY*, which separates data into tenants. This allows for faster reads when consuming data based on that pattern. For example, when architecting data lake zones, it is common to partition data on the ingestion date in the raw/bronze area, and partition data on the query request parameters on the exposition layer/gold.

Bucketing

Bucketing is another technique that's used to organize data within a table. It groups rows with similar values for a specified column into fixed-size buckets, which are stored as separate files on disk. By doing so, bucketing can reduce the amount of data that needs to be read when querying a specific subset of values, resulting in improved query performance.

Bucketing is generally used when the data access pattern isn't predictable and on a high-cardinality column. In addition, it is often used in conjunction with partitioning to create a multi-level data organization strategy. While partitioning divides data at a high level, bucketing further organizes data within each partition, creating a more granular and efficient data layout.

The following figure shows various bucketing techniques:

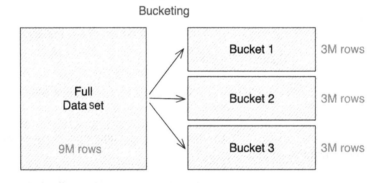

Figure 7.4: Bucketing techniques

In the preceding figure, the dataset is split into an equal number of rows in each bucket to improve global performance.

When implementing bucketing, it's essential to select an appropriate bucketing key and determine the optimal number of buckets. Like partitioning, choosing a bucketing key that corresponds to common query patterns will yield the best performance improvements. Additionally, selecting the right number of buckets is crucial for achieving a good balance between query performance and storage overhead. Too few buckets may lead to inefficient data organization, while too many buckets can result in excessive storage overhead and maintenance complexity.

Design by query

Design by query is an approach that helps you design your data models with a high focus on the queries your consumers are anticipating to run. In this method, the organization of data is guided by its expected consumption patterns. Unnecessary joins are eliminated, tables are flattened, and in some cases, only relevant columns are retained. For example, in the gold layer of the medallion architecture, this strategy is typically implemented.

Imagine that you're building a library. Instead of randomly arranging books, you organize them based on how frequently they're read and by whom. Much like this, the design-by-query approach assigns paramount importance to your data usage patterns. By doing so, it allows for a more efficient and streamlined data model that is highly responsive to the specific needs of its consumers.

Data can be organized using the previous patterns since instance data can be arranged using the partitioning pattern.

The following figure shows various design-by-query techniques:

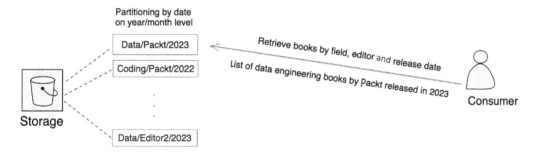

Figure 7.5: Design-by-query techniques

In conclusion, the design-by-query approach is an innovative method to tailor your data models based on anticipated queries. This strategy, which focuses on data consumption patterns, ensures efficient data organization, thereby leading to an optimized and responsive data model. By employing techniques such as data partitioning and intelligent data arrangement, we can significantly enhance data accessibility and efficiency. In essence, design by query revolutionizes the way we structure our data by placing the focus on the end consumer's needs, ensuring a smoother data interaction experience.

Clustering

Clustering is a powerful concept in the world of databases that's designed to enhance performance by organizing data so that it can be retrieved more efficiently. Clustering also differs from one technology to another.

Take the example of Cassandra, a popular NoSQL database known for its exceptional scalability and high availability. In Cassandra, data is distributed and organized using two concepts – partitioning and clustering. Partitioning tells the system how to spread data across its cluster nodes, while clustering defines how to organize data within a specific node.

Just like partitioning, clustering improves query performance by enabling direct access to requested data.

Z-ordering

By organizing data in a multidimensional space, Z-ordering can optimize data storage and increase query performance. It operates by using a space-filling curve, such as the Z-order curve or the Hilbert curve, to transfer multi-column values into a single value (the Z-order value). As a result of this procedure, data with comparable values is stored together on disk, reducing the quantity of data that must be read during query execution.

Z-ordering is very effective when dealing with huge datasets with various filtering criteria since it allows for better data locality and more efficient I/O operations. This technique may be used on both partitioned and non-partitioned tables, and it can be used with other data modeling strategies, such as partitioning and bucketing, to improve data organization and query speed even more.

Z-ordering can be a bit more complex than other data modeling techniques as it requires careful consideration of the columns to be included in the Z-order value calculation. Ideally, you should select columns that are frequently used in query predicates and have a high degree of similarity among their values. Additionally, it's important to ensure that the chosen columns are compatible with the chosen space-filling curve algorithm.

Views and materialized views

Views are virtual tables that represent a subset of data from one or more tables. They are built with SQL queries and can be used to simplify complex searches, encapsulate business logic, or give a unique data representation for each user. By centralizing and abstracting complex logic, views can improve the maintainability of your data architecture. However, if not constructed correctly, they can add a layer of complexity and influence performance.

Materialized views are like views, but their results are physically stored in a table. By precompiling and storing the results of complex queries, this method can greatly enhance query performance. However, materialized views require additional storage and need to be refreshed periodically to ensure data consistency, which can impact performance and maintenance efforts.

Use cases and benefits of advanced techniques

Now that we've looked at partitioning, clustering, bucketing, and Z-ordering, let's look at some of the applications and advantages of these advanced data modeling techniques:

- **Enhanced query performance**: These strategies can considerably minimize the quantity of data that needs to be read during query execution by arranging data more efficiently, resulting in shorter response times and improved overall system performance.

- **Scalability**: Partitioning and bucketing can aid in managing huge datasets by dividing them into smaller, more manageable chunks. This allows you to perform actions on specified partitions or buckets, which reduces the quantity of data that must be processed and allows your system to scale more effectively.

- **Data management**: Partitioning allows for more efficient data administration since you can add, drop, or reorganize partitions independently without affecting the remainder of the table.

- **Storage optimization**: Because rows with comparable values are stored together on disk, Z-ordering can help you optimize storage space by compressing data more effectively. This can result in substantial storage reductions, particularly for large datasets.

- **Flexibility**: These advanced techniques can be used with other approaches to data modeling, such as the star schema, snowflake schema, and normalization/denormalization, to construct a comprehensive data architecture tailored to your individual use case and performance constraints.

Defining the adapted strategy

Let's discuss crafting a top-notch strategy for data ingestion and storage, which is vital for managing, accessing, and analyzing your information effectively. In this section, we'll cover the basics of a data ingestion and storage strategy, setting the stage for the next subsections where we'll discuss evaluating your requirements, following best practices, and adjusting your strategy as necessary.

In the following subsections, we'll explore the process of defining an adapted data ingestion and storage strategy for your organization. We'll offer guidance on evaluating requirements and constraints, adopting best practices, and modifying your strategy as needed. By the end of this section, you'll have the know-how and tools to create a solid, efficient, and scalable data ingestion and storage strategy that suits your organization's unique needs.

Assessing requirements and constraints

Developing a data ingestion and storage strategy requires an in-depth understanding of your organization's unique requirements and constraints. This section will guide you through the process of assessing these factors, thereby helping you make informed decisions when you're defining your strategy.

Data sources and formats

So, what's a data ingestion and storage strategy all about? It's a thorough plan to ingest data from various sources and store it in the optimal storage option for your organization. Your organization will likely handle a variety of data sources and formats. Identifying these is crucial to building an efficient data ingestion and storage strategy. This plan should tackle the following aspects:

- **Data sources**: Recognize the types of data sources your organization uses, such as databases, log files, APIs, or social media. Knowing your data sources will help you determine how to ingest data efficiently and in a format compatible with your storage solution. For instance, real-time data streaming from social media APIs requires a different ingestion approach, such as using tools such as Apache Kafka, compared to batch ingestion of historical log files, which might be done through **Extract, Transform, Load** (ETL) processes.

- **Data formats**: Be familiar with the different data formats you'll be ingesting, such as structured, semi-structured, or unstructured data. This knowledge is essential for selecting the right storage solution and ensuring it works with your data processing and analytics tools. Structured data from databases is often directly ingestible into relational databases or data warehouses, whereas semi-structured or unstructured data, such as JSON from APIs or free-form text from social media, may require preprocessing or a data lake to accommodate the varied formats.

- **Data volume and growth**: Estimate the amount of data you'll be ingesting and storing, as well as how fast it will grow. This information will help you pick a storage solution that can scale with your data requirements.

- **Data access and analysis**: Think about how you'll access and analyze the data. Will you use APIs, SQL queries, or big data processing frameworks? This factor influences your choice of storage solution and impacts the overall efficiency of your data ingestion and storage strategy.

- **Data security and compliance**: Ensure your data ingestion and storage strategy adheres to relevant regulations and maintains your data's security and privacy. This might involve implementing encryption, access control, and monitoring.

- **Integration with existing systems**: Make certain your data ingestion and storage strategy integrate smoothly with your current systems, such as databases, analytics platforms, and business intelligence tools.

- **Flexibility and adaptability**: Remember that your organization's data landscape will change over time. Your data ingestion and storage strategy should be flexible and adaptable, accommodating changes in data sources, formats, and storage needs.

- **Data complexity**: Evaluate the complexity of your data. Is it hierarchical, relational, or flat? This information will help you choose a storage solution that can accommodate your data's structure.

- **Data velocity**: Consider how frequently your data is updated. High-velocity data might require real-time ingestion, while lower-velocity data may allow for batch processing. High-velocity data from online transactions or IoT devices necessitates technologies capable of streaming ingestion to handle the rapid flow of data, whereas data from monthly financial reports can be ingested in batches.

Organizational constraints

Every organization has its unique constraints that shape the data ingestion and storage strategy. These can include the following:

- **Budget**: Determine the financial resources available for data ingestion and storage. This will help you choose cost-effective solutions that meet your organization's needs without breaking the bank.

- **Staff skills**: Assess the expertise of your team. Are they familiar with certain tools or storage systems? This knowledge can guide you toward solutions that make the most of your team's skills or identify areas where training is needed.

- **Existing infrastructure**: Take stock of your organization's existing data infrastructure, including databases, analytics platforms, and other tools. Your strategy should integrate with and leverage these resources whenever possible.

- **Security and compliance**: Ensure your data ingestion and storage strategy complies with relevant regulations and maintains data security and privacy. This may involve implementing encryption, access controls, and monitoring.

- **Scalability**: Consider your organization's future growth. Will your data volume increase significantly? Your strategy should be scalable and adaptable to accommodate this growth.

Once you've assessed your requirements and constraints, you'll have a solid foundation for defining your data ingestion and storage strategy. In the next section, we'll dive into best practices for developing a strategy that balances flexibility and rigidity while promoting an iterative approach. By following these guidelines, you can create an effective strategy that meets your organization's needs and ensures the successful management, access, and analysis of your data.

Best practices for developing a strategy

Now that you've assessed your requirements and constraints, it's time to dive into the best practices for developing a data ingestion and storage strategy. These practices will help you create a strategy that balances flexibility and rigidity while embracing an iterative approach.

Iterative approach

An iterative approach to strategy development allows for continuous improvements and adjustments as your organization's needs evolve. Here's how to apply this approach:

- **Start small**: Begin with a simple, focused strategy that targets your most crucial data sources and storage needs. This will help you gain experience and insights that can be applied to future iterations.

- **Learn from experience**: Use each iteration as an opportunity to learn and refine your strategy. Gather feedback from stakeholders and identify areas for improvement.

- **Plan for incremental improvements**: Break down complex tasks into smaller steps, making them more manageable. Gradually build on your strategy as your organization's data ingestion and storage needs grow.

- **Embrace change**: Be prepared to adapt your strategy as your organization evolves, whether it's due to changes in technology, data sources, or business objectives.

Balancing flexibility and rigidity

A successful strategy strikes a balance between flexibility and rigidity, allowing your organization to adapt to change while maintaining stability. To achieve this balance, consider the following:

- **Establish clear goals**: Define the objectives of your strategy to ensure all stakeholders are aligned. This will help create a sense of direction and focus.

- **Create a framework**: Develop a framework for your strategy that outlines key components, such as data ingestion methods, storage solutions, and monitoring tools. This will provide a stable foundation while allowing for adjustments as needed.

- **Adapt to data source changes**: Stay informed of changes to your data sources, such as new formats or access methods. Update your strategy accordingly to maintain compatibility and efficiency.

- **Prioritize flexibility for evolving needs**: Keep in mind that your organization's data needs will change over time. Design your strategy with flexibility in mind to accommodate these changes.

- **Maintain rigidity for consistency**: While flexibility is important, some aspects of your strategy should remain consistent to ensure stability. For example, you should maintain a consistent naming convention and data structure across all storage solutions.

By following these best practices, you'll be on your way to developing a robust data ingestion and storage strategy that strikes the perfect balance between flexibility and rigidity. This approach will enable your organization to adapt to changing needs while maintaining a stable foundation for data management.

In the next section, we'll discuss how to evaluate and adjust your strategy through monitoring and metrics, ensuring continuous improvement. With these tools at your disposal, you'll be well equipped to optimize your data ingestion and storage strategy, making it a valuable asset for your organization's success. So, let's keep moving forward and explore these vital techniques!

Evaluating and adjusting the strategy

Once you've developed your data ingestion and storage strategy, it's essential to evaluate its effectiveness and make adjustments as needed. Let's look at how monitoring and metrics can facilitate continuous improvement.

Monitoring and metrics

Tracking KPIs and other metrics is crucial for evaluating the success of your strategy. By monitoring these metrics, you can identify potential issues and areas for improvement. Here are some metrics to consider:

- **Data ingestion speed**: Measure how quickly your system ingests data from various sources. Faster ingestion speeds help ensure timely access to data for analysis and decision-making.

- **Data quality**: Assess the accuracy and completeness of ingested data. High-quality data is essential for accurate analysis and insights.

- **Storage utilization**: Monitor storage usage to ensure your solutions are being used efficiently. This can help you identify opportunities for optimization and cost reduction.

- **System reliability**: Track the reliability of your data ingestion and storage systems. A reliable system minimizes downtime and ensures consistent access to data.

Continuous improvement

As you monitor metrics and gather feedback from stakeholders, use this information to make continuous improvements to your strategy. Here are some ways to achieve continuous improvement:

- **Regularly review metrics**: Schedule periodic reviews of KPIs and other metrics to assess your strategy's performance. This helps with identifying trends and areas for improvement.

- **Encourage feedback**: Create an open feedback loop with stakeholders, including team members and users. Their insights can help you fine-tune your strategy.

- **Test and optimize**: Experiment with different approaches to data ingestion and storage. Use A/B testing or other methods to identify the most effective solutions for your organization.

- **Stay informed**: Keep up to date with industry trends and emerging technologies. Incorporating new tools and techniques can help you maintain a cutting-edge strategy.

In conclusion, regularly evaluating and adjusting your data ingestion and storage strategy is essential for staying ahead in today's fast-paced data landscape. By monitoring metrics and embracing continuous improvement, you'll ensure that your strategy remains effective and adaptable, empowering your organization to make the most of its valuable data resources.

Summary

In this chapter, we journeyed through the crucial components of data ingestion and storage strategies. We emphasized the importance of a well-structured and adaptable data ingestion and storage plan for organizations to proficiently manage and utilize their data.

We explored the concept of design by query and how it revolutionizes data modeling by focusing on end user needs. We also learned about the power of clustering to enhance performance, and we dove into the intricacies of Z-ordering for optimizing data storage and improving query performance. We examined the role of views and materialized views and their impact on performance and complexity. We also discussed the strategy of read replication to balance the load and improve performance, especially under heavy load.

Furthermore, we discovered various advanced data modeling techniques, such as partitioning, clustering, bucketing, and Z-ordering, and acknowledged their benefits, which include enhanced query performance, scalability, and improved data management. These techniques also contribute to storage optimization and offer flexibility in designing a comprehensive data architecture.

As we move forward, remember that the key to success in mastering the art of data management lies in maintaining a flexible and adaptable approach. By staying current with industry developments and continuously refining your plan, you'll be primed to tap into your organization's full data resource potential.

As we transition into *Chapter 8*, we will delve into the vast landscape of strategies and methodologies used to consolidate disparate data sources into a unified, accessible format. We will examine different data integration models, as well as their benefits, drawbacks, and use cases, to offer a nuanced understanding of their application in diverse contexts.

8

Data Integration Techniques

This chapter provides a thorough investigation into the vast landscape of strategies and methodologies used to consolidate disparate data sources into a unified, accessible format. The first part of this chapter introduces two prominent data integration models – point-to-point and middleware-based integration. Each model's benefits, drawbacks, and use cases will be meticulously examined to offer you a nuanced understanding of their application in diverse contexts.

This chapter will then transition into a detailed exploration of various data integration architectures, namely batch, micro-batching, real-time, and incremental. Each architecture will be dissected to present you with their unique advantages, trade-offs, and potential applications, thereby providing a comprehensive view of their roles and performances in the data integration domain.

Then, this chapter will delve into commonly used data integration patterns, such as **Extract, Transform, Load** (**ETL**) and **Extract, Load, Transform** (**ELT**), with an additional focus on other patterns, such as **change data capture** (**CDC**) and data federation. Here, you will gain insight into the characteristics, implications, and examples of these patterns, facilitating a solid understanding of their practicality and effects.

Lastly, we'll embark on a tour of the critical data integration organizational models, which include the traditional monolithic architecture, the data mesh model, and the data lake architecture. Each model will be analyzed in terms of their definition, characteristics, and subsequent implications on organizational governance.

By the end of this chapter, you will be armed with the knowledge to compare these models effectively and receive expert recommendations to help you select the right approach for your data integration needs. This chapter's exploration of data integration techniques serves as a solid foundation for any individual or organization seeking to thrive in today's data-driven environment.

This chapter covers the following main topics:

- Data integration models – point-to-point and middleware-based integration
- Data integration architectures – batch, micro-batching, real-time, and incremental
- Data integration patterns – ETL, ELT, and others
- Data integration organizational models

Data integration models – point-to-point and middleware-based integration

Let's consider the importance of data integration in today's data-driven world. Organizations are constantly faced with a variety of data sources, formats, and technologies as they grow and adapt. For this reason, it can be difficult to get a complete, accurate, and current picture of the data environment of your organization. In this situation, data integration could be useful.

The process of merging data from several sources into a logical, consistent, and approachable structure is known as **data integration**. By integrating data to drive business choices and enhance overall performance, organizations may analyze, evaluate, and use data better. But how do we go about successfully integrating data? In this case, data integration models come into play.

In this chapter, we'll look at two popular methods of data integration: middleware-based integration and point-to-point integration. These models provide several methods for synchronizing and linking data between different systems, each with a unique set of advantages and disadvantages.

Point-to-point integration comprises directly linking two systems to facilitate data exchange. While this method is simple to implement, as the number of connections increases, it can become complicated to maintain.

On the other hand, middleware-based integration manages system connections and data flows through a solitary hub known as middleware. This approach can aid in simplifying things and enhancing scalability, but it could also introduce new levels of abstraction and possible weak points.

We'll examine these models' benefits and drawbacks as well as instances from the real world as we look at them in detail. You will gain a solid understanding of the various data integration models by the conclusion of this chapter and will be better equipped to select the one that best suits the requirements of your firm. So, let's get going and start networking!

Point-to-point integration

In this section, we'll look at the advantages, disadvantages, and uses of this popular data integration method. But first, let's make sure we're all on the same page regarding what point-to-point integration is.

Point-to-point integration involves directly linking two systems to ease data flow. Consider it as building a bridge between two systems, enabling data to flow freely from one system to the other. Because it is very simple and quick to apply, this method is typically utilized when dealing with a small number of systems. However, as the number of connections increases, so does the complexity of monitoring and maintaining these connections. So, let's go through the advantages and disadvantages of point-to-point integration.

The following figure represents a point-to-point integration model:

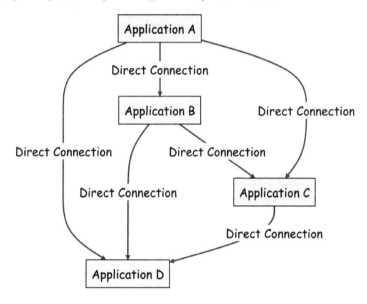

Figure 8.1 – Point-to-point integration model

The preceding figure depicts how point-to-point integration directly connects individual systems, creating a network of data bridges that can facilitate easy data flow, though this may result in a complex web of connections as the system count increases.

Advantages of point-to-point integration

Here are a few of the benefits of point-to-point integration:

- **Simplicity**: Directly connecting two systems may be a simple operation, especially if the systems are interoperable and use comparable data formats. When you're just starting or dealing with a small number of systems, this simplicity might be tempting.

- **Customization**: Developers may customize each connection to the individual needs and requirements of the systems involved using point-to-point integration. This can result in highly optimized networks that maximize data exchange efficiency.

- **Speed**: Because there is no need for additional processing or routing through a centralized hub, direct connections between systems can sometimes result in faster data transfer than other data integration models.

Disadvantages of point-to-point integration

Here are a few disadvantages of point-to-point integration:

- **Scalability**: As the number of systems grows, the number of connections required increases at a rapid rate, creating a tangled web of connections. This can make the overall integration process difficult to manage, maintain, and troubleshoot.

- **Traffic monitoring**: In this model, traffic is monitored directly by observing the connectivity and data sent from one application to another. Even if it allows quick problem detection, it becomes too complex and challenging to monitor as the number of connections grows, as described previously.

- **Maintainability**: Each direct connection may require custom coding, which can lead to high maintenance costs as developers must update and adapt each connection individually when systems change or new requirements arise.

- **Lack of reusability**: Since each connection is tailored to the specific systems involved, it's challenging to reuse code or configurations across multiple connections, leading to a less efficient and more time-consuming integration process.

- **Strong dependency and life cycle/change management**: Point-to-point integration creates a rigid dependency structure between systems, complicating life cycle and change management. Adjustments in one system can necessitate cascading changes across multiple connections, amplifying the complexity and risk of system updates.

- **Multi-level dependency**: The architecture may involve multi-level dependencies, where an issue in a primary connection (for example, between applications A and B) indirectly affects downstream applications (such as application D), even if they are not directly connected. This indirect impact highlights the fragility of the integration strategy in accommodating system changes.

- **Bottleneck/performance issues**: When multiple consumers are directly connected to the same producer (for example, application A serves applications B, C, and D), it can create performance bottlenecks. These bottlenecks arise as the producer struggles to manage concurrent requests efficiently, thereby impacting the overall performance and reliability of the integrated system.

Expert advice

Point-to-point integration is a straightforward way to connect systems, but it can quickly become unmanageable as the number of connections grows. A good rule of thumb is to limit the use of point-to-point integration to scenarios where you have less than 10 systems to integrate.

Now that we've covered the advantages and disadvantages, let's explore some real-life use cases and examples of point-to-point integration.

Technologies and use cases

Web services such as **Representational State Transfer (REST)**, **Simple Object Access Protocol (SOAP)**, **Secure File Transfer Protocol (SFTP)**, and **Simple Storage Service (S3)**, are examples of technologies that are used for point-to-point data interaction. Each of these technologies has benefits that satisfy different requirements.

However, it's important to note that beyond these modern web-based services, traditional ETL solutions also play a crucial role in point-to-point integrations, especially when connecting directly to producer application databases. For instance, in scenarios involving direct data extraction from a database, classic ETL tools can establish a direct connection to the database of a **customer relationship management (CRM)** platform such as Salesforce.

Take, for instance, a scenario involving Salesforce, a CRM platform. In this context, web services, especially RESTful APIs, can be a good choice for establishing a direct link with a billing system – for instance, when a new customer profile is added/edited in Salesforce. In this case, Salesforce can initiate an API call encapsulating customer data in JSON or XML format, which is then relayed over HTTP/HTTPS to the billing system to keep it updated.

The following figure shows how to integrate Salesforce with the billing system:

Figure 8.2 – Integrating Salesforce with the billing system

A common scenario for Salesforce integration arises when there's a requirement to funnel data into a centralized repository for reporting, such as an S3 data lake. Direct data transfer services such as AWS AppFlow, or tools such as Salesforce Data Loader paired with the S3 API, can be utilized. These solutions streamline the transfer of data from Salesforce to the S3 data lake, facilitating easier data aggregation and subsequent reporting.

The following figure shows how to integrate Salesforce with an S3 data lake:

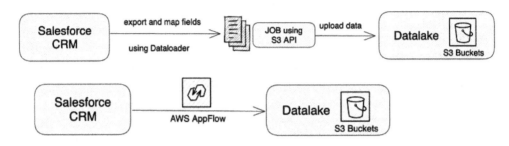

Figure 8.3 – Integrating Salesforce with an S3 data lake

The following is a non-exhaustive list of other use case scenarios where point-to-point integration can be suitable:

- **Use case 1**: A small business with limited systems

    Consider a small firm that manages its operations using just two or three systems, such as a CRM for customer data and an accounting system for financial data. With such a limited number of systems, a point-to-point link may be a simple and cost-effective approach to sync data between them, ensuring that customer and financial data are aligned and up to date.

- **Use case 2**: Connecting legacy systems

    Older legacy systems can sometimes be difficult to integrate with modern systems due to their unique data formats, protocols, or limited support for newer technologies. In these cases, point-to-point integration can be a viable option as developers can create custom connections tailored to the specific requirements and limitations of the legacy systems involved.

- **Use case 3**: Data migration projects

    When migrating data from one system to another, such as during a system update or transition to a new platform, point-to-point integration can be an effective method of moving data between old and new systems. Because integration is frequently temporary in many circumstances, the simplicity and speed of point-to-point integration might be beneficial.

    Finally, point-to-point integration offers a simple and adaptable way to link systems and share data. However, when more systems and connections are added, this technique could become cumbersome and challenging to manage. When reviewing your organization's data integration requirements, it is critical to compare the benefits and drawbacks of point-to-point connections with alternative models, such as middleware-based integration, which we will explore in the following section. When working with larger and more complicated system settings, point-to-point integration has considerable difficulties. Another solution that alleviates some of these constraints is middleware-based integration.

Choosing the right integration model is essential to the success of your data integration efforts, so keep that in mind as we continue our journey through data integration. When selecting the ideal solution, it's essential to consider the needs of your company, the number of systems involved, and the complexity of the data communicated. You will be better prepared to make informed judgments and improve your data integration processes if you carefully consider these criteria and comprehend the benefits and downsides of each integration strategy.

Stay tuned for the next section, where we'll examine middleware-based integration and go through its advantages, disadvantages, and use cases. You will be able to optimize the value of your data and make the best business choices thanks to this thorough understanding of data integration patterns.

Middleware-based integration

In this section, we'll look at middleware-based integration, which is an alternative to point-to-point integration that can help manage the complexity of merging various systems. Middleware-based integration uses a common hub or platform to connect disparate systems, applications, and data sources.

The following figure shows a middleware-based integration model:

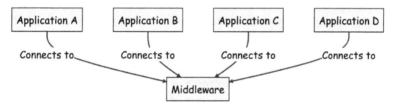

Figure 8.4 – Middleware-based integration model

For this type of architecture based on middleware, we generally use **message-oriented middleware (MOM)** and an **enterprise service bus** (**ESB**), technologies that are used for integrating disparate systems. They facilitate communication and data exchange between different applications and services. However, they differ in their capabilities, complexity, and use cases.

While MOM and ESB are commonly recognized technologies for integrating disparate systems, they are not the only solutions available. The DataHub model is another significant approach to middleware-based integration. This model is a centralized architecture that consolidates data from multiple sources into a single repository before it's distributed to various systems. This model is a powerful data integration mechanism that provides a unified view of information throughout the organization. Unlike MOM and ESB, which are primarily concerned with message and service orchestration, the DataHub approach prioritizes data centralization, management, and governance.

The primary focus of messaging systems, a key component of MOM, is to ensure message transfer across a network. They employ queues to balance the load effectively and topics to facilitate a publish-subscribe model. On the other hand, ESB extends these capabilities by adding additional features, such as orchestration, routing, and transformation.

Next, we'll go over the benefits and drawbacks of this technique, as well as look at real-world examples and use cases.

Advantages of middleware-based integration

Here are the advantages of middleware-based integration:

- **Scalability**: The capacity to scale successfully is one of the most significant advantages of middleware-based integration. Unlike point-to-point integration, middleware-based integration may support growth by adding new systems or applications without requiring considerable modification.

- **Flexibility**: Integration based on middleware provides better flexibility in merging disparate systems, applications, and data sources. This adaptability allows firms to adjust more readily to changing business needs and facilitates the smooth incorporation of new technology.

- **Reduced complexity**: By using a central hub, middleware-based integration simplifies the overall integration architecture. It minimizes the number of connections between systems, making it easier to manage, maintain, and troubleshoot integration issues.

- **Enhanced data governance**: Middleware-based integration promotes better data governance by providing a centralized location for data transformation, validation, and enrichment. This centralization ensures data consistency and quality across integrated systems.

- **Standardization**: Middleware-based integration encourages the adoption of standard data formats and communication protocols, facilitating smooth data exchange and reducing potential errors.

- **Traffic monitoring**: This model offers a centralized approach to traffic monitoring as it acts as a hub. It provides a holistic view of network health and advanced analytics, and it also facilitates load balancing across applications. This results in a more manageable and efficient system of traffic monitoring.

Disadvantages of middleware-based integration

Here are the disadvantages of middleware-based integration:

- **Cost**: Implementing middleware-based integration might be more expensive than point-to-point integration, especially when the initial investment in integration platforms or tools is considered. However, the long-term benefits of decreased complexity and increased scalability may outweigh this expense.

- **Vendor dependency**: Middleware-based integration often relies on specific platforms or tools, which may lock organizations into a particular vendor's ecosystem. This dependency can limit flexibility and make it more challenging to switch vendors or adopt new technologies in the future.

- **Potential latency**: Middleware-based integration can introduce additional latency into data exchange processes as data must pass through the central hub before reaching its destination. This latency may be an issue for organizations requiring real-time data integration.

> **Tip**
>
> Middleware-based integration can simplify and standardize your data integration process by using a central hub to manage connections and data flows. However, choosing the right middleware platform is crucial since different platforms may have different capabilities, costs, and compatibility with your existing systems.

Technologies and use cases

Technologies such as Apache Kafka, RabbitMQ, AWS Kinesis, and Azure EventHub can be used to implement a middleware-oriented data integration model where applications don't communicate directly with each other; instead, they connect to the central point, which is the middleware layer that handles communication between applications.

Take, for instance, a scenario that consists of a large e-commerce company that needs to track user behavior on its website in real time for personalized recommendations. When a user visits their website, every action generates events such as viewing a product, adding an item to the cart, or purchasing an item. These events are dispatched to a Kafka topic as messages using the AVRO format. AVRO, developed within Apache's Hadoop project, is a row-oriented framework for remote procedure calls and data serialization. It leverages JSON to define data types and protocols, ensuring data is serialized in a streamlined binary format.

Multiple services within the company are actively subscribed to various topics. The recommendation service utilizes user events to continually update its recommendation model for each individual. The anti-fraud service remains vigilant, monitoring transaction events for any suspicious activities. Simultaneously, the inventory service employs purchase events to ensure stock availability is up to date. Lastly, the analytics service taps into all the events, crafting comprehensive reports and extracting insights regarding users' behaviors. Kafka is a key player in this complex ecosystem. It not only ensures the consistent delivery of events to all these services, even when faced with millions of events per second, but it also decouples the services deftly. This elegant design allows each service to process events at its own pace while also allowing each to be scaled independently.

Here is a non-exhaustive list of other use case scenarios where middleware-oriented integration can be suitable:

- **CRM**: Middleware can integrate CRM systems such as Salesforce with other business applications such as email marketing tools, customer support systems, and social media platforms. This integration enables businesses to have a centralized view of customer data, streamline customer interactions, and provide personalized experiences.

- **Supply chain management**: Middleware can facilitate integration between different systems involved in the supply chain, such as suppliers, manufacturers, distributors, and retailers. By integrating these systems, businesses can optimize inventory levels, automate order processing, track shipments, and improve overall supply chain visibility.

- **Financial services**: Middleware can be used to integrate banking systems, payment gateways, and financial management software. This integration enables businesses to automate financial processes, such as payment reconciliation, funds transfer, and financial reporting, resulting in improved accuracy, efficiency, and compliance.

- **Human resources (HR) management**: Middleware can integrate HR systems with recruitment platforms, payroll systems, and employee performance management tools. This integration streamlines HR processes, such as employee onboarding, payroll processing, and performance evaluations, leading to increased operational efficiency and improved employee satisfaction.

- **Healthcare systems**: Middleware can integrate **electronic health record** (EHR) systems with laboratory information systems, radiology systems, and billing systems. This integration enables healthcare providers to access patient information, test results, and billing data in real time, improving patient care coordination and billing accuracy.

- **Manufacturing**: Middleware can integrate **manufacturing execution systems** (MESs) with **enterprise resource planning** (ERP) systems, **warehouse management systems** (WMSs), and logistics providers. This integration enables real-time visibility into production schedules, inventory levels, and shipment tracking, optimizing manufacturing and supply chain operations.

- **Travel and hospitality**: Middleware can integrate booking engines, **property management systems** (PMSs), customer loyalty programs, and payment gateways. This integration enables seamless booking and payment processes, centralized guest data management, and personalized guest experiences across various touchpoints.

- **Energy management**: Middleware can integrate smart energy meters, energy management systems, and billing systems. This integration enables real-time monitoring of energy consumption, automated billing and invoicing, and demand response management, helping businesses optimize energy usage and reduce costs.

- **Education management**: Middleware can integrate **student information systems** (SISs), **learning management systems** (LMSs), and online assessment platforms. This integration enables streamlined student enrollment, course management, and assessment processes, enhancing the overall learning experience.

- **Marketing automation**: Middleware can integrate **customer data platforms** (CDPs), marketing automation tools, and analytics platforms. This integration enables businesses to capture and analyze customer data, automate marketing campaigns, and measure the effectiveness of marketing efforts.

By examining these use cases and examples, we can see the versatility of middleware-based integration in addressing various integration challenges. Choosing the right middleware platform and tailoring it to an organization's specific requirements can significantly streamline the integration process and enable organizations to derive maximum value from their data and applications. As businesses evolve, middleware-based integration can serve as a critical component in supporting and enabling this growth, fostering innovation and efficiency across the enterprise.

Next, we'll discuss various data integration architectures.

Data integration architectures – batch, micro-batching, real-time, and incremental

When diving deeper into the world of data integration, it is critical to comprehend the many data integration designs available. Each architecture type has benefits and drawbacks that make it better suited for specific scenarios and use cases. We'll go over four possible data integration architectures in this section: batch, micro-batching, real-time, and incremental.

These designs can be thought of as the foundation of your data integration process. They govern how data is exchanged and processed between systems, and they have a large impact on the overall performance, scalability, and maintainability of any data integration solution. It is critical to select the appropriate architecture for your specific requirements since this will have a direct impact on the efficiency and efficacy of your integration efforts:

- **Batch data integration** is the process of grouping data into sets and processing it at regular intervals. This method is useful when data does not need to be processed immediately (low latency) and can be handled in huge chunks. It's frequently utilized in nightly or weekly data updates when the system can analyze data without interfering with other processes.

- **Micro-batching data integration** is a batch processing variant that handles smaller, more frequent data collections. This method creates a balance between batch processing efficiency and real-time integration timeliness. It's handy in situations where you need a more current picture of your data but don't need immediate updates.

- **Real-time data integration** is concerned with processing data as it is generated or received. This method is ideal for situations in which you need high reactivity to make quick decisions based on the most recent data. Real-time integration is frequently utilized in applications such as real-time fraud detection, where prompt response is required to limit risks.

The following figure shows the different data integration architectures:

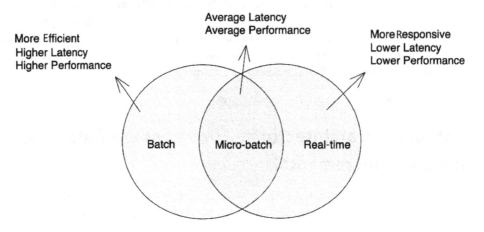

Figure 8.5 – Different data integration architectures

The previous three data integration architectures can be implemented either in a full or in an incremental integration. Full integration processes the entire dataset, proving particularly useful when changes in the data source are intricate and challenging to monitor. On the other hand, incremental integration only processes the data that has changed since the previous integration, which is a fast technique for handling data updates without having to process the complete data collection each time. When data changes often and reprocessing the complete dataset is time-consuming and resource-intensive, incremental integration is typically utilized.

Consider your organization's specific demands and requirements as we investigate these various data integration architectures. You'll be better equipped to choose the right architecture for your data integration projects if you understand the trade-offs and factors to consider.

Batch data integration

In this section, we'll dive deeper into batch data integration while looking at use cases, trade-offs, and things to consider while putting this architecture in place. Understanding the complexities of this technique will help you decide if it's the best fit for your data integration needs.

Batch data integration is a tried-and-true method for gathering and processing data in big groups, or "batches." Data is collected throughout time and then processed all at once over a predetermined time range. This method has various advantages, making it a popular choice for many businesses.

Advantages

Because it allows for bulk data processing, batch processing can be more resource-efficient than real-time processing. This can help reduce the strain on system resources and avoid performance concerns. Let's take a look at some more advantages:

- **Error handling is simplified**: Mistakes that occur during batch processing are frequently easier to discover and remedy because they affect an entire batch of data. This makes it easier to identify and resolve the problem.

- **Consistency**: By batch processing data, you may ensure that all data in each batch is consistent and up to date. This is especially beneficial for protecting data integrity and eliminating discrepancies that may result from real-time data processing.

- **Performance/efficiency**: Batch processing can be faster than micro-batch or real-time systems when handling large amounts of data. This is because it groups tasks and runs them all at once, which is more efficient. However, while batch processing can finish a full job quickly, it may not be as responsive as real-time systems. This means it might take longer to get feedback after making a request. But for large, non-responsive use cases, batch processing can be a very efficient choice.

Case studies

Batch data integration is ideal for cases where data does not need to be provided immediately and may be processed during off-peak hours. Among the most prevalent use cases, we have the following:

- **Data warehousing**: To combine and store massive volumes of data from multiple sources, data warehouses frequently rely on batch processing. This contributes to the warehouse containing a consistent snapshot of the data at a certain point in time.

- **Reporting and analytics**: When it comes to creating reports and doing analytics chores, batch processing is a popular option. You may verify that reports and analyses are based on a consistent dataset by processing data in batches, making it easier to make relevant conclusions.

- **Data backups**: Backing up data is an essential activity for any organization, and batch processing can be an efficient way to create regular backups. This guarantees that backup data is consistent and current.

Trade-offs

While batch data integration has many advantages, there are certain drawbacks to consider:

- One of the major disadvantages of batch processing is the inherent lag in data availability. Because data is only processed at planned time slots, it may not be appropriate for scenarios requiring real-time data access.

- You must also consider the impact of batch processing on system resources, particularly during peak hours. To meet this strain, you may need to plan batch processing during off-peak hours or devote additional resources.

> **Warning**
> Batch data integration can be efficient and consistent, but it also introduces data latency, which means that your data may not be up to date at all times. This can be a problem for scenarios where you need real-time or near-real-time data access, such as fraud detection or dynamic content generation.

Consider the following factors when establishing batch data integration:

- **Batch size and frequency**: The size and frequency with which the batches are handled have a direct impact on the performance and resource consumption of your integration solution. Achieving a balance between efficiency and data accuracy is crucial.

- **Error handling and recovery**: While not a drawback of batch processing itself, creating a solid error handling and recovery strategy is critical to ensuring the integrity of your data and reducing the risk of data loss. When properly implemented, batch data integration can enhance data consistency and integrity by including robust error handling and recovery mechanisms.

Finally, batch data integration might be a useful solution for firms that need to process huge volumes of data regularly. You can make an informed judgment about whether this architecture is the correct solution for your data integration needs by studying its use cases, trade-offs, and variables.

Micro-batching data integration

In this section, we'll investigate micro-batching data integration, including its use cases, trade-offs, and factors to consider when implementing this method. Understanding the nuances of micro-batching can help you decide if it's the appropriate fit for your data integration needs.

Micro-batching data integration falls between batch and real-time processing. This method processes data in smaller batches at more frequent intervals. Micro-batching provides a compromise between the efficiency of batch processing and the timeliness of real-time processing by breaking down data processing into smaller, more manageable portions.

Advantages

Here is a list of advantages of micro-batching data integration:

- **Increased data timeliness**: Because micro-batching allows for more frequent updates, the data is more current and the time it takes to propagate changes through the system is reduced

- **Scalability**: Processing data in smaller batches provides for more detailed control over resource allocation and can assist in minimizing system bottlenecks

- **Flexibility**: Micro-batching provides a flexible middle ground between batch and real-time processing, allowing enterprises to adjust their data integration strategy to their individual needs

Case studies

Micro-batching data integration is ideal for circumstances requiring a balance of data timeliness and resource efficiency. Among the most prevalent use cases, we have the following:

- **Near-real-time analytics**: Micro-batching enables near-real-time analytics, allowing organizations to access up-to-date insights without the resource overhead of true real-time processing

- **Log processing**: Log files are often generated continuously and can be processed using micro-batching to detect trends, errors, and other patterns more quickly than with traditional batch processing

- **Data streaming**: Micro-batching can be employed in data streaming scenarios, where data is ingested and processed in smaller batches to enable more timely decision-making and analysis

Trade-offs

While micro-batching data integration has many advantages, there are certain drawbacks to consider:

- **Complexity**: Micro-batching can be more complex to implement than traditional batch processing, as it requires more frequent data processing and may involve additional synchronization and coordination mechanisms

- **Resource usage**: While micro-batching is more resource-efficient than real-time processing, it may still consume more resources than batch processing, particularly if the micro-batches are processed at very frequent intervals

Factors to consider

When implementing micro-batching data integration, it's essential to consider the following factors:

- **Batch size and frequency**: Finding the right balance between batch size and processing frequency is crucial to optimizing resource usage and data timeliness. Smaller, more frequent batches will provide more up-to-date data but may consume more resources.

- **Latency requirements**: Evaluate your organization's latency requirements to determine if micro-batching is the right approach. If real-time processing is essential, micro-batching may not be sufficient to meet your needs.

- **Data consistency**: Ensure that data consistency is maintained across micro-batches, particularly when dealing with distributed data sources or systems that require synchronization.

- **Error handling**: When implementing micro-batching, consider how you should handle errors and exceptions that may occur during processing. Implementing robust error handling and monitoring mechanisms can help ensure the stability and reliability of your data integration pipeline.

- **Infrastructure and tooling**: Evaluate the existing infrastructure and tools within your organization to determine if they can support micro-batching. Some tools and platforms are better suited for micro-batching than others, so it's essential to consider compatibility and ease of integration when making your decision.

- **Resource allocation and optimization**: Micro-batching may require different resource allocation strategies compared to traditional batch processing. Carefully consider how to allocate resources, such as compute power and memory, to ensure optimal performance and efficiency.

- **Monitoring and management**: With more frequent data processing, efficient monitoring and management solutions are essential. Ascertain that you can successfully monitor the performance of your micro-batching processes and make necessary adjustments to maintain optimal performance.

Industry good practice

Micro-batching data integration is a popular choice for data streaming scenarios, where data is ingested and processed in smaller batches to enable more timely decision-making and analysis. Many modern data streaming platforms, such as Apache Kafka and AWS Kinesis, support micro-batching as a native feature or through integration with other tools.

In conclusion, micro-batching bata integration may be an appropriate approach for enterprises that require a balance of data timeliness and resource efficiency. You can make an informed judgment about whether this technique is the best fit for your data integration needs by considering its use cases, trade-offs, and various factors.

Real-time data integration

Now that we've looked at several data integration architectures, it's time to tackle one of the most desirable yet difficult types of data integration: real-time data integration. Real-time data integration has become a key tool for enterprises as the demand for quick access to data has increased. In this section, we'll go through the use cases, trade-offs, and factors to think about while establishing real-time data integration.

Use cases

Real-time data integration is particularly useful in scenarios where up-to-date information is crucial for decision-making. Here are some common use cases:

- **Fraud detection**: Financial institutions and eCommerce platforms need real-time data to detect fraudulent transactions and prevent financial loss.

- **Monitoring and alerting**: Real-time data integration helps organizations monitor their infrastructure, applications, and services to identify potential issues and send alerts immediately.

- **Personalized recommendations**: eCommerce and content platforms can leverage real-time data to offer personalized recommendations based on user behavior and preferences.

- **Real-time analytics**: Real-time data integration enables businesses to perform real-time analytics, providing insights for decision-making, trend analysis, and forecasting.

- **Dynamic content generation**: Platforms such as TikTok and Instagram can harness the power of real-time data to generate dynamic content feeds tailored to individual user behavior and preferences. By analyzing the user's interactions, such as likes, shares, comments, or time spent on certain types of content, these platforms can immediately adjust the feed to present content that aligns with the user's interests. This ensures a personalized and engaging user experience, which can increase both user satisfaction and platform engagement rates.

- **IoT device management and analytics**: Real-time data integration plays a critical role in the **Internet of Things (IoT)** ecosystem, enabling the continuous monitoring and management of IoT devices. It facilitates the immediate analysis of data generated by these devices, supporting predictive maintenance, real-time operational insights, and the optimization of IoT networks for enhanced efficiency and reliability.

Advantages

Here is a list of advantages of real-time data integration:

- **Immediate access to data**: Real-time integration ensures that data is available as soon as it is generated, enabling immediate access for analysis and decision-making

- **Enhanced decision-making**: With up-to-the-minute data, organizations can make informed decisions quickly, staying ahead of market trends and reacting to changes in real time

- **Improved customer experience**: Real-time data integration allows businesses to offer personalized experiences to customers by immediately responding to their actions and preferences

- **Increased operational efficiency**: Real-time insights into operations can help identify and address inefficiencies quickly, reducing downtime and optimizing performance

- **Better fraud detection and security**: The immediate analysis of transactions and user behavior can help in detecting fraudulent activities and potential security breaches as they happen

- **Dynamic content generation**: This enables platforms to provide content that is dynamically tailored to user preferences and behaviors, enhancing user engagement and satisfaction

- **Real-time analytics and reporting**: This allows you to analyze data and generate reports in real time, offering insights that can be acted upon immediately

- **Enhanced monitoring and alerting**: This allows organizations to monitor their systems and infrastructure in real time, providing immediate alerts in case of issues, thus minimizing potential damage or downtime

Trade-offs

While real-time data integration offers many benefits, there are trade-offs to consider:

- **Increased complexity**: Real-time data integration often involves complex architectures, making implementation and maintenance more challenging compared to batch or micro-batching

- **Scalability**: Handling high volumes of data in real time can be resource-intensive, requiring powerful infrastructure and robust systems to ensure smooth operations.

- **Cost**: The infrastructure, tools, and resources required for real-time data integration can be expensive, especially for organizations with tight budgets

Factors to consider

In deploying real-time data integration, a multitude of factors warrant careful deliberation, including latency, data volume, and data quality requirements, the choice of integration tools and technologies, and the need for fault tolerance and resilience. Handling sensitive data brings security and compliance to the fore, while constant monitoring and optimization are indispensable for optimal performance. These key elements, alongside others, are discussed in detail here:

- **Data latency requirements**: Evaluate your organization's data latency requirements to determine if real-time data integration is necessary. Some use cases may not require real-time data processing, and opting for micro-batching or batch processing may be more cost-effective and resource-efficient.

- **Data volume and velocity**: Assess the volume and velocity of data generated by your organization to ensure that your infrastructure and tools can handle real-time data integration. Consider factors such as data throughput, processing capabilities, and storage capacity.

- **Data quality**: Real-time data integration can introduce data quality issues, such as incomplete, inconsistent, or duplicate data. Implement data validation and cleansing techniques to maintain data quality and ensure accurate insights.

- **Integration tools and technologies**: Choose appropriate tools and technologies that support real-time data integration. Some popular options are Apache Kafka, Apache Flink, and Apache Nifi, all of which provide scalable and reliable real-time data processing capabilities.

- **Fault tolerance and resilience**: Ensure that your real-time data integration architecture is fault-tolerant and resilient. Implement mechanisms to handle failures, such as retries, backpressure, and data replication, to minimize the impact of system failures on data processing.

- **Security and compliance**: Real-time data integration often involves sensitive information, making security and compliance essential considerations. Implement data encryption, access control, and auditing mechanisms to protect your data and comply with regulatory requirements.

- **Monitoring and optimization**: Real-time data integration requires constant monitoring and optimization to maintain optimal performance. Implement monitoring solutions to track system performance and resource usage and adjust as needed to ensure smooth operations.

- **Data consistency**: Ensure the consistency of data across all systems involved in real-time integration. Real-time data processing can lead to consistency challenges, especially in distributed environments where data is replicated across different systems. Implement strategies such as transaction management, eventual consistency models, or distributed databases to maintain data accuracy and integrity across the ecosystem.

> Expert advice
>
> Real-time data integration can provide fast and reactive data access, but it also requires more complex and robust architectures to handle high volumes and velocities of data. To implement real-time data integration successfully, you need to consider factors such as latency requirements, data quality, fault tolerance, security, and compliance.

Finally, real-time data integration has the potential to deliver enormous benefits to companies by providing quick access to valuable insights and boosting decision-making capabilities. However, it is not without its difficulties and trade-offs, all of which must be examined properly. You may make informed decisions about whether real-time data integration is the appropriate choice for your company and how to deploy it effectively by assessing the use cases, trade-offs, and factors covered in this section.

Incremental data integration

In our investigation of alternative data integration designs, we've discovered that incremental data integration provides distinct advantages for firms that must deal with constantly changing data. This section will go over the use cases, trade-offs, and factors to think about while adopting incremental data integration in your business, highlighting how CDC plays a crucial role in this architecture.

The following figure represents the CDC integration model:

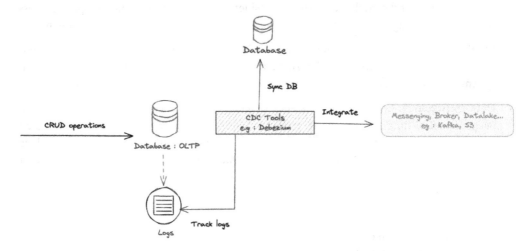

Figure 8.6 – CDC integration model

In this representation, the CDC integration model is based on log tracking to apply the same changes on another database. Incremental data integration, often synonymous with CDC, at its core, treats database alterations as events. Such a pattern is most beneficial in scenarios where processing only the change in data – rather than the entire dataset – is more efficient and resource-saving. Some common use cases are data synchronization, change tracking and auditing, incremental data loading, populating data lakes with fresh data, and data warehousing updates. By focusing on the changes detected through CDC mechanisms, organizations can significantly reduce processing time and resource consumption.

Use cases

Incremental data integration is most beneficial in scenarios where processing only the change in data is more efficient than processing the entire dataset. Here are some common use cases:

- **Data synchronization**: Incremental data integration is ideal for keeping data synchronized between different systems as it only processes new or updated data, reducing processing time and resource usage

- **Change tracking and auditing**: Incremental data integration can be employed to track changes in data over time, enabling organizations to maintain an audit trail for compliance and analysis purposes

- **Data warehousing**: In a data warehousing environment, incremental data integration can be used to efficiently update the warehouse with new or modified data from the source systems, reducing the impact on system performance and minimizing data latency

Trade-offs

As with any data integration architecture, there are trade-offs to consider when implementing incremental data integration:

- **Complexity**: Incremental data integration may require more sophisticated logic to identify and process data changes, increasing the complexity of the integration process.

- **Data consistency**: Since incremental data integration deals with changes in data, ensuring data consistency between source and target systems can be challenging, especially when dealing with data deletion or schema changes.

- **Change identification**: Identifying data changes accurately and efficiently is critical for incremental data integration. Inaccurate change identification can lead to data corruption, missed updates, or duplicate data.

Factors to consider

Delving into the nitty-gritty of incremental data integration, it's essential to understand that this process is primarily powered by CDC techniques. CDC mechanisms are pivotal for detecting data modifications in real time, enabling efficient data synchronization between source and target systems. This section outlines the important factors organizations need to address when leveraging CDC for incremental data integration, from selecting an appropriate change detection mechanism to managing data deletions and schema changes effectively. This ranges from selecting an appropriate change detection mechanism to efficiently handling data deletions and schema changes. Furthermore, we'll discuss the significance of tool selection and the necessity for constant monitoring and optimization:

- **Change detection mechanism**: Choose an appropriate change detection mechanism for your incremental data integration process. Options include timestamp-based, log-based, or snapshot-based change detection, each of which has its advantages and disadvantages.

- **Data consistency and integrity**: Implement data validation and reconciliation techniques to ensure data consistency and integrity between source and target systems. This may involve comparing source and target data, handling data conflicts, or using data lineage tracking to trace data changes.

- **Performance and resource usage**: Evaluate the performance and resource usage of your incremental data integration process. Ensure that it is efficient and scalable to handle the volume and velocity of data changes in your organization.

- **Data deletion handling**: Develop a strategy for handling data deletions in your incremental data integration process. This may involve marking deleted records as inactive or removing them from the target system entirely.

- **Schema change handling**: Establish a process for handling schema changes in the source system. This may involve automatically detecting and propagating schema changes or using schema versioning to maintain backward compatibility.

- **Integration tools and technologies**: Select the right tools and technologies that support incremental data integration. Some popular options include Apache NiFi, Talend, and Microsoft **SQL Server Integration Services** (**SSIS**), which offer features for handling data changes efficiently.

- **Monitoring and optimization**: Examine the performance and resource utilization of your incremental data integration process to find bottlenecks and areas for improvement. Optimize the process regularly to achieve peak performance, scalability, and dependability.

In conclusion, incremental data integration can deliver significant benefits to companies by reducing processing time and resource consumption associated with data integration operations. However, putting this architecture in place presents several obstacles and trade-offs that must be evaluated carefully. You may need to make well-informed decisions about whether incremental data integration is the appropriate choice for your business and how to implement it effectively by considering the use cases, trade-offs, and variables presented in this section.

> Tip
> Incremental data integration can reduce processing time and resource consumption by processing only the changes in data instead of the entire dataset. However, this approach requires accurate and efficient change detection mechanisms to ensure that no data is missed or duplicated. Some common change detection mechanisms are timestamp-based, log-based, and snapshot-based methods.

Next, we'll discuss data integration patterns.

Data integration patterns – ETL, ELT, and others

After looking at different data integration models and architectures, it's time to look at data integration patterns. These patterns describe best practices and approaches for combining data from several sources into a coherent and useful shape. You may solve unique integration difficulties and guarantee that your data integration efforts are efficient, accurate, and scalable by understanding and implementing these patterns.

This section will go through three major data integration patterns: ETL, ELT, and other notable patterns such as CDC and data federation. We'll go over the properties and ramifications of each pattern, as well as present examples to show you how these patterns might be used in real-world circumstances.

The most utilized patterns are ETL and ELT, which focus on how data is extracted, converted, and loaded into a target system. The key distinction between the two is in the order in which the transformation and loading phases are performed, which affects the processing efficiency, resource consumption, and the overall performance of your data integration process.

Finally, data federation is a design style that integrates data from multiple sources without physically moving or modifying the data. Instead, it produces a virtual, integrated representation of the data that users or applications may access and evaluate.

Keep in mind that there is no one-size-fits-all solution as we investigate these patterns. The optimum solution for your firm will be determined by your specific requirements, data sources, and integration objectives. Understanding these patterns will enable you to make more educated decisions about which technique is best suited to your data integration difficulties and goals.

The ETL pattern

This section will walk you through the ETL data integration pattern, which is one of the most well-known and extensively used methods for integrating data from multiple sources.

ETL is a data integration process that involves extracting data from various sources, transforming it to fit operational needs, and then loading it into a database or data warehouse. This process aligns closely with the schema-on-write pattern. In the schema-on-write pattern, data is validated against a schema before it's written into the database. During the transformation stage of ETL, data is often cleaned, enriched, and reshaped to match the target schema. This ensures that the data in the database is consistent, reliable, and ready for immediate querying and analysis.

We'll look at use scenarios and examples to assist you in understanding when and how to apply this method in your data integration projects, as well as the attributes and implications of the ETL pattern.

Characteristics and Implications

As a reminder, ETL is a sequential process involving three steps:

- **Extract**: Data is extracted from various source systems, which could be databases, files, APIs, or other data sources. The extracted data is often in different formats and structures.

- **Transform**: Data is transformed into a common, standardized format, which can involve cleansing, validating, enriching, and reformatting the data. The transformed data is often stored in a staging area before being loaded into the target system.

- **Load**: The transformed data is loaded into the target system, such as a data warehouse, data lake, or other storage solutions, where it can be analyzed and used for business intelligence, reporting, or other purposes.

To ensure that the destination system is kept up to date with the most recent data from the source systems, the ETL process is typically implemented as a batch process that runs at predetermined intervals, such as daily, weekly, or monthly.

There are several implications of using the ETL pattern:

- **Resource-intensive**: The transformation step may be computationally expensive, requiring significant processing power and memory, depending on the complexity of the changes and the volume of data being processed.

- **Data latency**: Due to the batch nature of the ETL process, there may be a delay between when data is obtained from the source systems and when it is available in the target system. This latency may hinder real-time reporting and decision-making.

- **Scalability**: As the number of data sources and transformations increases, ETL operations can become increasingly complicated, making it difficult to manage and expand the integration process.

Use cases and examples

Now that you understand the characteristics and implications of the ETL pattern, let's look at some use cases and examples where this approach is most applicable:

- **Data warehousing**: Many data warehousing operations rely on ETL to integrate, transform, and load data from diverse sources into a central repository for reporting and analysis. ETL operations are used to ensure that the data in the data warehouse is clean, consistent, and ready for analysis. A large store, for example, collects sales data from several point-of-sale systems and internet channels. The retailer extracts, cleans, and transforms the data into a standard format before loading it into a data warehouse for analysis and reporting via an ETL process.

- **Data migration**: ETL can be used to extract data from a source system, modify it as needed (for example, to fit the schema of the target system), and load it into the new system when businesses need to migrate data from one system to another. For example, suppose a corporation decides to transition from a classic CRM system to a cloud-based CRM platform. An ETL process is used to take customer data from the old system, clean and transform it, and then load it into the new CRM platform.

- **Data consolidation**: ETL methods can be used to consolidate data from multiple sources, resulting in a single and consistent representation of the data for analysis and reporting. For example, let's say that a healthcare company wishes to create a comprehensive view of patient records by integrating data from several EHR systems. An ETL procedure collects patient data from each EHR system, standardizes it, and feeds it into a central data repository.

The following code sample helps illustrate the steps involved in ETL. Data is extracted from the source, transformed using Python logic, and then loaded into a destination database:

```python
import sqlite3

def extract_from_source(conn):
    cursor = conn.cursor()
    cursor.execute("SELECT * FROM source_data")
```

```
    data = cursor.fetchall()
    return data

def transform_data(data):
    # Placeholder logic for transforming data
    transformed_data = [(f"transformed_{d[0]}",) for d in data]
    return transformed_data

def load_to_destination(conn, data):
    cursor = conn.cursor()
    cursor.executemany("INSERT INTO destination_data (name) VALUES (?)",
data)
    conn.commit()

source_conn = sqlite3.connect('source_database.db')
destination_conn = sqlite3.connect('destination_database.db')

# ETL Process
data = extract_from_source(source_conn)
transformed_data = transform_data(data)
load_to_destination(destination_conn, transformed_data)
```

To summarize, the ETL pattern is a powerful and extensively used approach for data integration, especially in cases where data consolidation, data warehousing, and data migration are important goals. However, the resource needs, data latency, and scalability issues that can accompany ETL operations must be considered.

> **Warning**
>
> ETL is a traditional and widely used data integration pattern that involves transforming data before loading it into the target system. This ensures that the data is consistent and ready for analysis. However, ETL can also be resource-intensive and introduce data latency. Moreover, ETL may not be suitable for scenarios where you need to store raw or unstructured data or explore different ways of transforming data.

You may make informed judgments about when and how to utilize this method in your data integration projects by studying the properties and implications of the ETL pattern and reviewing use cases and examples. As you work with data integration, you'll likely come across instances where ETL is the best answer, as well as situations where other patterns, such as ELT or real-time data integration, may be more appropriate. You will be better positioned to create and implement effective data integration solutions that match your organization's demands and support its goals if you are aware of these various patterns and their trade-offs.

The ELT pattern

The ELT pattern is critical to cover as we dive deeper into data integration patterns. The proliferation of cloud-based data warehouses and big data platforms has contributed to this strategy's rise in popularity in recent years.

ELT is a newer way of handling data. You get the data, put it into your system, and then make changes to it. This is often used with the schema-on-read pattern. In schema-on-read, you add the data to the system in its original form and only organize and structure it when you query it. This means you can use the same data in different ways and different structures, depending on what you need at the time. This gives you more flexibility and lets you explore your data more freely.

Let's take a closer look at the features and ramifications of ELT, as well as some use cases and examples that can shed light on the field's potential uses.

Characteristics and implications

Unlike the traditional ETL process, the ELT pattern switches the order of operations. First, data is extracted from source systems and then loaded directly into the target system, without undergoing any transformations beforehand. The transformation step takes place within the target system itself, leveraging its processing capabilities.

This pattern has some unique characteristics and implications, as follows:

- **Utilization of target system resources**: ELT takes advantage of the processing power of modern data warehouses and big data platforms, allowing for faster and more efficient data transformations. This approach can be particularly beneficial when dealing with large datasets as it offloads the resource-intensive transformation tasks from the integration tool to the target system.

- **Reduced data latency**: Since data is loaded directly into the target system before being transformed, ELT can reduce data latency compared to the ETL pattern. This characteristic is especially valuable in scenarios where near real-time data access is critical for decision-making and analysis.

- **Scalability**: As the target system handles the transformation tasks, the scalability of the ELT pattern depends on the processing capabilities of the target platform. Cloud-based data warehouses and big data systems are typically designed for high scalability, making ELT a suitable option for organizations with growing data volumes and processing requirements.

- **Complexity**: The complexity of the ELT pattern can vary depending on the target system and its built-in transformation capabilities. While some data warehouses offer user-friendly interfaces and tools for designing and executing data transformations, others may require more specialized knowledge and expertise.

Use cases and examples

Now that we've covered the characteristics and implications of the ELT pattern, let's explore some use cases and examples to better understand how it can be applied in real-world scenarios:

- **Cloud-based data warehousing**: Companies using Amazon Redshift, Google BigQuery, or Snowflake as their cloud data warehouse will find the ELT pattern useful. With the powerful data processing capabilities provided by these platforms, complicated transformations can be executed inside the target environment. This method not only boosts performance but also reduces complexity by reducing the requirement for specialized integration software.

- **Big bata analytics**: In the realm of big data, the ELT pattern can be an effective solution for integrating and processing vast amounts of data. Platforms such as Apache Spark and Hadoop allow for distributed data processing, enabling organizations to transform data at scale within the target environment. By using ELT in this context, businesses can efficiently prepare data for advanced analytics, machine learning, and other big data applications.

- **Data lake integration**: Data lakes store raw, unprocessed data from various sources, making them an ideal candidate for the ELT pattern. By loading data directly into a data lake and performing transformations using built-in processing tools, organizations can maintain a single source of truth for their data and streamline their analytics workflows.

The following code sample helps illustrate the steps involved in ELT. Data is directly loaded into a data warehouse, after which transformations are performed using SQL within the warehouse itself:

```python
import sqlite3

def load_to_data_warehouse(conn, data):
    cursor = conn.cursor()
    cursor.executemany("INSERT INTO raw_data_warehouse (name) VALUES (?)", data)
    conn.commit()

def transform_in_data_warehouse(conn):
    cursor = conn.cursor()
    cursor.execute("""
      INSERT INTO transformed_data_warehouse (name)
      SELECT 'transformed_' || name FROM raw_data_warehouse
      """)
    conn.commit()

# ELT Process
data = extract_from_source(source_conn)
warehouse_conn = sqlite3.connect('data_warehouse.db')
load_to_data_warehouse(warehouse_conn, data)
transform_in_data_warehouse(warehouse_conn)
```

> **Industry good practice**
>
> ELT is a newer and more flexible data integration pattern that involves loading raw data into the target system and transforming it on demand. This allows you to store more types and volumes of data and perform various transformations based on your needs. ELT is especially suitable for cloud-based data warehouses and big data platforms that have high processing power and scalability.

In summary, the ELT pattern offers a powerful alternative to the traditional ETL approach, particularly in scenarios where the target system has robust processing capabilities. By understanding the characteristics, implications, and use cases of the ELT pattern, you can make informed decisions about when and how to apply this method in your data integration projects. As you continue to explore data integration techniques, it's essential to consider the unique needs and requirements of your organization, as well as the specific capabilities of your target system.

Advantages and disadvantages of the ELT pattern

It's important to consider the advantages and disadvantages of the ELT pattern when deciding whether it's the right fit for your data integration needs. Here are some of the key points to consider.

Advantages:

Here is a list of advantages of the ELT pattern:

- **Performance**: By leveraging the processing capabilities of the target system, ELT can deliver better performance compared to ETL, especially for large datasets and complex transformations

- **Scalability**: The ELT pattern can easily scale with the growth of your data volumes and processing needs, provided that your target system is designed for high scalability

- **Data latency**: The ELT pattern can aid in reducing data latency by loading data into the target system before transformation, thereby granting you near-real-time access to your data for decision-making and analysis

Disadvantages:

And on the other hand, let us also mention the disadvantages of the ELT model

- **Security**: In some cases, loading raw data directly into the target system might pose security risks as sensitive data may be exposed during the transformation process. It's essential to implement proper data governance and security measures to mitigate these risks.

- **Complexity**: Depending on the target system, the ELT pattern may require specialized knowledge and expertise to design and execute data transformations. This can increase the complexity of your data integration processes and may require additional training or resources.

- **Vendor lock-in**: Relying on the target system's built-in transformation capabilities can lead to vendor lock-in, making it difficult to switch to a different platform in the future. It's crucial to carefully evaluate the long-term implications of adopting the ELT pattern and consider the potential costs and challenges of switching platforms.

With regards to cloud-based data warehousing, big data analytics, and data lake integration, the ELT design offers substantial benefits over conventional ETL approaches. You may make educated decisions about when and how to apply the ELT pattern in your data integration projects by first weighing its advantages and disadvantages. Keep in mind that your data environment's demands and requirements, the capabilities of your target system, and the overall aims of your data integration projects will all play a role in determining the best data integration strategy for your business.

The following table compares the usage ELT and ETL:

	ETL	ELT
Order of Operations	Extract data from the source, transform it, and then load it into the target system	Extract data from the source, load it into the target system, and then transform it
Schema	Requires a pre-defined schema (schema-on-write)	Supports schema-on-read, which allows more flexibility
Data Processing	Data is transformed before being loaded into the target system to meet the target data model's requirements	Data is loaded into the target system before being transformed
System Load	The processing load is on the ETL tool or source system, rather than the target system	The processing load is on the target system, which leverages its processing capabilities for potentially better performance
Data Availability	Data is available for analysis after the ETL process is completed	Data is available for near-real-time access after it's loaded, but transformations are completed later
Data Latency	May introduce latency as data is transformed before being loaded	Can potentially reduce data latency by transforming data after it's loaded
Security	Transforms data before loading it, potentially reducing exposure of sensitive data	It may expose sensitive data during transformation, requiring robust data governance and security measures
Complexity	It might require less specialized knowledge, depending on the transformation's needs	It may require specialized knowledge to design and execute transformations, possibly increasing complexity

Table 8.1 – Comparing ETL and ELT

In the realm of data integration, understanding the strengths and weaknesses of the ELT pattern is pivotal in making strategic decisions. This pattern, while effective in reducing data latency and enhancing performance and scalability, raises issues around security, complexity, and potential vendor lock-in. Despite these considerations, ELT provides significant benefits in the context of cloud-based data warehousing, big data analytics, and data lake integration, emerging as a preferred pattern over the traditional ETL approach. As with any technology, the choice between ETL and ELT should hinge upon your unique data needs, your target system's capabilities, and your overarching data integration objectives.

Other data integration patterns

In this section, we will delve into an additional data integration pattern – data federation – that can be extremely helpful in certain scenarios. When creating and implementing your data integration strategy, having a thorough understanding of these patterns, their use cases, and their benefits and drawbacks can help you make better judgments.

Data federation

Data federation is a data integration pattern that provides a unified view of data from multiple, disparate sources without the need for physically moving or copying the data. Instead, data federation relies on a virtual layer that consolidates and integrates data from various sources, making it available to users and applications as if it were a single, unified data source.

Characteristics and implications

Data federation has several key characteristics that set it apart from other data integration patterns:

- **Virtual integration**: Data federation does not require you to physically move or copy data, which can save time, resources, and storage space
- **Real-time data access**: By consolidating data from multiple sources in real time, data federation allows users to access the most current information without waiting for data synchronization processes
- **Flexibility and extensibility**: Data federation enables you to easily add or remove data sources, making it a flexible and extensible solution for managing changing data environments
- **Data abstraction**: Data federation provides a unified view of data, abstracting the underlying complexities of individual data sources and allowing users to interact with the data without needing to understand its source or structure

Use cases and examples

Data federation can be an effective solution for the following use cases:

- **Data consolidation**: Organizations with multiple, disparate data sources can use data federation to provide a single, unified view of their data, simplifying access and reporting

- **Real-time analytics and reporting**: By providing real-time access to data from multiple sources, data federation can enable real-time analytics and reporting, allowing decision-makers to access the most up-to-date information

- **Data virtualization**: Data federation can be used to create a virtual data layer that hides the complexity of the underlying data sources and structures, making it easier for users and applications to interact with the data

- **Data governance and compliance**: Data federation can help enforce data governance policies and compliance requirements by providing a centralized point of control for accessing and managing data from multiple sources

In conclusion, developing successful data integration strategies requires knowledge of the various data integration patterns and their benefits and drawbacks. CDC and data federation are alternatives to ETL and ELT that can be useful in some circumstances. Data integration processes can be optimized and desired outcomes achieved by carefully evaluating the use cases and characteristics of each pattern. Always keep in mind that your company's specific objectives and needs must be considered while determining the optimal data integration solution.

Tip

CDC is a specialized data integration pattern that captures changes in the source system and applies them to the target system in real time or near real time. CDC can improve data timeliness and reduce resource consumption by avoiding full or incremental loads. CDC can be implemented using various methods such as triggers, logs, or APIs.

Next, we'll discuss data integration organizational models.

Data integration organizational models

In the evolving landscape of data management, various organizational models have emerged, each offering distinct processes, implications, and governance strategies. This section delves into three key models: the traditional monolithic model, which is characterized by centralized data lakes and warehouses; the data mesh model, which emphasizes decentralization and domain-oriented control of data; and the data lake architecture, a hybrid approach that marries the benefits of its predecessors. By examining their definitions, characteristics, and organizational implications, we aim to provide a comprehensive understanding of these models. Finally, we'll compare these approaches and provide factors to consider when selecting the most appropriate model for your organization's unique needs.

Introduction to organizational approaches in data integration

Choosing an organizational model for data management significantly impacts a company's operational efficiency and strategic agility. The choice between traditional models such as the monolithic architecture and data lake, and newer ones such as data mesh, has far-reaching implications, influencing processes, data governance, and organizational structure. As we navigate this complex landscape, it's crucial to remember that the right data integration model can transform data from a mere resource into a strategic asset.

Overview and relevance

In the vast, interconnected world of data management and integration, an organization's chosen model for handling data can fundamentally shape its operational efficiency, strategic agility, and overall success. Navigating the different organizational models available, understanding their implications, and choosing the one most suitable to a given business context is of paramount importance. Hence, this section aims to provide a comprehensive overview and an incisive analysis of the different organizational models in data integration, focusing on their relevance in modern data-driven business environments.

The contemporary data landscape is characterized by complexity, diversity, and volume, brought about by a range of factors. These include the growth of digital technologies, the explosion of big data, the advent of AI and machine learning, and an increasing regulatory focus on data privacy and security. Amid this complexity, data integration emerges as a strategic necessity rather than a technical convenience. It's the underpinning process that enables organizations to aggregate, organize, and extract value from their diverse data sources.

However, how an organization goes about this process – its choice of a data integration model – can significantly impact its data infrastructure's efficacy, scalability, and manageability. Traditional models such as the monolithic architecture, data lake, and data warehouse, offer centralized control and standardization but can pose challenges in scalability and flexibility. In contrast, newer models such as data mesh propose a more decentralized and domain-oriented approach to address the limitations of the traditional models.

Recognizing the relevance of these organizational models is critical. It's not just about data management; it's about enabling effective data governance, improving data quality, driving business intelligence, and ultimately, leveraging data as a strategic asset. Thus, understanding the different organizational models in data integration, their strengths, and their challenges, can provide invaluable insights for businesses aiming to thrive in the data-driven digital economy.

The distinction between processes, implications, and governance

Delving into the organizational approaches to data integration requires a clear understanding of the distinctions between processes, implications, and governance since these aspects are intertwined yet unique in their roles within the data integration landscape.

Processes in data integration refer to the operational steps and techniques involved in merging data from diverse sources. It covers tasks such as ETL, data cleansing, validation, and more. The efficiency and efficacy of these processes often dictate the quality and usability of the integrated data, directly impacting an organization's ability to generate valuable insights.

Implications, on the other hand, denote the broader organizational impacts and considerations resulting from the chosen data integration approach. This includes aspects such as the required skills and resources, scalability, flexibility, cost implications, and effects on data privacy and security. For instance, while a monolithic architecture might streamline data integration processes, it may also necessitate a single point of control, potentially creating bottlenecks or single points of failure.

Governance in data integration is the overarching framework that guides how data is collected, stored, managed, and used within an organization. It involves defining and implementing policies, procedures, roles, and responsibilities to ensure data quality, security, and compliance. For instance, in the data mesh model, governance might involve defining the accountability of domain-oriented teams for the quality and security of their respective data domains.

While all three aspects are pivotal in shaping a data integration strategy, it's important to understand their unique roles and intersections. Effective processes can facilitate high-quality data integration, but without proper governance, organizations risk data inconsistency, non-compliance, and security vulnerabilities. Similarly, considering the implications of an approach can help ensure it aligns with an organization's resources and strategic objectives. The interplay of these factors makes choosing the right organizational model a complex but critical decision for any data-driven enterprise.

Traditional model – monolithic architecture

The traditional data management model, often referred to as the monolithic architecture, centralizes all of an organization's data into a single repository and features systems such as data lakes and data warehouses. Despite its ability to handle vast amounts of data, this model presents scalability and management challenges. It also has significant implications for data governance as it centralizes data responsibilities, potentially leading to bottlenecks and inflexibility in data governance.

Definition and characteristics

The traditional model for data integration, often referred to as the monolithic architecture, encompasses systems such as data lakes and data warehouses. This model is characterized by a centralized approach where all the data within an organization is gathered, stored, and processed in a singular, centralized repository.

In this architecture, a data lake serves as a vast storage reservoir that holds a massive amount of raw data in its native format until it is needed. This data could be structured, semi-structured, or unstructured, offering flexibility for diverse data sources. A data lake allows you to store all types of data, providing a broad overview for exploratory data analysis and machine learning.

A data warehouse, on the other hand, is a structured repository that's designed for analyzing and reporting structured and processed data. It is a highly curated environment where data is transformed into a format that can be easily used by business users, and it is optimized for analytical processing and business intelligence applications.

The traditional model is characterized by a few key features. Firstly, it centralizes data management, creating a single source of truth. This offers a consolidated view of business operations and facilitates comprehensive analytics. Secondly, the model is designed to handle massive amounts of data thanks to the capacity of data lakes and the organization of data warehouses. Finally, the model tends to be schema-on-write, meaning data must be cleaned, transformed, and structured before storage, which can ensure data quality and consistency but may involve significant processing time.

Despite its apparent strengths, the monolithic model comes with its challenges, especially concerning scalability and management. We'll explore these next.

Organizational implications and governance aspects

The traditional monolithic model has substantial implications for an organization's data governance policies and strategies. Being a centralized structure, it tends to concentrate data-related responsibilities in a single team or department, especially for governance. This team or department is typically responsible for managing, gathering, processing, and storing data from different sources and providing access to various stakeholders across the organization. While this can offer certain advantages, such as consistent data handling and a singular point of control, it also brings about notable challenges.

One of the most significant implications of this centralized structure is the potential bottleneck effect. As the sole entity responsible for data management, the central team can become overwhelmed with requests for data access, transformation, or analysis, leading to delays and inefficiencies. This scenario can also contribute to a lag in responsiveness when business units need quick access to data or need to adjust data processes due to changing business conditions.

The governance aspects of the monolithic model are closely tied to its centralized nature. In this context, data governance is about ensuring the availability, usability, integrity, and security of the data stored in the data lake or warehouse. This responsibility is typically vested in the central data team, which can establish and enforce data policies, procedures, and standards. They ensure that the data is accurate, complete, and reliable and that it is used appropriately and protected against unauthorized access or loss.

While this model provides a high level of control over data, it can lead to rigidity in data governance. Changes to data policies or processes may require extensive coordination and take considerable time to implement. This could be a potential disadvantage in rapidly changing business environments where agility and flexibility are highly valued.

In addition, this centralization of data governance could lead to a lack of ownership and accountability among other business units. Since data management is the responsibility of one team, other units might perceive data quality and accuracy as someone else's problem. This perception could negatively affect the overall data quality and integrity across the organization.

Another critical aspect is the potential for security and privacy concerns. With all the data centralized, the data lake or warehouse becomes an attractive target for malicious attacks. This concentration of data necessitates robust security measures to protect against potential breaches.

Lastly, the success of a monolithic architecture heavily depends on the skills and capabilities of the central data team. This requirement puts a high premium on recruiting and retaining highly skilled data professionals and maintaining up-to-date technological capabilities.

In conclusion, while the traditional model offers significant control over data, it also comes with organizational and governance implications that must be carefully managed. This is particularly true given the rapidly increasing volume, variety, and velocity of data in today's digital organizations, which can strain the capacities of a centralized model. As a result, many organizations are exploring alternative approaches, such as the data mesh model, which we will discuss next.

Data mesh model

This section presents an in-depth exploration of two modern data architectures: the data mesh model and the data lake architecture. The data mesh model represents a novel approach to data management, decentralizing responsibility across domain-oriented teams and treating data as a product. On the other hand, the data lake architecture focuses on storing raw data on a large scale, offering flexibility and scalability for diverse analytical needs. The implications of both models on organizational structure and governance will also be discussed, shedding light on their potential benefits and challenges.

Definition and characteristics

The data mesh model is an innovative approach to data architecture that shifts away from the traditional monolithic model, where data is collected, processed, and stored centrally. Instead, it introduces a decentralized paradigm that distributes the responsibilities of data across various domain-oriented teams and then through different roles. A key principle of data mesh is to treat data as a product, with individual teams owning and managing the data they generate as part of their daily operations.

In the data mesh model, data is no longer viewed as a byproduct or residue of business processes but rather as an integral component that drives value and is a key contributor to business objectives. As such, the teams generating and using the data are given the stewardship of their respective data domains. They become responsible for its quality, usability, and accessibility, bringing about an inherent sense of ownership that can significantly improve the overall quality and relevance of the data.

The data mesh model brings several defining characteristics that differentiate it from the traditional approach. Firstly, it is a distributed model, where each domain-oriented team operates independently, managing their data products. This structure fosters agility and responsiveness to business needs, as teams are empowered to make decisions and implement changes within their domains without going through a centralized entity.

Secondly, the data mesh model emphasizes the use of a domain-driven design. This design guides how data is modeled, stored, and processed, leading to better alignment with business needs and easier integration of data across different domains.

Thirdly, the model advocates for a technology-agnostic approach. It encourages the use of best-suited technologies for different data needs, promoting technological diversity and reducing the risk of vendor lock-in. The model also emphasizes interoperability, ensuring that different technologies can work together seamlessly.

Lastly, the data mesh model embodies a strong focus on data discovery and accessibility. It promotes the use of standardized metadata and well-defined APIs to expose data products, making it easier for other teams and stakeholders to find and use the data they need.

A critical part of this model is the role of the data product owner, a position that bears the responsibility for the success of the data product. The data product owner should have a deep understanding of both the domain and the data needs of consumers, and they ensure that the data product is reliable, accurate, and valuable.

To summarize, the data mesh model is a decentralized, domain-driven, and technology-agnostic approach that treats data as a product. It offers a potential solution to the scalability issues faced by traditional, centralized models, especially in organizations where data is generated across a diverse range of domains. However, it's important to note that while the data mesh model brings promising benefits, it also presents its own set of challenges, particularly in terms of governance, as we'll see in the following section.

The four pillars of the data mesh model

The data mesh model, while embodying a paradigm shift in data architecture, also introduces four fundamental pillars that support its principles and guide its execution. These pillars not only encapsulate the philosophical foundation of the data mesh approach but also provide a practical framework for organizations adopting this model:

- **Domain-oriented decentralized data ownership and architecture**: The first pillar is centered around the principle of decentralization, which is a break from the traditional, centralized data lake or warehouse approach. In the data mesh model, responsibility for data is distributed among various cross-functional, domain-oriented teams within an organization. Each of these teams owns and manages the data it generates, treating it as a product. This empowers individual teams to maintain the quality and reliability of their data and accelerates the delivery of valuable data products by reducing dependencies on centralized data teams.

- **Data as a product**: The second pillar, treating data as a product, revolutionizes how data is viewed within an organization. Traditionally, data has often been seen as a byproduct or residue of business operations. However, the data mesh model acknowledges data as an asset that drives insights and innovation. This pillar also necessitates the presence of a data product owner, a role that ensures the data product is fit for its intended use, aligns with the business objectives, and delivers value to its consumers.

- **Self-serve data infrastructure as a platform**: The third pillar emphasizes the need for a self-serve data infrastructure. To promote autonomy among the domain-oriented teams, they should be given the tools and platform to access, process, and distribute data without reliance on a central data team. This does not imply a lack of standards or governance, but rather the decentralization of control, with robust and standardized protocols and tools to ensure the security, privacy, and quality of data.

- **Federated computational governance**: The fourth and final pillar addresses governance in the data mesh model. As the model decentralizes data ownership, traditional governance methods become impractical. Hence, the data mesh model necessitates a federated governance approach. This approach allows for rules, policies, and standards to be defined at an organizational level, at which point they are implemented at the individual team level. This balances the need for control and standardization with the benefits of decentralization, facilitating trust and interoperability between different data domains.

Each pillar of the data mesh model is intertwined and mutually reinforcing. The shift toward domain-oriented, decentralized data ownership goes together with treating data as a product. Likewise, the self-serve data infrastructure and federated governance are necessary enablers of these decentralization efforts. These pillars serve as the compass for organizations navigating the journey of implementing a data mesh, grounding the transformation in concrete principles and practices.

Organizational implications and governance aspects

The application of the data mesh model carries significant implications for an organization's structure and governance policies. Its principles, while promising greater flexibility and responsiveness, necessitate fundamental changes in the way teams work and how data is managed within an enterprise.

From an organizational perspective, the decentralization of data ownership disrupts traditional hierarchies and power dynamics. Unlike monolithic models, where data governance is centralized, the data mesh paradigm necessitates that every domain-oriented team takes ownership of their data. These teams act as independent data custodians, treating their data as a product. This shift can cultivate a more collaborative and transparent culture within the organization, with data transparency and accountability becoming integral parts of team roles.

With the move toward a decentralized model, the role of the centralized data team also transforms. Rather than acting as the primary custodians and gatekeepers of all data, their role pivots towards providing the necessary infrastructure, tools, and guidelines for the domain teams to manage their data. This change necessitates the upskilling and reskilling of central data teams to understand the complexities of a self-serve data platform and the nuances of supporting domain teams.

A critical facet of this shift is the evolution of the data product owner role. In the data mesh model, the data product owner takes on the responsibility of ensuring the data product's fitness for its intended use, aligning it with business objectives, and ensuring it delivers value to its consumers. This role becomes instrumental in the functioning of the data mesh model and must be integrated effectively within the organization.

In terms of governance, the data mesh model introduces a federated governance approach, another significant departure from traditional models. This approach allows for rules, policies, and standards to be defined at the organizational level, but these are implemented at the individual team level. Governance becomes a shared responsibility, with each domain team having a role in maintaining data quality, privacy, and security. This federated model fosters local ownership while still maintaining the necessary checks and balances across the organization.

However, these shifts in organizational structures and governance also present challenges. For example, ensuring that each team is equipped with the necessary skills and resources to manage their data can be a considerable undertaking. Furthermore, implementing federated governance requires a delicate balance of autonomy and control, and getting this balance right can be complex and challenging.

In conclusion, the organizational implications and governance aspects of the data mesh model are both profound and promising. They signal a move toward more decentralized and agile data management structures, fostering greater collaboration, transparency, and accountability. However, these transformations also require significant change management efforts, underlining the importance of careful planning, clear communication, and ongoing support.

Data lake architecture

A data lake, in the realm of data architecture, is a unique model designed specifically to accommodate the challenges and leverage the potential of big data. As organizations continuously generate enormous volumes of data, the need for efficient storage and management solutions becomes a paramount necessity. The data lake architecture emerges as a robust solution to this need by providing a comprehensive platform for storing vast quantities of raw data.

One of the distinguishing features of a data lake is its ability to store raw, unprocessed data. In contrast to other data storage models, such as data warehouses or monolithic architectures, which necessitate that data be preprocessed, structured, and classified before storage, a data lake can ingest data in its rawest form. This feature is crucial as it allows for the inclusion of a wide range of data types, including structured data from relational databases, semi-structured data such as CSV or JSON files, and unstructured data such as emails, documents, and even binary data such as images, audio, and video files.

Another defining characteristic of data lakes is their schema-on-read approach. While traditional storage methods, such as data warehouses, require a predefined schema for data storage (known as schema-on-write), a data lake applies the schema only at the point of reading or extracting the data. This unique feature offers substantial flexibility, enabling the same data to be interpreted and analyzed in myriad ways depending on the specific requirements of the end-user. This results in a highly adaptable, agile data environment that can cater to a diverse array of analytical applications, from machine learning and predictive analytics to real-time reporting and advanced visualizations.

Furthermore, the scalability of data lakes is a significant attribute. As the volume of data generated by organizations continues to rise, the ability to seamlessly scale storage capacity up or down becomes critical. Data lakes, underpinned by cloud-based storage technologies, can be easily scaled, enabling organizations to manage their storage needs cost-effectively and pay only for the storage they use.

Another advantage of data lakes is their inherent openness. This openness extends to the type of data that can be stored and the variety of analytics tools and platforms that can be used in conjunction with a data lake. By breaking away from the constraints of proprietary systems, data lakes empower organizations to choose the tools and technologies that best align with their operational needs and strategic goals.

Despite these beneficial characteristics, it's crucial to recognize potential challenges. The flexibility and openness of data lakes can, without adequate structure and governance, lead to a "data swamp" scenario, characterized by a lack of organization and governance. Therefore, a well-designed data lake necessitates the implementation of robust data governance and data management strategies. These strategies are critical to maintaining data quality, ensuring data security, and preventing the accumulation of dark data, which is data collected but not used.

Organizational implications and governance aspects

The data lake architecture not only brings forth a set of robust capabilities but also triggers significant organizational implications. These implications often manifest in the realm of organizational structures, processes, and the overall strategic outlook of the enterprise.

A major implication is the transformation of organizational roles and responsibilities. Data lakes promote a data democratization culture where end users can directly access and analyze data, bypassing traditional gatekeepers such as IT departments. However, this democratization necessitates a change in the skillset of the workforce. Employees need to be proficient in data querying and analysis, making data literacy a critical competency in a data lake environment.

Another organizational implication concerns the reevaluation of existing business processes. Given the schema-on-read nature of data lakes, it's possible to derive diverse insights from the same dataset. This flexibility can lead to new analytical approaches that challenge established procedures. The potential to disrupt traditional ways of decision-making may meet resistance, necessitating careful change management.

Furthermore, the adoption of a data lake could steer an organization toward a more data-driven culture. With the availability of diverse data, organizations can use these insights to inform strategic decisions, leading to an increased reliance on data rather than intuition or experience. This cultural shift can have profound implications on the organization's overall strategy and competitive positioning.

These organizational implications underscore the need for robust governance in the data lake architecture. Data governance involves establishing rules, policies, and procedures to manage and ensure the quality, security, and usability of data.

For a start, data quality in a data lake is critical, given the adage "garbage in, garbage out." Policies should be in place to ensure data is well-described, accurate, and relevant. This might involve the implementation of data cataloging tools or automated data quality checks.

Data security and privacy are also key governance aspects. As data lakes store a vast amount of potentially sensitive data, mechanisms should be established to ensure data protection. This can include encryption, access controls, and anonymization techniques.

Finally, governance plays a role in preventing the data lake from becoming a "data swamp," an environment where data is disorganized, redundant, and of questionable value. This necessitates a clear data strategy that outlines what data should be stored, who has access, and how it will be maintained.

In conclusion, the adoption of a data lake architecture implies a series of organizational changes, touching upon roles, competencies, processes, and culture. Simultaneously, it calls for a robust governance structure that guarantees data quality, security, and value. Navigating these implications and governance aspects requires a thoughtful approach, alignment with the overall business strategy, and a commitment to building a data-driven culture.

Comparing the different models and choosing the right approach

Comparative analysis of different data management models offers a solid basis for decision-making when considering the specific requirements of an organization. Here, we'll compare the traditional (monolithic) architecture, the data mesh, and the data lake models:

Aspect	Traditional (Monolithic) Model	Data Mesh Model	Data Lake Model
Definition	A centralized data store where data from multiple sources is integrated into one comprehensive and easily managed system.	A decentralized data management approach that emphasizes domain-oriented decentralized data ownership and architecture.	A large centralized repository with raw data held in its native format, processed data, and oriented business case data.
Data Structure	Highly structured, often in a relational database form.	This depends on the interlaying technology. However, it can accept structured to unstructured data, depending on the domain context.	It can implement all data natures, but it generally deals with unstructured and semi-structured data, which provides high flexibility.

Aspect	Traditional (Monolithic) Model	Data Mesh Model	Data Lake Model
Scalability	Depending on the underlying technology, this is generally limited due to its monolithic nature. It's more complex to scale as the volume of data increases.	Depending on the underlying technology, it is generally highly scalable as it's mainly implemented on distributed technologies.	It has high scalability due to its distributed nature and flattened architecture.
Governance	Centralized, with data managed and controlled by central IT teams.	Decentralized, with governance distributed across domains since each domain can scale independently.	Can be implemented in both centralized or decentralized governance but requires robust governance to avoid becoming a "data swamp."

Table 8.2 – Comparing the traditional (monolithic), data mesh, and data lake models

This comparison provides a high-level overview of the different models. Choosing between these models should involve detailed consideration of specific organizational needs, including the volume and variety of data, the desired level of data democratization, and the capacity for data governance. Additionally, the current state of data architecture and the readiness of the organization to adopt a new model should also be factored in.

Factors to consider in choosing an approach

When selecting a data architecture approach for your organization, several crucial factors should be considered to ensure an effective and efficient implementation. This section highlights the factors to consider when choosing between traditional models, data mesh, and data lake:

- **Volume and velocity of data**: The amount of data your organization handles and the speed at which this data is generated are vital factors. Traditional models might struggle with large-scale, real-time data, while data lake and data mesh are designed to handle big data environments more efficiently.

- **Data variety**: The diversity of data types, structures, and sources your organization manages can influence the architecture selection. For highly varied data, the flexibility of a data lake or a data mesh could provide the necessary accommodation.

- **Data governance**: It's essential to consider how you want to manage and control data. If your organization prefers centralized governance, traditional models may be suitable. However, for distributed data governance, a data mesh is a better fit. Data lakes require robust governance to prevent them from becoming data swamps.

- **Organizational structure**: The way your organization operates also matters. If your organization is highly siloed or segmented, the data mesh approach may enable better cross-functional data usage.

- **Scalability needs**: If your organization anticipates significant growth or scaling in the future, it's better to select a model that can comfortably accommodate that growth, such as a data mesh or data lake.

- **Data access and democratization**: If promoting widespread data access across the organization is a priority, then the data mesh, with its distributed ownership, might be the best fit.

- **Resources and skills**: Implementing new data architectures requires specific technical skills and expertise. Make sure you evaluate the available resources and skill sets within your organization.

- **Current infrastructure**: Lastly, take stock of your current data architecture and infrastructure. Moving from a traditional model to a data mesh or data lake can require significant restructuring and resources.

Remember, each architecture has its strengths and limitations. It's essential to evaluate these factors in the context of your organizational goals, technical capabilities, and strategic direction. There is no one-size-fits-all solution, and the best approach depends on your unique circumstances and needs.

Recommendations and best practices

As organizations venture into data integration, certain recommendations and best practices can help pave the path toward successful implementation and optimization of either traditional, data mesh, or data lake models.

First, let's look at traditional models:

- **Data consistency**: In traditional architectures such as data warehouses, it's crucial to ensure data consistency and quality. Implement strict ETL processes and regular data audits.

- **Scalability planning**: Even if your organization chooses a traditional model, considering future scalability needs is crucial. Adopt practices that allow for a smooth transition toward more scalable architectures, such as data lakes or a data mesh, when needed.

Now, let's look at data lake models:

- **Prevent data swamps**: Implement robust data governance and management strategies to avoid your data lake turning into a data swamp. Metadata management, access controls, and data cataloging can help maintain order and usability.

- **Security measures**: Due to the openness of data lakes, security becomes paramount. Implement strong access controls and encryption mechanisms to protect sensitive information.

Finally, let's look at data mesh models:

- **Promote data ownership**: Foster a culture of data ownership among different domain teams. Encourage teams to take responsibility for the quality and security of their data

- **Establish clear data contracts**: For seamless cross-functional data usage, establish clear data contracts outlining the format, content, and quality of the data provided by each team

Here are some general best practices:

- **Agile practices**: Regardless of the chosen architecture, incorporating agile practices in data management, such as iterative development and continuous integration, can yield beneficial results.

- **Continuous learning**: Data architectures are continually evolving. Maintain a culture of continuous learning and stay updated on the latest trends and advancements.

- **Invest in talent**: Investing in training existing staff and hiring new talent with the required skillset is crucial. This ensures that your organization has the necessary expertise to manage and optimize the selected data architecture.

- **Tailor to your needs**: Each organization is unique, and what works for one might not work for another. Tailor your data strategy to your organization's specific needs, goals, and capabilities. A custom approach rather than a one-size-fits-all strategy often yields the best results.

Remember, these recommendations only serve as a guide. Each organization needs to adapt and modify them according to their unique circumstances and objectives. With thoughtful planning and execution, any organization can leverage its chosen data architecture to achieve its strategic goals.

Summary

This chapter provided an extensive overview of various data integration techniques, aiming to equip you with an understanding of diverse models, architectures, and patterns employed in data integration. This chapter began by comparing point-to-point integration and middleware-based integration, elaborating on their respective advantages, disadvantages, and use cases. Then, we transitioned to a comprehensive review of data integration architectures while discussing the mechanics, trade-offs, and applicability of batch, micro-batching, real-time, and incremental data integration. Next, we explored popular data integration patterns, including ETL and ELT, along with several others, such as CDC and data federation. Finally, we covered data integration organizational models, providing a deep dive into the traditional (monolithic) architecture, the data mesh model, and the data lake architecture. We concluded by offering guidance on choosing the right integration model, with a detailed comparison and practical recommendations for businesses.

The next chapter will build on these foundations and explore data transformation and processing.

9

Data Transformation and Processing

In today's data-centric world, the art and science of data transformations form a cornerstone of any data integration process. Their importance lies in their ability to modify or rearrange data in ways that render it primed for analysis, display, or subsequent processing. By understanding and leveraging data transformations, we can unlock the latent potential of data, offering insights that might otherwise remain obscured.

The primary aim of this chapter is to elucidate what data transformations are and to explore their most prevalent types, including filters, aggregations, and joins. We recognize that each dataset, with its unique characteristics and challenges, requires a tailored approach. Thus, our goal is to empower you with the knowledge and tools to discern which strategies are best suited for your specific data needs.

Data transformations are not merely about understanding data, but acting upon that understanding. It's about bridging the gap between raw data and actionable insights. Therefore, our objectives stretch beyond theoretical knowledge. We aspire to provide practical insights by diving into real-world use cases and tangible examples, ensuring that you not only grasp the concepts but can apply them effectively.

By the end of this chapter, you will have a comprehensive understanding of different data transformation strategies. You will be able to discern and apply appropriate transformation techniques based on specific data challenges. You will also appreciate the value of these methods in the broader context of data integration. Finally, you will have an enhanced readiness to tackle the multifaceted challenges posed by diverse data types and formats.

Embark on this journey with us as we navigate the intricate pathways of data transformation, charting a course from the wilderness of raw data to the structured landscapes of insightful information.

The following topics will be covered in this chapter:

- The power of SQL in data transformation
- Data transformation possibilities

- Massively parallel processing
- Spark and data transformation
- Different types of data transformation

The power of SQL in data transformation

While SQL is a universally understood language in the data world, mastering its use for data transformations often represents a small yet significant gap to bridge. We'll aim to close this gap, enabling you to fully leverage SQL's power in transforming and molding data to your specific needs.

A brief history of SQL

To fully appreciate SQL's power in data transformation, you must first understand its origins and the context in which it was created. SQL, or **Structured Query Language**, was developed by IBM researchers Raymond Boyce and Donald Chamberlin in the early 1970s. **Structured English Query Language (SEQUEL)** was the name given to the language at first. Due to trademark issues, the name was later changed to SQL.

The primary motivation for the development of SQL was to provide a more accessible and efficient way to interact with relational databases. Database systems at the time were based on complex, low-level languages that were difficult to use and necessitated extensive knowledge of the underlying data storage mechanisms. SQL emerged as a game-changing solution, providing users with a simpler, more intuitive way to define and manipulate data in relational databases.

SQL's main goal in development was to provide a more accessible and efficient way to interact with relational databases. Database systems at the time relied on complex, low-level languages that were difficult to use and required extensive knowledge of the underlying data storage mechanisms. SQL emerged as a revolutionary solution, providing a simpler, more intuitive way for users to define and manipulate data in relational databases.

SQL as a standard for data transformation

SQL has a few key features that make it an invaluable tool for data transformation tasks:

- **Declarative nature**: SQL is a declarative language, which means that users only need to specify what they want to achieve, rather than how to achieve it. This stands in stark contrast to procedural languages, where users must define the step-by-step process for data manipulation. The declarative approach makes SQL more accessible to non-programmers and streamlines the process of writing and understanding complex queries.

- **Expressiveness**: SQL's rich syntax allows users to easily express a wide range of data transformations, including filtering, aggregation, and joining operations. Its powerful built-in functions and operators enable users to perform complex calculations, string manipulations, and date operations with minimal effort. This expressiveness translates to increased productivity for data professionals working with relational databases.

- **Standardization**: SQL's standardized syntax ensures that queries written for one RDBMS can be easily adapted to work with another. This greatly simplifies the process of migrating data between different database systems and promotes collaboration among teams working with various RDBMSs. The SQL standard has evolved over the years, with new features and improvements being added regularly. This ensures that the language stays relevant and continues to meet the evolving needs of data professionals.

- **Optimization**: One of the key advantages of SQL is that the query optimizer, a component of RDBMSs, data warehouses, or some advanced distributed processing engines accepting SQL syntax such as Spark, takes care of determining the most efficient way to execute a given query. This relieves users from the burden of optimizing their queries manually, allowing them to focus on the logic of the data transformation instead. As database systems continue to improve, so do their query optimizers, resulting in better performance for SQL-based data transformations.

- **Extensibility**: SQL's extensible nature allows vendors to add custom functions, data types, and operators to their RDBMS implementations. This means that SQL can be tailored to handle specific data transformation requirements that may be unique to a particular RDBMS or application. Users can also create their **user-defined functions** (**UDFs**) to implement custom logic within SQL queries, further enhancing the language's capabilities for data transformation tasks.

Finally, the historical context of SQL, combined with its powerful features, standardization, and extensibility, make it an indispensable tool for data transformation in relational databases. As you learn more about data transformation concepts and techniques, you'll discover that SQL plays an important role in enabling users to perform complex operations on their data.

As we proceed, it is critical to recognize SQL's versatility in addressing various data transformation challenges. Its continued presence in the world of data management attests to its adaptability and ability to evolve in response to the ever-changing needs of data professionals.

By learning SQL, you will have a powerful tool for managing and transforming data in relational databases. As you progress through this chapter and learn more about data transformation techniques, you'll realize how useful SQL can be for a variety of data integration tasks.

SQL is undeniably a critical skill for anyone working with data because it is a language that has stood the test of time and continues to be a cornerstone of modern data management. So, whether you're a seasoned data professional or just getting started in the world of data transformation, embracing SQL and its capabilities will undoubtedly help your career.

SQL's historical context and powerful features make it not only a necessary tool but also an intriguing subject for anyone interested in data transformation. As you learn about and use SQL in your projects, you will undoubtedly appreciate its elegance, simplicity, and vast capabilities for transforming and managing data within relational databases.

Next, we'll study data transformation possibilities.

Data transformation possibilities

Why do we need to change raw data? One of the reasons is that it can be full of errors or missing pieces, and it's not uniform. Different data formats and styles can make it hard to use. To solve these issues, data needs to be processed and transformed. This makes it accurate, consistent, and easy to use.

The goal is not just to fix errors but also to create new and more meaningful data. We clean and reorganize the data and mix it in new ways. This leads to fresh insights that can be used in reports or to make predictions.

This new, smarter data helps data-driven companies make better decisions. Instead of guessing or making assumptions, they can base their strategies on real, solid data. So, data processing and transformation not only solve problems but also help create valuable new insights.

Let's say you're a data analyst at a big retail company who's studying customer buying trends. Your data is spread across various databases, each with unique naming and date formats. To handle this, you'd use data processing and transformation. This not only makes the data consistent and easy to analyze but also creates new, meaningful data.

This process involves cleaning, reorganizing, and mixing the data in different ways to extract new insights. These insights are used for detailed reports and accurate predictions, helping the company make better decisions. Instead of making guesses, the company can now rely on solid data. In short, data processing and transformation correct issues and create valuable insights.

In this section, we will illustrate examples using SQL syntax, which allows us to better understand the concepts. However, note that these transformations can be achieved with all data transformation solutions.

> **Expert advice**
> Raw data is often messy, incomplete, inconsistent, or incompatible with your analytical or processing goals. Data transformation helps you clean, restructure, and enrich your data, making it more suitable for your needs.

Next, we'll study some of the most used processing operations.

Filters

Data that meets specific criteria can be extracted using a filter and combined with other datasets. The primary goal of filtering is to pare down data to the essentials so that it may be faster to process, analyze, and glean insights. To better appreciate the use of filters and learn how to implement them effectively, we will examine several filtering algorithms and real-world examples of filter usage in this section.

Filtering data is one of the most common operations in data transformation. In SQL, the WHERE clause allows you to apply conditions to filter rows based on specific criteria. Here's an example:

```
SELECT * FROM employees WHERE salary > 50000;
```

This query retrieves all rows from the employees table where the salary is greater than 50,000. The WHERE clause can be combined with various logical operators, such as AND, OR, and NOT, to create more complex filters.

Hopefully, this helps illustrate the concept of filtering. Let's assume you work for a marketing agency and have access to a massive dataset detailing the demographics and spending habits of thousands of consumers. Your boss has tasked you with conducting research to determine whether consumers might be interested in a new product targeted toward metropolitan women aged between 25 and 35. The dataset needs to be filtered according to these parameters so that only the genuine consumers are considered.

Filters can be applied to your data in a variety of ways. Some frequent ways are as follows:

- **Equality filters**: Equality filters are used to find entries that have the same value or a collection of values. For example, you may choose all consumers of a certain gender or from a given geography. Depending on whether you're comparing to a single value or a set of values, equality filters can be applied using the = (equals) or in operators.

- **Range filters**: With range filters, you can select data points that lie inside a specified numerical range. Assuming we run a marketing firm, we might use age as a filter and focus on clients who are between the ages of 25 and 35. Many range filters make use of the > (greater-than), < (less-than), >= (greater-or-equal-to), and <= (less-than-or-equal-to) comparison operators.

- **Pattern matching filters**: Pattern matching filters are used to pick records that contain specified characters or match a specific pattern. This method is very handy when working with text data, such as names or addresses. Wildcard matching (using * or ? characters) and regular expressions are two common pattern-matching strategies.

- **Compound filters**: In many cases, you'll need to apply multiple filters simultaneously to narrow down your data effectively. Compound filters allow you to combine multiple filtering criteria using logical operators, such as AND and OR. In our marketing agency example, we would need to apply a compound filter to select customers who meet all three criteria: gender, age, and location.

Now that we've explored the different types of filters let's look at some real-world examples:

- **Example 1**: E-commerce store

  An online retailer may decide to follow up with customers who have spent more than $500 in the last 6 months to learn more about their shopping preferences. The "total spent" column's range filter and the "last purchase date" column's date filter would be used for this purpose.

- **Example 2**: Employee database

  The HR team may want to see who among the staff has been performing well and has put in enough time to merit promotion. They would use range filters on the "performance rating" and "years of service" columns and an equality filter on the "job title" column to eliminate people who are currently in management positions.

Finally, filters are a crucial data transformation tool for extracting the most relevant details from large datasets. Learning and applying various filtering procedures will help you save time and effort during data analysis, allowing you to focus on really gaining insights and making data-driven decisions.

Expert advice

While simple, filters are an invaluable tool for simplifying data. By incorporating them early in the transformation steps, you may focus on the most relevant data subset for your research, improving processing efficiency and focus. Furthermore, they improve speed by eliminating redundant data, reducing both validation time and storage space. Don't be afraid to use them liberally and adapt as your needs change.

Aggregations

Information processing is highly dependent on aggregations. They make it feasible to organize and synthesize information for improved comprehension and more enlightened decision-making. In this section, you'll discover what data aggregation is, why it's useful, and some real-world applications.

Essentially, aggregations are operations that accept several input values and produce a single output value that summarizes the input values. They compact huge datasets to make their analysis and interpretation simpler. Let's look at some frequent examples of aggregating functions:

- SUM: Calculates the total of a set of numeric values.

- COUNT: Determines the number of items in a dataset.

- AVERAGE: Finds the mean value of a set of numeric values.

- MEDIAN: Determines the middle value of a set of numeric values.

- MIN/MAX: Identifies the smallest or largest value in a group of values.

- MODE: Finds the most frequently occurring value in a group.

- GROUP BY: Arranges data into groups. It's typically used in combination with other aggregation functions, such as SUM, COUNT, MAX, MIN, and AVG.

Aggregations are crucial for summarizing and analyzing data. SQL provides a suite of aggregate functions, including COUNT, SUM, AVG, MIN, and MAX, to perform calculations on a group of rows. To group rows based on certain columns, you can use the GROUP BY clause. Here's an example:

```
SELECT
  department,
  COUNT(*) AS employee_count,
  AVG(salary) AS average_salary
FROM
  employees
GROUP BY
  department;
```

This query calculates the number of employees and the average salary for each department. The GROUP BY clause groups the data by the department column, while the COUNT and AVG functions perform the calculations.

Warning

Aggregations are useful for summarizing and analyzing data, but they also involve a loss of information. When you aggregate data, you reduce its granularity and detail, which may affect the accuracy or completeness of your results. Always consider the trade-offs between aggregation level and information quality.

Let's dive into some practical use cases and examples of aggregations in action.

Use case 1 – sales analysis

Suppose you are a business owner interested in analyzing your sales data to discover the optimal pricing, promotional, and inventory management strategies. When data is aggregated, patterns and trends that were not obvious in the original dataset become visible.

The SUM function can be used to calculate total sales for a specified category, whereas the AVERAGE function can be used to get the average selling price of an item. You can use the COUNT tool to calculate the number of daily or weekly transactions, which can be utilized to identify periods of peak sales and refine promotional efforts.

The following table presents a snapshot of sales data for an electronics store:

Transaction_ID	Product_Category	Quantity	Price
1	Electronics	2	150
2	Clothing	3	40
3	Electronics	1	300
4	Clothing	5	30

Table 9.1 – Sales data of an electronics store

Using aggregations, you can answer questions such as the following:

- What is the total revenue for each product category?
- What is the average price of items in each category?
- How many transactions occurred in each category?

Use case 2 – social media analysis

To fine-tune your content strategy, let's say you're in charge of the company's social media accounts and you want to gauge your followers' degree of interest. Data aggregation can reveal when your followers are most active and which types of posts they prefer to read.

You can use the COUNT function to determine which posts are garnering the most attention by tallying the number of likes, comments, and shares for each. The AVERAGE function can also be used to calculate the average level of engagement with a given post across different time frames (weekdays versus weekends, for example) and content categories (such as videos, images, or text updates).

The following table presents a snapshot of engagement data for your social media:

Post_ID	Content_Type	Likes	Comments	Shares
1	Image	150	20	10
2	Video	300	50	25
3	Text	75	10	5

Table 9.2 – Engagement data for your social media

Using aggregations, you can answer questions such as the following:

- What is the average number of likes, comments, and shares per content type?
- Which content types receive the most engagement?
- When do posts receive the most engagement?

In conclusion, aggregations are a powerful tool for analyzing and summarizing large datasets. They enable you to extract valuable insights from raw data, helping you make data-driven decisions and improve your strategies.

Use case 3 – customer segmentation

Suppose you oversee marketing, and you want to create more targeted campaigns for specific client segments. With the support of aggregated data, you may learn more about your audience and customize your messaging.

The AVERAGE function can be used to get the average expenditure of various demographic groups, whereas the COUNT function can be used to determine the number of persons in a certain age group or geographic region. Mode can also be used to evaluate which product categories are most well-liked by various client groups, hence guiding product suggestions and marketing activities.

The following table presents a snapshot of customer data for your shops:

Customer_ID	Age	Location	Purchase_Value
1	28	New York	150
2	35	Chicago	300
3	42	New York	75

Table 9.3 – Shops customer data

Using aggregations, you can answer questions such as the following:

- What is the average purchase value for each age group or location?
- How many customers are in each segment?
- What are the most popular product categories among different customer segments?

Use case 4 – website analytics

As the site's owner, you should analyze visitor statistics to improve site operation and user happiness. By aggregating data, you may identify patterns in user behavior and utilize that knowledge to influence design, content, and marketing decisions.

For instance, the COUNT function can be used to determine the total number of visitors, page views, and sessions for a certain time interval (such as daily, weekly, or monthly). You can use the AVERAGE tool to determine how long customers stay on your site on average or what percentage of them leave quickly.

The following table presents a snapshot of analytics data for your website:

Date	Unique_Visitors	Page_Views	Sessions	Session_Duration	Bounce_Rate
2023-04-25	1,000	4,000	1,500	3.5	40%
2023-04-26	1,200	5,000	1,800	4	35%

Table 9.4 – Website analytics data

Using aggregations, you can answer questions such as the following:

- What is the average number of unique visitors, page views, and sessions per day?
- How has the site's traffic changed over time?
- Which pages or sections of the site have the highest bounce rates?

Aggregates are a powerful tool for data analysis that may be utilized to reveal previously hidden insights and assist strategic decision-making. As you engage with multiple datasets, aggregations will play an important role in your data transformation and processing activities.

Joins

In the world of data transformation and processing, **joins** play a significant role in merging data from several sources to generate a comprehensive and holistic perspective of the data at hand. Joins let you construct associations across distinct datasets based on shared properties or keys, giving you insights you could not have gleaned from the data alone. In this section, we'll explore several types of joins and their use cases, giving you a solid foundation in this fundamental data transformation technique.

SQL joins enable the combination of data from multiple tables based on a common key. There are several types of joins, including inner join, left join, right join, and full outer join. Here's an example of an inner join:

```
SELECT
  e.first_name,
  e.last_name,
  d.department_name
FROM
  employees e
JOIN
  departments d
ON
  e.department_id = d.id;
```

This query combines data from the `employees` and `departments` tables based on the common key, `department_id`. The `JOIN` keyword, followed by the `ON` clause, specifies the condition for the join operation.

Use cases and examples

Here are some examples to help you understand the different possibilities offered by this function:

- **Use case 1**: Combining customer and order data

Imagine that you work for an e-commerce company and have two datasets holding customer information and order details, respectively. To acquire a deeper insight into your clients' purchasing tendencies, you must integrate these databases.

The following table shows a snapshot of the customer data:

Customer_ID	Name	Email	Location
1	Alice's store	alice.store@email.com	New York
2	Bob Market	bob.market@email.com	California

Table 9.5 – Customer data

The following table shows a snapshot of the order data:

Order_ID	Customer_ID	Product	Quantity	Total_Price
1	1	Shoes	2	100
2	2	T-Shirt	1	20
3	1	Headphones	1	50

Table 9.6 – Order data

By joining these two tables on the `Customer_ID` field, you can analyze the combined data to answer questions such as the following:

- What is the total spending of each customer?
- Which products are popular among customers from different locations?

The following table shows an aggregation of `Total_Price` per `Customer_ID`, which is the total spending of each customer using the sum operation on total prices and joining and aggregating on the customer:

Customer	Total_Price
Alice's store	150
Bob Market	20

Table 9.7 – Aggregation result

- **Use case 2**: Combining employee and department data

Suppose you work in HR and you have two datasets – one with employee information and another with department details. To analyze employee distribution across departments, you need to join these datasets using a join operation.

The following table shows a snapshot of the employee data:

Employee_ID	Name	Job_Title	Department_ID
1	Jane Doe	Analyst	100
2	John Smith	Developer	200
3	Mary Johnson	Manager	300
4	Ronald Tim	Developer	300

Table 9.8 – Employee data

The following table shows a snapshot of the department data:

Department_ID	Department_Name	Location
100	Finance	New York
200	IT	California
300	HR	Texas

Table 9.9 – Department data

By joining these two tables on the `Department_ID` field, you can analyze the combined data to answer questions such as the following:

- How many employees work in each department?
- Which departments have the highest concentration of specific job titles?

Now that we've looked at some use cases, let's dive into the different types of joins:

- **Inner join**: An inner join combines rows from two tables based on a specified condition, returning only the rows that meet the condition. In other words, the resulting dataset contains only the rows with matching values in both tables. Using the `Customer` and `Order` tables, an inner join on `Customer_ID` would only return the rows where a match exists in both tables.

- **Left join (left outer join)**: A left join returns all the rows from the left table (the first table) and the matching rows from the right table (the second table). If no match is found, `NULL` values are returned for the columns from the right table. In the `Employee` and `Department` tables, a left join on `Department_ID` would return all the rows from the `Employees` table and the matching rows from the `Departments` table. If an employee's department isn't found in the `Departments` table, `NULL` values would be displayed for the department-related columns.

- **Right join (right outer join)**: A right join is like a left join but returns all the rows from the right table and the matching rows from the left table. If no match is found, `NULL` values are returned for the columns from the left table. In the `Employee` and `Department` tables, a right join on `Department_ID` would return all the rows from the `Departments` table and the matching rows from the `Employees` table. If a department doesn't have any employees in the `Employees` table, `NULL` values will be displayed for the employee-related columns.

- **Full outer join**: A full outer join returns all the rows from both tables, with `NULL` values in the columns where no match is found. In the `Customer` and `Order` tables, a full outer join on `Customer_ID` would return all rows from both tables, with `NULL` values in the order-related columns for customers without orders and in the customer-related columns for orders without a matching customer.

- **Cross join**: A cross join, also known as a Cartesian join, returns the Cartesian product of the two tables – that is, every combination of rows from the first table with rows from the second table. Cross-joins can result in a significantly larger dataset, so they should be used cautiously. In the `Employee` and `Department` tables, a cross-join would return a dataset with every employee paired with every department, regardless of whether the employee works in that department or not.

- **Self-join**: A self-join is a join operation where a table is joined with itself, usually to establish a hierarchical or recursive relationship. Self-joins are typically used with tables that have a foreign key referencing their primary key. In an `Employee` table with a manager column referencing the `Employee_ID` value of another employee, a self-join could be used to find the direct subordinates of a specific manager.

Warning

Joins combine data from different sources but can be slow and tricky with big datasets. To improve joins, pick the right type, use indexes, avoid extra joins, and always check results for accuracy.

In conclusion, joins are powerful tools in data transformation and processing that allow you to combine and analyze data from diverse sources. By understanding the distinct types of joins and their use cases, you can effectively work with datasets and gain insights that would otherwise be hidden in isolated data silos. As you continue to explore data transformations, remember that joins are just one of many techniques that can help you unlock the full potential of your data.

Conclusion

As demonstrated previously, SQL is a powerful language for performing data transformations such as filtering, aggregation, and joining. Because of its versatility, expressiveness, and standardized syntax, it is a must-have tool for data professionals working with structured datasets that accept SQL syntax, such as RDBMSs and data warehouses. You'll be better equipped to handle complex data transformation tasks and derive meaningful insights from your data if you understand and master SQL.

SQL has many data transformation methods and operators for filtering, aggregating, joining, and more. To maximize SQL's capabilities, learn its syntax, semantics, and database system features and extensions. Practice developing clear, succinct, and efficient SQL queries for complicated data transformation scenarios. In the sections that follow, we will continue our investigation of data transformation and processing, delving into diverse types of transformations such as event processing and batch processing, as well as various transformation patterns such as Lambda and Kappa architectures. With this knowledge and your newly acquired SQL skills, you'll be prepared to take on even the most difficult data transformation projects.

Massively parallel processing

Massively parallel processing (**MPP**) engines and databases represent a distinct type of data processing system, specifically designed to execute complex analytical queries over large data volumes. They employ a divide-and-conquer methodology, enabling speedy data processing by distributing data across multiple nodes for simultaneous processing.

At their core, MPP engines harness the power of parallelism. Each node operates independently of the others, working on its portion of the data. Every node has storage, memory, and processing units, ensuring that there is no bottleneck in terms of resources. This distribution of data and computation is what grants MPP engines and databases their scalability and efficiency. As data grows or the demand for faster insights increases, additional nodes can be incorporated into the system seamlessly.

What sets MPP engines and databases apart from traditional databases is their architectural design. They use a shared-nothing architecture, which, unlike shared-memory or shared-disk architectures, minimizes contention for resources and avoids single points of failure. Each node operates autonomously, making it less likely for a single failure to impact the entire system. If a node fails, the system automatically redistributes its data to other nodes, ensuring continued operation without significant performance impact.

In this big data era, MPP engines and databases have gained prominence for their ability to handle voluminous data effectively and deliver insights rapidly. They are becoming an integral part of the data strategy of many organizations, particularly those dealing with vast amounts of complex, multidimensional data. The following figure illustrates the architecture of an MPP engine:

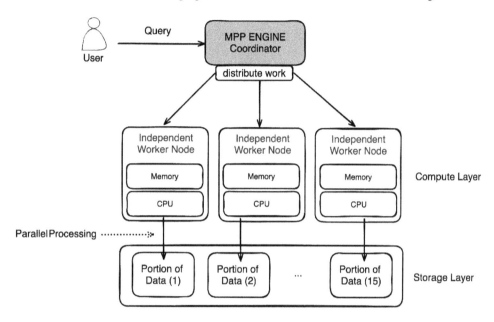

Figure 9.1 – MPP engine architecture

The preceding figure shows a user submitting a query to the MPP engine, which then coordinates the distribution of work across multiple independent processing nodes, each with its own CPU and memory. These nodes are part of the compute layer and perform parallel processing on different portions of data, which are part of the storage layer.

In the sections to follow, we will explore some use cases and examples of MPP databases, discuss their advantages and challenges, look at data modeling considerations in MPP, and discuss ways to optimize data exposition with MPP databases and their integration with other data exposition technologies.

Use cases and examples

MPP databases, with their ability to process enormous amounts of data rapidly, find widespread use across industries and applications. This section will dive into several use cases where MPP databases have proven to be instrumental, each accompanied by a representative example:

- **Data warehousing and business intelligence** (**BI**): Organizations frequently utilize MPP databases for data warehousing and BI applications. They serve as robust solutions for storing, analyzing, and retrieving large volumes of data, allowing businesses to generate valuable insights. For example, a large eCommerce company could use an MPP database to analyze customer behavior data across millions of transactions. This could include analyzing trends, purchasing patterns, and seasonal demand, which could then drive business strategies.

- **Financial services**: In the financial sector, MPP databases are often employed for risk management, fraud detection, and high-speed trading analytics. An investment bank, for instance, could leverage an MPP database to analyze trading data in real time. By processing vast quantities of trade data swiftly, the bank can make quick decisions, manage risks effectively, and ensure regulatory compliance.

- **Telecommunications**: Telecommunication companies deal with huge amounts of data generated from various sources, including call detail records, network logs, and customer data. An MPP database could help a telecom company analyze network performance across different regions and times, enabling them to optimize network resources and improve service quality.

- **Healthcare**: In the healthcare industry, MPP databases can be used for large-scale genomic research, patient data analysis, and real-time monitoring of vital signs. For instance, a healthcare research institute could use an MPP database to analyze the genomic data of thousands of patients, helping to identify patterns and correlations that can lead to the development of new treatments or personalized medicine.

- **Internet of Things (IoT)**: With the rise of IoT devices, the amount of data that's generated has skyrocketed. MPP databases are suitable for storing and processing IoT data due to their ability to handle high data velocity, variety, and volume. An IoT solution provider could use an MPP database to analyze data from thousands of sensors in real time, leading to better decision-making and improved operational efficiency.

- **Social media analytics**: MPP databases are used in social media analytics to analyze user behavior and trends, as well as to generate insights for targeted advertising. For instance, a social media platform could use an MPP database to analyze user interactions and trends across billions of posts, enabling it to customize user feeds and provide targeted ad content.

In each of these examples, the distinguishing feature of MPP databases is their ability to process vast amounts of data quickly and efficiently. The architecture of MPP databases, which separates computation and storage across multiple nodes, enables them to excel in scenarios where traditional databases may falter under the data's sheer weight. In the subsequent sections, we will delve into the benefits and challenges of MPP databases and explore data modeling within them to maximize data exposition.

Advantages and challenges

MPP databases present a compelling choice for modern organizations dealing with massive amounts of data. Yet, they also come with unique challenges. To help you make a balanced decision, we'll explore both aspects.

Advantages

Here are some of the benefits of using MPP solutions:

- **Scalability**: MPP databases are horizontally scalable, which means they can handle increased data volume by simply adding more nodes to the system. This scalability feature makes MPP databases an excellent solution for big data applications where data volume can grow exponentially.

- **Performance**: MPP databases distribute data across multiple nodes, and queries are processed in parallel. This approach significantly reduces query response time, even when dealing with voluminous datasets. Therefore, MPP databases are particularly beneficial in scenarios that require real-time or near-real-time analytics.

- **High availability and fault tolerance**: MPP architectures provide in-built redundancy. If a node fails, other nodes can pick up the slack, ensuring that the system remains available. This redundancy also contributes to fault tolerance as the data is not lost if a node fails.

- **Flexibility**: MPP databases often provide flexible data models, which can support structured, semi-structured, and unstructured data. This flexibility allows organizations to deal with varied data types common in big data scenarios.

- **Efficient joins across multiple data sources**: One of the prominent advantages of MPP databases is their ability to efficiently handle joins across different data sources. As data is distributed across multiple nodes, an MPP system can execute complex join operations in parallel, resulting in faster data integration and query response. This feature is particularly advantageous when combining data from disparate sources, making MPP databases an ideal choice for situations that require complex data analysis and cross-referencing.

Challenges

Here are some of the challenges of using MPP solutions:

- **Complexity**: The setup, configuration, and management of MPP databases can be complex. They require specialized knowledge to handle data distribution, load balancing, and fault tolerance mechanisms. This complexity may necessitate trained personnel, adding to the operational cost.

- **Cost**: While MPP databases offer significant advantages, they can also be expensive, especially for large-scale deployments. Costs can arise from licensing, maintenance, and the necessary hardware for running multiple nodes. However, this high cost can be mitigated through the use of MPP databases in a **Software-as-a-Service (SaaS)** model.

- **Data skew**: In MPP systems, data is distributed across nodes for parallel processing. However, if data is not evenly distributed, some nodes may have a higher workload than others, leading to performance issues. This data skew can be a challenge in effectively utilizing an MPP system.

- **Network latency**: Since MPP databases rely on distributing data and processing across nodes, network latency can impact performance. If the inter-node communication is not fast enough, it can create bottlenecks and slow down data processing.

- **Vendor lock-in**: Many MPP solutions are provided by specific vendors and migrating data to another system can be difficult and time-consuming. This scenario potentially creates vendor lock-in, limiting flexibility in changing or upgrading the data solution.

In conclusion, MPP databases offer robust solutions for dealing with massive data volumes and delivering high-speed analytics. However, organizations must be aware of and prepared to tackle the challenges these systems present. The key is to match the requirements of the use case with the capabilities of the MPP system, ensuring the benefits outweigh any potential drawbacks. With thoughtful planning and execution, MPP databases can provide significant value in today's data-driven landscape.

> **Warning**
>
> MPP databases offer significant advantages for big data processing, but they also come with unique challenges. They require specialized knowledge to set up, configure, and manage effectively. They can also be expensive, especially for large-scale deployments. They may face issues such as data skew, network latency, or vendor lock-in that can affect performance or flexibility. Therefore, organizations should carefully evaluate the benefits and drawbacks of using MPP databases for their specific use cases and requirements.

Data modeling in MPP

Data modeling is a crucial aspect of using MPP databases effectively. It involves shaping data in a manner that suits the capabilities of MPP databases, helping to maximize their performance and efficiency. This process can be different compared to traditional relational databases due to the distinct nature of MPP architectures.

In an MPP system, data is partitioned across multiple nodes. Therefore, the data model should be designed to ensure that data is evenly distributed among these nodes to avoid data skew. This balanced distribution helps in load balancing and allows for efficient parallel processing. Also, the data model should limit the necessity for cross-node communication, which could cause performance bottlenecks.

The following figure illustrates the impact of an uneven distribution of data on performances:

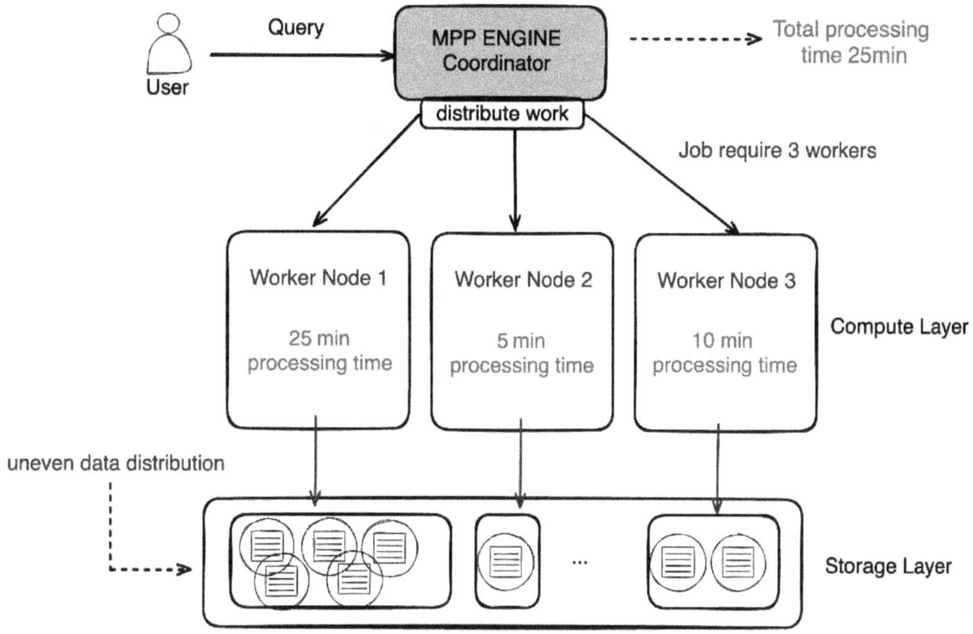

Figure 9.2 – The impact of an uneven distribution of data on performances

In the preceding figure, node 1 requires 5x the amount of time to handle data, which implies that nodes 2 and 3 are put in an idle state and increase the total processing time.

A common approach in data modeling for MPP databases is partitioning data according to the most suitable pattern to make the data evenly distributed. Denormalization is also a recommended approach. By reducing the number of joins required to access related data, the MPP system can execute queries more efficiently. It's important to mention that denormalization is a trade-off as it can increase storage requirements and complexity in data management.

Data modeling should also consider the types of queries that will be executed on the database. Designing the model so that it aligns with frequent query patterns can significantly enhance performance. This approach, often termed as **design by query**, can involve tactics such as co-locating related data on the same node.

A well-designed data model can help businesses leverage the full power of MPP databases, including their capabilities in handling large data volumes and executing complex analytical queries. However, it requires careful planning, understanding the nuances of MPP architecture, and potentially modifying traditional data modeling practices.

In conclusion, effective data modeling is vital to unlocking the potential of MPP databases. It plays a pivotal role in achieving high-performance data analysis and making data more accessible, thereby contributing to more informed business decisions.

Next, we'll study Spark and data transformation.

Spark and data transformation

Spark's adaptability combines SQL's familiarity with algorithm development's power. It allows changes ranging from SQL procedures to advanced algorithms. Mastering Spark for data transformation unlocks strong capabilities for comprehensive data analysis and processing, adapted to varied demands and use cases.

A brief history of Spark

Apache Spark, commonly known as Spark, is an open source distributed computing system written in Scala that provides a fast and general-purpose framework for big data processing and analytics.

Spark is primarily utilized in programming languages such as Scala, Python, and R.

It was initially developed at the **Algorithms, Machines, and People Lab (AMPLab)** at the University of California, Berkeley, in 2009.

Spark was created to address the limitations of the existing batch processing system, Hadoop MapReduce, by introducing in-memory computing and a more versatile programming model. The project was motivated by the need for a unified framework that could handle various data processing workloads, including batch processing, interactive queries, streaming, and machine learning.

The development of Spark was led by Matei Zaharia, who started the project as a research project during his PhD studies. In 2010, Spark was open sourced under a BSD license and gained significant traction in the big data community.

One of the key innovations introduced by Spark is its **resilient distributed dataset (RDD)** abstraction, which provides fault-tolerant distributed data processing. RDDs allow data to be stored in memory across a cluster of machines, enabling faster and more efficient data processing compared to disk-based systems such as Hadoop MapReduce.

As Spark gained popularity, it attracted the attention of industry players, leading to the creation of Databricks, a start-up founded by the original creators of Spark. Databricks offers a cloud-based platform built on top of Spark, providing enhanced scalability, ease of use, and additional features.

Over the years, Spark has evolved and matured, with significant contributions from the open source community. It has become one of the most widely adopted big data processing frameworks, used by organizations of all sizes and across various industries.

Spark's versatility and performance have made it a popular choice for a wide range of use cases, including data warehousing, ETL processes, real-time analytics, machine learning, and graph processing.

Using Spark for data transformation

Developing with Spark for data transformation offers several key advantages. Here are some of the key advantages of using Spark for data transformation:

- **Speed and performance**: Spark is designed to handle large-scale data processing and analytics tasks efficiently. It leverages in-memory computing, allowing it to cache data in memory and perform operations much faster compared to disk-based systems such as Hadoop MapReduce. This speed and performance make Spark ideal for processing and transforming large datasets.

- **Ease of use**: Spark provides a high-level API that makes it easy to write code and perform complex data transformations. It offers APIs in multiple languages, including Scala, Java, Python, and R, making it accessible to developers with different programming backgrounds. Spark's intuitive and expressive syntax allows developers to write concise and readable code, reducing the development time and effort required for data transformation tasks.

- **Versatility**: Spark supports a wide range of data processing tasks, including batch processing, interactive queries, streaming, and machine learning. This versatility makes it a powerful tool for various data transformation requirements. Whether you need to perform simple data filtering and aggregation or complex transformations involving joins, window functions, or graph processing, Spark provides the necessary capabilities.

- **Scalability**: Spark is designed to scale horizontally, meaning it can handle increasing workloads by adding more machines to the cluster. It distributes data and computations across multiple machines, allowing it to process massive datasets efficiently. Spark's ability to scale seamlessly makes it suitable for handling big data transformation tasks, where data volumes can be substantial.

- **Integration with existing ecosystems**: Spark integrates effortlessly with a range of widely used big data solutions such as Hadoop, Hive, and HBase. It offers the flexibility to read and write data across multiple data storage options, including HDFS, Amazon S3, and relational databases. This integration allows you to leverage existing data infrastructure investments and easily incorporate Spark into your data transformation pipelines.

- **Rich ecosystem and community support**: Spark has a vibrant and active open source community, constantly contributing to its ecosystem. It offers a wide range of libraries and extensions for specialized use cases, such as Spark SQL, Spark Streaming, MLlib, and GraphX. These libraries provide additional functionalities and simplify complex data transformation tasks, making it easier for developers to achieve their goals.

Examples of using the Spark DataFrame API

To better understand how to transform data using Spark in both Python and Scala, let's examine some specific examples.

Load CSV file: Imagine that you're using Spark to load a CSV file stored on AWS S3 using the DataFrame API.

Here's how you would do this with Python:

```
employee_csv_path = "s3://hr_bucket/employee.csv"
employees_df = spark.read.csv(employee_csv_path, header=True,
inferSchema=True)
```

Here's how you would do this with Scala:

```
val employee_csv_path = "s3a://your_bucket_name/employee.csv"
val employees_df = spark.read.csv(employee_csv_path).option("header",
"true").option("inferSchema", "true")
```

Filter: You can use filters to retrieve all the information from the `employees` DataFrame where the salary of the employees is greater than $50,00.

Here's how to do this with Python:

```
# Filter employees with salary greater than $50,00
filtered_employees_df = employees_df.filter(employees_df.salary >
50000)
```

Here's how to do this with Scala:

```
import org.apache.spark.sql.functions.col
// Filter employees with salary greater than $50,00
val filtered_employees_df = employees_df.filter(col("salary") > 50000)
```

Logical operator: You can combine multiple conditions using logical operators such as && (AND) and || (OR).

You can do this with Python like so:

```
filtered_employees_df = employees_df[(employees_df['salary'] > 50000)
& (employees_df['age'] > 30)]
With Scala:val filtered_employees_df = employees_
df.filter(col("salary") > 50000 && col("age") > 30)
```

This example filters employees with a salary greater than $50,000 and an age greater than 30.

You can use the ! (NOT) operator to negate a condition.

Here's how to do this with Python:

```
filtered_employees_df = employees_df[employees_df['salary'] > 50000]
```

Here's how to do this with Scala:

```
val filtered_employees_df = employees_df.filter(!(col("salary") <=
50000))
```

This example retrieves employees with a salary greater than $50,00 by negating the `salary <= 50000` condition.

Aggregations: In Spark, you can leverage the power of the DataFrame API to perform aggregations. The DataFrame API provides functions such as COUNT, SUM, AVG, MIN, and MAX for performing calculations on a group of rows. To group rows based on specific columns, you can use `groupby`, which is the same as the SQL function.

You can do this using Python like so:

```
aggregated_employees = employees_df.groupby('department').
agg(employee_count=('department', 'count'), average_salary=('salary',
'mean')).reset_index()
```

You can do this using Scala like so:

```
val aggregatedEmployees = employees.groupBy("department")
  .agg(count("*").as("employee_count"), avg("salary").as("average_
salary"))
```

In the preceding code, we used Spark's DataFrame API to perform the aggregations. First, we used the GROUPBY function to group the rows by the `department` column. Then, we used the `agg` function to calculate the count, `(COUNT("*"))`, and the average salary, `(avg("salary"))`, of the employees.

Joins: Spark allows you to combine data from multiple DataFrames based on a common key. Spark supports several types of joins, including inner join, left join, right join, and full outer join.

Here's an example of using an inner join in Python:

```
joinedData = employees.join(departments, employees['department_id'] ==
departments['id']) \
    .select(employees['first_name'], employees['last_name'],
departments['department_name'])
```

Here's an example of using an inner join in Scala:

```
val joinedData = employees.join(departments, employees("department_
id") === departments("id"))
  .select(employees("first_name"), employees("last_name"),
departments("department_name"))
```

In the preceding code, we used Spark's DataFrame API to perform the join operation. We started by using the join function to join the `employees` and `departments` DataFrames based on the common `department_id` and `id` keys, respectively. The `===` operator specifies the join condition. Then, we used the `select` function to select the desired columns from the joined DataFrame, namely `first_name` and `last_name` from `employees` and `department_name` from `departments`.

Comparing the SQL and Spark DataFrame API approaches

In this section, we'll compare the SQL and Spark DataFrame API approaches. SQL is a simple query language, whereas the Spark DataFrame API is a robust interface for structured and semi-structured data. We'll compare these two approaches' usability, performance, versatility, and interoperability. The comparison in the following table will help you choose the right data transformation tool:

	SQL	Spark
Syntax and Query Language	SQL.	DataFrame API in Scala, Python, Java, and R.
Data Manipulation and Transformation	It provides a wide range of operations, such as SELECT, WHERE, GROUP BY, JOIN, and more. It also supports complex transformations through SQL queries.	It offers a rich set of functions and transformations, such as filtering, aggregation, joins, window functions, and more. It also provides a flexible and powerful API for transforming data.
Performance and Scalability	It relies on the underlying database engine, and its performance varies based on the database system. It can handle large datasets efficiently, depending on the database optimization techniques that are used.	It's optimized for distributed processing, making it suitable for big data processing. It also leverages the in-memory computation and parallel processing capabilities of the Spark engine, leading to high-performance data transformations.
Ecosystem and Integration	It's widely supported by various relational database systems and can be integrated with other tools and frameworks specific to the database system.	It's part of the Apache Spark ecosystem with good integration with other Spark components. It offers seamless integration with various data sources and third-party libraries.

	SQL	Spark
Flexibility and Expressiveness	It offers a comprehensive set of operations to manipulate and analyze data. It also provides a wide range of built-in functions and the ability to define and use **user-defined functions (UDFs)** for custom transformations.	It provides a rich set of functions and transformations, allowing for complex data processing. It also supports the creation and usage of UDFs for custom logic and data transformations. Furthermore, it offers a flexible programming model for advanced data manipulation. UDFs can be programmed using Java, Python, Scala, and R.
Language Support	It's supported by a wide range of programming languages.	It's primarily used with Scala, but it also supports Python, Java, and R. It enables developers to work with their preferred language for data transformation tasks.
Debugging and Optimizations	It provides query optimization techniques specific to the database system. It also offers detailed debugging capabilities and query profiling tools for performance tuning.	It offers detailed debugging capabilities and built-in optimizations. It also provides various optimization techniques such as predicate pushdown, column pruning, and data caching. This allows developers to optimize and fine-tune data transformation jobs.
Real-Time Stream Processing	It provides limited real-time capabilities that mostly focus on batch processing. It also supports streaming via specialized extensions such as Apache Kafka integration.	It supports real-time stream processing through Spark Streaming. It also provides a unified programming model for batch and stream processing. This enables developers to build real-time data pipelines and analytics applications.

	SQL	Spark
Community and Support	It's supported by a vast community and resources specific to the database system. Database vendors provide documentation, forums, and support channels.	It has a large and active community with extensive documentation and support and offers online resources, forums, and user groups for assistance. It also provides enterprise-level support through Databricks and other vendors.

Table 9.10 – SQL and Spark comparison

This comparison highlights SQL's sophisticated data manipulation and transformation capabilities, performance scalability dependent on the database engine, and broad language compatibility. SQL has limited real-time capabilities.

Spark, with its in-memory compute and parallel processing, handles huge data well. It supports Spark Streaming and complicated data processing with a flexible programming model.

SQL and Spark have different strengths, so which one you should choose depends on the data transformation task.

Next, we'll study several types of data transformation.

Different types of data transformation

Data transformation is a critical component of any data integration process, and understanding the various types of transformations is essential for effective data management. This section provides a friendly introduction to the types of transformations you might encounter on your data journey.

First, we will discuss batch processing, which is our first data transformation method. Batch processing deals with data transformations in chunks or groups. This method is frequently used when it is more efficient to process multiple data points at the same time or when the data does not require immediate analysis. Examples of common use cases include generating daily sales reports and updating a recommendation system overnight. Then, we will discuss event and stream processing, which are two other data transformation methods that are closely related, each playing a crucial role in handling real-time data. Event processing focuses on immediately handling individual events or data points as they occur. This method is particularly effective in scenarios that demand rapid action or analysis, such as fraud detection or monitoring user behavior on a website.

On the other hand, stream processing deals with continuous data flows. It continuously analyzes and processes data, making it indispensable in a world where vast amounts of data are generated rapidly. Stream processing is particularly beneficial for real-time analytics, social media monitoring, and IoT devices. By investigating these various transformation types, you will be better equipped to select the best approach for your specific data integration requirements. In the following sections, we'll go over the characteristics, use cases, and examples of each type to give you a solid understanding of how they can be applied to different scenarios.

Batch processing

In today's data-driven world, it's essential to understand how to manage and process information effectively. Batch processing transforms enormous datasets by grouping related data elements. This method is best for batch processing vast amounts of data on a daily, weekly, or monthly basis.

Batch processing optimizes computing resources, increases performance, and maintains data integrity with a static copy. With massive datasets and complicated operations, it may not be suitable for rapid analysis.

Industries employ batch processing. Retailers and banks utilize it for inventory management and risk analysis. It simplifies medical billing, insurance claims processing, and patient data analysis. Data warehousing requires it for efficient ETL processes.

In short, batch processing is an efficient data transformation approach for large datasets when real-time analysis isn't needed.

Batch processing has several key features that distinguish it from other data transformation techniques:

- **Scheduled processing**: Unlike event-driven systems, batch processing usually operates on a predetermined schedule. Data is collected and processed at specific intervals, such as daily, weekly, or monthly.

- **High throughput**: Batch processing is designed to handle large volumes of data, making it well-suited for tasks that involve processing extensive datasets. By grouping data and processing it in parallel, batch systems can achieve a high level of throughput.

- **Resource optimization**: Batch processing allows for more efficient use of computing resources. By scheduling processing during periods of low demand or utilizing idle resources, batch systems can minimize the impact on overall system performance.

- **Data consistency**: Batch processing ensures data consistency by working on a snapshot of the data at a given point in time. This approach avoids the challenges of real-time data processing, such as handling incomplete or rapidly changing datasets.

While batch processing has many advantages, it's essential to be aware of its limitations. Due to its scheduled nature, batch processing may not be suitable for situations where real-time analysis is critical. Additionally, managing and maintaining batch systems can be complex, particularly when dealing with large datasets and intricate workflows.

Batch processing has a wide range of applications across various industries. Some of the most common use cases are as follows:

- **Financial services**: Banks and financial institutions often rely on batch processing for tasks such as end-of-day account reconciliations, report generation, and risk analysis. These tasks typically involve processing vast amounts of data, making batch processing an ideal solution.

- **Retail**: In the retail sector, batch processing is commonly used for inventory management, sales analysis, and customer segmentation. By processing data in batches, retailers can efficiently analyze large datasets and make informed decisions about inventory levels, pricing strategies, and marketing campaigns.

- **Healthcare**: Batch processing is frequently employed in healthcare settings for tasks such as medical billing, claims processing, and patient data analysis. By working on large volumes of data simultaneously, batch systems can streamline operations and ensure accurate, consistent results.

- **Data warehousing**: In data warehousing, batch processing is a popular choice for ETL operations. These processes involve extracting data from various sources, transforming it into a standardized format, and loading it into a data warehouse for analysis. Batch processing allows ETL operations to be executed efficiently, ensuring timely and accurate data updates.

In conclusion, batch processing is a robust and flexible method of data transformation that works exceptionally well when dealing with massive datasets. You can decide if batch processing is the best method for your project if you are familiar with its benefits, drawbacks, and features. Batch processing can be a powerful data transformation tool when real-time analysis is unnecessary, and efficiency is the top priority.

Stream processing

In this age of instant information, there is a growing need for real-time data processing. Stream processing is a technique that's designed specifically to address this need. In this section, we'll explore the world of stream processing and uncover the key features and challenges it presents.

Functionality of stream processing

Stream processing is an approach to data transformation that operates on continuous, real-time data streams rather than batches of data. Unlike batch processing, which groups data and processes it in scheduled intervals, stream processing handles data as it flows through the system. This real-time approach enables businesses to react and make decisions more quickly, capitalizing on emerging trends and opportunities.

Here are some essential characteristics of stream processing:

- **Continuous data processing**: Stream processing is designed to handle data as it arrives, with no need to wait for a complete set of data before processing can begin. This approach enables rapid, real-time analysis and decision-making.

- **Time-sensitive**: Stream processing is particularly suited for applications that rely on timely information. By processing data as it is generated, stream processing helps ensure that the latest data is always available for analysis.

- **Scalability**: Modern stream processing systems such as Kafka are built to handle varying volumes of data. As data streams grow, stream processing systems can expand to accommodate the increased workload, ensuring consistent performance even as data volumes change.

Although stream processing offers many advantages, it also presents some challenges:

- **Data quality**: As stream processing operates on real-time data and distributed architectures with many events arriving at the same time, it must contend with issues such as missing, out-of-order, or duplicate data points. Addressing these issues requires robust error handling and data cleansing strategies.

- **Latency**: Stream processing systems must be able to process data quickly to maintain real-time performance. Balancing the need for low-latency processing with the complexity of the processing tasks can be a challenging endeavor.

- **Resource management**: Stream processing systems must manage resources efficiently to maintain consistent performance under varying workloads. This may involve optimizing the use of computing resources or implementing backpressure mechanisms to prevent data loss or system failure.

Stream processing has found applications across various industries, including the following:

- **Financial services**: Stream processing enables real-time risk analysis, fraud detection, and trading systems. By analyzing financial data in real time, financial institutions can make more informed decisions and respond to market changes more quickly.

- **IoT and smart cities**: Regarding IoT and smart city applications, stream processing plays a crucial role in analyzing sensor data in real time. This allows systems to react quickly to changing conditions and make data-driven decisions to optimize resource usage, traffic flow, or energy consumption.

- **Social media and web analytics**: Stream processing is an essential tool for analyzing user behavior and engagement on social media platforms and websites. By processing data streams in real time, businesses can gain insights into user preferences and trends, enabling them to optimize their marketing efforts and improve customer experiences.

- **Telecommunications**: In the telecommunications industry, stream processing is used for real-time network monitoring, call detail record analysis, and **quality of service (QoS)** management. This enables providers to quickly identify and resolve network issues, ensuring a high level of service for their customers.

In conclusion, stream processing is a powerful data transformation technique, particularly well-suited for real-time data processing applications. By understanding the features, benefits, and challenges associated with stream processing, you can determine if it's the right fit for your project. When the need for real-time analysis and decision-making is paramount, stream processing can be a game-changer in your data transformation toolbox.

Windowing in stream processing

Windowing is a crucial concept in stream processing, allowing us to make sense of continuous data streams by dividing them into manageable chunks for analysis. In this section, we'll explore the concept of windowing, the different types, and how it can be applied to stream processing tasks. Please note that windowing can also be implemented by micro-batching engines such as Spark. Windowing is the process of segmenting a data stream into finite windows. By grouping events that occur within these windows, we can perform meaningful analysis of the data, such as calculating aggregates, detecting trends, or identifying patterns. We will examine the various sorts of windowing strategies used in stream processing, each with its own advantages and uses.

Fixed (tumbling) windows

In this approach, the data stream is divided into fixed-size, non-overlapping time intervals. Each event belongs to exactly one window, and once a window has been processed, it is discarded.

The following figure illustrates fixed windows:

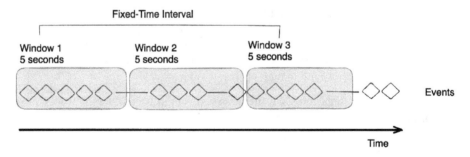

Figure 9.3 – Fixed windows

As illustrated in the figure, fixed windows are useful for calculating aggregates over uniform time intervals, such as hourly or daily summaries.

Sliding and hopping windows

Sliding and hopping windows overlap and continuously slide along the data stream, creating a new window at regular intervals. This technique allows for more frequent analysis of the data, providing a smoother and more up-to-date view of the information. Sliding windows are ideal for monitoring real-time trends or detecting patterns that may span multiple fixed windows.

The following figure illustrates sliding and hopping windows:

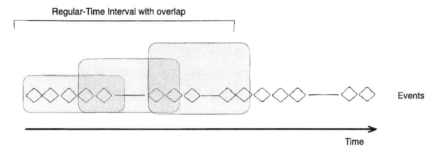

Figure 9.4 – Sliding and hopping windows

A hopping window is more structured around a schedule, advancing at regular time intervals from the start of the time series and generating outputs for each specific period. On the other hand, a sliding window operates on an event-driven basis, moving forward and producing outputs only when there are new data points available in the time series for evaluation.

Session windows

Session windows are designed to capture periods of activity in the data stream, such as user sessions on a website. They dynamically adjust their size based on the presence or absence of events within a specified timeout period.

The following figure illustrates session windows:

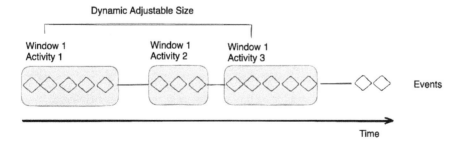

Figure 9.5 – Session windows

Session windows are particularly useful for analyzing user behavior as they can provide insights into individual sessions without being constrained by fixed time intervals.

Global windows

Global windows encompass the entire data stream, treating it as a single window.

The following figure illustrates global windows:

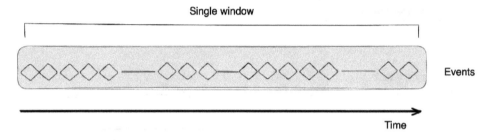

Figure 9.6 – Global windows

This approach is suitable for situations where the complete dataset must be considered for analysis, such as detecting global patterns or processing data streams with irregular event patterns.

- **Windowing** plays an essential role in stream processing by enabling the analysis of time-based patterns and trends within the data. To choose the appropriate windowing technique for your stream processing task, consider the following factors:

- **Time sensitivity**: If your analysis requires up-to-date results, sliding windows may be more suitable. For less time-sensitive tasks, fixed or session windows might be more appropriate.

- **Event patterns**: Consider the patterns within your data stream. If events are irregular or based on user activity, session windows might be the best choice. If events are evenly distributed over time, fixed or sliding windows may be more suitable.

- **Analysis goals**: Your analysis goals will also influence your choice of windowing technique. For instance, if you aim to calculate aggregates over uniform time intervals, fixed windows are an excellent choice. If you want to detect patterns that span multiple time intervals, sliding windows may be more appropriate.

In summary, windowing is an indispensable technique in stream processing, helping to make sense of continuous data streams and enabling time-based analysis. By understanding the various types of windowing and considering your specific stream processing goals, you can choose the right technique to unlock valuable insights from your data.

Event processing

Event processing, similar to stream processing, is a method that focuses on handling data in real time, allowing for swift decision-making and immediate responses to emerging situations. But compared to stream processing, event processing is centered around discrete events, where each event is considered individually and triggers specific actions or responses.

Event processing shines when it comes to dealing with data that needs immediate attention. For example, consider scenarios such as monitoring stock market fluctuations or detecting anomalies in a production line – time is critical! This method ensures prompt action and reduces the likelihood of missing valuable information by focusing on each event as it occurs.

So, what is an "event" in this context? An event is any noteworthy occurrence or change in the status of a system. A user activating a button on a website, a temperature sensor picking up an unexpected spike, or a sales tally in an inventory system are all examples of such events. Each of these is an example of a situation that might cause a given system response.

Event processing has a few key characteristics that set it apart from other methods:

- **Near-real-time processing**: Events are processed as they occur, without delays or waiting for additional data. This enables rapid analysis and decision-making based on the most up-to-date information.

- **Event-driven**: The system responds to specific events rather than processing data in batches or according to a predetermined schedule. This ensures that relevant actions are taken as soon as an event is detected.

- **Scalability**: Just like stream processing, event processing systems are designed to handle high volumes of data and adapt to fluctuating workloads, making them suitable for a wide range of applications.

Faster decision-making, improved responsiveness, and the ability to manage massive amounts of data in near-real-time are just a few of the many benefits of event processing. However, there are obstacles to overcome. It takes specialized knowledge and equipment to successfully implement an event processing system. In addition, it can be challenging to keep data quality and consistency high when dealing with real-time data from multiple sources.

The **Command Query Responsibility Segregation** (**CQRS**) pattern can be a key enabler in overcoming the challenges that are faced in implementing an event processing system. It divides a system's tasks into two major groups: commands that alter the state and queries that read the state. This division significantly improves the handling and scalability of event processing systems. When it comes to event processing, the command aspect oversees processing the incoming events, while the query aspect manages real-time read operations, guaranteeing prompt responses. By separating these tasks, CQRS can boost response speed and support immediate action in line with the event's characteristics.

Additionally, CQRS supports event-driven architectures, where system changes trigger events that propagate throughout the system. This matches up well with the event-driven nature of event processing, assisting in keeping system-wide data consistency. The events produced by CQRS can serve as a dependable source of truth, allowing for system state reconstruction at any moment and ensuring data accuracy and integrity.

Plus, because of CQRS's asynchronous nature, it boosts the scalability of event processing systems. Since read and write operations are separated, they can be individually scaled depending on their workload, thereby offering a solid solution for managing vast volumes of data.

Despite these challenges, event processing has become an indispensable tool for many businesses and industries. Here are a few examples of its applications:

- **Financial services**: Some banks and financial institutions use event processing to monitor transactions for fraud, manage risk, and analyze market trends in real time. This allows them to respond quickly to potential threats and make well-informed decisions.

- **Manufacturing**: In manufacturing settings, event processing can help monitor equipment performance, detect anomalies, and optimize production processes. By acting on real-time data, businesses can minimize downtime and reduce costs.

- **Smart cities**: Event processing is essential for managing traffic, optimizing public transportation, and monitoring environmental conditions in smart cities. Real-time data analysis helps improve city planning and resource allocation, making urban living more efficient and sustainable.

- **Healthcare**: In healthcare, event processing can help monitor patient conditions, track equipment usage, and optimize hospital operations. Real-time data analysis can lead to improved patient care and more efficient healthcare systems.

Focusing on what's happening now helps you respond quickly and not miss anything important. But what is an "event" in the first place? A notable change in the status of a system can be thought of as an event. Some examples of such events are when a user clicks a button on a website, when a temperature sensor registers an unexpected rise, and when an inventory system records the sale of an item. All of these indicate system events that may set off certain responses.

The difference between stream processing and event processing

Event processing and stream processing are distinct yet complementary data processing techniques. Event processing focuses on reacting to individual, discrete events, which makes it ideal for scenarios that require immediate action, such as fraud detection. Stream processing, on the other hand, deals with continuous data flows and analyzing and processing data in real time, which is useful in applications such as real-time analytics and IoT device monitoring. While event processing homes in on single-event granularity, triggering specific responses, stream processing maintains a broader view, analyzing data trends over time. Together, these methods form a comprehensive approach to handling diverse real-time data needs in various technological and business contexts.

Summary

This chapter examined various data transformation methodologies, tools, and use cases, including filters, aggregations, and join. Each operation's utility and function were stated, which enabled us to cover practical applications.

Next, we explored data transformation use cases in sales analysis, social media analysis, customer segmentation, and website analytics. These case studies demonstrate the concepts' efficacy.

SQL and Spark, two key data transformation tools, dominated this chapter. SQL, a popular query language, is used to change data, whereas Spark is a powerful data processing engine. We compared SQL and Spark's DataFrame API to show these tools' adaptability.

Finally, we discussed the main data transformation techniques, which include event, batch, and stream processing. We emphasized their unique features and usefulness before covering windowing. After, you learned about data transformations through practical examples and were provided with a thorough comparison of various technologies. This discussion will help you choose data transformation technologies and procedures for your needs.

In the next chapter, we'll explore data transformation and strategies such as the Lambda and Kappa architectures and data quality transformations.

10
Transformation Patterns, Cleansing, and Normalization

In this chapter, we'll learn about transformation patterns and their role in data management. The Lambda, Kappa, and Microservice architectural patterns will be covered in the following sections. We'll also cover important data transformation methods, such as cleansing, normalization, masking, de-duplication, enrichment, validation, and standardization.

Data workers, like you, must understand these transformation patterns and methods. In a data-driven world, the ability to analyze raw data is invaluable. This expertise is crucial for data scientists preparing data for machine learning models, analysts gaining insights, and database administrators assuring data governance and security.

The Lambda, Kappa, and Microservice designs enable you to construct robust data pipelines for large and diversified data sources. Understanding data infrastructure construction is crucial in a business setting where fast and accurate information can affect decision-making.

Data cleansing, normalization, masking, de-duplication, enrichment, validation, and standardization are crucial procedures in preparing raw data for analysis or other data operations. These processes ensure data quality, conform with data privacy laws, and optimize storage and processing resources.

Transformation patterns and strategies improve data professional skills. They provide the instruments to maximize data accuracy, reliability, and security. These insights will help us through data transformation.

The following topics will be covered in this chapter:

- Transformation patterns
- Data cleansing and normalization

Transformation patterns

Data transformation has given rise to several different architectural patterns for more effective data management, processing, and storage. These patterns offer a roadmap for developing software that can cope with the growing volume, velocity, and variety of data. The Lambda, Kappa, and Microservice architectures will be discussed in this section as they are all examples of common transformation patterns.

Choosing the correct transformation pattern is crucial if a business is to maximize the value of its data and data assets. Different situations call for the use of different design patterns due to their strengths and weaknesses.

When deciding between different transformation patterns, it's important to think about things such as scalability, flexibility, maintainability, and fault tolerance. Consider your organization's specific requirements and constraints, such as its available funds, personnel, and technology.

In the following sections, we'll examine the aforementioned transformation patterns in greater depth, exploring their underlying principles, example applications, and overall benefits. The details of each pattern will help you select the best architecture for your data transformation tasks.

Keep in mind that there is no one-size-fits-all answer as you delve into these transformation patterns. Your data landscape, requirements, and objectives are specific to your business, so the best strategy will vary. If you weigh the benefits and drawbacks of each pattern and tailor them to your business's needs, you can create a data transformation system that will help you gain new insights and make more informed decisions.

Lambda architecture

Lambda architecture is a popular data processing pattern that provides a comprehensive approach to handling massive datasets. It combines both batch processing and stream processing to deliver a balanced solution for processing large volumes of data with low latency. In this section, we'll explore the components, benefits, and use cases of Lambda architecture.

The foundation of Lambda architecture is built on three layers: batch, speed, and serving. Let's take a closer look at each layer:

- **Batch layer**: This layer handles large-scale, computationally intensive batch processing tasks such as managing historical data. Precomputed views, also known as batch views, are created and sent to the serving layer after the data has been processed in bulk.

- **Speed layer**: The speed layer, also known as the real-time layer, is responsible for handling data in real time as it is received. It supplements the batch layer with low-latency processing to ensure that insights can be drawn from data in real time. The speed layer produces real-time perspectives, and the serving layer combines them with batch perspectives.

- **Serving layer**: Lambda architecture's final layer, the serving layer, oversees presenting a consolidated view of both the precomputed batch views and the real-time views. It facilitates straightforward data queries so that users can gain insights that are both timely and accurate.

The following figure shows an example of Lambda architecture:

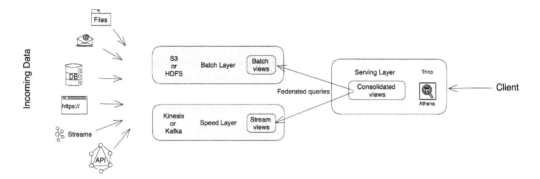

Figure 10.1 – Lambda architecture

The serving layer runs federated queries across various data sources, compiling them into a cohesive view for clients using technologies such as AWS Athena or Apache Trino/Presto. The stream layer can be powered by technologies such as Amazon Kinesis, Azure EventHub, or Apache Kafka. Lastly, the batch layer accumulates and processes data in batches, employing technologies such as Amazon S3, ADLSv2, or Hadoop HDFS for storage. Although additional technologies such as EMR or Spark are generally implied in such processes, they've been omitted from the preceding diagram for simplicity.

One of Lambda architecture's main benefits is that it can create data processing systems that are robust, scalable, and easy to maintain. It guarantees that problems in either the batch or the speed layers won't affect each other. Because of this partition, each component can be independently scaled to meet the growing demands of the business.

Lambda architecture is particularly well-suited for scenarios where organizations require real-time analytics alongside historical data processing. Lambda architecture can track stock market trends and analyze data to foresee future fluctuations, such as in the banking sector. The same holds for the retail industry, where it can be used to analyze customers' actions in real time and shed light on their past purchases.

However, Lambda architecture also has its disadvantages. One major issue is the duplication of the effort required to maintain two independent processing layers, each with a code base and supporting infrastructure. As a result, there may be more opportunities for errors and higher costs associated with maintenance. In addition, redundancy and an increase in storage needs can result from processing data in both the batch and speed layers.

Despite these drawbacks, Lambda architecture continues to be a popular option for companies seeking to create highly scalable and robust data processing systems. Companies can reduce complexity by experimenting with Lambda architecture's many variants, such as those that streamline the speed layer or employ a unified processing framework that caters to both batch and stream processing.

In conclusion, Lambda architecture offers a reliable method of handling massive amounts of data, with the added benefits of providing accurate historical records and timely in-the-moment insights. It allows businesses to construct scalable, fault-tolerant, and easily maintained data processing systems by capitalizing on the benefits of both batch and stream processing. Lambda architecture is still a viable choice for businesses with varied data processing needs, even though it presents some difficulties, such as complexity and redundancy.

Kappa architecture

Kappa architecture is an alternative data processing pattern that addresses some of the complexity and redundancy concerns associated with Lambda architecture. It simplifies the data processing landscape by focusing on a single stream processing layer instead of two separate layers for batch and stream processing. In this section, we will dive into the components, benefits, and use cases of Kappa architecture.

Kappa architecture is built on two main components: a stream processing layer and a serving layer. Let's examine each component:

- **Stream processing layer**: This layer is responsible for processing data in real time as it arrives. It ingests the data, processes it, and generates views or insights that can be served to end users. In Kappa architecture, the stream processing layer is designed to handle both real-time and historical data processing tasks.

- **Serving layer**: Like Lambda architecture, the serving layer in Kappa architecture is responsible for presenting the processed data to users. It combines the real-time views generated by the stream processing layer with any historical data that has been processed, enabling users to access a unified view of the data.

One of the key advantages of Kappa architecture is its simplicity. Utilizing a single stream processing layer for both real-time and historical data reduces the complexity and maintenance burden associated with managing separate layers and code bases in Lambda architecture. This simplification also results in reduced storage requirements as there is no need to store the same data in multiple layers.

Kappa architecture is particularly well-suited for situations where real-time processing is the primary focus, and historical data processing can be handled through the same stream processing infrastructure. For example, in the logistics industry, Kappa architecture can be used to track and analyze real-time vehicle movements while also providing historical analysis for route optimization. Similarly, in the social media space, Kappa architecture can be employed to analyze user interactions and content trends in real time while offering insights into historical trends.

Despite its benefits, Kappa architecture is not without its challenges. One of the main concerns is that stream processing systems may not be as mature or optimized for large-scale data processing as batch processing systems. Additionally, some organizations might find it challenging to adapt their existing batch-processing workflows to work within the constraints of a stream-processing system.

To overcome these challenges, organizations can explore hybrid approaches that combine elements of both the Lambda and Kappa architectures, depending on their specific data processing requirements. For instance, they can utilize a stream processing layer for real-time data processing while retaining a separate batch processing layer for heavy, resource-intensive tasks that are not time-sensitive.

The following figure shows an example of Kappa architecture:

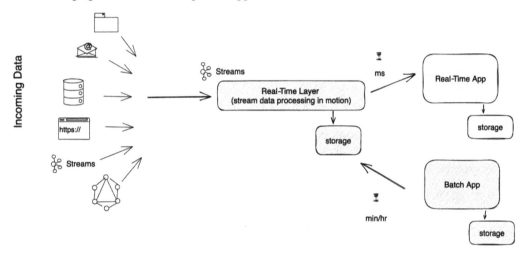

Figure 10.2 – Kappa architecture

In conclusion, Kappa architecture offers a streamlined alternative to Lambda architecture by focusing on a single stream processing layer for both real-time and historical data processing. This simplification results in reduced complexity, maintenance overhead, and storage requirements. While Kappa architecture may not be suitable for all use cases, especially those that require significant batch processing capabilities, it remains an attractive option for organizations that prioritize real-time data processing and are willing to adapt their existing workflows to fit within a stream processing framework.

Microservice architecture

Microservice architecture is a software development approach that structures applications as a collection of loosely coupled, independently deployable services. In the context of data transformation and processing, this approach allows organizations to create flexible, scalable, and resilient data pipelines by breaking down complex data workflows into smaller, manageable components. In this section, we'll discuss the core principles, benefits, and use cases of Microservice architecture in data processing.

Microservice architecture follows a few guiding principles:

- **Modularity**: Each microservice is designed to perform a specific function or process a particular type of data, allowing for a clear separation of concerns. This modularity makes it easier to develop, test, and maintain individual components of a data pipeline.

- **Decentralization**: Microservices are developed and managed independently, often by separate teams. This decentralization facilitates parallel development, reduces interdependencies between components, and enables faster deployment of new features and enhancements.

- **Scalability**: Microservices can be easily scaled to meet changing data processing demands. By isolating resource-intensive processes into separate services, organizations can scale only the components that require additional resources, optimizing resource usage and minimizing costs.

- **Resilience**: The loosely coupled nature of microservices ensures that the failure of a single component does not bring down the entire data pipeline. This resilience makes it easier to diagnose and fix issues while maintaining overall system stability.

Microservice architecture offers several advantages for data transformation and processing:

- **Flexibility**: By breaking down complex data workflows into smaller, more manageable components, organizations can easily adapt their data pipelines to changing requirements or incorporate new data sources without disrupting the entire system

- **Faster development and deployment**: With clearly defined responsibilities for each microservice, development teams can work independently and in parallel, accelerating the development and deployment of new features and improvements

- **Improved fault tolerance**: The failure of a single microservice has a limited impact on the overall system, allowing for more robust data pipelines with built-in redundancy and failover mechanisms

- **Simplified maintenance**: The modular design of microservices makes it easier to identify and fix issues within specific components, reducing the time and effort required for maintenance and troubleshooting

Here are some of the practical applications of Microservice architecture in data processing:

- **E-commerce platforms**: Microservices can be separated into various domains, with each managed as a separate set of services and processing pipelines, such as customer profiles, product catalog updates, cart management, and purchasing and transaction processing, ensuring smooth and efficient data management across the platform

- **IoT data processing**: In the context of the **Internet of Things** (**IoT**), microservices can efficiently process large volumes of data from multiple sources, such as sensors, devices, and gateways, allowing organizations to derive valuable insights from their IoT infrastructure

- **Fraud detection**: In financial institutions, microservices can be used to analyze various data streams for signs of fraudulent activity, enabling real-time detection and prevention of fraud

- **Social media analytics**: Microservices can process and analyze vast amounts of social media data, such as user profiles, interactions, and content, helping organizations gain insights into customer preferences, trends, and sentiment

The following figure shows an example of Microservice architecture in the context of data transformation:

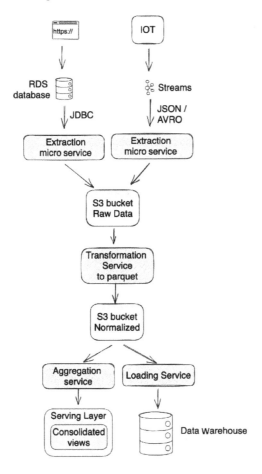

Figure 10.3 – Microservice-based architecture

In conclusion, Microservice architecture offers a flexible, scalable, and resilient approach to data transformation and processing. By breaking down complex workflows into modular components, organizations can adapt their data pipelines more easily, accelerate development and deployment, and maintain system stability. While implementing microservices may require an initial investment in infrastructure and development practices, the long-term benefits of this approach make it a compelling choice for organizations dealing with complex and dynamic data environments.

Case study – an e-commerce platform that uses a microservice for data engineering

In the context of an eCommerce platform, microservices play a crucial role in building a robust and efficient data engineering pipeline. These modular and independent components excel in handling various data processing tasks specific to the eCommerce domain, such as customer profiles, product catalog updates, and transaction processing.

To develop an eCommerce data engineering pipeline using Microservice architecture, consider the following steps:

1. **Identify the eCommerce data processing requirements**: Understand the specific data processing needs of your eCommerce platform. This includes tasks such as managing customer profiles, updating the product catalog in real time, and processing transactions securely and efficiently.

2. **Design microservices for eCommerce data processing**: Break down the data processing tasks into smaller, self-contained microservices. For example, you can create separate microservices for customer profile management, product catalog updates, and transaction processing. This modular approach facilitates agility, scalability, and ease of maintenance.

3. **Define communication protocols**: Establish clear communication protocols between the Microservices. Utilize messaging systems such as Apache Kafka and RabbitMQ or implement REST APIs for seamless inter-service communication.

4. **Implement data pipelines**: Develop the necessary components within each microservice to process and transform the eCommerce data. This may involve tasks such as data ingestion, data cleaning, data enrichment, and other relevant operations. Ensure that each microservice performs its specific data processing task effectively and reliably.

5. **Orchestrate the pipeline**: Employ a workflow management tool such as Apache Airflow to orchestrate the eCommerce data processing pipeline. This allows you to manage dependencies between microservices, schedule tasks, and monitor the overall pipeline performance.

6. **Incorporate data storage and retrieval**: Integrate suitable data storage solutions such as relational databases, NoSQL databases, object storage, or distributed filesystems within the microservices. This ensures efficient storage and retrieval of eCommerce data for each specific processing task.

7. **Implement fault tolerance and monitoring**: Implement fault tolerance mechanisms such as retries, error handling, and circuit breakers to ensure the resiliency of the eCommerce data processing pipeline. Set up monitoring and logging systems to track the performance and health of each microservice.

By following these steps, you can develop a robust and scalable data engineering pipeline for your eCommerce platform using Microservice architecture. This approach enables efficient data management, agile processing of customer profiles, real-time product catalog updates, and secure transaction processing, thereby enhancing the overall performance and user experience of your eCommerce platform.

Transformation patterns comparison

In this section, we will compare the Lambda, Kappa, and Microservice architectures. This comparison aims to illuminate the distinct advantages and challenges associated with each pattern. By examining real-world applications and theoretical considerations, we can better understand the operational nuances that differentiate these architectures. It is important to discern these transformation patterns' unique strengths and applications so that you can choose the most appropriate for specific scenarios.

Here is a comparative table that highlights the key aspects of each pattern:

Feature	Lambda Architecture	Kappa Architecture	Microservice Architecture
Processing	Batch and real-time	Stream (real time)	Service-oriented
Complexity	High	Medium	Variable
Flexibility	Low to medium	Medium to high	High
Data Handling	Comprehensive	Streamlined	Decentralized
Scalability	Scalable with effort	Naturally scalable	Highly scalable
Use Case	Complex analytics	Real-time analytics	Independent, scalable services
System Management	More challenging	Simpler than Lambda	Depends on the service's design

Figure 10.1 – Comparison of each transformation pattern

In comparing transformation patterns such as Lambda, Kappa, and microservice, it's crucial to understand their distinct applications and limitations. Lambda architecture is ideal for handling massive datasets where both batch and real-time processing are required, offering a comprehensive view of data at the cost of complexity in managing two distinct paths. Kappa architecture, on the other hand, simplifies this by using a single-stream processing pipeline, making it more straightforward but potentially less versatile for complex batch-processing tasks. Finally, Microservice architecture excels in scenarios demanding high scalability and flexibility, thus enabling independent scaling and development of services. However, this may introduce overhead in data management and inter-service communication.

When choosing the best pattern, consider your specific use case requirements: Lambda for comprehensive batch and real-time processing, Kappa for streamlined real-time processing, and Microservice for flexibility and scalability in service development and deployment. The decision should align with your data processing needs, system complexity tolerance, and scalability requirements. Next, we'll discuss data cleansing and normalization.

Data cleansing and normalization

Having high-quality data is essential in the data processing and transformation industry. Messy, inconsistent, or incorrect data can produce questionable conclusions and should be avoided at all costs. This is where the need for data normalization and cleansing becomes apparent. In this section, we'll delve into these two methods and examine their significance in preserving data quality.

Data cleansing, also known as data scrubbing, is the process of inspecting data for mistakes and then fixing (or removing) them. Errors in data entry, technical difficulties, and even representational differences can all contribute to these problems. Your data will be more useful for analysis, reporting, and decision-making if you take the time to clean it first.

Here are a few examples of typical data-cleansing activities:

- Fixing misspelled words and typos
- Creating a universal time and date format
- Adding or editing data to complete a record
- The process of locating and fixing anomalies

However, data normalization is a method that's used to create a standard format for data, making it more manageable and comparable across different sets. Data normalization, or the process of converting information into a standardized format, is useful because it can facilitate less duplication, higher quality data, and easier analysis and reporting. It's crucial when you're dealing with information from various sources, some of which may use different file formats or have different organizational schemes.

There are many possible methods of normalization, including the following:

- Adjusting numbers to fit a standard format (for example, converting temperatures into Celsius)
- Quantitatively rescaling data to a more manageable range (such as 0 to 1)
- Categorizing and encoding qualitative information (for example, converting text labels into numerical codes)
- Converting all dates and times into a standard format, such as the ISO 8601 standard, to avoid inconsistencies when integrating data from multiple sources

To ensure your data is fit for analysis, reporting, and decision-making, it must undergo cleansing and normalization. You can help your company maximize its data resources and make better, data-informed decisions by investing in these methods. Next, we'll dive into greater detail on specific data cleansing and normalization techniques, as well as other data processing methods that can further improve the quality and usability of your data.

Data cleansing techniques

If you care about the integrity and accuracy of your data, you must regularly cleanse it. Datasets can be cleaned of mistakes, inconsistencies, and inaccurate information using several methods. To help you make sure your data is clean and ready for analysis, we'll go over some of the most popular methods for doing so:

- **Removing duplicate records**: Duplicate records can cause confusion and lead to inaccurate conclusions during data analysis. Identifying and removing these duplicates is crucial for maintaining data quality. When using criteria such as matching unique identifiers or other key attributes, techniques such as deduplication or record linkage can be used to find and merge or eliminate duplicates.

- **Fixing typographical errors**: Typos and spelling mistakes can compromise the quality of your data and make it difficult to analyze. To correct these errors, you can use techniques such as spell-checking, dictionary-based validation, or even machine learning algorithms such as Levenshtein distance to identify and fix potential typos in your data.

- **Handling missing values**: Missing values can lead to incomplete or biased analysis, making it crucial to address them during data cleansing. There are several techniques to handle missing values:

  - **Imputation**: Replacing missing values with an estimate, such as the mean or median of the available data

  - **Deletion**: Removing records with missing values, which can be useful when the amount of missing data is minimal and doesn't significantly impact the analysis

  - **Interpolation**: Estimating missing values based on neighboring data points, which can be particularly useful for time series data

- **Correcting outliers**: Outliers are data points that differ significantly from the rest of the dataset. While some outliers represent genuine anomalies, others may result from errors or inconsistencies in the data. Outlier detection methods such as standard deviation, **interquartile range** (**IQR**), or clustering algorithms can be used to identify and correct or remove these problematic data points.

- **Standardizing data formats**: Inconsistent data formats can make it difficult to combine and analyze datasets. Standardizing formats for dates, times, currencies, and other data types ensures that your data is consistent and easy to work with. Techniques such as parsing, formatting, and conversion can be used to transform data into a standard format.

- **Categorizing and encoding data**: Categorical data, such as text labels or codes, can be challenging to analyze and compare. Categorizing and encoding this data can make it more manageable and easier to analyze. Techniques such as label encoding, one-hot encoding, or target encoding can be used to transform categorical data into a numerical format that's easier to work with in analysis and machine learning algorithms.

- **Validating data consistency**: Ensuring that your data is consistent across different records and sources is crucial for maintaining data quality. Techniques such as cross-field validation, referential integrity checks, or rule-based validation can be used to verify that data values are consistent with one another and conform to predefined rules and constraints.

- **Enriching data**: Sometimes, data cleansing may also involve enriching your dataset by adding new information or deriving additional insights. This can be done through techniques such as data augmentation, feature engineering, or external data integration.

By employing these data cleansing techniques, you can improve the quality and reliability of your data, ensuring that it's accurate, consistent, and ready for analysis. In the next section, we'll explore data normalization techniques that can help you further organize and structure your data for more efficient processing and analysis.

Data normalization techniques

Data normalization is a vital process for structuring and organizing data in a way that reduces redundancy and simplifies analysis. By normalizing your data, you can improve its consistency, integrity, and ease of use, making it more accessible and valuable to your organization. In this section, we'll explore various data normalization techniques that can help you streamline and optimize your data for better processing and analysis:

- **Min-max scaling**: This technique scales numeric data to a specific range, usually between 0 and 1. Min-max scaling is done by subtracting the minimum value from each data point and dividing the result by the range of values. This approach is particularly useful when comparing data with different scales or units, but it can be sensitive to outliers.

- **Z-score normalization (standardization)**: Z-score normalization, also known as standardization, involves transforming data so that it has a mean of 0 and a standard deviation of 1. This technique is useful for comparing data that follows a normal distribution or when using machine learning algorithms that assume data is standardized. To apply z-score normalization, subtract the mean from each data point and divide the result by the standard deviation.

- **Log transformation**: Log transformation can help you manage data with skewed distributions or exponential growth patterns. By applying the natural logarithm to each data point, you can reduce the impact of extreme values and make the data more symmetric. Log transformation is often used in financial, economic, or biological data analysis.

- **Box-Cox transformation**: Box-Cox transformation is a family of power transformations that can help stabilize the variance and normalize the distribution of data. By applying a parameter (Lambda) to the data, Box-Cox can find the most suitable transformation for your dataset. This technique is useful when the data doesn't follow a specific distribution pattern, and you need a flexible approach to normalization.

- **Feature scaling**: In some cases, you may need to scale individual features within a dataset to ensure they have equal importance during analysis. Techniques such as min-max scaling, z-score normalization, or robust scaling (which uses the median and interquartile range) can help you achieve this. Feature scaling is essential when working with machine learning algorithms that are sensitive to the scale of input features, such as linear regression or support vector machines.

- **One-to-N encoding**: When working with categorical data, it's often necessary to convert the data into a numerical format for analysis. One-to-N encoding, also known as one-hot encoding, creates binary features for each category, allowing you to represent categorical data in a more structured and machine-readable format.

- **Database normalization**: Database normalization is a technique for organizing data within relational databases to minimize redundancy and improve data integrity. By following a set of normalization rules (or normal forms), you can create a more efficient database schema that supports data consistency and reduces the risk of anomalies during data updates. Common normalization forms include **first normal form** (**1NF**), **second normal form** (**2NF**), and **third normal form** (**3NF**), each with its specific requirements and constraints.

- **Text normalization**: Text normalization is the process of transforming textual data into a consistent format that's easier to analyze. Techniques such as case folding (converting all text into lowercase), removing special characters, stemming (reducing words to their root form), and lemmatization (converting words into their base form) can help standardize textual data and improve its quality for analysis.

By applying these data normalization techniques, you can create a more structured, consistent, and accessible dataset that's easier to analyze and use within your organization. In the following sections, we'll explore additional data processing techniques, such as data masking, de-duplication, validation, and standardization.

Data masking

Data masking is a technique that replaces sensitive information with fictional or obfuscated data, ensuring privacy and compliance while still allowing the data to be used for testing, analysis, or training purposes. There are several methods for data masking, including the following:

- **Substitution**: This involves replacing sensitive data with randomly generated data of the same type to ensure that the structure remains intact but the information is no longer identifiable

- **Shuffling**: This involves randomly rearranging the data within a column and then breaking the connection between sensitive data and other attributes while preserving the overall data distribution

- **Masking out**: This involves obscuring portions of sensitive data, such as replacing certain characters with symbols or placeholders, to make it difficult to identify the original information

- **Generalization**: This involves replacing specific data with broader categories or ranges, thus reducing the level of detail while maintaining some degree of usefulness

Data de-duplication

Data de-duplication is the process of identifying and removing duplicate records from a dataset. Duplicate data can negatively impact data quality, leading to inaccurate analysis and decision-making. Here are some techniques that can be used for data de-duplication:

- **Exact match**: Identifying duplicate records by comparing all attributes for exact matches

- **Fuzzy matching**: Comparing records based on a similarity score, allowing for variations in spelling, formatting, or data entry errors

- **Record linkage**: Using algorithms and probabilistic techniques to identify and match related records across datasets, even when they don't share a common unique identifier

Data enrichment

Data enrichment is the process of enhancing raw data by incorporating additional information from external sources. This process can significantly improve the value and utility of your data, leading to more insightful analysis and better decision-making. In this section, we'll delve into the concept of data enrichment, its benefits, and some practical approaches to enriching your data.

Data enrichment can be thought of as the art of adding context to your data. By supplementing the raw data with extra information, you can reveal hidden connections, identify trends, and uncover new insights. Data enrichment can be applied to a wide range of data types, including customer data, financial data, geospatial data, and more.

There are several benefits to data enrichment, including the following:

- **Improved data quality**: Enriching your data can help fill in gaps, correct inaccuracies, and provide a more complete picture of the information at hand

- **Enhanced analysis**: By adding context to your data, you can uncover new insights and perform more in-depth analysis, ultimately leading to better decision-making

- **Personalization**: Enriched data can enable a more personalized user experience as you can tailor products, services, or marketing efforts based on the enhanced information

- **Compliance**: In some cases, data enrichment can help organizations comply with regulations by ensuring that they have accurate and up-to-date information

To enrich your data, there are several practical approaches to consider:

- **Data integration**: Data integration involves combining data from different sources to create a unified view. This process can involve joining datasets, merging records, and mapping fields between sources.

- **Data augmentation**: Data augmentation involves adding new attributes to your data, such as demographic information, industry classifications, or geospatial coordinates. This can be done through various techniques, including web scraping, APIs, or purchasing data from third-party providers.

- **Data linkage**: Data linkage is the process of connecting records from different datasets based on shared attributes, such as an ID, email address, or phone number. This can help you uncover relationships between data points that may not have been apparent in the raw data.

- **Data validation**: Data validation involves checking the accuracy and completeness of your data. This can include verifying addresses, email addresses, or phone numbers, as well as ensuring that mandatory fields are populated and that data values fall within expected ranges.

- **Feature engineering**: Feature engineering is the process of creating new variables or features from existing data to improve the performance of machine learning models. This can include techniques such as one-hot encoding, binning, or aggregating variables.

In conclusion, data enrichment is a powerful process that can greatly enhance the value of your data. By integrating, augmenting, and validating your data, you can unlock new insights and improve decision-making. As you embark on your data enrichment journey, keep the different approaches and techniques available in mind, and choose the ones that best suit your specific needs and goals.

Data validation

Data validation is the process of ensuring that data meets specific criteria or follows predefined rules. By validating data, you can identify errors, inconsistencies, or inaccuracies and take corrective actions. Here are some techniques you can use for data validation:

- **Range checks**: This involves ensuring that numerical data falls within a specified range of acceptable values

- **Format checks**: This involves verifying that data adheres to a specific format, such as dates, email addresses, or phone numbers

- **Consistency checks**: This involves ensuring that data is consistent across related records or fields

- **Referential integrity checks**: This involves confirming that relationships between data entities are maintained, such as foreign key constraints in databases

Data standardization

Data standardization is the process of transforming data from various sources into a common format, enabling easier comparison, analysis, and integration. Standardizing data ensures consistency and improves data quality, making it more valuable for decision-making. Let's look at some techniques for data standardization:

- **Unit conversion**: This involves converting data into a standard unit of measurement, such as converting temperatures into Celsius or distances into kilometers

- **Date and time formatting**: This involves ensuring that date and time values follow a consistent format across the dataset

- **Text formatting**: This involves standardizing text data, such as capitalization, spelling, or abbreviations, to ensure consistency

- **Categorical encoding**: This involves transforming categorical data into numerical or binary formats that can be easily processed and analyzed

By applying these data cleansing, normalization, and additional techniques, you can improve the quality, accuracy, and reliability of your data, leading to better insights and decision-making within your organization.

Summary

In this chapter, we explored various architectural patterns and techniques for data transformation and cleansing. We understood the Lambda, Kappa, and Microservice architectures, highlighting their strengths and use cases. We also delved into data cleansing and normalization, discussing techniques such as data masking, de-duplication, enrichment, validation, and standardization. Finally, we provided a comprehensive summary of this chapter's key concepts and concluded with an overview of the topics covered.

Moving on to the next chapter, the focus shifts to exposing and accessing data through different technologies and APIs.

11

Data Exposition and APIs

Upon completing the data transformation, modification, and retrieval procedures, it's fundamentally important to circulate this information efficiently and securely to a range of stakeholders, from internal teams to external partners and even customers. There are numerous methods available to meet this demand. This chapter aims to provide an in-depth look into various facets of data exposure and the role **application programming interfaces** (**APIs**) play in this domain. Our journey begins with understanding the concept of data exposition, its importance, and the many ways in which it can be achieved for both internal and external usage. We will delve into the intricacies of the exposition model and the contrast between task services and entity services, with a special focus on **Representational State Transfer** (**REST**) APIs.

In the chapter, we will look at the many methods for exposing data, ranging from stream expositions to data APIs. Each technique has its own set of use cases, benefits, and challenges. We will look more closely at stream processing technologies, as well as present a practical case study demonstrating the real-time exposure of warnings and KPIs in a manufacturing application.

In addition to stream expositions, we will discuss the exposure of flat files and data APIs such as **Open Database Connectivity** (**ODBC**)/**Java Database Connectivity** (**JDBC**), GraphQL, and **Open Data Protocol** (**OData**). A critical piece of this exploration involves understanding data modeling and the use of various engines for data exposition.

As we progress, the spotlight will be on APIs, where we will discuss the best practices for API design, versioning, security, and documentation. We will discuss the numerous factors that must be considered during API implementation and dive into technical elements such as scalability, performance, and error handling. We will also cover API testing, life cycle management, strategy and governance, planning and roadmaps, and the need for monitoring and analytics to better equip you.

Finally, we'll conclude this chapter with a comparative analysis of different data exposure solutions, providing a comprehensive summary that will enable you to make informed decisions. This chapter promises to be an enlightening journey, arming you with the knowledge you need to efficiently expose data and implement APIs in your organization.

The following topics will be covered in this chapter:

- Understanding the strategic motives for data exposure

- Going through the data exposition technologies

- A focus on APIs and strategy

- A comparative analysis of data exposure solutions

Understanding the strategic motives for data exposure

Exposing data from analytics platforms has become an integral part of modern data-driven operations. This process allows raw data from diverse sources, including databases, logs, IoT devices, and third-party APIs, to be accessed and analyzed centrally. As a result, it helps facilitate well-informed strategic decisions and propels business growth.

Data exposure between profiles

Within an analytics platform, the seamless and efficient exchange of data between various user profiles – such as data scientists, data analysts, and other stakeholders – is of paramount importance. These diverse roles, each with their unique requirements and perspectives, constitute the collective intelligence of an organization's data operations.

Data scientists, for instance, often require raw, unfiltered data to build predictive models and explore intricate patterns and relationships within the data. On the other hand, data analysts might need aggregated and preprocessed data to generate descriptive and diagnostic insights that can be readily communicated to business stakeholders.

Thus, an effective analytics platform must support varied data needs and facilitate easy data sharing and collaboration among different user profiles. This can be achieved by incorporating flexible data access controls, intuitive data discovery features, and robust data lineage capabilities.

Moreover, as these roles often work in tandem, providing the capability for seamless handoffs of data and insights across these profiles can enhance the overall productivity and efficacy of data-driven initiatives. This necessitates the analytics platform to support a variety of data formats, interfaces, and export options that cater to different user profiles' tooling preferences and technical proficiencies.

When designing or selecting an analytics platform, considering the dynamic interplay and data exchange requirements among various user profiles is crucial to foster collaboration, enhance user satisfaction, and drive more impactful data-driven decisions.

Data exposure for external usage

These analytics platforms feature a broad range of tools for visualizing and interpreting data in a user-friendly way. To make the most of these capabilities, data must be exposed or made accessible to these platforms. Organizations typically establish data pipelines to pull data from its origin and load it directly onto the analytics platform. This practice ensures the availability of the most accurate and current data for analysis, proving critical for maintaining data accessibility.

However, the potency of an analytics platform is not confined to data consumption. It also lies in its data output capabilities. Once data has been analyzed, it can be exposed or output in a variety of formats for further utilization. These formats might include visual reports, raw data exports, or APIs that enable other systems to directly query the processed data.

It's noteworthy that many external operational platforms are increasingly interested in using the data from analytics platforms. One key reason behind this interest is the readiness of the data. The data on an analytics platform has typically undergone extensive processing, making it "analysis-ready." It is clean, transformed, and often enriched with additional context. This readiness reduces the time and effort required by operational platforms to use this data, leading to efficient and faster data-driven actions.

The ability to query or extract data from an analytics platform is extremely useful, whether it's for extracting processed data for further analysis in separate statistical tools, feeding machine learning models, populating dashboards in a business intelligence tool, or using the data in external operational platforms. It gives a single perspective of data, facilitates real-time decision-making, and improves data mobility, making it a critical component in attaining business goals in today's data-driven environment.

Exposition model

The exposure of data through APIs involves the use of a variety of protocols, each with its unique characteristics and advantages. These protocols facilitate the transfer of information and render data accessible to a broad spectrum of professionals, ranging from data engineers and data scientists to data analysts. A comprehensive understanding of these protocols is vital for leveraging data APIs effectively.

These protocols serve as the communication rules that standardize how requests for data are made and how responses are returned. They help in abstracting the complexities of data exchange, making it possible for different profiles with varying levels of technical expertise to interact with the data effortlessly.

The following figure shows an exposition model:

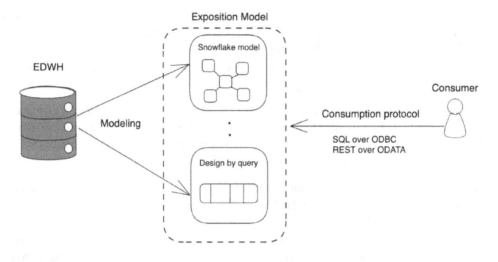

Figure 11.1 – Exposition model

A wide range of professionals are interested in leveraging data for various purposes. For example, data engineers focus on establishing data processing frameworks and pipelines, while data scientists concentrate on developing predictive or analytical models. Meanwhile, data analysts use the data to derive key performance indicators that inform decision-making. The diverse requirements for the same foundational data set make accessibility and ease of use crucial priorities for modern businesses. Therefore, to optimally expose data and unlock its potential, it is crucial to align the choice of protocols with the specific requirements of each user profile. This tailored approach not only enhances data utilization but also ensures a more efficient, streamlined data flow within the organization, driving more informed and effective decision-making processes.

Data exposition service models versus entity exposition service models

We can observe a clear dichotomy in the ways data exposition services models, which can broadly be divided into data exposition services and entity exposition services. Each kind is important and is tailored to fulfill certain needs in data operations.

Data exposition services, such as REST APIs or file transfers, are specifically engineered to address a predefined and formalized need. These services streamline data delivery, offering packaged solutions that cater to explicit demands. For instance, a REST API can be designed to deliver a specific service based on datasets or part of them by performing specific operations, while file transfers can be set up to provide data files that have been pre-processed or formatted to meet a distinct requirement. These services thrive on their ability to provide focused, targeted solutions, enabling efficient utilization of resources and effective responses to specific needs.

On the other hand, entity exposition services allow unrestricted access to data, providing the capability to navigate through the information without use limitations. Protocols such as OData and GraphQL, or queryable engines, fall into this category. These services facilitate the complete exploration and manipulation of data entities. They provide users with the flexibility to query and retrieve data based on their unique requirements, offering broader and more dynamic access to the data. This unrestricted access can be pivotal in scenarios where needs are dynamic, and the ability to explore and manipulate data freely is essential.

These two categories of services, while different in their operation, work together to offer comprehensive solutions in the data management landscape, each serving unique needs in specific contexts.

A focus on REST APIs

Web APIs, which often employ HTTP protocols, form the backbone of data sharing and communication between applications across the internet. They offer controlled, secure access to functionality and data that can be consumed by other software applications. Access typically involves specific, targeted data that optimizes efficiency and network resources.

Focusing on **Representational State Transfer** (**REST**), we'll explore its unique advantages and challenges. REST is a popular methodology for developing distributed applications due to its simplicity and statelessness. REST APIs leverage HTTP methods to access and modify data across XML, JSON, and HTML media types. They are especially effective for public APIs accessed by numerous devices and for creating services for widespread developer adoption.

However, REST APIs can present many challenges, such as the data overhead when over-fetching and under-fetching data. Over-fetching refers to situations where a client downloads more data than required, whereas under-fetching happens when an API endpoint doesn't deliver enough data. Both scenarios can impair application performance and network utilization efficiency. Another notable challenge while designing an API in analytics or big data contexts is the protocol overhead and the excessive data in headers, cookies, and metadata compared to the actual useful data in requests and responses. This can cause bandwidth inefficiency, increased latency, and slower performance.

It's important to keep these considerations in mind while designing and implementing APIs for optimal results.

Next, we'll discuss data exposition technologies.

Going through the data exposition technologies

As we saw earlier, data needs vary widely, both in terms of user profiles and specific requirements. That's why it's essential to have tailored data exposition methods to meet each type of need. Depending on the size of the organization and the volume of the associated data, it may be beneficial to utilize one or multiple exposition systems.

Streams expositions

Data streaming is an advanced practice in data engineering that involves making data available in real time as it is generated.

This practice grants immediate access to data from various sources, such as sensors, social media platforms, and financial transactions.

The advantages of data streaming are particularly significant in fast-paced sectors such as finance, manufacturing, transportation, and logistics, where swift, informed decisions can influence competitiveness.

This chapter delves into the technology and applications associated with data streaming that serve data to third-party applications while highlighting the benefits and challenges.

Although stream processing primarily focuses on data handling rather than exposition, we haven't delved into it before. Therefore, we propose that you take some time to explore and review some stream processing technologies and their effective usage for exposing data, shedding light on their unique aspects and relevance in the context of real-time data availability.

Use cases and examples of streams as an exposition technique

Real-time data streaming is crucial for decision-making, monitoring, and prediction across several industries.

Here are some practical examples:

- **Finance**: Financial institutions can utilize real-time data streams to gain insights into market trends and execute trades promptly. For instance, these institutions can monitor stock price changes and track various investment portfolios' performance, enabling them to make informed decisions about buying and selling stocks. Real-time data streams also aid in detecting anomalies and risks, thus helping mitigate potential losses.

- **Manufacturing**: Manufacturers can leverage data streams from IoT sensors to get real-time data on production processes and equipment health. This data helps optimize production processes, anticipate equipment maintenance needs, and minimize downtime.

- **Social media**: Social media platforms use data streams to track user behavior and deliver tailored content to users in real time. By analyzing real-time data streams, these platforms can offer personalized content recommendations, targeted ads, and customized user experiences.

- **Healthcare**: In the healthcare sector, data streams from wearable devices or medical equipment provide valuable insights to medical professionals, enabling them to deliver better care and make informed decisions.

- **Energy**: In the energy sector, data streams are essential in predicting energy demand, optimizing power distribution, and monitoring equipment health.

- **Retail**: Retailers can benefit from data streams by using them to track customer behavior and manage inventory effectively.

Advantages and challenges of exposing streams

Exposing data streams offers numerous benefits, such as real-time data access, improved decision-making, and enhanced monitoring capabilities.

However, challenges also arise, including managing data volume, processing, and security.

Here are the advantages:

- **Real-time data access**: Allows for data to be accessed and analyzed as it is generated
- **Immediate insights for decision making**: Enables quick analysis and interpretation of data for informed decisions
- **Improved operational efficiency**: Optimizes business processes and reduces costs using real-time data
- **Enhanced customer experiences**: Personalizes customer experiences and provides better service using real-time data

Here are some of the challenges:

- **High data volume and velocity**: Managing and processing large volumes of data generated at high speeds can be challenging.
- **Complex data processing**: Real-time data streams often require sophisticated processing techniques to extract meaningful information from the input stream.
- **Security concerns**: Real-time data streams can pose security risks, such as unauthorized access and data breaches. The **General Data Protection Regulation** (**GDPR**) requires organizations to protect personal data in real-time data streams with appropriate security measures, process data lawfully and transparently, provide clear privacy notices, and demonstrate compliance through audits.

Stream processing technologies

Various technologies have emerged to address the challenges associated with processing and managing data streams.

These technologies focus on enabling real-time processing, scalability, and fault tolerance.

Some popular stream processing technologies are as follows:

- **Apache Kafka**: A distributed streaming platform designed for high-throughput, fault-tolerant, and scalable data streaming. Kafka is widely used for building real-time data pipelines and applications that require processing data streams.

- **Apache Flink**: A fastened reliable large-scale data processing engine, Apache Flink is tailored for distributed, stateful computations over data streams. It provides high-throughput, low-latency processing and can recover from failures, ensuring the continuous flow of data.

- **Amazon Kinesis**: A managed service from **Amazon Web Services** (**AWS**) that enables the collection, processing, and analysis of real-time streaming data. Kinesis offers seamless integration with other AWS services, scalability, and high availability.

- **Google Cloud Dataflow**: A fully managed service for stream and batch data processing provided by Google Cloud Platform. Dataflow is designed for high performance and offers autoscaling, strong consistency, and fault tolerance.

- **Apache Samza**: A distributed stream processing framework that can process millions of events per second. Samza offers stateful processing and integrates with Apache Kafka for data ingestion and Apache Hadoop **Yet Another Resource Negotiator** (**YARN**) for resource management.

- **Apache Storm**: A fast and reliable distributed stream processing system, Apache Storm is designed for real-time data processing. Storm offers fault tolerance, scalability, and strong consistency and can process millions of records per second.

Case study – a manufacturing application to expose alerts and KPIs in real time

Let's consider a manufacturing application that uses sensors to monitor equipment health and production processes.

The following figure shows the architecture of a manufacturing application exposing a KPI and alert stream:

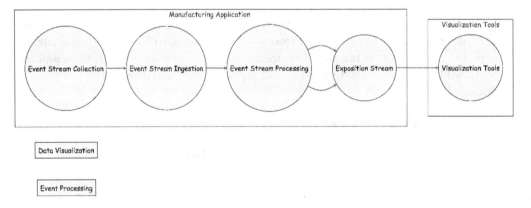

Figure 11.2 – Architecture of manufacturing an application exposing a KPI and alert stream

The preceding figure represents the integration of various solutions that contribute to establishing an architecture that is well suited to the specific context of the organization:

- **Event stream collection**: The sensors that are installed on manufacturing equipment continuously generate real-time data regarding various operating parameters such as temperature, pressure, and vibration. This data is an example of an event data stream.

- **Event stream ingestion**: The raw data from the sensors is ingested into a data pipeline using a real-time data streaming technology such as Apache Kafka. Kafka is capable of handling high volumes of data in real time and is fault-tolerant, making it suitable for this application.

- **Event stream processing**: Once ingested, the data is processed in real time using a stream processing technology such as Apache Flink. Flink can handle large-scale data processing tasks and provides low-latency, high-throughput processing capabilities. During this stage, the raw data is cleaned, transformed, and structured into a format suitable for analysis. In this step, business events such as alarms and KPIs are produced as events and are sent to an exposition stream that can be consumed by third-party applications. This allows other applications to receive real-time updates on the status of the manufacturing processes and equipment health.

- **Exposition stream**: By exposing data in a stream, third-party applications can consume processed events such as alerts and KPIs. This integration can be achieved by integrating the alert and KPI exposition stream with various visualization tools, dashboards, or applications, enabling users to view and analyze the data in real time and make informed decisions.

The following figure shows the process of sending alerts and KPIs to an exposition stream:

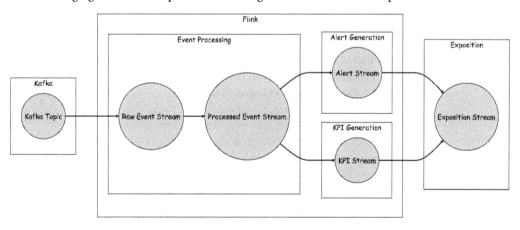

Figure 11.3 – Processing alerts and KPIs that have been sent to an exposition stream

Using an exposition stream for real-time data access enables third-party applications to leverage processed events such as alerts and KPIs effectively. This process not only facilitates instant insights but also promotes data-driven decision-making. Visual tools and dashboards enhance this process by making the data more accessible and user-friendly. As illustrated in the preceding figure, this system optimizes the use of alerts and KPIs, transforming them into valuable, actionable insights that are delivered directly through the exposition stream.

Let's go through an example of the code structure with Flink to implement this architecture:

1. First and foremost, as an example, you'll need to include the following library:

    ```
    import org.apache.flink.api.common.functions.MapFunction;
    import org.apache.flink.streaming.api.datastream.DataStream;
    import org.apache.flink.streaming.api.environment.
    StreamExecutionEnvironment;
    ```

2. Next, we must define the main function, which serves as the architectural backbone of the entire data processing pipeline:

    ```
    public class EventStreamProcessingExample {
        public static void main(String[] args) throws Exception {
            // Set up the execution environment
            StreamExecutionEnvironment env =
    StreamExecutionEnvironment.getExecutionEnvironment();
            // Create a stream from the ingested data
            DataStream<RawEvent> ingestedStream = env.addSource(new
    KafkaEventSource());
            // Apply cleaning, transforming, and structuring
    operations
            DataStream<Event> processedStream = ingestedStream
                    .map(new CleaningTransformation())
                    .map(new Transformation())
                    .map(new StructuringTransformation());
            // Send the processed events to the Exposition Stream
            processedStream.addSink(new KafkaExpositionSink());
            // Create alerts based on specific events
            DataStream<Alert> alertStream = processedStream
                    .filter(event -> event.getMeasurement() > 100)
    // Example condition for generating an alert
                    .map(new AlertCreation());
            // Send the alerts to relevant stakeholders
            alertStream.addSink(new AlertSink());
            // Execute the job
            env.execute("Event Stream Processing");
        }
    ```

3. Then, we must define the public static classes – `RawEvent`, `Event`, and `Alert` – and implement the following MapFunctions:

- `CleaningTransformation`

- `Transformation`

- `StructuringTransformation`

- `AlertCreation`

4. Last but not least, we must define the source and sink event:

```
// Implement the Kafka source and sink for ingesting and
emitting events
    public static class KafkaEventSource implements
SourceFunction<RawEvent> {
        // Implementation for reading events from Kafka
        // ...
    }
    public static class KafkaExpositionSink implements
SinkFunction<Event> {
        // Implementation for writing events to Kafka
        // ...
    }
    public static class AlertSink implements SinkFunction<Alert>
{
        // Implementation for sending alerts to relevant
stakeholders
        // ...
    }
}
```

This pipeline example offers a comprehensive demonstration of how to efficiently ingest, process, and expose real-time event data. Utilizing Apache Flink as the core engine for stream processing, it handles everything from data cleaning and transformation to alert generation. The integration with Kafka serves as both the data source and sink, making this architecture highly extensible and capable of handling high data volumes.

Exposing flat files

To transfer flat files, you can use several protocols that have been developed to facilitate these operations, among which **File Transfer Protocol (FTP)**, **Web Distributed Authoring and Versioning (WebDAV)**, and others such as **Hypertext Transfer Protocol (HTTP)**, **Secure Copy Protocol (SCP)**, and **SSH File Transfer Protocol (SFTP)** stand out.

FTP, an internet standard protocol, is one of the earliest methods used to transfer files between hosts over a TCP-based network. It uses a client-server architecture where a client initiates a connection to a server to download or upload files. FTP can handle large files and directories, but it lacks encryption for data transfer, making it less secure.

To address this security issue, SFTP was introduced. It operates over **Secure Shell** (**SSH**) connections, providing the functionality of FTP, but with a secure, encrypted connection.

WebDAV, an extension of the HTTP protocol, enables users to manage and edit files on a remote web server. Unlike FTP, WebDAV supports file locking and versioning, thus preventing conflicts when multiple users edit a file simultaneously.

SCP is based on the BSD RCP protocol, which is another method for secure file transfer. Like SFTP, it uses SSH for data transfer, providing security during the transmission.

HTTP isn't traditionally used for file transfers, but its widespread use on the web has led to its application for this purpose. HTTP servers can make files available for download and modern web technologies allow file uploads as well.

Each protocol comes with its advantages and limitations, and the choice depends on factors such as security needs, file size, compatibility, and the nature of the data being transferred. Regardless of the protocol chosen, effective file transfer is a fundamental aspect of data management and accessibility in our interconnected digital world.

Exposing data APIs

The primary objective of data exposure through data API protocols is to facilitate access to data for various applications, with a specific emphasis on data analytics and machine learning. These use cases require protocols that are inherently data-oriented and simplify data manipulation, unlike service-oriented protocols such as REST web APIs.

Data APIs enable us to securely access, analyze, and visualize data from disparate sections of our system or even external systems. They offer a standardized methodology for data requests and retrieval. For instance, a business intelligence tool might utilize a data API to aggregate information from multiple databases.

Such data exposition protocols often necessitate the remodeling of data to cater more effectively to consumption queries. The remodeling often involves data rearrangement, reorganization, and aggregation, ranging from simple aggregates to more complex ones.

Typically, in data warehouses with a governed data size or databases with an unpredictable consumption pattern, the exposition model relies on flat tables, star, or snowflake schema models. However, when dealing with massive data volumes or when usage patterns are known, the "design-by-query" pattern becomes incredibly useful. This pattern models the data precisely as expected by consumers, reducing the amount of data that's fetched, processed, and transmitted. The modeling process leverages processing engines discussed in depth in previous chapters.

These protocols and exposition models offer numerous benefits, such as simplifying data manipulation and enhancing performance when dealing with large data batches. This is particularly relevant in analytics and data science use cases that routinely handle large volumes of data.

For example, data manipulation is streamlined due to the close association between querying and processing languages and the data model itself. This relationship aids in circumventing the complexities of unsuitable data handling methods prevalent in service-oriented technologies such as REST API.

In conclusion, data APIs are an efficient mechanism for data publication and utilization for analysis and other applications. They offer a safe and structured conduit to data stored in multiple locations within or outside an organization. It's vital to consider the unique needs of your system and use cases when designing and exposing your data.

Furthermore, web APIs, an evolving segment within data exposition, deserve special attention. As the digital environment continues to evolve, these technologies are crucial in enabling targeted and efficient data access. This discussion will delve into the specifics of exposing web APIs while focusing on REST and GraphQL, and also highlight additional protocols such as WebSocket, SOAP, and gRPC to provide a holistic view of the topic.

> **Performance warning**
>
> Performance considerations are crucial when employing data APIs, especially when selecting the right protocols. Using inappropriate protocols such as REST APIs for large-scale data exposition could lead to bottlenecks due to rapid requests, HTTP protocol overheads, and extra mapping operations from data models to result models. To mitigate this, remember to implement pagination strategies, which can efficiently manage large datasets and significantly enhance performance.

ODBC/JDBC

Both the ODBC and JDBC APIs allow software to communicate with a database. Both provide a standard interface for communicating with databases. These protocols are frequently employed when an RDBMS or **Enterprise Data Warehouse** (**EDWH**) system is utilized as the data's underlying storage layer. Not only that, but with the emergence of modern technologies such as Apache Hive, Apache Presto/Trino, or AWS Athena, it is easy to utilize such protocols in data lake or lakehouse systems. Those protocols are primarily consumed using SQL or some of its derivates to query and manipulate data and get as near to data as feasible.

ODBC provides a universal API for connecting to relational, flat, or hierarchical databases. Since ODBC is not tied to any specific platform or programming language, it can be used with any system that implements the ODBC protocol. This adaptability makes ODBC an attractive option for exposing data APIs, particularly when working with disparate systems.

Consider, for example, a big retail company that you might be familiar with. They have stores in different parts of the world, and all of these stores produce a million of transactional data. This data is usually stored in databases that are specific to each location and can be in different types of RDBMSs, such as PostgreSQL, MySQL, or SQL Server.

Imagine you're the data architect in this company. You're tasked with bringing all this data together for important business insights such as tracking sales trends, managing inventory, and understanding customer behavior.

Here's where the magic of ODBC API comes into play. This tool allows you to tap into each of these databases with its SQL querying abilities, no matter where they're located or what type of RDMS they are. It's like having a universal key to all the data treasure chests!

Now, this data can be kept in any type of central repository, including a data warehouse or a data lake. Once that is done, it can be organized in a way that works for your analytics program. A star schema could be a suitable fit in this instance to cover most of the use cases, with sales serving as the central fact table and product, store, customer, and time as dimensions branching out from it. Utilizing modeling patterns such as **design-by-query**, which categorizes and orders data according to consumption questions, might help improve performance for use cases that demand a greater focus on efficiency because it streamlines the process of finding data.

GraphQL

GraphQL is a query language as well as an API runtime. It was built by Facebook to address the shortcomings of REST APIs. The fundamental advantage of GraphQL is that it allows clients to request only the information they require, which can significantly reduce network traffic. It is constantly read, edited, and updated (subscriptions). The ability to adapt offers the potential to improve network efficiency and productivity. However, for simple use cases, a GraphQL API may be more complex to develop than a REST API. Because it is so new, developers may face a steeper learning curve.

Consider a mobile app development company building an application for a music streaming service. The app needs to display information about the artists, albums, and songs. Traditional RESTful services would require separate endpoints for each data type, leading to multiple network requests and potentially over-fetching data. With REST APIs, you might have to hit an endpoint such as `/artists/{id}` to get artist details, then `/artists/{id}/albums` to fetch their albums, and subsequently `/albums/{id}/songs` to get the songs in each album.

In this situation, using GraphQL can significantly improve the efficiency of data retrieval operations. GraphQL, with its flexible querying capabilities, allows clients to specify exactly what data they need, reducing the amount of data that's transferred over the network. The app can make a single, succinct request, like so:

```
{
  artist(id: "123") {
    name
```

```
    albums {
      title
      songs {
        name
        duration
      }
    }
  }
}
```

This single request will return the artist's name, the titles of their albums, and the name and duration of each song on those albums. The server will return a JSON object that exactly matches these characteristics, giving the app just the data it needs – nothing more, nothing less. This use case highlights how GraphQL can simplify data requirements for client apps by lowering the quantity of data that's fetched and delivered and the number of network requests. It demonstrates the strength of GraphQL in delivering efficient, flexible, and powerful APIs, making it a popular choice for modern online and mobile apps.

OData

OData is an open standard that allows for the creation and consumption of queryable and interoperable RESTful APIs in a simple and standard way. It enables full **Create, Read, Update, Delete (CRUD)** support via standard HTTP protocols. It's a great option for exposing data over the web because it lets clients query and alter data using conventional HTTP protocols. Data can be stored in a wide range of places, from relational databases and filesystems to CMS and static web pages, so OData APIs come in handy when accessing this information.

Suppose you have an API that exposes a list of employees in a company. A basic OData endpoint for this data might look something like this:

```
https://api.yourcompany.com/odata/Employees
```

You can then use OData's query features to filter, sort, and shape this data directly from the URL. For example, to return only employees that have a last name starting with `'A'`, you could use the following URL:

```
https://api.yourcompany.com/odata/
Employees?$filter=startswith(lastName, 'A') eq true
```

`$filter` is a system query option that's defined by OData to filter the results. `startswith(lastName, 'A') eq true` is the filter expression, which means it only returns employees where it's true that their `lastName` property starts with `'A'`.

Similarly, you can use OData's query features to sort the data:

```
https://api.yourcompany.com/odata/Employees?$orderby=lastName
```

In this example, the `$orderby` query option will sort the employees by their last name in ascending order. These are just a few instances of what OData can do. The protocol adds numerous new features for altering and querying data.

Data modeling

Data modeling is crucial for maximizing the effectiveness of data exposure. Its primary purpose is to optimize data retrieval, reducing the time required to fetch data and minimizing computational processes such as joins. In essence, data modeling provides a high-level blueprint dictating the organization, storage, and accessibility of data.

One widespread technique in data modeling to optimize data retrieval is data flattening. This practice transforms hierarchical data structures into a "flat" table format, reducing the operations necessary to extract data and subsequently accelerating retrieval times. However, it's important to note that data flattening can lead to redundancy and potential loss of certain data element relationships.

Another pivotal aspect of data modeling is the control and reduction of data depth. Data depth refers to the degree of nested data structures within a dataset. Too much depth can introduce complexity and slow down data access and processing times. It's essential to manage this depth effectively – limiting excessive nesting can enhance data interpretability, speed up access, and simplify data manipulation.

Particularly in analytics contexts where historical data is significant, managing the depth of data history becomes vital. Storing and accessing vast amounts of historical data can severely impact performance. Hence, it's advisable to carefully consider the depth of data history needed for your use cases and apply appropriate strategies to limit the depth, such as data archiving or summarization, thereby optimizing performance.

The concept of **design by query** is another key data modeling consideration. This strategy involves modeling data so that it aligns closely with anticipated query patterns. By doing so, response times are improved, and unnecessary data processing is minimized. This approach is especially beneficial when dealing with large datasets and known usage patterns.

Lastly, which underlying data storage technology is chosen can greatly influence your data modeling approach. Choices range from traditional RDBMSs to NoSQL databases and modern data lakes. Each offers unique characteristics impacting data retrieval efficiency – an RDBMS may be perfect for complex queries on structured data, while NoSQL databases or data lakes offer more scalability and flexibility for unstructured or semi-structured data.

In conclusion, effective data modeling is pivotal for efficient data exposure. By carefully considering aspects such as data flattening, data depth control, design by query, and the appropriate choice of data storage technology, organizations can significantly enhance their data accessibility and retrieval performance.

Exposing data via an engine

We'll now examine data exposition and specific solutions and integrated engines to achieve it. Dedicated solutions include API creation, deployment, monitoring, and retirement with security and performance optimization. Then, we'll discuss **massively parallel processing** (**MPP**) and NoSQL databases' advantages and optimization methodologies for data exposure. These solutions should be chosen based on an organization's needs to maximize data presentation.

Dedicated solutions

The all-inclusive management of an API's lifespan is a cornerstone of these dedicated data exposition solutions, encompassing everything from the design and deployment stages to versioning, monitoring, and eventual retirement of APIs. Tools such as graphical design interfaces, code generation capabilities, testing suites, and version control systems ensure APIs remain effective, relevant, and updated, aligning with evolving data and business requirements.

Data security is integral to these solutions, offering a breadth of features from authentication and authorization to encryption and auditing, all of which are designed to safeguard data. This intricate web of security mechanisms restricts data access to authorized users and ensures data transmissions occur securely.

These solutions also prioritize performance optimization, a crucial attribute that ensures prompt data delivery, even under high-demand circumstances. Features ranging from load balancing to caching and query optimization bolster the system's ability to handle extensive loads effectively. For instance, in-memory data grid solutions such as Hazelcast can dramatically enhance performance by caching frequently accessed data.

Dedicated data exposition solutions, including prominent open source options such as Apache Kafka and Tyk, offer an array of capabilities, from data ingestion and processing to comprehensive API life cycle management. Platforms such as MuleSoft, Apigee, and Kong offer superior API management capabilities, covering everything from design and deployment to versioning and monitoring.

Moreover, these solutions ensure smooth integration with other systems and services, a critical factor in creating a holistic data infrastructure capable of managing diverse data sources and targets. This interoperability enables the solution to effectively interact with other components in an organization's tech stack, such as databases, data lakes, and business intelligence tools.

In conclusion, choosing dedicated data exposition solutions should be driven by their robust capabilities across these vital areas. While the specific solution that's chosen may depend on an organization's unique needs and context, these foundational functionalities undeniably form the backbone of effective data exposition.

Integrated engine

For efficient data exposure, MPP and NoSQL databases are important data management solutions. MPP databases thrive in large-scale OLAP-oriented data processing because of their analytics-optimized engines, parallel-processing capacities, and meticulous data modeling. On the other hand, NoSQL databases are valued for their scalability and data modeling flexibility since they necessitate customized techniques that are matched with their non-relational structure. Both systems, when expertly connected with other data technologies, can serve as the foundation for a versatile, all-encompassing data architecture.

MPP engine

Optimizing data exposition with integrated MPP databases involves careful data structuring, querying, and accessing, paying heed to the unique capabilities of MPP architectures. This includes designing data models and queries for efficient data distribution across all nodes, optimizing data layout with appropriate partitioning and indexing strategies, and fine-tuning queries to maximize parallel processing. Regular monitoring and adjustments are crucial for maintaining optimal performance.

Integrating MPP databases with other data exposition technologies can further enhance their efficiency. Near-real-time data handling benefits from the parallel processing abilities of MPP systems when coupled with dashboarding and reporting technologies such as Tableau, PowerBI, and others. Lastly, data storage systems such as data lakes or NoSQL databases can complement MPP for data storage and processing.

NoSQL databases

Optimizing data exposition with NoSQL databases involves strategic data modeling, query tuning, and continuous performance monitoring tailored to NoSQL's unique, non-relational characteristics. Key strategies include designing data models in line with NoSQL's various data modeling types and storage formats, understanding and leveraging the query language of the specific NoSQL database, and periodically adjusting system parameters and resources for peak efficiency. Integrating NoSQL databases with data exposition technologies such as streaming tools, web APIs, and various data storage systems can significantly enhance data handling, accessibility, and performance. Web APIs such as REST and GraphQL or gRPC-based solutions can also be beneficial and can provide efficient data exposure, depending on the system's needs.

By harmonizing these strategies, organizations can greatly improve their data infrastructure's utility and performance.

Next, we'll focus on APIs and strategy.

A focus on APIs and strategy

The critical role of APIs in the realm of data integration is a subject of increasing importance. APIs, in essence, are sets of instructions or rules that enable different software applications to communicate and exchange data. They provide a structured method for diverse systems to interconnect, fostering a higher degree of interoperability among various software components. By offering a clear and consistent means for data exchange, APIs act as critical facilitators for seamless and efficient data integration.

Data integration itself is an essential process within the wider context of data management. It involves combining data from different sources into a unified, coherent view. This process is crucial for numerous tasks, from simple data analysis to more complex operations such as business intelligence, machine learning, and decision support systems. As the amount and variety of data grows, the importance of robust data integration strategies cannot be overstated.

Combining APIs with data integration workflows offers considerable benefits. Firstly, data integration can help reduce the amount of data to be fetched by the API and organize it in the most efficient way to be consumed by the consumers. Second, APIs simplify the process of obtaining data from different sources by providing a standardized method for requesting and receiving data. Third, APIs can be used to automate data integration processes, reducing the need for manual intervention and the risk of errors. Lastly, APIs support real-time data integration, allowing systems to pull the latest data from various sources as needed. Despite the apparent simplicity of APIs, they are powerful tools that can drive more efficient, flexible, and robust data integration. The following sections will delve deeper into API design best practices, implementation considerations, and the overall API strategy. We will explore how organizations can effectively leverage APIs to enhance their data integration efforts, address challenges, and seize opportunities in our increasingly data-driven world.

API design best practices

When it comes to building APIs, simply having a functional solution isn't enough. The design of an API can significantly influence the user experience and the ease of integration, thus having long-term implications for the API's success. High-quality APIs tend to follow a set of best practices in their design, including aspects such as versioning, security, and documentation.

API versioning

API versioning is one of the fundamental principles that ensures the evolution of an API over time. As applications grow, their requirements change, which often leads to necessary changes in the API's structure or behavior. These changes can potentially disrupt existing API consumers if they're not managed properly. Thus, API versioning comes into play.

Versioning involves indicating a specific API version that the client wishes to interact with. If the client doesn't specify a version, they interact with the most current version. There are multiple approaches to API versioning, each with its pros and cons.

The most popular strategies include URI versioning, where the version number is part of the API's URI, and request header versioning, where the version number is included in the HTTP header. Less commonly, versioning can be included as a query parameter.

URI versioning is straightforward to implement. However, it can lead to URL pollution if not managed carefully. Request header versioning is more elegant and doesn't impact the URL structure, but it's less visible and can complicate debugging.

When implementing versioning, it's crucial to have a clear policy about supporting older versions, deprecation, and user communication. This ensures that API consumers have ample time to adjust their systems when changes occur, reducing disruption and maintaining a positive developer experience.

API security

Security is a cornerstone of any API design. With APIs acting as gateways to potentially sensitive data and services, robust security measures are non-negotiable.

Authentication and authorization are fundamental aspects of API security. Authentication confirms the identity of the user or system trying to access the API, while authorization determines what that user or system is allowed to do. APIs can use different mechanisms for authentication, such as API keys, OAuth, or **JSON Web Tokens (JWT)**.

Data confidentiality and integrity are also essential. Encryption, both in transit and at rest, ensures that the data cannot be read if intercepted. Using HTTPS for data in transit is the standard practice. Data integrity checks, such as digital signatures or checksums, can verify that the data hasn't been tampered with during transmission.

Rate limiting is another important security consideration. It involves limiting the number of API requests a client can make in a specific period. This helps prevent abuse, protect the API from being overwhelmed, and maintain quality of service for all users.

Lastly, input validation and error handling should be carefully designed to prevent attacks such as SQL injection and avoid revealing sensitive information in error messages. All user inputs should be treated as potentially dangerous and be thoroughly validated before processing.

API documentation

Well-crafted API documentation is one of the most valuable assets for an API's user base. It acts as a guide, offering users clear and concise instructions about how to interact with the API effectively. Effective documentation accelerates adoption and usage, reduces integration errors, and improves the overall developer experience.

API documentation should be comprehensive and cover all aspects of the API, including endpoints, request/response formats, error codes, and common usage examples. It should also be structured and organized in a user-friendly manner, making it easy to find relevant information quickly.

The documentation should represent the current state of the API and should be updated regularly as the API evolves. This is where versioning intersects with documentation. To avoid confusion and guarantee users have the relevant information for the API version they're using, each version of an API should have its own set of documentation.

Tools such as Swagger or Postman can help automate the documentation process and maintain accuracy. Additionally, these tools can generate interactive documentation, enabling users to make live API calls directly within the documentation, enhancing their understanding and testing capabilities.

In conclusion, API versioning, security, and documentation form the backbone of API design best practices. Implementing these elements thoughtfully can significantly enhance the utility, usability, and longevity of an API, creating a positive experience for all stakeholders. However, these are not exhaustive, and other considerations, such as performance, scalability, and integration with other systems, play significant roles in designing successful APIs.

Integration with other systems and services

Successful APIs are not islands but integral parts of a broader system landscape. Their design must consider easy integration with various other systems and services, which may range from cloud services to **enterprise integration patterns (EIPs)** and third-party applications.

Integration with cloud services is becoming increasingly important as many companies transition to cloud-based architectures. These services provide vast capabilities and resources that can augment the functionality and efficiency of your API. For example, cloud storage services can handle large datasets, cloud databases can provide scalable and reliable data persistence, and cloud-based machine learning services can add advanced analytical capabilities to your API. When designing APIs, consider how they will interact with these services, including aspects such as authentication, data transfer methods, error handling, and FinOps. EIPs offer time-tested solutions for various challenges that arise when integrating different systems. They provide a standardized way to deal with common integration scenarios such as data transformation, message routing, or handling asynchronous messaging. By aligning your API design with relevant EIPs, you can enhance its compatibility with other systems and simplify integration tasks.

Third-party applications are another crucial consideration. These might be customer-facing apps that use your API to provide functionality to their users or internal apps that utilize your API for data access or processing tasks. The design of your API can have a significant impact on the user experience of these apps. Ensuring that your API follows industry standards, has a stable and well-documented interface, and provides efficient and reliable service can greatly facilitate integration with these applications.

Also, APIs should be designed with flexibility in mind, allowing easy expansion or modification to support new integration scenarios as they arise. This includes designing for extensibility, providing clear and comprehensive documentation, and implementing robust error handling to ensure graceful failure and easy troubleshooting during integration.

In essence, an API's ability to integrate seamlessly with various systems and services forms a fundamental aspect of its success. Given the diverse array of potential integrations, this is a complex task that demands careful planning and thoughtful design. However, the payoff in terms of broader API applicability, increased adoption, and improved user satisfaction makes this effort worthwhile.

API implementation considerations

It's important to realize that API implementation isn't just about creating an API. The goal is to design and implement a strong, scalable, cost-effective, and performant API that gives users a smooth experience. Well-implemented APIs are stable, easy to use, and can gracefully handle failures and scale with demand. Therefore, API implementation is important. Your API's success and sustainability depend on them; thus, they should be part of your API strategy from the start. Scalability, speed, and error handling are an API implementation's three most important characteristics.

Scalability

Scalability is the cornerstone of a successful API and its ability to accommodate growth over time. APIs must demonstrate resilience and adaptability as their user base expands, data volume increases or the frequency of calls escalates.

The underlying architecture of an API plays a significant role in ensuring scalability. Microservice architecture, for instance, can improve scalability. It decomposes the API into small, independent services, allowing individual components to scale independently based on demand.

Rate limiting is another important scalability strategy. By placing a cap on the number of requests a consumer can make within a certain time, you ensure that the system doesn't get overwhelmed by too many simultaneous requests.

Furthermore, the use of cloud-based solutions can aid in scalability. Cloud platforms often provide auto-scaling features, which automatically adjust the available resources based on the load. This means that during periods of high demand, the cloud platform will automatically allocate more resources to your API, and during periods of low demand, it will reduce the resources, thereby optimizing costs.

Performance

API performance has a direct impact on the user experience and your API's reputation. Consumers expect rapid, consistent responses from APIs.

There are various techniques to enhance API performance. For example, using HTTP/2 can reduce latency and allow for multiplexing, while Gzip compression can make API responses smaller and faster to transmit.

Another way to enhance performance is by paginating the API responses, especially for APIs that return large datasets. Pagination ensures that the response is not too large as it could otherwise result in timeouts or performance issues.

Furthermore, adopting a **content delivery network** (**CDN**) can enhance performance by caching the API's responses at the edge locations, thereby reducing the time taken to deliver responses to the consumers.

Error handling

Robust error handling is a testament to a well-implemented API. A good API not only needs to function correctly but also fail correctly.

Graceful degradation is a useful strategy here. This principle is about building your API in such a way that, even in the event of a failure, the API can continue to operate but provide a reduced level of functionality.

In addition to sending error messages, the API could implement an exponential backoff strategy, advising the consumers to progressively increase the wait time between retries, thus minimizing the load on the server during an error state.

Also, consider implementing a dead-letter queue, a service that collects failed requests for later analysis. This way, you can study why certain requests fail and improve your system based on your findings.

In conclusion, an API's implementation isn't just about getting the job done – it's about how well it's done, ensuring that it's scalable, performs optimally, and handles errors efficiently. Each of these areas is a field of study and is worth understanding deeply for anyone serious about API development.

FinOps

In the cloud context, FinOps for APIs is essential, particularly with the pay-as-you-go pricing model of cloud services. Since cloud providers usually charge for data exiting their systems, it's crucial to design APIs that minimize outbound data transfers to manage costs effectively. Efficient FinOps strategies include monitoring and optimizing API usage with a focus on data transfer efficiency. Implementing caching and selecting efficient data formats are key to reducing data egress charges and outbound data costs. Regular adjustments to resource allocations, informed by API usage patterns, help in balancing performance with cost. This approach ensures that outbound data is managed wisely to avoid unnecessary expenses, maintaining an optimal balance between functionality and expenditure.

API testing

API testing is an indispensable part of the API life cycle that's vital for ensuring the stability, security, and efficiency of your APIs. Different types of testing can be conducted throughout the life cycle, each focusing on different aspects of the API and serving distinct purposes.

Unit tests are the first line of defense. They are designed to test individual components or functionality in isolation to ensure that each part of the API works correctly. Unit tests help developers identify issues early in the development cycle and make debugging easier by narrowing down the potential causes of an error.

Integration tests come next, focusing on the interactions between different components of your API. They validate that multiple units work together correctly, ensuring that the API behaves as expected when different parts interact. This kind of testing is critical because even if individual units work perfectly in isolation, issues may arise when they interact.

Load tests aim to test the API's ability to handle many simultaneous requests and assess how the API performs under high traffic or data load. Load testing can uncover issues related to the API's scalability and help you understand how your API will perform under peak load conditions, providing valuable insights for capacity planning and optimization efforts.

Finally, **security tests** are crucial for any API. APIs often act as gatekeepers to sensitive data, and any security vulnerability can lead to severe consequences. Security testing aims to uncover vulnerabilities such as unauthorized data access, SQL injection, and **cross-site scripting** (**XSS**). Regular security testing can help ensure that your API stays resilient against various attack vectors and that any new changes don't introduce additional vulnerabilities.

The frequency and rigor of each type of test depend on the API's criticality, its usage patterns, and the sensitivity of the data it handles. But as a rule, regular and comprehensive testing should be a cornerstone of your API implementation strategy.

API strategy and governance

Developing and maintaining an API strategy and governance structure is integral to managing the growth and usage of APIs within an organization. It comprises creating effective plans and roadmaps, constant monitoring and data analysis, and a life cycle approach to API management. Let's delve deeper into each of these crucial elements.

Planning and roadmaps

To kickstart the API strategy, the organization must first lay down its objectives. Clearly defining the API's business value is crucial. It could be enhancing the customer experience, integrating with third-party services, or driving innovation and new business models.

Next, it's about putting these ideas into a structured roadmap. This roadmap represents a sequence of actions or stages leading to a particular long-term goal. It's crucial that it is built while keeping the organization's long-term strategy in mind and that it is flexible enough to adapt to changing circumstances. It should include details on resource allocation, anticipated challenges, and the estimated timeline for the API's rollout.

A well-thought-out roadmap aids in envisioning how the API will evolve with time and how it aligns with the organization's objectives. An API roadmap is not a one-and-done document; it should be revisited and revised regularly as the business, technology, and market landscapes evolve.

Monitoring and analytics

After the APIs are live and in use, the next crucial aspect of API strategy and governance is continuous monitoring and analysis. Monitoring involves tracking the performance of APIs, detecting problems before they become critical, and ensuring that the **service-level agreements** (**SLAs**) are being met. The data that's collected during monitoring, such as error rates, latency, and throughput, can help identify bottlenecks and areas for improvement.

On the other hand, API analytics focuses on understanding the usage patterns, user behaviors, and business value derived from the APIs. It can offer insights into which features are popular, help spot trends, identify peak usage times, and even detect potential misuse or abuse of the APIs. Analytics can also inform decision-making regarding future enhancements and aid in making informed business decisions.

API life cycle management

Lastly, API life cycle management focuses on the holistic care of an API, from inception to deprecation. It requires regular review and updates to ensure the API continues to deliver its intended value.

The API life cycle includes several stages – planning, designing, implementing, testing, deploying, managing, versioning, and, eventually, retiring. Each stage requires its unique set of best practices and considerations. For instance, during the versioning stage, it's crucial to manage different versions of the API effectively. It ensures smooth transitions and reduces disruptions for the users.

Similarly, deprecation and retirement must be handled delicately, giving users ample notice and alternative options if possible. Therefore, API life cycle management should aim at minimizing disruptions while continually improving the API to meet evolving needs.

To supplement life cycle management, governance policies should be in place to control who can make changes to the API, what changes are allowed, and how those changes should be documented and communicated. This ensures consistency and reliability, building trust among users and developers.

In conclusion, the importance of API strategy and governance can't be overemphasized. Through strategic planning, consistent monitoring and analysis, and comprehensive life cycle management, organizations can create and maintain robust, secure, and valuable APIs, thereby reaping substantial business benefits.

Next, we'll discuss a comparative analysis of data exposure solutions.

A comparative analysis of data exposure solutions

Each technology has a unique purpose, use case type, and set of operations they excel in. They also employ different querying approaches and data fetching/access types. While some technologies are push/pull in nature, others focus on pull mechanisms. The following table highlights the unique advantages and potential warnings associated with each technology. This comparative analysis can assist in making informed decisions when choosing a technology that best fits specific data needs and application requirements.

The following table provides a comparative overview of various data technologies – Stream, ODBC/JDBC, OData, GraphQL, and REST APIs:

	Stream	ODBC/JDBC	ODATA	GraphQL	Rest API
Purpose	Analytics and operational	Analytics and operational	Analytics and operational	Mainly operational	Operational and data query
Use Case Type	Real-time analytics and event processing	Reporting and dashboarding	N/A	Web/desktop-based apps	Web/desktop-based apps
Operations	Publish, notify, and subscribe	Projection, aggregation, and joins	Data access and manipulation	Real-time updates, single-page applications, and CRUD operations	CRUD operations
Querying Approach	Topic-centric	Data-centric	Data-centric	Data-centric	Service-centric
Data Fetching/ Access Type	Continuous streaming	Direct and on-demand	On-demand and granular	On-demand, granular, and stream	On-demand and granular
Push/Pull	Push/Pull	Pull	Pull	Push/pull	Pull
Querying Language	Dependent on the streaming platform (for example, SQL-like for Kafka or binary)	Mainly SQL	REST and SQL	GraphQL	REST

	Stream	**ODBC/JDBC**	**ODATA**	**GraphQL**	**Rest API**
Advantage/ Warning	**Advantage:** Real-time data processing	**Advantage:** Widely used and robust	**Advantage:** Standardized and supports CRUD operations	**Advantage:** Highly flexible and avoids over-fetching/under-fetching	**Advantage:** Simple and widely used
	Warning: Can be complex to manage	**Warning:** Can be limited by the capabilities of the underlying database	**Warning:** May require a complex setup	**Warning:** Can be complex to set up	**Warning:** Can lead to over-fetching/ under-fetching

Table 11.1 – A table for comparing exposition solutions

Finally, the variety of data technologies – Stream, ODBC/JDBC, ODATA, GraphQL, and REST APIs – meets a wide range of application needs, from real-time analytics to ordinary CRUD operations. Each technology has its own set of advantages and disadvantages that must be addressed based on the specific use case and operational requirements.

Streaming platforms can analyze data in real time, making them excellent for real-time analytics and event processing. Because it is extensively used and robust, ODBC/JDBC is frequently used for reporting and dashboarding. ODATA provides a consistent way to CRUD activities, although it may necessitate a complex setup. GraphQL stands out for its great flexibility, which prevents over-fetching and under-fetching of data, whereas a REST API, due to its simplicity and widespread use, may cause over-fetching or under-fetching.

Understanding these various qualities can help you select the most appropriate technology and its optimization for data-intensive applications. As data requirements change, it's critical to constantly review and select the appropriate technology for your individual needs to balance the ease of setup, flexibility, robustness, and specific data processing requirements.

Summary

This chapter delved into the diverse ways to expose data using various technologies and APIs. We started by examining different data exposition technologies such as Streams, REST APIs/GraphQL, WebSocket, SOAP, and gRPC, emphasizing the strengths and challenges of each. Through real-world use cases, we discussed their applications, their different access types, the protocols used, and their roles in both NoSQL and RDBMS environments.

Then, we explored the crucial stage of data preparation and the importance of security in data exposition. We discussed techniques for reducing data history and the various data modeling methods that are aimed at performance enhancement and retrieval time reduction. Essential security measures such as anonymization, encryption, role-based access control, and authentication were also covered.

The focus then shifted to APIs and their strategies, exploring their significance in data integration. We reviewed API design best practices, including versioning, security, and documentation, and the considerations necessary for implementing APIs. An in-depth discussion about API scalability, performance, error handling, and testing provided a thorough understanding of API implementation considerations. This chapter wrapped up with an overview of API strategy and governance, including planning, monitoring, and life cycle management, as well as a brief look at MPP databases.

This chapter was enriched with a deep dive into MPP databases, where we examined their use cases, advantages, challenges, data modeling, and optimization strategies. It concluded by discussing the possibilities when integrating MPP databases or NoSQL databases with other data exposition technologies.

Moving forward to the next chapter, we will shift our focus to data preparation and analysis. This next chapter will explore why, when, and where to perform data preparation, strategies for choosing the right transformations, and key concepts for reporting and self-analysis. As we delve deeper into these topics, we will be building upon the concepts and techniques that were introduced in *Chapter 9*, providing you with an even broader understanding of the data management ecosystem.

12
Data Preparation and Analysis

Preparing and analyzing data is an important part of data science and analytics. As data sets grow in size and complexity, effective data preparation and analysis are more crucial than ever before for making informed decisions and gaining useful insights. This chapter goes into the procedures, tactics, and governing factors of carrying out such endeavors.

In the first part of the chapter, we break down what data preparation is, when it's needed, and where it's done. Data quality, scalability, reporting needs, data storage, governance, and cooperation are just a few of the things that affect when and where data preparation takes place.

Going further, we will delve into data transformation, discussing methods, options, and consequences. We'll discuss how to create a plan for transforming data, how to choose the best data transformations, and how to put that plan into action while maximizing its effectiveness. You'll get an understanding of the many methods of transformation, the criteria that go into choosing one, and how these ideas play out in actual applications.

Finally, we'll go into the final stages of data preparation and analysis: reporting and self-analysis. Best practices for report layout, data quality and consistency, and reader-specific reports are all things you'll learn. We will also offer self-analysis techniques and tools to help you better interpret data on your own and present that data in a meaningful and aesthetically appealing way.

By the end of this chapter, you will have a solid grounding in the fundamentals of data cleaning and analysis. You will have mastered the skills necessary to comprehend data needs, evaluate data quality, and coordinate tactics with analytics and reporting objectives. You'll learn to pick the right transformations for your data, put them into action, and maximize their effectiveness. You'll also be able to self-evaluate, adjust to new data requirements, and create effective reports. Your data handling skills will be greatly enhanced, and you'll be able to make important contributions to your company's data-driven decision-making using the information you've gained.

The following topics will be covered in this chapter:

- Why, when, and where to perform data preparation
- Strategy and the choice of transformations
- Key concepts for reporting and self-analysis

Why, when, and where to perform data preparation

In the dynamic world of data management and analysis, the preparation of data holds a pivotal role. This section aims to shed light on the key components and concepts of data preparation. It also underscores its significance in the broader framework of data integration.

Data preparation is often likened to setting the stage before a grand performance. It's the process of cleaning, structuring, and enriching raw data to improve its quality and usefulness. Similar to a well-prepared stage enhancing an artist's performance, well-prepared data can significantly improve the accuracy and reliability of data analysis, thereby leading to more insightful and actionable business intelligence.

First and foremost, let's delve into the essence of data preparation. At its core, it's about making raw data more suitable for analytics or other business processes. This involves various sub-processes, including data cleansing, data transformation, and data enrichment. Data cleansing corrects or removes data that is incorrect, incomplete, improperly formatted, or duplicated. Data transformation converts data from one format or structure to another, making it more accessible or suitable for specific uses. Data enrichment, on the other hand, enhances data with additional information to increase its value.

The importance of data preparation in data integration can't be overstated. Data integration involves consolidating data from various sources to provide a unified view, aiding in better decision-making. However, data from different sources often comes in different formats and structures and may contain errors.

For example, if inconsistent data formats are not addressed during preparation, the integrated data may contain errors that distort analysis results and lead to incorrect conclusions.

In a retail scenario, if product names aren't standardized across stores during data preparation, inventory analysis on the integrated data won't be accurate since the same product will appear under multiple names.

As another example, if there are numerous duplicate records in the raw data and these are not deduplicated during preparation, any aggregated metrics calculated on the integrated data will be inflated. In a customer database, if duplicate customer profiles aren't removed, the number of unique customers will be overestimated, skewing customer segmentation analysis.

This is where data preparation steps in, tidying up the data to ensure it's in a suitable state for integration. By aligning disparate data into a unified structure, eliminating inconsistencies, and enriching it with relevant information, data preparation enhances the effectiveness of data integration.

However, there are several difficulties associated with data preparation. The sheer amount of information presents one of the biggest obstacles. Maintaining data security and privacy while dealing with data in multiple formats are additional difficulties. Despite these challenges, good data preparation can greatly enhance the results of data integration.

Data preparation also involves a set of key components that contribute to its execution. These include data profiling, data validation, data standardization, and data matching. Data profiling involves examining the data to understand its structure, content, and quality. Data validation ensures that the data complies with the defined business rules and standards. Data standardization brings the data into a common format, allowing for better compatibility and comparison. Lastly, data matching identifies, links, or merges related entries within or across data sets.

The following screenshot shows the various aspects of data preparation:

Figure 12.1 – Various aspects of data preparation

In conclusion, data preparation is the critical step that guarantees the quality and usability of data, making it the backbone of data integration. A thorough familiarity with data structures and formats is required for this assignment. But when done right, it lays the path for solid, trustworthy, and insightful data analysis, which is priceless in the age of data-driven decision-making. You will have in-depth knowledge of the significance and application of data preparation after reading this section, as we delve deeper into its complexities.

Factors influencing when to perform data preparation

When contemplating the data preparation stage in data integration, one aspect that demands meticulous thought is the timing of the event. The question of 'when' is often critical, tied intrinsically to aspects such as data quality, system performance, and analytical requirements. To make an informed decision, let's dissect these elements further.

Data quality and consistency

The initial quality and consistency of data arriving in your system primarily dictate when data preparation should take place. The quality of data is a multi-faceted characteristic, usually gauged through parameters such as accuracy, completeness, consistency, reliability, and relevance. Each of these attributes bears its weight in deciding the optimal time for data preparation.

For example, consider a scenario where the incoming data streams frequently display inconsistency or contain a high proportion of missing or erroneous values. In such a case, performing data preparation early becomes paramount. By starting the data preparation process early, inconsistencies can be recognized and amended before they percolate through the system and instigate errors or inaccuracies in subsequent data processing and analysis.

However, in situations where data quality is consistently high with minimal missing or incorrect values, an alternate strategy might be more efficient. Batching the data and preparing it in larger, less frequent intervals can help economize computational resources needed for data preparation, thereby reducing the overall intricacy of the data integration process.

Imagine a climate study organization that gathers weather data from stations worldwide. The data, including temperatures, humidity, and wind speeds, comes in various qualities with occasional inconsistencies and missing values.

The organization uses tools such as Amazon S3 for storing data and Apache Spark for integration, quality checks, advanced data tasks, and machine learning.

Data from different weather stations may not follow the same format or units – some might record temperature in Celsius, others in Fahrenheit. So, it's crucial to normalize data for consistency and further analysis. Also sometimes, data from some stations might have missing values because of equipment issues or transmission errors. It's important to identify and handle these early to maintain the accuracy of the analysis. The system could fill in missing values with techniques such as interpolation or machine learning predictions based on past data and other variables' relationships.

However, since most weather station data is consistent and high quality, the organization batches the data to optimize computational resources used for data preparation. They store raw data from reliable stations in Amazon S3 and prepare it in larger, infrequent intervals. This saves computational resources and simplifies the overall integration process.

Performance and scalability

The overall performance of your data integration system and its ability to scale up also heavily influence when data preparation should occur. The timing of data preparation can have a ripple effect on the data pipeline's performance. If data preparation happens too early, it might lead to a bottleneck, impeding the overall system performance, which is generally the case with architectures based on ETL patterns. On the other hand, if data preparation is postponed excessively, the system might find it challenging to process large volumes of data efficiently, causing potential performance degradation and the potential for data loss.

Scalability is an equally crucial factor in this equation. As the volume of data to be handled rises, the system should be capable of scaling proportionately to manage the increased workload, which is generally the case with architectures based on ELT patterns such as data lake-based architectures.

Scalability refers to the ability of data systems and processes to handle increased data volume efficiently. As the volume of data needing preparation grows, the workflows and infrastructure must be able to scale up accordingly. Scalability issues arise when data pipelines are unable to process larger amounts of data within a reasonable time frame. This can lead to delays, lagged insights, and reduced organizational agility. Therefore, when designing data preparation architecture, scalability is a key consideration.

Scalability often hinges on the timing of data preparation. If executed correctly, data preparation can amplify the system's scalability by ensuring that data is consistently available in a format that can be processed and analyzed with ease.

Also, it's important to note how preparing data influences system performance when reading or writing data. The approach to data preparation can directly affect the system's efficiency depending on its requirements.

In systems where data reading is frequent, it's usual to prepare data in a way that benefits the user. By arranging and shaping data to align with how it's meant to be accessed, you can cut down on processing time. This might mean setting up schemas and indexes to streamline data retrieval. Preparing data might also involve denormalization, where you purposefully keep duplicate data to boost read speed, or sorting data based on common access patterns.

On the other hand, in systems where data writing is more common, it often works best to keep data in its initial form as long as possible. This delays processing and transformation steps, providing better scalability. By moving data transformation to later stages, you can process incoming data faster and more efficiently, avoiding potential bottlenecks.

However, keep in mind that this strategy might up computational and storage needs when it's time to read or analyze the data. This is because more work will be needed to prepare the data. So, it's crucial to strike a balance depending on your system's unique performance needs.

In summary, the timing of data preparation plays a significant role in system performance and scalability. This demands careful planning and design to ensure data preparation aids the system in meeting performance goals and scaling efficiently as data quantity and complexity grow. It's a delicate balance requiring a deep understanding of your system's needs, data characteristics, and organizational demands.

Use case requirements

The timing of data preparation also correlates with the requirements of the use case tasks that follow. If the objective is real-time analytics, data preparation and integration need to occur almost simultaneously with data arrival. This will ensure that the data is clean, consistent, and ready for analysis, providing users with the most accurate and up-to-date information. Any delay in data preparation can render the insights outdated.

On the other hand, if the analytical and reporting tasks are not time-sensitive and are more focused on historical trends, data preparation can be performed in batches at regular intervals and/or during non-peak hours. This method helps optimize the use of system resources, improves overall performance and allows for a more in-depth cleaning and transformation process, ensuring that the data is as accurate and consistent as possible.

Therefore, the timing of data preparation is not an arbitrary choice but a strategic decision with ramifications on the effectiveness and efficiency of the data integration process. It demands a comprehensive understanding of the quality and consistency of data, the system's performance capabilities and scalability, and the specific needs of downstream analytics and reporting tasks. A well-planned data preparation schedule can ensure that data is available for analysis whenever required, thereby empowering timely and informed decision-making. In the following section, we'll delve deeper into the factors determining where to perform data preparation.

Strategic planning and goal alignment are also essential factors to consider when deciding on the timing of data preparation. Every business has specific goals and objectives that it aims to achieve. The timing of data preparation should be aligned with these goals.

Resource optimization

Finally, resource optimization is a critical aspect to consider when deciding on the timing of data preparation. Data preparation can be a resource-intensive process, involving significant computational power and storage capacity. Therefore, the timing of data preparation should be strategically planned to optimize the use of available resources.

For example, if the data integration system is less busy during off-peak hours, it might be beneficial to schedule data preparation tasks during these times. This would allow the system to utilize its resources more efficiently, without affecting the performance of other critical tasks.

In conclusion, the timing of data preparation is a complex decision that involves a careful consideration of various factors. It's not just about when the data arrives in the system, but also about the quality and consistency of the data, the performance and scalability of the system, the specific requirements of analytics and reporting tasks, efficient data management, strategic planning, and resource optimization. By understanding and considering these factors, businesses can make more informed decisions about the timing of data preparation, ultimately leading to more efficient and effective data integration processes.

Factors influencing where to perform data preparation

Deciding where to perform data preparation is a crucial step in the data integration process. It's like picking the ideal location for your favorite game – the success of your strategy largely depends on it. The right choice can lead to streamlined processes, efficient collaboration, and improved data governance. Let's dive into some factors that can guide this decision.

Data storage and processing systems

Think about the device you're using to read this. Your choice was influenced by factors such as storage capacity, processing power, and the kind of tasks you planned to perform, right? Similarly, in the data world, the selection of data storage and processing systems significantly impacts where data preparation takes place.

If your organization deals with hefty data volumes or complex data types, you might lean towards powerful, distributed processing systems such as Hadoop or Spark. These systems are designed to handle heavy-duty processing tasks, making them excellent places for data preparation. On the other hand, if your data volume is manageable, traditional databases or even in-memory computing platforms might be sufficient.

Data governance and compliance

Let's say you're planning a surprise party for a friend. You wouldn't organize it in a place where surprise parties are against the rules, would you? Similarly, data preparation should happen in a location that respects data governance policies and regulatory compliance.

Data governance involves a set of practices ensuring high data quality throughout the complete lifecycle of data. It's like the rulebook for managing, improving, and protecting your data. The location of data preparation must align with these rules. For instance, some regulations might prohibit the transfer of data across borders. In such cases, data preparation needs to occur within the allowed geographical confines.

Collaboration and accessibility

Consider your favorite social networking app. It's popular because it promotes collaboration and is readily accessible, right? Likewise, data preparation should take place in a location that encourages collaboration and is easily accessible.

In today's interconnected world, teams often span across different geographical locations. The chosen location for data preparation should allow multiple users to access, modify, and work on the data simultaneously, fostering collaborative work. Technologies such as cloud-based data platforms have made this easier than ever, providing scalable, secure, and accessible solutions.

Remember, the 'where' of data preparation isn't a one-size-fits-all answer. It varies based on your data, your organization's needs, and the available technology. It's like picking the right venue for an event. The right place sets the stage for success, so choose wisely!

The impact of data volume and variety

Think about your local library. A small one may be perfect for a town with a few hundred residents, but it would struggle to serve a bustling city of millions. Similarly, the volume and variety of your data can heavily influence where you choose to perform data preparation.

Imagine having to process a few gigabytes of structured data – a traditional relational database system might be perfectly adequate. However, if you're dealing with petabytes of unstructured data, you'd need something more robust, such as a distributed processing system or a data lake. The location of your data preparation activities should ideally align with the scale and complexity of your data.

Security and privacy considerations

Remember those secret notes you passed around in school? You didn't want them falling into the wrong hands, right? Similarly, data often contains sensitive information that requires strict security measures.

Data breaches can have catastrophic consequences, ranging from financial losses to damage to an organization's reputation. Therefore, the location of data preparation should be secure, providing features such as encryption, access control, and audit trails. In many cases, this might mean choosing an on-premises solution over a cloud-based one, or vice versa, depending on which offers better security mechanisms.

Cost and resource availability

Picture this – you're planning a trip. You wouldn't book a hotel that's way out of your budget, would you? The same principle applies to data preparation. The costs associated with different locations for data preparation can vary widely, and it's essential to consider these while making your decision.

The costs aren't just monetary – they also include the resources required to set up and maintain the chosen location. Do you have the necessary hardware and infrastructure for an on-premises solution? Do you have the bandwidth needed for a cloud-based system? These are crucial questions to ask while deciding where to perform data preparation.

Integration with existing systems

Think about your home entertainment system. Adding a new device can be tricky if it doesn't play nicely with your existing setup. Similarly, the location of your data preparation activities should integrate seamlessly with your existing data architecture.

If your organization already uses a specific platform or system for data storage or analysis, it might be best to choose a location for data preparation that works well with these existing systems. This could mean less disruption, a lower learning curve, and quicker implementation.

Conclusion

In conclusion, choosing the right location for data preparation is a critical decision that can significantly influence your data integration process's efficiency and effectiveness. It's like finding the right home for your data – get it right, and you'll have a solid foundation for all your subsequent data activities. Next, we'll delve into developing a data transformation strategy, another vital aspect of data preparation. In our next section, we will shift our focus to the 'how' of data preparation – developing a robust data transformation strategy.

Next, we'll discuss strategy and the choice of transformations.

Strategy and the choice of transformations

In the vast field of data analysis, having a sound data transformation strategy is vital. Such a strategy streamlines the process of converting raw data into a more useful and appropriate format for analysis and decision-making. This section will delve into how to develop a data transformation strategy, focusing on understanding data requirements, assessing data quality and performance, and aligning with analytics and reporting goals.

Developing a data transformation strategy

Embarking upon the terrain of data transformation strategy, it's analogous to the work of an architect. Rather than building physical structures, however, we are curating the trajectory and architecture of data. It's indeed an exhilarating task.

Understanding your data requirements

Recognizing your data requirements is the first and foremost step in crafting a data transformation strategy. Imagine you're a detective, and the data is your case – you need to understand its nature, its characteristics, and its complexity.

Consider the nature of the data you're dealing with. Is it structured or unstructured? Structured data, such as that found in relational databases, follows a specific format, making it easier to manage and query. Unstructured data, such as social media posts or customer reviews, lacks a predefined format or organization, requiring additional processing to extract value.

The volume of data you're dealing with is another essential aspect. The size of your dataset can impact your choice of transformations, the hardware and software you use, and even the time it takes to perform the transformations. It's essential to have a clear idea of the amount of data you will be processing to ensure you have the necessary resources and capabilities in place.

Additionally, what kind of information is captured within the data? This can greatly influence the type of transformations needed. For instance, data about customer behavior might need a different transformation than financial data.

The goal of data transformation is not just to change the data's form but to make it more useful for your specific needs. This leads us to another important consideration: the intended outcome of your transformations. Are you preparing the data for a machine learning model, a statistical analysis, or business reports? Different goals necessitate different types of transformations.

Yet, a critical question remains at the center of this process: what is the data needed for? It is vital to understand not only what data you currently have but also what data you need to achieve your objectives. This involves considering the specific metrics or variables that are necessary for your analysis, the level of detail required (such as transaction-level data, aggregated data), and the time that the data should cover. Defining your data needs will provide a clear direction for your data transformation strategy, helping you focus on the most relevant data and transformations.

Assessing data quality and performance

Data quality is a comprehensive evaluation of the suitability of your data for your purposes. Think of it as a health check for your data. You wouldn't want to build a tower on a shaky foundation, would you?

Data quality refers to the data's accuracy, completeness, consistency, validity, and timeliness. High-quality data should accurately reflect the real-world construct they represent, be free of inconsistencies and errors, and be up to date. Poor data quality can lead to inaccurate analysis results, misguided decisions, and a loss of trust in the data and the systems that generate it.

Moreover, identifying the need for data plays a crucial role in maintaining data quality. For instance, if you have determined that you need real-time data for certain analyses, it's essential to ensure that your data systems can reliably provide up-to-date information. Conversely, if you need historical data, your focus should be on data preservation and archiving strategies.

Data performance, on the other hand, refers to how well your data can be processed. It's all about the speed, efficiency, and reliability of your data processing tasks. Good performance ensures that your data transformations run smoothly and quickly, allowing you to deliver insights on time. Performance is especially important when dealing with large volumes of data, where inefficiencies can slow down your operations and consume valuable resources.

Aligning with analytics and reporting goals

Data transformation is not an end but a means to an end. The final piece of the data transformation strategy puzzle is aligning your transformations with your analytics and reporting goals.

Think of your analytics and reporting goals as your destination, and your data as the vehicle that gets you there. Your transformation strategy is the roadmap that guides your journey.

Who will use the transformed data? What questions do they need to answer? What decisions will they make based on the data? These are all questions that can help you align your transformation strategy with your analytics and reporting goals.

Remember, the goal is to satisfy the need for data. The transformed data should not only be of high quality and aligned with the strategic goals, but it should also meet the specific data needs of different users. Whether it's providing accurate sales data for a business analyst, granular customer behavior data for a data scientist, or aggregated financial data for a CFO, ensuring that the transformed data meets these needs is a crucial part of your data transformation strategy.

If your users are data scientists developing predictive models, your transformation strategy might need to focus on preparing data for machine learning algorithms. If your users are business analysts, your strategy might need to emphasize making the data understandable and actionable.

Likewise, your organization's **Key Performance Indicators** (**KPIs**) and strategic goals should guide your transformation strategy. By focusing on the data that's most important to your organization's success, you can ensure your efforts are well-directed and impactful.

In conclusion, developing a data transformation strategy is like building a house. Just as you wouldn't start without a blueprint, understanding your data requirements, assessing your data quality and performance, and aligning with your analytics and reporting goals form the blueprint for your data transformation strategy.

So what does this mean practically? If you were building a house, you'd need to know the size, layout, and purpose of each room before you started. Similarly, understanding your data requirements involves knowing what kind of data you have, what you need it to do, and what form it needs to take to meet those needs.

You wouldn't build your dream home on a shaky foundation, would you? The same applies to data transformations. It's essential to perform a thorough check-up on your data's quality and performance before you begin. Just as a doctor would check for any underlying conditions before recommending a course of action, assessing your data's health can help you identify and address any potential problems early on.

Finally, think about your dream house again. Would you design it without considering the needs and preferences of the people who will be living in it? Of course not! In the same way, your analytics and reporting goals need to be at the forefront of your data transformation strategy. After all, data is only as valuable as the insights and decisions it enables.

Creating a robust and effective data transformation strategy may seem like a daunting task but remember that it's a process. As you work through each step, you'll build a deeper understanding of your data and how to transform it into a powerful tool for decision-making. Just like building a house, it takes time, effort, and patience, but the result is worth it: a wealth of valuable insights that can help drive your organization's success. So, it's time to roll up your sleeves, dive into your data, and start building your transformation strategy!

Data needs identification: from goals to detailed data sources

Data needs identification is a pivotal part of any data transformation strategy. It entails understanding the organization's analytics and reporting goals, translating these goals into data requirements, and defining the data sources that need to be captured. This process creates a seamless transition from high-level goals (gold/insight) to detailed data needs (silver), leading to the identification of the necessary data sources (bronze).

Understanding the reporting goals and KPIs

Identifying reporting goals and **KPIs** is the first step in data needs identification. This is where the organization's strategic objectives and operational targets translate into quantifiable metrics. Reporting goals and KPIs essentially function as the guiding star for all data-related initiatives, forming the top layer – the gold layer – in our data hierarchy.

For example, a retail business might have a reporting goal to increase customer retention. The KPI for this goal could be the rate of repeat customers. This top layer of insight not only sets the overall direction for the data transformation strategy but also serves as the reference point for all subsequent layers.

Identifying the detailed data needs

With a clear understanding of the reporting goals and KPIs, the next step is to identify the detailed data needs. This means understanding the specific types of data required to calculate your KPIs and answer your reporting questions. This represents the silver layer in our data hierarchy.

To continue with our retail example, to calculate the rate of repeat customers (our KPI), we would need detailed data about individual customer transactions. This might include the customer ID, the date of purchase, the items purchased, the total amount spent, and so on. Identifying these detailed data needs ensures that the organization can accurately track its KPIs and achieve its reporting goals.

Defining the data sources to be captured

Once the detailed data needs have been identified, the final step is to define the data sources that need to be captured. This is the bronze layer of our data hierarchy, where raw data is collected and stored for future processing.

In our retail example, the data sources could include transaction records from both online and physical stores, loyalty program databases, and **customer relationship management** (**CRM**) systems. It's essential to ensure that these data sources can provide the detailed data needed to track our KPIs.

Importantly, this stage also involves considering the structure and format of the data sources. Do they provide structured data that can be easily processed, or unstructured data that requires more extensive transformation? Understanding this will help shape the data transformation strategy.

Conclusion

The process of data needs identification creates a clear link between high-level goals and the raw data that underpins them. By moving from goals to detailed data needs, and from detailed data needs to data sources, an organization can ensure that its data transformation strategy is rooted in its operational and strategic objectives.

The process may be complex, requiring careful thought and coordination across different areas of the organization. However, it's a critical investment that will pay dividends in the form of more accurate reporting, better decision-making, and ultimately, an increased ability to meet organizational goals.

In essence, data needs identification as a bridge between the gold of insight and the bronze of raw data. By crossing this bridge, an organization can ensure that its data transformation strategy is not just technically sound, but also strategically aligned, creating a firm foundation for data-driven success.

Selecting appropriate data transformations

In this section, we shall delve deeply into data transformations, particularly focusing on commonly used techniques and factors that guide the selection of these transformations. Let us proceed with this analysis.

Common data transformation techniques

In the world of data analysis and modeling, a wide variety of data transformation techniques exist, each suitable for circumstances and data types. Let's delve into some of the most widely utilized techniques:

- **Normalization**: Frequently used in database management, normalization aims to reduce data redundancy and improve data integrity. It organizes data into tables where each data item has only one occurrence. This technique improves the efficiency of database operations.

- **Scaling**: This method is applied to adjust the range of data values. It's often used in machine learning to ensure that all features contribute equally to the model's performance. There are different methods of scaling such as Min-Max scaling and Z-score standardization.

- **One-hot encoding:** A crucial technique in handling categorical data for machine learning algorithms. This process converts categorical data into a binary vector representation, making it easier for algorithms to understand and process.

- **Binning**: This procedure involves grouping continuous data into different categories or ranges, known as bins. It's useful for reducing the effects of minor observation errors and the impact of outliers, thereby leading to a more robust model.

- **Imputation**: A technique that handles missing data by substituting them with statistical estimates such as the mean, median, or mode. For more complex scenarios, methods such as regression imputation or multiple imputation can be used.

- **Log transform**: This transformation method is useful when dealing with skewed data. It can help to normalize the distribution and manage the impact of outliers.

Factors influencing transformation choice

The selection of a transformation technique is often governed by a blend of various elements:

- **Nature of data**: The type, distribution, quality, and volume of data play a significant role in selecting an appropriate transformation. For instance, categorical data might require one-hot encoding, while continuous data may be better suited for scaling or binning.

- **Analysis or modeling requirements**: Different analytical methods and machine learning algorithms require data in distinct formats. As such, understanding the specific prerequisites of your chosen method is crucial to making an informed transformation choice.

- **Desired outcome**: The goal of the analysis or modeling also influences the selection of transformation. For instance, if the objective is to reduce the impact of outliers, binning might be an appropriate choice.

- **Computational efficiency**: The computational cost and time of executing transformations can also influence the choice, especially in large datasets. Some transformations may be computationally expensive and hence may not be suitable for very large datasets.

Case studies and examples

To illuminate these concepts, let's consider a couple of illustrative examples:

- **Example 1**: Customer segmentation: An e-commerce company wants to segment its customers based on purchasing behavior. The raw data includes various categorical data such as product categories and continuous data such as purchase amounts. The data scientist might choose a one-hot encoding for the categorical data and binning for the continuous data to create meaningful customer segments. Also, scaling may be necessary to ensure different variables contribute equally to the segmentation algorithm.

- **Example 2**: Predictive maintenance: A manufacturing company intends to predict machine failures using sensor data. The data contains missing values due to occasional sensor malfunctions. The data scientist may opt for imputation to fill these gaps, knowing that the chosen machine learning algorithm can't handle missing data. Also, as sensor readings can vary widely, normalization or scaling could be applied to manage this range.

The following screenshot shows a machine failure prediction use case:

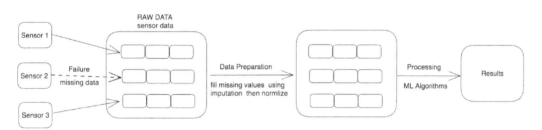

Figure 12.2 – Machine failures prediction use case

- **Example 3**: Real estate pricing: In a real estate pricing model, log transformation can be applied to manage the skewness in house prices. Similarly, one-hot encoding could handle categorical variables such as neighborhood or house type. Furthermore, given the impact of outliers in such datasets, binning or winsorizing could be used.

- **Example 4**: Algorithmic trading platform: An algorithmic trading company needs to optimize its stock trading algorithms by leveraging historical stock market data. The raw data contains stock prices, trading volumes, volatility measurements, news sentiment scores, and macroeconomic indicators. The data scientists need to transform this data into a format suitable for time series analysis and machine learning modeling. The following are some of the key transformations they apply:

  - Log transforms to normalize skewed price distribution data. This allows more accurate modeling of price movements.

- One-hot encoding of categorical variables such as stock sectors, ratings, and news sentiment scores. Enables the models to interpret the categories.

- Feature scaling of values such as trading volumes, volatility, and economic indicators. Normalizes the data to a standard range so all features can be compared.

- Time series formatting such as lagging and rolling windows. Analyzing temporal relationships and trends is key for forecasting.

- Imputation of missing values using interpolation or related data. It prevents models from disregarding records with gaps.

- Binning/discretization of continuous data such as prices into price change buckets. It reduces the effects of noise on raw prices.

In conclusion, the choice of data transformations is a careful balance between the nature of the data, the requirements of the analysis or modeling, the desired outcomes, and computational efficiency. By understanding the available techniques and the factors that influence their selection, data scientists can make more informed choices, boosting their analysis's effectiveness and accuracy.

Implementing and optimizing data transformations

In the final part of our exploration of data transformations, we'll dive into the practical aspects of implementing, monitoring and optimizing data transformations. We'll also discuss the need for flexibility in adapting to evolving data needs.

Best practices for implementation

Embarking on the journey of implementing data transformations, there are several best practices to consider that could make the process smoother and more effective:

- **Understand the data**: Before beginning any transformation, it's vital to understand the data, its context, and its structure. This knowledge can guide the selection of the most suitable transformations.

- **Automate where possible**: The use of automation can significantly reduce the time and effort involved in implementing transformations, especially in cases of large datasets or complex transformation pipelines.

- **Document the process**: Thorough documentation is essential for traceability, troubleshooting, and knowledge transfer. It should include details about the data, the chosen transformations, the reasons behind these choices, and the expected outcomes.

- **Test and validate**: Test the transformations on a subset of the data first. This step can identify issues earlier in the process and make them easier to correct. Validation should also be performed to confirm that the transformations have the expected results and don't introduce errors.

- **Involvement of stakeholders**: Besides data scientists and engineers, it's also crucial to involve stakeholders in the data transformation process. Their input can help to align the transformation with business needs and increase the acceptance and use of the outcome.

- **Iteration and improvement**: Data transformation is often an iterative process. Once you have applied a transformation, evaluated the result, and received feedback from stakeholders, you can refine the transformation and repeat the process.

Monitoring and optimizing performance

Monitoring is crucial to ensure that transformations are functioning as intended and that performance is maintained over time. Optimization, on the other hand, is the process of refining transformations to improve efficiency and effectiveness:

- **Monitoring tools**: Many tools are available to monitor the performance of data transformations, providing insights into run times, error rates, resource utilization, and more.

- **Regular review**: Regularly reviewing the performance data can help identify trends, spot issues early, and assess the impact of any changes or optimizations.

- **Optimization techniques**: Depending on the performance data and the specific issues identified, different optimization techniques can be applied. This could include adjusting parameters, redesigning transformations for greater efficiency, or updating hardware or software resources.

- **Proactive approach**: Rather than reacting to issues after they occur, take a proactive approach by setting up alerts based on the performance metrics. This way, you can address potential problems before they have a significant impact.

- **Use of machine learning**: Advanced techniques such as machine learning can help to optimize data transformations. For example, machine learning algorithms can identify patterns in the transformation errors and suggest corrections.

Adapting to evolving data needs

In our rapidly changing data landscape, the ability to adapt is key. Data needs can evolve due to many factors, such as changes in data sources, updates in business requirements, or advances in technology and analytics techniques:

- **Flexible design**: Design transformations with flexibility in mind, allowing for easy adjustments as data needs change. This could mean using modular structures, parameterization, or designing for scalability.

- **Continuous learning**: Stay abreast of the latest trends, tools, and techniques in data transformation. This knowledge can help to foresee necessary adaptations and make informed choices about how to evolve.

- **Feedback loops**: Create feedback loops with stakeholders to understand changing data needs and priorities. Regular communication can provide early warning of changes and give valuable input into how transformations should adapt.

- **Investment in skills and tools**: As data needs evolve, so do the required skills and tools. Investing in ongoing training for your team and keeping your software tools up to date is essential.

- **Data governance**: Evolving data needs often involve changes in the data's scale, complexity, and sensitivity. Therefore, good data governance practices are crucial to ensure data privacy, security, and compliance are maintained.

Case examples

To bring these points to life, consider the following scenarios:

- **Scenario 1**: A finance company implements a transformation pipeline for loan application data. They automate the process using ETL tools, documenting each step meticulously. Over time, they monitor the transformation's performance, using these insights to optimize the pipeline, reducing run times and error rates.

- **Scenario 2**: A healthcare analytics team designs a flexible transformation process to clean and normalize patient data. When a new data source is introduced, they can quickly adapt the transformations to incorporate this new data, avoiding disruptions to their analysis workflows.

- **Scenario 3**: A marketing agency designs a flexible transformation pipeline to handle customer data from various sources. Over time, they encounter performance issues due to increased data volume. By regularly monitoring the performance, they can identify the bottleneck and optimize the pipeline by distributing the transformations across multiple servers.

- **Scenario 4**: An e-commerce company implements a transformation to derive insights from their sales data. When the company expands to new markets, the characteristics of the sales data change significantly. Thanks to their flexible design and ongoing communication with stakeholders, they can quickly adapt the transformation to handle the new data, ensuring continuous insights for their business decisions.

These examples illustrate that the implementation of data transformations is not a one-off task but a continuous process of monitoring, optimizing, and adapting. By following the best practices and staying flexible, organizations can ensure their data transformations continue to meet their evolving data needs and contribute to their business success.

In conclusion, implementing data transformations is a practical and iterative process. With careful attention to best practices, regular monitoring and optimization, and a flexible mindset toward evolving data needs, data scientists can create robust, efficient, and adaptable transformation pipelines. This approach enables them to unlock the full potential of their data, delivering insightful and accurate analytics and reporting.

Next, we'll discuss key concepts for reporting and self-analysis.

Key concepts for reporting and self-analysis

In our journey through data preparation and analysis, we've witnessed the significance of cleaning, transforming, and integrating data. However, these tasks are simply a prelude to the climax: gleaning insights from our data. The peak of this process is reached when we effectively report and analyze the data, applying the fruits of our labor to drive informed decision-making. Within this context, understanding the key concepts of reporting and self-analysis is crucial. These concepts serve as a compass, guiding us through the complex maze of data analysis and interpretation.

Reporting and self-analysis are, in essence, the processes through which we extract value from our well-prepared data. These practices allow us to transform raw data into meaningful insights, enabling us to gain a clearer understanding of our business, our customers, and our market.

Reporting refers to the systematic presentation of data and findings. It is the bridge that connects data with decision-makers, transforming numbers and figures into comprehensible insights that can be acted upon. Reporting is not merely a task of data visualization; it is the art of telling a story with data, where the narrative is driven by the business objectives and questions at hand.

Self-analysis, on the other hand, involves directly interacting with the data, probing it from different perspectives, and making sense of the patterns it reveals. It is the practice of exploring and interpreting data independently, without the need for predefined reports or advanced analytics tools. In essence, self-analysis is a way of 'conversing' with data, enabling individuals to question, listen to, and learn from it.

Reporting and self-analysis serve as tools to harness the value of data, with each offering unique advantages and challenges. Reporting converts data into actionable insights, providing a structured narrative to guide decision-making, while self-analysis allows for a more explorative and personalized interaction with data. However, reporting can sometimes oversimplify complex data or miss nuanced insights. In contrast, self-analysis demands a higher level of data literacy and can be time-consuming. Both approaches are needed in a comprehensive data strategy, enabling organizations to make informed decisions based on a blend of structured reports and individual data exploration.

The importance of these practices in data preparation and analysis cannot be overstated. They not only bring value to the data but also help identify areas of improvement in data quality and transformation. They provide a feedback mechanism that iteratively enhances the entire data life cycle. By understanding the key components and concepts in reporting and self-analysis, we gain a deeper appreciation of the complexity and beauty of the data journey.

The following screenshot shows the various aspects of reporting and self-analysis:

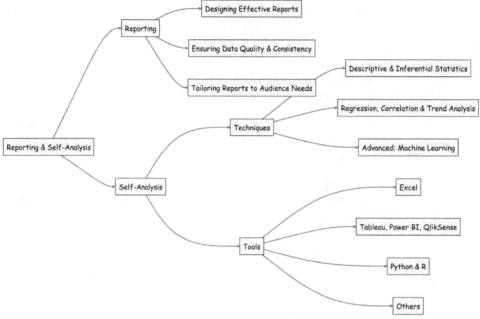

Figure 12.3 – Various aspects of reporting and self-analysis

As we dive into the key components and concepts of reporting and self-analysis, we will discuss the mechanics of designing effective reports, tailoring outputs to diverse audiences, and ensuring the quality and consistency of data. We will also explore various techniques and tools for self-analysis, providing a toolkit for you to effectively interpret and leverage your data. With this foundation, you'll be prepared to drive actionable insights from your data, fueling informed decisions and strategic foresight.

Reporting best practices

Reporting forms an integral part of the data analysis process, turning raw data into actionable insights. In this section, we will delve into the essentials of effective reporting. This includes the design aspects that enhance comprehensibility, the necessary steps for ensuring data quality and consistency, and the importance of tailoring the report to cater to the needs of the specific audience. Understanding and applying these facets ensures that reports not only accurately reflect the data, but also facilitate informed decision-making by delivering insights in an accessible and meaningful way.

Designing effective reports

Creating informative, easy-to-understand reports is critical to conveying findings from a dataset. The design of a report directly impacts the clarity of the presented information and the audience's ability to extract value from it.

A well-structured report should have a clear and concise headline, followed by an introductory summary that outlines the report's purpose. This establishes context and provides an overview of what to expect. Next, the body of the report should detail the data, incorporating a logical progression of ideas supported by charts and graphs that best represent the information. Simplicity and consistency should be guiding principles in report design; excessive colors or overly complicated charts can detract from the data's story.

Each visual should be designed for comprehension, with labeled axes and clear legends where necessary. Finally, the report should conclude with a summary of the findings and any derived insights or recommendations. This structure assists the reader in following along and understanding the narrative the data is telling.

Here is an example of visualization:

Figure 12.4 – First example of visualization

And this is another example of visualization:

Figure 12.5 – Second example of visualization

For example, to effectively visualize changes in data over time, various chart types can be employed, each offering unique insights. Bar charts, in the first example, represent values through the heights of bars, ideal for comparisons against a baseline, while line charts, in the second example, use connected points to illustrate trends where baselines are less meaningful or data points are numerous.

Ensuring data quality and consistency

Ensuring data quality and consistency is critical to reliable reporting. Data quality encompasses the accuracy, completeness, and dependability of the data. Ensuring quality begins with careful data collection, where efforts should be made to minimize errors. This quality control continues through data cleaning and preparation phases, where duplicate data is removed, missing values are addressed, and inconsistencies are resolved.

Data consistency refers to maintaining uniformity in data over time and across various reports. This allows users to accurately compare and analyze data, a process aided by adhering to a standard format and terminology. Regular data audits are an effective tool for maintaining data quality and consistency and help ensure the integrity of the data being reported.

Tailoring reports to audience needs

A successful report must be tailored to the needs of the intended audience. Different stakeholders will have different requirements based on their position within the organization. For example, executives may seek a high-level overview, analysts may require granular data for in-depth examination, and clients might need a progress update on specific projects.

To effectively tailor a report, it is crucial to understand the audience. Once the audience's needs are understood, the report's content, detail level, and data visualizations can be adjusted accordingly. Using language and terminology familiar to the audience will enhance comprehension. Providing context will further aid understanding and give the data relevance. Highlighting the key insights or takeaways that matter most to the audience ensures the report is not only informative but also valuable.

In conclusion, trying to create a one-size-fits-all report to serve multiple needs and audiences is often counterproductive. This approach, usually taken to conserve time, reduce maintenance efforts, or save costs, or from a concern about data inconsistency across reports, can lead to inefficiencies. Moreover, overloading a report with information "just in case" can make it unnecessarily complex. Best practice suggests simplicity is key – the more straightforward the report, the more effective it is likely to be in communicating the intended insights. Mastering these areas allows for the creation of powerful reports that drive informed decision-making and action.

Self-analysis techniques and tools

The increasingly data-driven nature of modern business environments has made self-analysis an essential skill. In this section, we will examine this skill from a broad perspective, highlighting the techniques, tools, and real-world examples that best illustrate its efficacy. By understanding how to apply self-analysis effectively, one can unlock greater value from data and foster a more proactive approach to decision-making and problem-solving.

The process heavily relies on the user's level of knowledge and expertise. Inaccuracies and misinterpretations can easily arise from a misunderstanding of the data, leading to flawed conclusions. Thus, ensuring users have a comprehensive understanding of the data and its context is important for reliable and effective self-analysis. That's why a data governance system is essential for knowledge dissemination.

Overview of self-analysis techniques

The essence of self-analysis in a data context is the ability to use analytical techniques to derive insights from data without reliance on a dedicated analytics team. It helps individuals to engage with data directly, turning it into actionable insights. The range of techniques applied in self-analysis is broad, covering basic statistical analysis to complex machine learning models.

Descriptive statistics serve as the foundation of self-analysis, providing basic information about data distribution, such as mean, median, mode, and range. Additionally, inferential statistics allow users to make predictions or generalizations about a population based on a sample data set. Beyond these, regression analysis, correlation analysis, and trend analysis are other commonly used techniques that can reveal patterns and relationships within the data.

For more advanced self-analysis, machine learning algorithms may be employed. Techniques such as decision trees, clustering, and principal component analysis can help identify complex patterns and dependencies. Machine learning methods are particularly effective when dealing with large and complex data sets where traditional statistical methods may fall short.

Tools for self-analysis and visualization

Several software tools have been developed to facilitate self-analysis. They offer varying levels of complexity and customization, allowing users to choose the one that best suits their needs. For instance, Excel remains a popular choice for simple data manipulation and analysis. With its in-built functions for statistical analysis and charting capabilities, Excel is a powerful tool for basic self-analysis.

For more advanced analysis, tools such as Tableau, Power BI, and QlikSense provide a range of capabilities, from data integration and transformation to advanced data visualization. They have intuitive, drag-and-drop interfaces that make complex analysis accessible to non-technical users. Additionally, they feature robust visualization options that can turn analytical results into clear, visually compelling narratives.

Python and R are programming languages that are extensively used for more complex analysis and are particularly favored by those proficient in coding. With a wide range of packages and libraries for data manipulation, statistical analysis, machine learning, and visualization, they offer unparalleled flexibility and power.

Case studies and examples

To illustrate the power of self-analysis, consider the example of a retail company looking to understand its sales performance. Using self-analysis techniques, the company's managers could use Excel to calculate descriptive statistics for their sales data, revealing important metrics such as average sales value, sales variance, and seasonal trends. They could then use a tool such as   Tableau to visualize these metrics, producing a comprehensive sales dashboard that communicates the state of sales in the company.

For more complex scenarios, consider a telecommunications company seeking to reduce customer churn. Using a machine learning library in Python, an analyst could perform cluster analysis to segment the customer base into different groups based on usage patterns. They could then run a decision tree algorithm to identify the key factors contributing to churn within each group. With these insights, the company could develop targeted retention strategies, improving customer satisfaction and reducing churn.

In both examples, self-analysis enables individuals to engage directly with the data, empowering them to uncover insights and make informed decisions that drive value for their organizations.

Summary

In this chapter, we explored the critical components and best practices for data preparation and analysis. Starting with an examination of the importance and components of data preparation, we delved into the factors influencing when and where to perform data preparation, highlighting the need for considering data quality, scalability, storage, governance, and accessibility.

The chapter then transitioned into the strategy and choice of transformations. A detailed discussion was conducted on how to develop a data transformation strategy, the considerations for selecting appropriate data transformations, and the implementation and optimization of these transformations. The main emphasis was on understanding data requirements, assessing data quality and performance, and aligning the strategy with analytics and reporting goals.

In the final section, we dealt with the key concepts for reporting and self-analysis, where we discussed how to design effective reports, ensure data quality and consistency, and tailor reports to audience needs. We also outlined an overview of self-analysis techniques, the tools available for self-analysis and visualization, and provided some illustrative examples and case studies.

The upcoming chapter will provide an in-depth look into Workflow Management, Monitoring, and Data Quality within the context of data integration. It will cover best practices for workflows, event management, and data governance.

13

Workflow Management, Monitoring, and Data Quality

In this chapter, we will delve into the crucial components of workflow management, event management, and data quality within the context of data integration. We will explore the fundamental concepts and significance of efficient workflow and event management in orchestrating data integration processes seamlessly. Key components such as workflow design, execution, scheduling, automation, error handling, and recovery will be discussed, along with best practices to ensure smooth and effective workflow management.

Event-driven architecture emerges as a powerful paradigm for event management, enabling real-time event processing, routing, monitoring, and alerting. We also explore the various monitoring techniques and tools that are essential for keeping a close eye on data integration workflows and ensuring their smooth functioning.

Data quality and data observability take center stage as vital factors for maintaining high-quality data throughout the integration process. Further, we will look into techniques such as data profiling, validation, cleansing, and enrichment, along with data quality metrics and KPIs, to assess and improve data integrity. Moreover, we'll explore tools for data observability, which empower data professionals to monitor and enhance data accuracy and reliability.

By understanding these key areas, this chapter equips data practitioners with essential knowledge and strategies to optimize data integration processes, ensure data quality, and implement effective workflow and event management practices. Let's explore the core pillars that support seamless data integration in the modern data stack.

The following topics will be covered in this chapter:

- Going through the concepts of workflow management, event management, and monitoring
- Understanding data quality and data observability

Going through the concepts of workflow management, event management, and monitoring

In the next section, we explore three pivotal components that enable efficient data integration: **workflow management**, **event management**, and **monitoring**. We will demystify how tasks are co-ordinated, events are handled, and operations are observed to maintain high standards of performance and data quality. By examining these interconnected elements, readers will gain a comprehensive understanding of the essential building blocks for effective data integration.

First, we will delve into workflow management—the processes for designing, automating, scheduling, and optimizing data integration workflows. Next, we will discuss event management and event-driven architectures, which allow for the real-time processing and routing of events within data pipelines. Finally, we will explore various monitoring techniques and tools that provide visibility into data integration workflows, helping ensure smooth functioning.

Together, these areas provide the foundation for seamless data movement, transformation, and monitoring across complex data landscapes. Gaining expertise in workflow management, event management, and monitoring is key to implementing robust, efficient, and reliable data integration.

Introduction to workflow and event management

Data integration relies on workflow and event management. They orchestrate data movement and transformation, ensuring accuracy, consistency, and timeliness. We will discuss these procedures and their importance to data integration in this introductory section.

Data integration "workflows" transform and move data. Data extraction, transformation, validation, and loading are more complex workflow steps than copying data from one database to another (often abbreviated as **extract, transform, and load** (ETL). Workflow management emphasizes workflow planning, execution, monitoring, and optimization.

Data ingestion, processing, and delivery depend on workflow management. It streamlines data migrations and transformations, improving data integration. Effective workflow management automates these operations, reducing manual intervention and error. Well-designed workflows make data integration smooth, consistent, and reliable for complex data scenarios and high data volumes.

Event management parallels workflow management. In data integration, an **event** is a data change that causes a specific action or series of actions. This could be a source system receiving new data or a processing error.

Event management detects, processes, and responds to these events. **Event-driven architecture** (EDA) software components produce and react to events to integrate data. Dynamic data integration allows for real-time responses and adaptive processing.

Event management also strengthens data integration systems. It detects errors, alerts, and recoveries, minimizing data flow disruption. It also automates data operations in response to triggers, improving system agility.

Data integration requires workflow and event management. They balance structure and flexibility, allowing data systems to handle routine and unexpected data scenarios. In the following sections, we will discuss workflow and event management best practices, error recovery methods, and monitoring tools.

Overview and importance of data integration

Workflow and event management form the backbone of any **data integration** process. In essence, they act as the orchestrators, defining how data moves across different systems and platforms, how it is processed and transformed, and how potential issues or errors are addressed.

The term **workflow** refers to a defined sequence of tasks that process data from one form into another. This could involve extracting data from source systems, applying transformations to prepare it for analysis, loading it into a target data warehouse, and so forth. Each task in a workflow is linked to the others, often in complex ways, with the output of one task serving as the input for the next. Workflow management, therefore, revolves around designing, executing, and monitoring these sequences to ensure data flows smoothly and efficiently.

Event management, on the other hand, deals with the detection, processing, and response to events that are related to the occurrences that affect the system's operation. In the context of data integration, an event could be anything from the completion of a data extraction task to an error during data transformation. Event management ensures that such occurrences are promptly detected, the appropriate responses are triggered, and stakeholders are alerted if necessary.

Both workflow and event management are crucial to data integration for several reasons:

- They ensure efficiency by automating repetitive tasks and reducing manual intervention
- They enhance data consistency and accuracy by enforcing standardized procedures for data handling
- They aid in error detection and recovery, thus ensuring the reliability of the integration process
- They provide visibility into the data integration process, allowing better monitoring, optimization, and control

Overall, effective workflow and event management are indispensable for a robust, reliable, and efficient data integration process.

Key components and concepts

When focusing on workflow and event management, there are a few key components and concepts that form the foundation of these areas:

- **Tasks**: In the context of workflow management, tasks are the individual operations that are carried out. A task could be as simple as retrieving data from a source system or as complex as running a data transformation algorithm.

- **Workflow**: A workflow is essentially a sequence of tasks organized to accomplish a specific goal, such as the complete integration of data from multiple sources. Workflows can be linear or complex, involving multiple branches, conditional logic, and iteration logic.

- **Workflow engine**: This is the system that executes the workflows. It manages the state of the workflow, controls the execution order of tasks, and manages dependencies between tasks. Workflow engines come in various types to suit different needs and technical expertise, such as the following:

  - **UI-based/no-code**: This is for non-programmers, such as those who use Microsoft Power Automate, and it offers a graphical interface for workflow creation. **Code-based:** This is targeted at developers, such as those who use Apache Airflow, requiring coding for complex workflows. **Description-based**: A middle ground using declarative languages, exemplified by AWS Step Functions, defining the workflows in JSON for serverless applications or Kestra with YAML syntax.

- **Events**: Events represent a change in the state of a system or process that is relevant to the business. In the context of data integration, an event could be a new file arriving in a directory, a task failure, or the completion of a data load.

- **Event handlers**: These are procedures that define how to respond to an event. For example, if an error occurs during a data transformation task, an event handler might be set up to send an alert to the data engineering team.

- **Event queue**: This is a data structure that stores events as they occur. The events stay in the queue until they are processed by the event handlers.

- **Monitoring**: This involves the continuous observation of workflows and events to ensure that everything is operating as expected. It could involve checking that tasks are completed on time, that data quality metrics are within acceptable ranges, and that no errors or warnings are being generated.

Understanding these fundamental components and concepts is essential for effective workflow and event management. These elements work together to provide a framework that enables automation, error detection and handling, scheduling, and visibility into the data integration process.

Workflow management best practices

Data integration requires workflow management best practices. These best practices ensure workflow design and execution are structured and sequenced properly. The scheduling and automation of workflows improve resource efficiency and reduce manual labor. Despite the best procedures, errors are unavoidable, making error management and recovery of data crucial. These elements detect and fix problems, minimizing disturbances. This section covers data integration workflow management in detail.

Workflow design and execution

Efficient workflow management centers around the core principles of designing and executing workflows. Let's begin by clarifying the meanings of these terms in the following subsections.

Workflow design

A workflow is created by generating a plan that defines the sequence of actions required to perform a certain task. These activities can be as simple as retrieving datasets or as sophisticated as changing raw data into an analyzable format. A well-designed workflow outlines the linkages and interdependence between tasks and offers clear instructions for each one. This includes deciding on the order in which steps should be accomplished as well as the conditions under which they should be completed.

Workflow design can be performed manually using code or through the utilization of user-friendly graphical interfaces in advanced workflow management systems. These visual interfaces enable users, including nontechnical individuals, to visually map out workflows, making the process more intuitive and accessible.

Workflow execution

Workflow execution refers to the actual implementation of the tasks outlined in the workflow design. A crucial component in this process is the workflow engine, a piece of software responsible for interpreting the workflow design and ensuring the correct execution order of tasks.

During workflow execution, the engine tracks the status of each task, handles error situations, and manages the required resources. It also monitors task completion and schedules subsequent tasks based on their dependencies.

A well-designed and correctly executed workflow in the context of data integration can efficiently extract data from source systems, apply transformations, and load it into a target system with minimal human intervention. This strategy significantly improves data operations efficiency, minimizes the risk of errors, and ensures data availability when and where it is required.

Consider that you're integrating multiple data sources, including CRM and ERP, and marketing automation tools to have a holistic customer view. The design of this workflow will involve identifying the data sources, the types of data they contain, and how they relate to each other. The execution involves extracting data from each source, transforming it into a consistent format, and loading it into your data warehouse or a unified database.

For instance, a part of the workflow could be to extract customer data from the CRM, combine it with sales data from the ERP, and load this combined data into a data warehouse daily. This would allow teams across the organization to have a daily updated view of each customer's interaction and purchasing habits.

To summarize, the design and execution of workflows play a vital role in data integration processes, impacting both efficiency and the quality of the output. This field requires a deep understanding of the tasks involved, as well as the ability to anticipate and manage dependencies and potential issues.

Workflow scheduling and automation

Two essential elements of effective workflow management encompass workflow scheduling and automation, which have a profound impact on enhancing the dependability and productivity of data integration processes.

The following image captures the management of scheduling and automation:

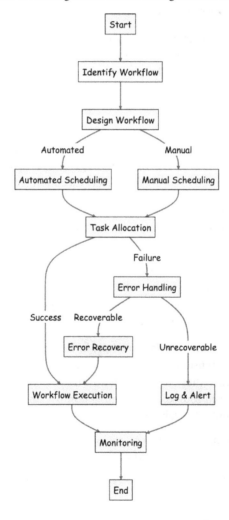

Figure 13.1 – Workflow management of scheduling and automation

The preceding screenshot provides a comprehensive overview of workflow scheduling and automation, including the key steps involved, from workflow identification to execution. It also highlights robust error handling, outlining how the system recovers if failures occur during workflow execution. With this holistic representation, we gain valuable insights into achieving efficient and resilient automated processes through thoughtful workflow design.

Workflow scheduling

Workflow scheduling entails strategically planning task execution within a workflow to achieve optimal performance. This entails resource allocation and task timing so as to minimize conflicts, delays, and resource wastage. In the context of data integration, scheduling can be complex due to task interdependencies, varying execution times, and resource limitations. Nevertheless, proficient scheduling is vital as it enables seamless operation and enhances workflow efficiency.

Scheduling can be based on time, the triggering of tasks at specific intervals, or event-based situations, where tasks are initiated in response to predefined conditions or events. This flexibility empowers organizations to adapt their data workflows to diverse operational requirements, providing optimal control over data processes.

Workflow automation

Workflow automation streamlines business processes by reducing manual tasks. Within data integration, it boosts efficiency by automating steps such as data extraction, transformation, loading, and error handling.

Workflow automation spans across multiple stages of data integration, automating tasks, such as extracting data from various source systems and pushing processed data into target systems or dashboards. It not only enhances efficiency and speed but also improves accuracy by minimizing the potential for manual errors.

Furthermore, automation tools often offer robust error-handling capabilities. They can identify, log, and occasionally rectify errors without human intervention, ensuring resilience and continuity in data processes.

By using our previous example, the data ETL jobs need to run on a regular basis. This can be scheduled and automated using various data integration tools or platforms. These tools allow you to schedule workflows to run at specified times or in response to certain triggers.

For example, you might schedule the ETL job to run every night at 2 am when the load on the system is low. Or you could set it up to run in response to a specific trigger, such as the arrival of new data in the CRM or ERP systems.

To summarize, scheduling and automation are pivotal in executing workflows as they enable efficient resource utilization, streamline operations, reduce manual intervention, and enhance the overall accuracy and dependability of data integration processes. Their appropriate implementation is imperative for organizations striving to optimize their data operations.

Error handling and recovery

Efficiently managing data workflows is fundamental for smooth and reliable data integration. Error handling and recovery strategies are pivotal components of proficient workflow management, safeguarding the resilience and dependability of data integration processes.

Error handling

Error handling encompasses the procedures implemented to effectively manage any exceptions that arise during workflow execution. In the context of data integration, these exceptions may stem from various factors such as data anomalies, system failures, or network issues.

The initial step in error handling involves real-time error detection, which can be achieved through meticulous logging and alert systems. These systems meticulously record unusual events and promptly notify the appropriate personnel to initiate corrective measures. The seamless integration of these systems within workflows ensures continuous monitoring for discrepancies and anomalies.

Once an error is detected, it is crucial to have mechanisms in place to comprehensively understand the nature of the error. Detailed error messages, diagnostic data, and tracebacks serve as invaluable resources, providing insights into the specific cause and location of the error.

Error recovery

Error recovery is the process of rectifying errors and restoring the workflow to a state of normal operation. An effective recovery strategy ensures that workflows can recuperate from errors with minimal disruption or data loss.

In data integration workflows, recovery may involve re-running specific tasks, reprocessing data, or, in certain cases, manual intervention to address the issue. Depending on the nature of the error, recovery procedures can be automated or require manual intervention.

A common error recovery technique in data workflows is checkpointing, which involves periodically saving the workflow's state. In the event of an error, the workflow can be rolled back to the most recently saved state, minimizing the loss of progress.

Even with the best design and automation in place, issues can occur in any workflow. These could be caused by several factors, such as changes in the data format or connectivity issues with one of the data sources.

Let's say that the ERP system is down for maintenance when the ETL job is scheduled to run. A good workflow system would have robust error handling and recovery processes in place to address such occurrences. It might, for instance, send an alert to the system administrator about the issue, skip the ERP data for this run, and proceed with the rest of the workflow or even retry the job after a certain period of time.

The recovery aspect comes into play if the workflow fails completely due to an error. The system should be able to recover from the failure without causing data loss or corruption. For example, if the workflow fails during the transformation stage, it should be able to roll back the transaction so that you can fix the issue and re-run the workflow without losing any data.

In conclusion, the implementation of robust error handling and recovery strategies significantly enhances the reliability and resilience of data integration workflows. These strategies preserve the integrity of data processes, mitigating the impact of errors and minimizing downtime. It is essential to tailor these processes to the specific needs and constraints of your organization's data integration workflows.

Event management best practices

EDA is a new method of data integration and cutting-edge computing. EDA focuses on "events" that highlight major system changes, unlike request-response systems. This design promotes real-time responses and activities through event producers, consumers, and channels. Asynchronous transmission and rapid data processing are EDA benefits. This section explains EDA's concepts, models, capabilities, applications, and key elements to help organizations use it to improve agility and responsiveness.

Event-driven architecture

At the intersection of data integration and modern computing lies the concept of an EDA. This structure hinges upon the principle of responding to actions, known as **events**, which can be defined as significant changes in a state within a system.

In the framework of an event-driven architecture, the production, detection, and reaction to events form the nucleus of all functionalities. This is a departure from the traditional request-response model seen in other systems, wherein communication is typically initiated by a requesting component. In contrast, EDA promotes a more dynamic and responsive system that is closely aligned with real-time business needs.

An EDA comprises three fundamental components: event producers, event consumers, and an event channel. The event producers are the components that generate events and push them to the event channel. An event channel, in turn, serves as a conduit that transports events from producers to consumers. The event consumers are components that are interested in types of events and react to them accordingly.

One of the standout advantages of event-driven architecture is the capacity for asynchronous communication. This means components can continue with other tasks without having to wait for a response from the event they have produced. As such, it allows for a loose coupling of services, fostering a more scalable and resilient system.

Another notable advantage is the inherent real-time nature of EDA, which is particularly useful when dealing with streaming data. By processing events as they occur, businesses can derive instant insights and promptly respond to changes.

In essence, event-driven architectures represent a paradigm shift towards building dynamic, real-time, and responsive data integration systems. As more organizations recognize the advantages of real-time data processing, we can expect the prominence of EDA to continue to rise.

Let's consider an example of an event-driven architecture in a retail e-commerce system. In this system, there are various events that occur, such as user login, item added to cart, order placed, and payment made. Each of these events signifies a change in state in the system and triggers certain actions.

It's essential to grasp the three foundational pillars that underpin the seamless interaction and flow of information:

- **Event producers**: Different parts of the system generate events. For instance, the user interface might produce a user login event when a customer signs in. When a customer adds an item to their shopping cart, the shopping cart service produces an item added to cart event.

- **Event channel**: Once these events are produced, they are pushed to an event channel. This channel could be a message queue, such as Apache Kafka, Azure EventHub, AWS Kinesis, and RabbitMQ, that acts as a pipeline for events, ensuring they are delivered to the right event consumers.

- **Event consumers**: On the other side, there are event consumers waiting for these events. These could be other parts of the system or services that react to these events. For instance, the inventory service might be a consumer for the order placed event, reducing stock levels in response to the event. Similarly, a recommendation service might be a consumer using the item added to cart event, and it uses this information to update the recommendation for that user.

This approach allows the different services in the system to operate independently and asynchronously, improving the system's scalability and resilience. Additionally, by reacting to events as they occur, the system can provide a more dynamic and real-time user experience. For example, the recommendation service can instantly update recommendations as soon as a new item is added to the cart, improving the shopping experience for the user.

EDA delivery models

In **EDA**, the concepts of **push** and **pull** refer to how events are transmitted between producers and consumers.

Push model

In this approach, event producers actively send or "push" events to the consumers or an intermediary channel as soon as they occur. This method ensures the immediate delivery and processing of events, making it ideal for scenarios where real-time reaction is crucial. The push model is characterized by its proactive nature, where the producer dictates the event flow. It is beneficial in situations where prompt response to events is critical and where the event rate is manageable by the consumers. For example, RabbitMQ employs a push model.

Pull model

Contrarily, the pull model requires the consumers to periodically check or "pull" for new events from a source or channel. This model is more controlled and can be better for scenarios where events do not require immediate attention or where the consumer's capacity to handle incoming events is variable. The pull model is reactive, allowing consumers to dictate the pace at which they receive and process events. The pull model is often preferred in scenarios where consumers need to control the intake. It's also useful in cases where the processing can afford some delay or needs to happen at specific intervals. For example, Apache Kafka or AWS Kinesis employ a pull model.

EDA delivery semantics – exactly once, at least once, at most once, and others

Delivery semantics in EDA define how the system ensures the delivery of events between producers and consumers, and there are at least three types:

- **Exactly once**: This ensures that each event is delivered and processed exactly once, eliminating duplicates and preventing data loss. It's the most stringent and complex to implement, requiring sophisticated mechanisms to track and manage event delivery. This semantic model is ideal for financial transactions, billing systems, or any domain where data accuracy and consistency are critical. The complexity and overhead are justified by the need for precision and reliability.

- **At least once**: Here, the system guarantees that events are delivered at least once. This may result in duplicate processing, so consumers need to be idempotent (able to handle duplicate messages without adverse effects). It's simpler than exactly once but still ensures no data loss. This model is common in order processing systems or any system where ensuring the delivery of every event is crucial, even if it means processing some events multiple times.

- **At most once**: In this approach, events are delivered once or not at all. It's the simplest but also the riskiest, as it can lead to data loss. This semantic model is suitable for non-critical data where the loss of some events is acceptable. This model is suitable for logging, monitoring systems, or scenarios where speed is more critical than completeness, and the occasional loss of events is acceptable.

Each delivery semantic model has its own set of trade-offs and is chosen based on the specific requirements and constraints of the use case at hand.

Event processing and routing

Event processing and routing are critical aspects of an event-driven architecture. In order to define the appropriate behavior for processing events, it is necessary to take into consideration the type and number of occurrences of each event, while routing determines how these events traverse through the system to reach the appropriate destinations. Together, they form the backbone of any effective event-driven system, enabling real-time responses and actions based on incoming events.

In an event-driven architecture, event processing begins when a certain predefined event occurs. An event could be anything from a user clicking a button on a website or a change in data values to a system error or status update. The central principle of event processing is that specific actions or reactions are triggered in response to these events. This could involve launching certain processes, activating specific functions, or updating system values.

For example, imagine a data integration workflow where an event is triggered whenever a new batch of data arrives from a data source. The event processing mechanism could be set up to initiate a data cleansing process each time this event occurs, ensuring that the incoming data are ready for further integration steps.

On the other hand, event routing is concerned with the path that an event follows after it has been generated. This involves directing the event to the right place in the system so that the appropriate processing actions can take place. Effective routing ensures that events reach the correct destination without unnecessary delays, supporting seamless operations in an event-driven architecture.

Continuing with our previous example, after the data cleansing event is triggered, the routing system could direct this event toward the necessary data cleansing functions. Depending on the complexity of the system and the event at hand, this might involve multiple steps, such as first routing the event to a validation function before directing it to the data cleansing function.

Both event processing and routing are crucial in facilitating responsive, dynamic, and flexible systems capable of real-time decision-making and process execution. They serve as key components in modern data integration strategies, especially when dealing with diverse and rapidly changing data sources.

CQRS and EDA connection

Modern data integration involves understanding the link between **command query responsibility segregation (CQRS)** and **event-driven architecture (EDA)**. Both concepts, while different, overlap in system design.

CQRS divides commands that change a system's state from queries that read it. This matches EDA's focus on events. In event-driven systems, CQRS commands can be seen as events. When a command happens, it changes the state, creating an event that moves through the EDA system. Both CQRS and EDA work asynchronously, and CQRS helps event systems by splitting reading and writing actions. In EDA, events can be sent without waiting for a result, making things quicker. Commands in CQRS can start state changes, and queries can read these changes.

In short, combining CQRS and EDA is useful for creating efficient systems. Using them together ensures smooth data flow, effortless modifications, and swift reactions from the system to any changes or requests.

The following screenshot illustrates a schematic representation of the integration of CQRS and EDA within a system:

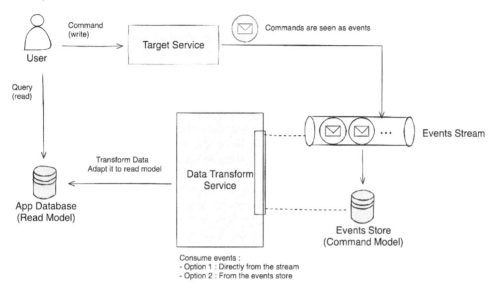

Figure 13.2 – Integration of CQRS and EDAIt

The preceding figure outlines the process flow from a user command to the eventual data read, highlighting the asynchronous nature of these patterns. Here, user commands (writes) are sent to a target service, which treats these commands as events. These events are then channeled through an events stream, which is then stored in the event store (command model); this represents the command model. A separate data transformation service adapts these data into a read model adapted to the consumption queries, which is stored in an application database. The user can then query this read model to read the latest data.

For a real-world example, consider an online shopping platform during a flash sale. A user places an order (write command) that is captured as an event and sent to the event stream. The event is stored and processed asynchronously, ensuring the system remains responsive. Meanwhile, the user continues shopping, unaffected by backend processes. The inventory and order status (read queries) are updated as the events are processed, providing real-time feedback to the user.

Event monitoring and alerting

Event monitoring and alerting are essential components of an event-driven architecture that ensure smooth and efficient operations. Through continuous observation and timely notifications, they help maintain the health and performance of a system, allowing for the swift identification and resolution of issues that could impact data integration processes.

Let's delve deeper into the two key components of this process: event monitoring and alerting.

Event monitoring

Event monitoring involves continuously tracking the events occurring within a system. It assesses the system's operational state and detects any significant changes or anomalies that might indicate potential issues. This information is vital for maintaining optimal system performance and facilitating proactive troubleshooting.

To illustrate the event monitoring process, consider a data processing system where each processed dataset generates an event. Event monitoring, in this context, would entail tracking these events to assess the frequency, volume, and success rate of data processing operations. If there's a sudden drop in event generation or a surge in errors, it might signify an issue within the processing mechanism, requiring immediate attention.

Event alerting

Event alerting, meanwhile, is the process of notifying relevant parties when specific conditions are met within the system. Alerting mechanisms can be designed around various parameters, such as error thresholds, operational statuses, or performance metrics. By promptly informing stakeholders of critical situations, alerting systems facilitate rapid response and issue resolution, minimizing downtime and disruption.

For example, if the monitoring mechanism identifies a substantial increase in processing failures in the same data processing system, an alert might be promptly sent to the data operations team. Depending on the severity and type of the problem, the alarm could be delivered through email, SMS messages, or even in-app notifications.

In essence, event monitoring and alerting work in conjunction to keep the system's stakeholders informed about its current state and any potential issues. They foster operational efficiency and system robustness, which are vital for any data integration effort in today's fast-paced and data-driven environment.

Monitoring techniques and tools

Monitoring is essential for data integration across systems. Complex workflows require proactive oversight. Monitoring goes beyond observation to prevent problems, optimize operation, and preserve data. Various methods handle unique problems to do this. The development of specialized technologies has made data integration monitoring more comprehensive and efficient.

Overview of monitoring techniques

Monitoring plays a crucial role in data integration by ensuring the smooth functioning of workflows and event management processes. A well-designed monitoring system can proactively identify potential issues, enhance system performance, and facilitate efficient data integration.

In the context of data integration, monitoring techniques can be categorized into four main types:

- **Log monitoring**: This technique involves regularly examining logs to detect abnormal behavior, failures, or specific patterns. Automated log monitoring systems can scan logs for anomalies, error codes, or predefined patterns and trigger alerts when necessary.

- **Performance monitoring**: Performance monitoring focuses on tracking **key performance indicators** (**KPIs**) such as response time, throughput, and CPU usage. Monitoring these metrics provides insights into the overall health and performance of the system. Deviations from normal values can indicate underlying issues that require attention.

- **Real-time monitoring**: Real-time monitoring involves the continuous tracking of system operations as they happen. This technique enables the instant detection of issues, enabling a quick response and minimizing potential disruptions. Real-time monitoring is particularly critical in high-stakes data integration environments where even minor downtime can have significant consequences.

- **Proactive monitoring**: Proactive monitoring involves setting up automated processes to identify potential issues before they escalate into significant problems. This can range from simple tasks, such as monitoring disk space, to complex activities, such as using predictive models to forecast system behavior based on historical data.

In conclusion, the selection of monitoring techniques depends on the specific requirements of the data integration project. Often, a combination of multiple techniques is employed to establish a comprehensive monitoring setup. Effective monitoring not only ensures system health but also contributes to more efficient, reliable, and trustworthy data integration operations.

Monitoring tools for data integration

As our knowledge of data integration processes expands, so does the range of tools available for monitoring these workflows. The following monitoring tools are essential in ensuring the smooth functioning of data integration and providing valuable insights and alerts for potential issues.

- **Log analysis tools**: Tools such as Splunk, Logstash, and Graylog are effective for analyzing logs generated by data integration processes. They enable the real-time processing of large volumes of log data, making it easier to identify patterns, anomalies, and potential issues.

- **Performance monitoring tools**: **New Relic**, **AppDynamics**, and **Dynatrace** are examples of tools that provide insights into the performance of data integration systems. They track metrics such as CPU usage, memory consumption, response time, and throughput. These tools help identify performance bottlenecks and ensure optimal system operation.

- **Alerting and visualization tools**: Visualization tools such as **Kibana** and **Grafana** present collected metrics and data in a graphical format. Meanwhile, alerting tools such as **PagerDuty** or **OpsGenie** can be configured to send notifications based on predefined rules and thresholds, enabling quick response to emerging issues.

- **Data integration platforms**: Comprehensive data integration platforms such as **Talend**, **Informatica**, and **Azure Data Factory** often include built-in monitoring capabilities. These tools can monitor data pipelines, track data lineage, validate data, and provide alerts for errors or failures.

- **Cloud monitoring tools**: With the increasing adoption of cloud-based data integration, specific monitoring tools have emerged for cloud environments. Examples of this include **Amazon CloudWatch**, **Google Stackdriver**, and **Azure Monitor**, which provide insights into cloud resources and applications, ensuring the system's health and performance.

In conclusion, the selection of monitoring tools for data integration depends on project requirements, system complexity, and the underlying infrastructure. Employing a well-suited set of monitoring tools contributes significantly to the robustness, efficiency, and reliability of data integration operations.

The following screenshot illustrates examples of monitoring tools:

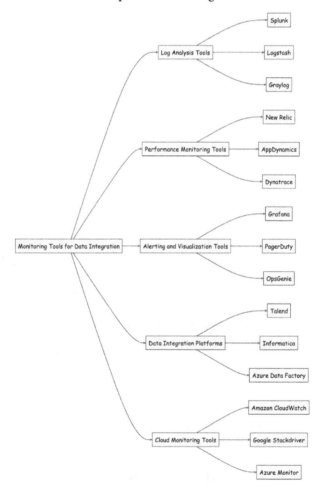

Figure 13.3 – Examples of monitoring tools

This screenshot provides a visual representation of the diverse tools available for data integration. It highlights the variety of specialized tools that cater to different aspects of monitoring, from log analysis and real-time tracking to alerting and more.

Next, we'll discuss data quality and data observability.

Understanding data quality and data observability

Data quality and data observability are two vital and interconnected facets of robust data management strategies. Ensuring data quality involves various techniques and methodologies to enhance the accuracy, consistency, completeness, and relevance of data. On the other hand, data observability involves providing visibility into the data pipeline, allowing organizations to trace data's journey, detect anomalies, and ensure its reliability. Together, these elements help enterprises build a strong data foundation, leading to more reliable insights and informed decision-making.

Introduction to data quality and observability

Data quality and observability form the backbone of reliable and insightful data analytics. When we speak of data quality, we are referring to the degree of excellence exhibited in the data content using various dimensions, such as accuracy, consistency, completeness, and reliability. Data observability, on the other hand, is an extension that involves actively monitoring and analyzing the data quality and the processes involved in data ingestion, storage, and management. Observability ensures that we have visibility into how the data is flowing through different systems and can act on any issues before they escalate. Both these components are critically intertwined and play a monumental role in ensuring that the data serves its purpose efficiently and effectively in any given data integration process.

Incorporating data quality and observability into existing **master data management** (**MDM**) systems is needed for leveraging and enhancing the company's data governance framework. It improves decision-making and standard adherence for unified data asset management. In the forthcoming sections, we will dive deep into the specifics of each and explore their relevance and applications.

Overview and importance of data integration

Data quality and observability are foundational elements that uphold the pillars of data integration. They contribute towards the establishment of a cohesive, reliable, and transparent data landscape that not only ensures the seamless flow of information but also safeguards its integrity and consistency throughout its life cycle.

Data quality is at the helm of effective data integration, directly influencing the reliability and utility of the integrated data. In an era marked by the exponential growth of data, ensuring that the data we are integrating is accurate, complete, consistent, and up-to-date is imperative. The quality of data underpins the efficacy of business decisions and strategies, thereby underlining its significance. For instance, an enterprise integrating data from disparate sources to fuel its machine learning models must ensure high data quality. Any inaccuracies, inconsistencies, or gaps can derail the accuracy of predictions and lead to misinformed strategies. Hence, maintaining high data quality is indispensable for reaping the full benefits of data integration.

On the other hand, data observability extends the concept of monitoring from just the operational aspects to the actual data flowing through the integration pipelines. It is about having clear visibility into the behavior of data as it moves across different systems and processes, thereby understanding how it changes, where it fails, and how it affects the overall performance of the data integration setup. It is akin to having a GPS for your data, tracing its journey through the intricate maze of integration workflows. This observability allows for proactive issue detection, speedy troubleshooting, and more resilient data integration processes.

In conclusion, high data quality and robust data observability go hand in hand in bolstering the efficiency and effectiveness of data integration. Together, they drive value for businesses by facilitating well-informed decision-making, ensuring regulatory compliance, and enhancing customer experiences. Without ensuring these, organizations risk making ill-informed decisions based on faulty data, leading to poor outcomes. Therefore, they are crucial for any organization that seeks to harness the power of data in a meaningful and impactful manner.

Key components and concepts

In the realm of data quality and observability, the key components and concepts form a critical framework that allows businesses to optimize their data integration efforts. At the very heart of data quality, we find elements such as accuracy, completeness, consistency, and timeliness, which together serve as the cornerstone for any effective data integration strategy.

Accuracy relates to how well the data reflects reality, underscoring the necessity for precise and error-free information. This is particularly relevant for businesses that rely heavily on data-driven insights, where even minor inaccuracies can lead to significant misinterpretations. Completeness, on the other hand, implies that the integrated data contains all the necessary elements for comprehensive analysis. Incomplete data can be misleading, leaving room for potential oversights or skewed conclusions.

Consistency refers to the uniformity of data across different sources and systems, which is crucial for maintaining the integrity of data when integrating from disparate sources. This consistency reduces confusion and helps ensure that the data behaves predictably, further supporting accurate and reliable analytics. Timeliness denotes the availability of data when needed. With fast-paced business environments, data must be current and readily available to cater to ever-evolving demands and decision-making needs.

In terms of data observability, the following key concepts are included:

- **Visibility**: This refers to the transparency in data movement across systems and processes, aiding in the prompt detection and rectification of errors or issues.

- **Traceability**: This ensures the ability to track data transformations through the integration pipeline, providing valuable insights into data provenance and fostering trust in data outputs.

- **Monitoring**: As the final component, it involves keeping a vigilant eye on the data's behavior and the operational aspects of data integration. This encompasses identifying anomalies, ensuring data quality, and maintaining performance standards, thus fortifying the overall integrity and robustness of the data integration setup.

Together, these components and concepts establish a robust foundation for data quality and observability, driving effectiveness in data integration practices and facilitating informed business decision-making.

Data quality techniques

Organizations use a range of interrelated data management methods to turn raw data into an asset. From data profiling and validation to data cleansing and enrichment, each stage ensures data quality and usability. These practices provide a complete data governance approach when combined with data quality metrics and KPIs. This allows data-driven decision-making and organizational performance by enabling continuous improvement and strategy alignment.

Data profiling, validation, cleansing, and enrichment

Data profiling and validation are integral to maintaining high-quality data within an organization. **Data profiling** refers to the process of examining the data available in an existing database and collecting statistics or informative summaries about said data. This process offers a comprehensive view of the nature and organization of the data, providing insights into patterns, anomalies, and dependencies that can be vital in making data-driven decisions.

For instance, data profiling may reveal common attributes or recurring patterns, which can inform how new data are integrated and how existing data are maintained. It can also highlight anomalies, which may represent errors or inconsistencies in the data. Understanding these abnormalities can assist in enhancing the robustness of data cleansing procedures. Data profiling might further illuminate dependencies between various data elements, which can be vital in managing relationships within the data and ensuring its overall integrity.

The steps of **validation**, **cleansing**, and **enrichment** are vital, offering an exhaustive examination of data to spot and rectify errors, discrepancies, or voids. These processes are elaborated on in *Chapter 10, Transformation Patterns, Cleansing and Normalization*, in the *Data cleansing and normalization* section. In summary, data profiling, validation, cleansing, and enrichment are key activities that improve data quality by guaranteeing accuracy, completeness, and dependability in order to make educated decisions and plan strategically. Profiling and validation give a full understanding of data structure and quality, highlighting anomalies such as discrepancies or missing information. Cleansing corrects these mistakes, whereas enrichment adds useful external information, making data a more valuable resource. Together, these processes dramatically increase the usability of data, allowing organizations to make more data-driven decisions.

Data quality metrics and KPIs

Data quality metrics and KPIs help managers assess data quality and reliability.

Data quality metrics measure accuracy, completeness, consistency, timeliness, and uniqueness. Accuracy metrics measure the percentage of records that meet validation rules, while completeness metrics measure the percentage without missing values. Timeliness can be measured by the percentage of records updated within a given timeframe, and uniqueness metrics can determine a dataset's duplicate rate. These metrics help organizations objectively evaluate data quality and identify areas for improvement.

KPIs measure an organization's data quality. Data quality KPIs may include the time to resolve data quality issues, the percentage of data errors found post-release or customer complaints about data quality. KPIs help assess an organization's data management practices and data quality goals.

These metrics and KPIs assess and improve. Monitoring these indicators helps organizations identify and fix data quality issues, improving data quality over time. Quality data improves analytics, decision-making, customer satisfaction, and business success.

Finally, data quality metrics and KPIs help assess, improve, and maintain data quality. Data-driven decision-making and improved business performance help them achieve strategic goals.

Data observability techniques and tools

Data observability, a notion that extends beyond conventional monitoring approaches, is becoming a crucial aspect of efficient data management. It provides comprehensive knowledge of the behavior of data as they pass through multiple processing and transformation steps. Observability is not only about discovering problems; more crucially, it enables teams to determine why a problem arose and how to resolve it.

Data observability centers on three fundamental characteristics: **controllability**, **visibility**, and **predictability**. The capacity to change the behavior of data systems to improve operations is highlighted by controllability. Visibility is the perception of data states and changes throughout all phases. Finally, predictability emphasizes the potential to properly estimate system actions based on observable patterns, hence leading to better-informed decision-making.

Data observability comes into play, particularly during data debugging, error tracking, and system optimization. It provides a clear view into the entire data lifecycle, aiding in the identification of bottlenecks, inefficiencies, and inaccuracies in real time. This holistic visibility can lead to more reliable data processing, driving better business decisions and outcomes.

To achieve data observability, it's essential to implement comprehensive logging and telemetry strategies, use metrics that reflect data health and performance, and create effective alerting systems for timely issue detection. However, given the massive volume and complexity of modern data ecosystems, manual observability practices may prove inefficient and error-prone. This is where data observability tools come into play, which we will discuss in the following sections.

Remember, implementing data observability is not a one-size-fits-all proposition. It requires a thoughtful approach that considers the unique needs, challenges, and goals of your data operations. As we move forward, we will delve deeper into the techniques and best practices to achieve effective data observability.

Tools for measuring and improving data observability

As data systems grow increasingly complex, leveraging specialized tools for measuring and enhancing data observability becomes an indispensable strategy. These tools facilitate in-depth visibility into data flows and transformations, making it easier to monitor system health, trace issues, and improve performance.

A key class of these tools includes those dedicated to comprehensive logging and telemetry. Solutions such as **Logstash, Fluentd**, and **Graylog** provide powerful mechanisms for collecting, processing, and visualizing log data. They can track everything from basic system events to detailed data transformations, offering critical insights into the operational state of your data workflows.

On the metrics and alerting front, tools such as **Prometheus** and **Grafana** are renowned. These platforms facilitate real-time monitoring and alerting based on predefined thresholds. They help detect anomalies, predict system behaviors, and understand the impact of changes in your data systems.

In the realm of data profiling and quality measurement, solutions such as **Informatica**, **Talend**, and **Trifacta** come into play. They offer advanced capabilities to inspect, validate, and cleanse data. They can provide metrics related to data quality, such as completeness, uniqueness, validity, and timeliness.

For distributed tracing, which is essential for understanding complex data pipelines, tools such as **Jaeger** and **Zipkin** can be instrumental. They provide a way to visualize how data flows through the system, making it easier to identify bottlenecks and points of failure.

In addition to the previous tools, new platforms such as **Datadog** offer versatile and comprehensive monitoring services that can be aptly positioned in the domain of data observability. Datadog combines the features of several different categories, making it a multifaceted tool suitable for a broad range of tasks. Lastly, solutions such as **Apache Atlas** and **Collibra** offer capabilities around metadata management and lineage tracking. They help trace the journey data take from source to consumption, offering clarity about their transformation and dependency.

The following screenshot represents the various tools for observability:

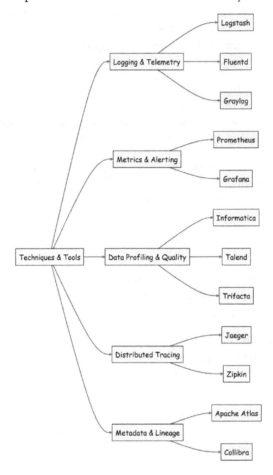

Figure 13.4 – Various tools for observability

In summary, the landscape of tools for data observability is diverse and rich. Picking the right ones depends on your specific needs and the nature of your data ecosystem. In the upcoming section, we'll discuss best practices and use cases, further illustrating how to leverage these tools effectively in your data operations.

Best practices and use cases

Data observability encompasses various facets, and implementing best practices is indispensable for leveraging its full potential. One such best practice is ensuring comprehensive data documentation. It is crucial to document data sources, transformations, and workflows so that data lineage and metadata are well understood. This leads to better insights and troubleshooting capabilities.

Another imperative practice is to incorporate real-time monitoring and alerting mechanisms. Keeping tabs on data pipelines and being alerted to anomalies as they occur is vital. Modern observability tools enable not just monitoring but also provide the context needed to understand why something has occurred, which dramatically reduces the time of resolution.

The practice of setting tangible data quality metrics and KPIs is equally important. These metrics might include accuracy, completeness, and timeliness. Establishing clear standards allows teams to measure against them and ensure that data are trustworthy and usable.

The use of automated data validation is also a best practice. This involves creating automated tests to ensure that data is accurate, consistent, and adheres to defined standards. Automation minimizes human error and ensures more reliable data.

Furthermore, data observability is about having a unified view of data from different sources. Adopting tools that can bring together logs, metrics, and tracing under a single pane is recommended.

In terms of use cases, data observability is critical in ensuring high availability and performance in e-commerce platforms. Real-time monitoring and alerting can be used to detect and rectify issues before they affect the customer experience.

Another use case can be seen in healthcare, where ensuring the quality and reliability of data is paramount. Data observability practices in such an environment can lead to better patient outcomes by ensuring that healthcare professionals have access to accurate, timely, and complete patient data.

In conclusion, employing data observability best practices, such as thorough documentation, real-time monitoring, and automated validation, is key to maximizing data reliability and performance. Whether it's improving the customer experience in e-commerce or patient outcomes in healthcare, data observability is an essential tool for any data-driven organization.

Summary

In conclusion, this chapter has provided a comprehensive exploration of essential components in data integration, including workflow and event management, monitoring techniques, and data quality practices. Understanding the significance of efficient workflow design, event-driven architecture, and real-time monitoring has proven vital for optimizing data integration processes.

Moreover, the focus on data quality techniques, data observability, and the use of relevant tools has been instrumental in ensuring data accuracy and reliability. By implementing these best practices, organizations can maintain a seamless and robust data integration framework, enabling them to derive valuable insights and make informed decisions.

In the next chapter, we will explore the key aspects of data lineage, governance, and compliance.

14
Lineage, Governance, and Compliance

With a solid understanding of workflow management, monitoring, and data quality, we now turn our focus to the equally critical aspects of data integration: lineage, governance, and compliance. In this chapter, we explore techniques for creating and visualizing data lineage, as well as tools and platforms for effective lineage management. We also delve into data governance, addressing best practices, frameworks, and the pivotal role of data catalogs and metadata management. Additionally, we explore compliance considerations and strategies, highlighting regulatory requirements and how to align data integration practices with compliance objectives. Through case studies and examples, we gain valuable insights into real-world implementations of lineage, governance, and compliance, demonstrating their significance in ensuring data integrity, accountability, and adherence to regulatory standards. Let's explore these essential aspects that safeguard the trustworthiness and reliability of data integration in the modern data stack.

The following topics will be covered in this chapter:

- Understanding the concept of data lineage
- Adhering to regulations and implementing robust governance frameworks

Understanding the concept of data lineage

Data lineage refers to tracing the origins and journey of data as it moves through various systems and transformations. Understanding data lineage provides transparency into how data is sourced, integrated, and processed. This visibility enables troubleshooting data issues, ensuring compliance with regulations, and making data-driven decisions with confidence. Effective data lineage relies on techniques such as metadata management, data mapping, and visualizations to capture the flow of data. Data governance frameworks leverage lineage to improve data quality and trust. Overall, comprehensive data lineage is crucial for modern data integration, fostering accountability and reliability in data analytics.

Overview of data lineage

Comprehending data lineage is essential due to its role in tracing errors back to their source, ensuring compliance with data regulations, making informed business decisions, and enhancing the overall understanding of the data's context. It provides transparency, fosters confidence in the data's integrity, and provides an understanding of its impact on information, reports, and decision-making processes.

A significant aspect of data lineage lies in its criticality for **data integration**. In the context of data integration, where data from multiple sources is combined into a unified view, understanding the path that data takes is vital. Data lineage provides **visibility** into the data's journey from its source through its transformation and final presentation. This visibility is particularly valuable when handling large volumes of data from multiple sources, a common scenario in today's data-driven businesses.

Without a clear understanding of data lineage, integrating data can lead to inaccuracies, inconsistencies, and misunderstandings. These issues, in turn, can result in flawed business decisions, regulatory noncompliance, and a general lack of trust in the data's reliability. Therefore, effective data lineage helps mitigate the risks associated with data integration.

Moreover, data lineage supports data governance by enhancing data **quality**, **integrity**, and **reliability**. It allows organizations to track how data is used, shared, and transformed, enabling efficient data auditing and compliance with data protection regulations.

In data troubleshooting, data lineage acts as a roadmap, providing visibility into the entire data landscape. It enables organizations to identify and rectify data issues, discrepancies, and bottlenecks swiftly and accurately. Furthermore, in situations where data anomalies are identified, data lineage allows organizations to trace back through the data's journey to locate the source of the problem.

In summary, data lineage plays an integral role in data integration by providing visibility into the data's journey, supporting data governance, aiding in compliance, and facilitating troubleshooting. With the rising importance of data in decision-making and the increasing regulatory focus on data integrity and privacy, understanding data lineage is becoming a non-negotiable aspect of data management strategies for modern organizations.

Techniques for creating and visualizing data lineage

Creating and visualizing data lineage involves the process of mapping data from its source to its destination and capturing its transformations along the way. The objective is to gain a clear understanding of how data moves and evolves throughout the enterprise ecosystem.

To create data lineage, organizations primarily use the following techniques:

- **Manual tracking**: This is the simplest approach, where individuals document data movements and transformations as they occur. Although it offers the highest level of detail and customization, it's time-consuming, prone to human error, and difficult to scale, making it less feasible for larger and more complex environments.

- **Automated lineage extraction**: In contrast to manual tracking, automated extraction uses software to track and record data movements automatically. This software can either be a standalone data lineage tool or form part of a broader data governance or data management platform. It works by tapping into data logs and metadata repositories or using APIs to capture data movements and transformations. This method is faster, more accurate, and scalable but might not capture every detail.

- **Hybrid approach**: A hybrid approach combines manual and automated tracking to maximize the benefits of both. For example, automated tools can be used to capture most of the data lineage information, while manual processes document exceptions or complex transformations that the automated tools cannot handle.

Visualizing data lineage refers to the process of presenting data lineage information in a clear, easy-to-understand format. It's typically performed using data lineage tools that can generate diagrams or other visual representations. The visualizations usually display nodes (representing data points or databases) and arrows or lines (indicating data movement or transformations).

For effective visualization, it's crucial to decide the level of granularity. While high granularity provides detailed information about transformations at each step, it can make the visualization complex and difficult to understand. In contrast, lower granularity offers a more straightforward, high-level view of the data journey but may omit vital details.

Another critical aspect of visualizing data lineage is ensuring the information is easy to navigate. This can be achieved by using color-coding, grouping related data elements, or incorporating interactive features that allow users to zoom in or out and expand or collapse sections of the lineage.

Finally, visualizing data lineage should not only focus on the past and present state of the data but also provide capabilities to model potential future changes. This can be particularly useful for assessing the impact of planned data transformations or migrations.

In conclusion, creating and visualizing data lineage requires a combination of the right techniques and tools tailored to an organization's specific needs and data complexity. While the process can be complex and time-consuming, the insights and control it provides make it a vital component of any robust data management strategy.

Tools and platforms for data lineage management

The management of data lineage is a complex task, requiring specialized tools and platforms designed to automatically track, store, and visualize data's journey throughout the organization. Let's explore some of these tools and platforms and how they contribute to effective data lineage management.

Data lineage tools

The market offers a diverse range of data lineage tools that can serve different types of organizations and their unique needs. The choice often depends on factors such as the size of the organization, the complexity and volume of data, budget constraints, and specific use cases that the tool is needed to address.

Some leading tools in the field include the following:

- **Apache Atlas**: As a powerful open-source tool, Apache Atlas offers a scalable platform for metadata management and data governance, with data lineage visualization being one of its core features. It's highly interoperable and offers native integration with various **Hadoop** components, providing an excellent framework for enterprises heavily relying on the Hadoop ecosystem for their data solutions.

- **Collibra**: Collibra data lineage automatically maps data relationships in context, visualizing the data's journey through systems, transformations, and reports. This way, it helps organizations to understand their processes better, ensure compliance, and make informed business decisions.

- **Informatica**: This robust, enterprise-level data integration tool provides an extensive suite of data management solutions. Among its many features, it offers sophisticated data lineage capabilities that enable businesses to track data from end-to-end, helping them comply with regulations and conduct in-depth impact analysis.

- **Talend**: Known for its data integration and data integrity platforms, Talend offers comprehensive data lineage features as a part of its suite. Talend users can track the data life cycle from origin to endpoint, which aids in maintaining data accuracy and regulatory compliance.

- **IBM InfoSphere Information Governance Catalog** (IGC): The IGC is an interactive, web-based tool that enables users to explore, understand, and analyze information. It provides capabilities to create, manage, and share a trusted business glossary and to derive the lineage of data.

- **Marquez**: Marquez is an open source metadata service from WeWork that offers an efficient way to capture and store data lineage information, covering data sources, datasets, and the jobs that produce them. Its strength lies in its ability to integrate with existing job schedulers and its compatibility with both SQL and NoSQL databases. With Marquez, users can visualize the flow of data, which improves their understanding of data transformations. Moreover, its focus on open standards promotes interoperability and flexibility, thus allowing organizations to tailor Marquez to their specific needs.

These tools typically provide capabilities such as automated metadata harvesting, data lineage visualization, impact analysis, and data discovery. They help in regulatory compliance, risk management, data governance, and improving overall trust in data.

It's important to note that the most effective tools are those that can integrate well with the existing data infrastructure, allowing for seamless lineage tracking across different systems and platforms. For example, a data lineage tool should be able to interface with databases, data warehouses, data lakes, ETL tools, BI tools, and any other technologies involved in the data life cycle.

Further, a good data lineage tool should provide both high-level and granular views of data lineage. High-level views are useful for understanding the overall flow of data, while granular views allow for the detailed inspection of transformations at each step.

In conclusion, a wide array of tools and platforms are available for managing data lineage, each with its strengths and considerations. Choosing the right tool involves understanding the organization's unique requirements and carefully assessing the capabilities of each tool against those requirements. Regardless of the choice, a good data lineage tool is an essential component of any data management strategy, providing transparency, facilitating compliance, and fostering trust in data.

OpenLineage format

OpenLineage is an open source initiative that aims to standardize data lineage collection, providing a universal and straightforward solution to a problem that's typically been challenging due to disparate data systems and tools. OpenLineage's universal model allows data engineers, data scientists, and other data-focused roles to accurately track and understand data as it flows across various platforms and processes.

The goal of OpenLineage is to create a unified and platform-agnostic model that enables the easy tracking of data lineage across numerous sources and systems. This approach reduces the complexity that's often associated with tracing data flows, especially in diverse data ecosystems.

OpenLineage isn't tied to a particular tool or platform, a characteristic that further bolsters its versatility. Its open standard encourages cross-platform compatibility, allowing it to operate seamlessly across an assortment of data tools and infrastructure. This flexibility facilitates a more inclusive and comprehensive overview of data lineage.

This initiative takes a practical approach to data lineage by focusing on operational metadata. Unlike traditional metadata that might solely represent the design or intent, operational metadata conveys what is happening as data moves and transforms. By focusing on this aspect, OpenLineage provides a realistic and valuable picture of data lineage.

At its core, OpenLineage is about creating transparency and confidence in data systems. Its common model promotes clarity, allowing organizations to maintain a high level of trust in their data operations. With OpenLineage, businesses can pinpoint exactly where their data has originated from and how it has evolved, leading to more informed and data-driven decisions.

In essence, OpenLineage aims to be a transformative force in the realm of data management. Its universal, adaptable, and transparent approach to data lineage offers a potential solution to one of the industry's most pressing and complex problems. Its emergence might well mark a pivotal moment in the advancement of data lineage understanding and management.

Benefits of using OpenLineage in data lineage management

First and foremost, OpenLineage's **standardization of lineage** metadata across diverse data systems and tools is a major boon. It eliminates the necessity to create custom lineage tracking solutions for each unique tool in a data stack, which significantly reduces time, effort, and the potential for errors.

The **flexibility** of OpenLineage is another standout benefit. Its platform-agnostic approach ensures seamless integration across numerous data systems. This compatibility makes it a versatile tool for organizations that leverage a wide array of data technologies, thereby enabling a more comprehensive lineage overview.

With its focus on operational metadata, OpenLineage offers a **realistic and accurate depiction** of data flows. By providing insights into actual data transformations and movements, it enables more informed decision-making and troubleshooting. This tangible information can prove instrumental in resolving data inconsistencies or errors.

OpenLineage also facilitates **regulatory compliance** and **data governance**. Offering a clear and detailed understanding of data sources, transformations, and destinations helps ensure that data is managed according to policies and regulations. This capability is especially beneficial for industries subject to stringent data regulations.

Additionally, OpenLineage bolsters data confidence within organizations. With its clear tracking of data lineage, it provides **transparency** into how data is handled and transformed. This transparency results in a higher level of trust in the data and its resultant insights, making data-driven decisions more reliable.

Finally, being an open source initiative, OpenLineage benefits from **community contributions**. This collaborative approach ensures continuous improvement and adaptability to new technologies or changes in the data landscape. Consequently, users of OpenLineage can be confident that the tool will evolve in tandem with industry advancements.

In conclusion, OpenLineage offers a wealth of benefits in data lineage management, from the enhanced integration and understanding of data flows to improved data governance and trust. By adopting OpenLineage, organizations can simplify and enrich their data lineage practices, leading to greater efficiency and more informed decision-making.

Practical implementation of OpenLineage

In practice, implementing OpenLineage involves defining lineage events and integrating these events with the data tools used within an organization. Let's delve into a basic example of how to utilize OpenLineage's APIs to create a lineage event:

```
from openlineage.client import OpenLineageClient
from openlineage.run import RunEvent, RunState, Run, Job, Dataset
open_lineage_client = OpenLineageClient(url="http://localhost:5000/
api/v1/lineage")
```

```
run_event = RunEvent(
  eventType=RunState.COMPLETE,
  eventTime="2023-01-01T12:00Z",
  run=Run(
    runId="abc123"
  ),
  job=Job(
    namespace="aws_s3",
    name="data-processing-job",
    facets={}
  ),
  inputs=[
    Dataset(
      namespace="aws_s3",
      name="s3://mybucket/input-data.csv",
      facets={}
    )
  ],
  outputs=[
    Dataset(
      namespace="postgres",
      name="jdbc:postgresql://database.example.com:5432/output",
      facets={}
    )
  ],
  producer="https://github.com/OpenLineage/OpenLineage/tree/0.0.1/
integration/common/openlineage/common/provider"
)
open_lineage_client.emit(run_event)
```

This Python code snippet utilizes an OpenLineage Python client to create and emit a run event indicating the completion of a job. The event encapsulates important details, such as the job name and namespace, the runID and the datasets used as inputs, and the datasets generated as outputs. After defining the event, the emit() function sends it to the OpenLineage server.

The preceding example assumes a locally running OpenLineage server and a Python environment with the OpenLineage client installed. In a real-world scenario, the server could be hosted remotely, and the job, run, and dataset details would be dynamically populated based on the actual data processing job.

In essence, OpenLineage's technical implementation revolves around constructing and emitting these lineage events across the various data operations in your system, thereby enabling detailed lineage tracking. By integrating such code snippets within data processing jobs, OpenLineage weaves an intricate web of data lineage, painting a comprehensive picture of your data's journey.

Data lineage in data governance, compliance, and troubleshooting

Data lineage is an essential element in the robust functioning of an organization's data infrastructure. It plays a pivotal role in data governance, compliance, and troubleshooting, forming the backbone of effective data management.

Data governance refers to the overall management of the availability, integrity, and security of data in an enterprise. It relies on the traceability and visibility of data, both of which are provided by data lineage. Understanding the path that data takes from its source to its endpoint allows organizations to assess the validity and reliability of their data. By having a clear picture of where data originates, how it's transformed, and where it's utilized, businesses can ensure that the information used in their decision-making processes is accurate and timely. Consequently, data lineage aids in improving the quality of business insights, thereby enhancing strategic decision-making.

In a world increasingly driven by data, compliance with data protection regulations has become crucial. Industries such as finance, healthcare, and e-commerce are subjected to stringent data protection laws. In this context, data lineage is instrumental in demonstrating compliance with these regulations. By tracing the journey of data, organizations can provide tangible proof of how data is sourced, processed, stored, and protected. This traceability is invaluable in the event of audits or regulatory checks, as it provides a comprehensive view of the data's lifecycle and the measures taken to protect it.

Troubleshooting is another area where data lineage proves invaluable functionality. When data inconsistencies or errors arise, understanding the path that the data has taken can significantly speed up the resolution process. Without data lineage, isolating the source of an error can be like finding a needle in a haystack, especially in complex, large-scale data ecosystems. However, with a clear view of the data's lifecycle provided by data lineage, pinpointing where transformations might have gone wrong becomes a more manageable task. This facilitates quicker error detection, correction, and overall system recovery.

Moreover, data lineage is not merely a tool for post-issue rectification; it also aids in proactive issue prevention. By regularly reviewing and analyzing the lineage of data, potential problems can be identified and rectified before they escalate into more significant issues.

Data lineage also plays a vital role in ensuring business continuity. During system migrations or upgrades, understanding the data's journey can help ensure that no critical data are lost or misinterpreted. This is critical in maintaining the integrity of business operations and ensuring a smooth transition during system upgrades.

In conclusion, data lineage forms a crucial aspect of an organization's data management strategy, contributing significantly to data governance, compliance, and troubleshooting. By providing transparency and traceability, it strengthens the reliability and integrity of the data, improves compliance with regulations, and enhances the efficiency of troubleshooting processes. Therefore, investing in robust data lineage practices is a smart move for any data-driven organization, leading to improved data quality, regulatory compliance, and operational efficiency.

While understanding the origins and transformations of data is crucial, equally vital is implementing robust governance practices and ensuring regulatory compliance. Data lineage provides transparency into data flows, but effective data governance gives structure and oversight to data management activities. Further, adherence to compliance requirements is imperative for operating legally and ethically. As we have seen, data lineage maps out the data journey. Now, let's explore how data governance frameworks and compliance strategies build on lineage capabilities to create a controlled, trustworthy data environment. With the right governance policies and compliance measures in place, organizations can manage integrated data responsibly and extract maximum value while minimizing risk.

Adhering to regulations and implementing robust governance frameworks

Data governance denotes the strategic, organizational approach taken to manage the availability, usability, quality, and security of data within an enterprise. It encompasses the policies, procedures, standards, and technologies that organizations implement to manage and ensure their data's integrity. In essence, data governance provides a strategic framework for data management, aiming to ensure that data assets are formally managed throughout the enterprise.

Compliance, on the other hand, refers to the process of adhering to established guidelines or specifications, such as laws, regulations, standards, and policies, that govern how organizations should handle, store, process, and protect data. In the context of data, compliance generally indicates conformity to laws, regulations, standards, and internal policies that dictate how data should be handled, stored, processed, and protected.

Examples of regulation laws and regulations that explain how organizations should handle, store, process, and protect data can be seen in the following:

- Data protection and privacy regulations such as GDPR, CCPA, and HIPAA dictate how personal data must be managed

- Industry-specific regulations such as PCI-DSS for payment card data, GLBA for financial data, and HITECH for healthcare data

- International data transfer regulations, such as EU-US Privacy Shield, provide frameworks for moving data across borders

- Government data handling standards for public sector organizations

- Organizational data security policies, retention policies, and classification schemes

- Data quality standards, such as ISO 8000 and DAMA-DMBOK, provide data management best practices

- Industry data formats and schemas such as FHIR for healthcare, ACORD for insurance, and XBRL for finance

- Open data standards, such as schema.org, DCAT, and data catalogs, enable interoperability

Data governance and compliance are intertwined concepts, as effective data governance practices can aid organizations in achieving regulatory compliance. Data governance sets the standard for data management activities, such as data quality, lineage, privacy, and security. When done effectively, it creates an environment conducive to meeting compliance requirements, which often dictate specific standards for many of these same activities.

Considering the ever-evolving landscape of data-related regulations, including the **General Data Protection Regulation (GDPR)** in the European Union and the **California Consumer Privacy Act (CCPA)** in the United States, compliance has emerged as a vital aspect of data management. These regulations impose stringent rules regarding the collection, storage, processing, and sharing of personal data, necessitating a rigorous approach to data governance.

While data governance focuses on maximizing the value of data, compliance is primarily risk-oriented, aiming to mitigate the legal and reputational risks associated with noncompliance. However, compliance should not be seen merely as a form of risk mitigation. Adherence to regulatory standards can enhance an organization's reputation, foster customer trust, and provide a competitive edge.

Data governance and compliance, therefore, serve as complementary aspects of a broader data management strategy. Data governance provides the framework and direction for managing data, while compliance ensures that the organization meets external regulatory requirements and internal data standards. Together, they facilitate an organized, controlled environment for data that balances the need for accessibility with the necessity of safeguarding sensitive information.

This is a succinct introduction to the concepts of data governance and compliance. As we proceed further, we will explore the key components of data governance and compliance in more detail, as well as their significance in data integration and the best practices to be implemented.

Data governance best practices

Data stewardship and **ownership** are vital components of a robust data governance framework, ensuring the management, integrity, and value of an organization's data. Data stewards oversee data assets, implementing measures for data quality and facilitating accessibility, while data owners have legal rights and control over the data, ensuring compliance and making strategic decisions. Together, data stewardship and ownership foster accountability and effective data management, minimizing risks and maximizing the benefits of data assets.

Data governance frameworks

Data governance frameworks serve as the structural backbone that guide the successful implementation and operation of data governance within an organization. These frameworks delineate the necessary **roles**, **responsibilities**, **procedures**, and **standards** required to manage and protect data assets effectively.

An efficient data governance framework is a combination of people, processes, and technologies. People form the governance team, including data stewards, data owners, and other key stakeholders.

Processes outline the standards, policies, and procedures for data management. Technology involves the tools and systems that support these processes and allow for the management and monitoring of data.

The following screenshots represent an example of a governance framework and all the various roots:

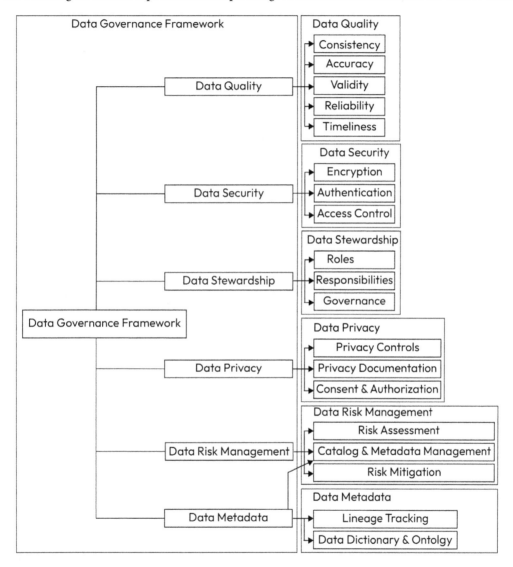

Figure 14.1 – Example of data governance framework

In the previous schema, the following elements are included:

- **Data governance framework**: The overarching framework

- **Data quality**: Focuses on data accuracy, consistency, and other quality dimensions
- **Data security**: Deals with data encryption, access control, and authentication
- **Data stewardship**: Involves roles, responsibilities, and governance mechanisms
- **Data privacy**: Includes privacy controls, documentation, and consent processes
- **Data risk management**: Involves risk assessments, compliance management, and risk mitigation strategies
- **Data metadata**: Deals with cataloging, lineage tracking, and data dictionaries

As is evident, the scope of data governance encompasses a wide array of themes, each with its own complexities and nuances. To provide a more targeted and insightful perspective, we will zero in on select aspects in the subsequent sections, enriching our overall understanding and aligning it with the overarching vision for data governance.

Establishing roles and responsibilities is a critical component of a data governance framework. A well-defined structure includes roles such as data stewards who are responsible for ensuring data quality, and data owners who have ultimate responsibility for data assets. Additionally, data users, who consume data for various business functions, and data custodians, who handle technical aspects of data management, are also crucial parts of the framework.

A robust data governance framework provides the foundation for consistent data handling practices. It standardizes how data is defined, stored, and accessed across the organization, facilitating data integration and interoperability. Standardization ensures that data quality is maintained, reducing the risks of errors and misunderstandings.

A data governance framework also outlines the data lifecycle, which is the stages that data passes through from creation to deletion. This lifecycle includes acquisition, storage, maintenance, usage, and the disposal of data. By defining this lifecycle, the framework ensures that data is handled appropriately at each stage, thereby maintaining its quality and integrity.

A data governance structure must also include accountability and transparency. **Accountability** guarantees that everyone involved in data management knows their roles and is held responsible for their actions. **Transparency** enables all stakeholders to understand how and why data decisions are made, as well as giving insight into data governance procedures.

A robust data governance framework also provides data security and privacy rules and processes. Given the growing significance of data breaches and severe data protection requirements, such as the GDPR, securing data security and privacy is critical. As a result, the framework should describe policies for access control, data encryption, and data anonymization.

The following screenshots represent the main relationship between data framework tools after the implementation of a data governance framework:

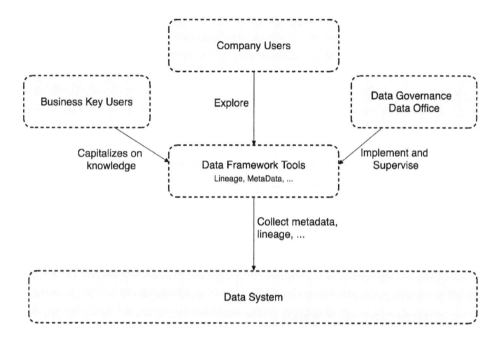

Figure 14.2 – Relationship between data framework tools and implementation

Implementing a data governance framework focuses initially on establishing roles, responsibilities, and processes, followed by deploying tools to support these processes. These tools evolve over time, starting with metadata capture and augmenting with functional information, eventually extending to observability. This phased approach ensures a solid foundation for governance while allowing for the progressive enrichment of tools to support an evolving data ecosystem.

The initial phase of establishing a data governance framework focuses on defining roles, responsibilities, and processes. Subsequently, tools are introduced to support these processes, evolving over time from metadata capture to enhancing functional information completeness. Eventually, this extends to data observability. Tools are selected, overseen, and implemented as per the governance team's directives, which may be centralized or distributed. While some metadata completion is automated, manual input is essential for functional knowledge, aiming to facilitate decision-making data access. The ongoing maintenance burden of this system should not be underestimated.

Technology is critical in enabling a data governance structure. Tools for data cataloging, metadata management, data quality control, and data lineage are essential for enforcing and sustaining the framework's norms and processes. Furthermore, the framework should have a data quality management approach. This includes creating data quality standards and defining data quality indicators, as well as developing data validation, cleaning, and enrichment methods.

To summarize, a data governance framework is an essential tool for ensuring that data is managed in accordance with the organization's business objectives and legal obligations. Role definition, standardization, lifecycle management, accountability, transparency, data security, privacy, data quality management, and the use of suitable technology are all critical components.

Organizations may gain better control over their data assets, increase data quality, promote effective data integration, maintain regulatory compliance, and ultimately drive improved decision-making by carefully creating and executing a data governance framework. The following sections will delve deeper into some of these key components of a data governance framework.

Data catalogs and metadata management

Data catalogs and **metadata management** play a crucial role in effective data governance. They provide the necessary structure and insight into an organization's data assets, facilitating their appropriate use and management. This segment will discuss these components in detail, emphasizing their importance and best practices in their implementation.

Data catalogs act as a comprehensive inventory of an organization's data assets. These catalogs serve as a centralized repository where data from various sources is indexed and organized. They facilitate the easier discovery, understanding, and management of data, providing users with a clearer overview of the available data, their sources, and their usage.

A well-structured data catalog should provide context for each data asset, which is typically achieved through metadata. Metadata is data about data, and it provides descriptive, structural, and administrative details about data assets. Descriptive metadata includes elements such as data names, descriptions, and tags. Structural metadata provides information about data organization, such as data types and relationships. Administrative metadata covers information such as data ownership, privacy status, and usage history.

Metadata management is the process of collecting, organizing, maintaining, and using this metadata. Good metadata management practices enable organizations to understand their data better, thereby improving data quality, consistency, and reliability. By providing context for each data asset, metadata management aids in the effective use of data catalogs.

One key aspect of metadata management is the creation and enforcement of metadata standards. These standards ensure consistency in metadata collection and use, making data assets more usable and manageable. These standards might include naming conventions, data typing rules, and mandatory metadata fields.

Data catalogs and metadata management together support data discoverability. They allow users to search and filter data assets based on different criteria, such as data source, data type, or data owner. This functionality is crucial in large organizations where data assets can span across various departments and systems.

Furthermore, data catalogs often incorporate data lineage information, which is crucial for understanding the origin of data and their transformation over time. This information aids in assessing data quality, validating compliance, and troubleshooting data issues.

The process of populating a data catalog and managing metadata is often facilitated by metadata extraction and scanning tools. These tools automatically extract metadata from data sources and populate the data catalogs, reducing manual effort and increasing accuracy. Moreover, they enable real-time updates to the catalogs as changes occur in the data landscape.

Data catalogs also play a significant role in data security and privacy. By tracking data ownership and privacy status, data catalogs help enforce access controls and privacy policies. This feature is particularly critical in the context of regulations such as GDPR, which demand strict controls over personal data.

In summary, data catalogs and metadata management form a critical component of a robust data governance framework. They provide the visibility and control necessary to manage data assets effectively. By adopting best practices in data cataloging and metadata management, organizations can ensure their data are easily discoverable, well-understood, and appropriately used and protected. This allows organizations to leverage their data more effectively, leading to better decision-making and improved compliance with regulations. The next section will further discuss the topic of data stewardship and ownership, another crucial aspect of data governance.

Data stewardship and ownership

In data governance, two pivotal concepts are **data stewardship** and **data ownership**. Both represent integral facets of managing and safeguarding data, ensuring its integrity, usability, and value for an organization.

Data stewardship pertains to the responsibility and practices involved in managing an organization's data assets. Data stewards are often individuals or teams appointed to manage the lifecycle of data within an organization. Their responsibilities can range from defining data quality standards and implementing data privacy measures to facilitating data accessibility for end-users. They act as the custodians of data, overseeing its proper use, maintenance, and protection.

A key function of data stewards is to ensure data quality. They implement procedures for data cleansing, validation, and enrichment to maintain accurate, up-to-date data. They also monitor data usage and interactions, intervening when necessary to correct inconsistencies or prevent data misuse.

Data ownership, on the other hand, refers to the individual or entity that has legal rights and complete control over a set of data. Data owners are typically responsible for what data is collected, how it's used, and who can access it. They are accountable for meeting regulatory compliance and ethical standards in data handling.

The clarification of data ownership is crucial in data governance as it establishes who has the ultimate authority and responsibility over data assets. This determination can help prevent data misuse, foster accountability, and facilitate better decision-making.

Together, data stewardship and data ownership form an integral part of a robust data governance framework. These roles bring order and accountability to data management, helping organizations to capitalize on their data assets while minimizing risks. In the following sections, we will delve deeper into compliance considerations and strategies, which is another essential aspect of data governance.

Compliance considerations and strategies

We now turn to the crucial aspect of **compliance considerations** and **data integration strategies**. This section provides an overview of the regulatory requirements that organizations must follow when integrating data from various sources. It explores the importance of compliance to ensure privacy, security, and data integrity and offers valuable insight into effective strategies and case studies that demonstrate successful compliance implementation.

Overview of regulatory requirements

In today's data-driven society, regulatory standards are critical for safeguarding the protection and privacy of people's information. Organizations must follow these standards to preserve data governance and ethical practices. Let's look at regulatory requirements and their relevance.

The **General Data Protection Regulation** (**GDPR**), for example, focuses on protecting individuals' personal data inside the **European Union** (**EU**). It establishes principles for data collection, storage, processing, and sharing while stressing openness, consent, and the rights of persons. Organizations that handle the data of EU individuals must comply with the GDPR.

Several limits exist in the United States depending on the type of business and data. The **Health Insurance Portability and Accountability Act** (**HIPAA**), for example, governs healthcare data privacy and security, whereas the **Gramm-Leach-Bliley Act** (**GLBA**) safeguards financial data. Furthermore, the **California Consumer Privacy Act** (**CCPA**) regulates California residents' personal data. Adherence to these criteria necessitates the implementation of suitable protections to protect data privacy, security, and individual rights.

Regulations tailored to the industry are also essential. The **Payment Card Industry Data Security Standard** (**PCI DSS**) establishes criteria for enterprises that handle credit card information with the goal of preventing fraud and safeguarding cardholder data.

International data exchanges need enterprises that consider cross-border data flow restrictions. The EU-US Privacy Shield and **Standard Contractual Clauses** (**SCCs**) establish legal foundations for data transfers across countries with varying privacy laws.

Organizations must employ comprehensive data protection methods, such as encryption, access restrictions, and secure storage, to comply with regulatory obligations. Regular risk assessments, incident response plans, and continuous monitoring are all critical procedures.

Noncompliance with regulatory regulations can result in serious penalties such as costly fines, legal ramifications, and harm to one's reputation and consumer confidence. As a result, firms must keep up-to-date with developing legislation, change their procedures accordingly, and cultivate a culture of compliance.

Organizations that prioritize regulatory compliance demonstrate their commitment to responsible data management, create consumer trust, and reduce the risks associated with data breaches and privacy violations.

Compliance strategies for data integration

Compliance strategies for data integration are crucial in ensuring that organizations adhere to regulatory requirements and maintain ethical data practices. These strategies encompass various approaches and measures to achieve compliance while effectively integrating data. Let's explore an overview of compliance strategies for data integration.

One fundamental strategy is conducting a comprehensive data inventory and assessment. This involves identifying all data sources, understanding their characteristics, and assessing their compliance status. By mapping the data landscape, organizations can identify potential compliance risks and develop appropriate mitigation strategies.

Another key strategy is implementing data governance frameworks. These frameworks provide the structure and guidelines for managing data in a compliant manner. They define roles, responsibilities, and processes to ensure data quality, security, and privacy. By establishing data governance practices, organizations can enforce compliance throughout the data integration lifecycle.

Data anonymization and pseudonymization are effective strategies to protect privacy during data integration. Anonymization involves removing or encrypting **personally identifiable information (PII)** from datasets, making it impossible to identify individuals. Pseudonymization replaces direct identifiers with pseudonyms, allowing data to be processed while protecting individual identities. By applying these techniques, organizations can reduce privacy risks and comply with regulations such as the GDPR.

Implementing data access controls and encryption mechanisms is another critical strategy. Access controls restrict data access to authorized individuals, ensuring that only those with proper permissions can view and manipulate sensitive data. Encryption adds an extra layer of protection by encoding data, rendering it unreadable without the appropriate decryption keys. These measures safeguard data integrity and confidentiality, addressing compliance requirements related to data security.

Regular data monitoring and auditing are essential strategies to ensure ongoing compliance. By continuously monitoring data activities and conducting regular audits, organizations can promptly identify and address compliance gaps or violations. This allows for timely corrective actions and demonstrates a commitment to maintaining compliance in data integration processes.

Collaboration with legal and compliance teams is also crucial. These teams provide expertise in interpreting and applying regulatory requirements to data integration practices. Their involvement ensures that compliance considerations are properly incorporated into the organization's data integration strategies and processes.

Lastly, organizations should stay updated with evolving regulatory landscapes. Compliance requirements are subject to change, and organizations must adapt their strategies accordingly. Monitoring regulatory updates and engaging in industry discussions can help organizations proactively adjust their data integration strategies to meet new compliance standards.

By adopting effective compliance strategies for data integration, organizations can mitigate risks, protect data privacy, and maintain regulatory compliance. These strategies provide a framework for responsible data practices while enabling organizations to leverage the value of integrated data for informed decision-making and innovation.

Case studies and examples

Case studies and examples play a vital role in understanding and illustrating the practical implementation of compliance strategies in data integration. By examining real-world scenarios and their outcomes, organizations can gain insights into effective approaches and learn from successful implementations. Let's explore some case studies and examples that highlight the importance of compliance strategies in data integration.

One notable case study is the implementation of a data governance framework in a healthcare organization. By adopting a comprehensive framework that incorporated data stewardship, ownership, and metadata management, the organization was able to establish clear accountability and ensure compliance with regulatory requirements, such as HIPAA. This case study demonstrates how a well-defined data governance framework can support data integration while maintaining compliance with industry-specific regulations.

Another example focuses on a financial institution that successfully implemented data anonymization techniques for regulatory compliance. By applying anonymization methods to customer data, such as replacing personally identifiable information with pseudonyms, the institution ensured compliance with data privacy regulations such as the GDPR. This case study showcases how compliance strategies, specifically data anonymization, can enable organizations to leverage data for analysis and integration while safeguarding privacy.

In the realm of data security, a case study involving a multinational corporation highlights the importance of encryption in data integration. By implementing robust encryption mechanisms during data transfer and storage, the organization effectively protected sensitive data and complied with data security regulations. This example emphasizes the significance of encryption as a compliance strategy to mitigate security risks in data integration processes.

Furthermore, an example from the retail industry demonstrates the impact of data monitoring and auditing in ensuring compliance. By implementing regular data audits and monitoring data activities, a retail company identified and addressed data integrity issues, ensuring compliance with regulations such as **Sarbanes-Oxley (SOX)**. This case study highlights the role of ongoing data monitoring as a compliance strategy to maintain data integrity and meet regulatory requirements.

Another case study showcases the benefits of collaboration between legal and compliance teams in data integration. In a telecommunications company, close collaboration between these teams helped interpret complex regulatory requirements and develop compliance strategies tailored to the organization's data integration processes. This example emphasizes the value of cross-functional collaboration in ensuring compliance and aligning data practices with legal obligations.

These case studies and examples demonstrate the practical application of compliance strategies in data integration. They highlight the importance of data governance frameworks, data anonymization, encryption, data monitoring, collaboration, and other strategies in achieving compliance objectives. By analyzing these real-world scenarios, organizations can gain valuable insights into the successful implementation of compliance strategies and adapt them to their own data integration processes.

Overall, case studies and examples provide tangible evidence of the benefits of compliance strategies in data integration. They serve as practical illustrations of how organizations can navigate regulatory requirements, protect data privacy, ensure data security, and maintain integrity throughout the data integration journey. By studying these examples, organizations can enhance their understanding of compliance best practices and develop effective strategies tailored to their unique data integration needs.

Navigating the labyrinth of data governance

Implementing a data governance framework might appear straightforward, but you can encounter many challenges, as discussed in the following subsections.

Fostering internal change for effective data governance

Incorporating a successful data governance framework isn't just about introducing new systems; it's about fostering an inclusive culture of change within the company. Comprehensive change management, combined with prior training, ensures that every stakeholder understands the new processes and their roles. Moreover, involving employees at every level in the transition promotes ownership and acceptance of the changes. This internal support is crucial for mitigating resistance, ensuring smoother implementation, and embedding the governance practices into the company's fabric for lasting success.

Complexity of data lineage and management

Maintaining up-to-date, comprehensive data lineage amidst the ever-evolving data landscape is a formidable challenge. Organizations grapple with the intricacies of tracing data origins, transformations, and flow through complex systems. This task becomes increasingly daunting with the expansion of data sources and the intricate web of processes involved in modern data ecosystems. Ensuring accuracy and clarity in data lineage not only demands meticulous attention but also a robust framework to manage the sheer complexity and dynamic nature of data assets.

Bridging theory and practice in data governance

Translating theoretical data governance frameworks into practical, actionable strategies can be a steep hill to climb. Organizations often find it challenging to align the idealized models of governance with the ground realities of their data infrastructure. The gap between conceptual frameworks and their implementation can lead to confusion, inefficiencies, and missed opportunities. It is crucial for businesses to navigate this divide with a pragmatic approach, ensuring that theoretical guidelines are adaptively applied to meet the unique demands and constraints of their data environments.

Summary

Throughout this chapter, we embarked on a comprehensive exploration of the multifaceted domains of lineage, governance, and compliance in the context of data integration. We began by understanding the pivotal role of lineage in tracing the origin and transformation journey of data. The knowledge acquired here equips readers with the ability to visualize and comprehend the entire lifecycle of data, from their inception to their eventual consumption, ensuring transparency and trust.

Diving deeper, we tackled the concept of governance, which emphasized the importance of protocols, standards, and best practices in managing data. This section imparted crucial skills on maintaining data's credibility, ensuring its consistency, and safeguarding its integrity, irrespective of its source or destination.

Lastly, the deep dive into compliance illuminated the intricate web of regulatory requirements that modern data operations must adhere to. Readers have been equipped with the knowledge to navigate this complex landscape, ensuring that data not only serves its intended purpose but also complies with legal and ethical standards.

In summing up this enriching chapter, it's evident that the knowledge and skills acquired here lay a robust foundation for any data professional. They act as a compass, guiding them through the challenges of modern data integration, ensuring transparency, credibility, and compliance.

This chapter provided an in-depth look at three critical pillars of trusted data integration: understanding data lineage, implementing robust data governance, and ensuring regulatory compliance. Next, we will explore practical applications and architectural patterns for real-time data integration.

15

Various Architecture Use Cases

In this book, we have journeyed through the intricacies of data integration, and this chapter is the culmination of all the knowledge amassed. Here, we dive into the practical application of the principles and techniques discussed throughout the preceding chapters.

This chapter explores various data integration architectures for real-time, cloud, geospatial, and IoT analysis. Each use case presents the unique requirements and challenges stemming from diverse data sources and business needs based on our own experience. Proper tools, techniques, and architectural patterns empower effective integration, but factors such as scalability, heterogeneity, spatial relationships, and security must be addressed. By choosing optimal architectures tailored to specific integration needs, organizations can harness data-driven insights across pivotal domains. Looking ahead, emerging trends, such as machine learning and new technologies, will shape the data integration landscape.

By the end of this chapter, you will have developed an understanding of the distinct challenges and opportunities of real-time, cloud-based, geospatial, and IoT data analysis in the context of the broader themes of the book. You will be able to recognize the architectures best suited for each data integration domain, drawing connections to the foundational principles discussed in chapters 1 to 14. You can process the practical acumen to apply these architectures effectively in real-world scenarios.

Join us in this chapter, as we weave together the threads of knowledge from the entire book, showcasing the architectures that power the diverse terrains of data integration.

The following topics will be covered in this chapter:

- Data integration for real-time data analysis
- Data integration for cloud-based data analysis
- Data integration for geospatial data analysis
- Data integration for IoT data analysis

Data integration for real-time data analysis

Modern data-driven decision-making relies on real-time data processing and examination to help companies adapt to changing situations. Businesses across sectors need continuous analytics in today's fast-paced and connected environment.

Real-time acquisition and interpretation of data enables companies to make well-timed and informed choices by collecting, analyzing, and decoding information as soon as possible. This method allows firms to react swiftly to market trends, consumer behavior, and operational issues, providing a competitive edge.

IoT, social media, and streaming services have expanded the need for real-time analytics. These technologies produce massive volumes of data requiring quick processing and review to gain insights.

Real-time analytics can detect abnormalities, uncover patterns and trends, enhance processes, and improve user experiences. It enables companies to rapidly comprehend their data and make strategic decisions.

Conducting these kinds of analytics poses challenges. To obtain reliable insights, organizations must consider data latency, scalability, and quality. They need robust infrastructure, sophisticated analytical tools, and rapid data processing frameworks to examine continuously incoming data.

This section discusses real-time analytics needs, problems, and best practices. We will examine the tools, technologies, and architectural patterns that enable real-time data integration. Organizations can make significant decisions by understanding it.

> **Expert tips**
>
> To mitigate the risk of setting unattainable goals, it's advisable to shift the conversation towards continuous rather than real-time data processing. This approach can help manage expectations regarding costs, infrastructure needs, and skill requirements that might otherwise be overwhelming for your organization.

Requirements for real-time data integration

In the context of real-time data analysis, it is first necessary to identify the needs of at least three fundamental axes:

- **Latency**: Low latency is needed for real-time insights and quick reactions to changing situations. Real-time data must be handled and analyzed quickly. Reduce data processing, transmission, and transformation delays to reduce latency. High-speed networks, algorithm optimization, and distributed computing architectures that minimize data pipeline latency can achieve this.

- **Scalability**: This entails handling increased data quantities and data sources without compromising performance. Real-time analytics involves processing enormous, continuous data streams. Scalable architectures and technologies let enterprises process high-velocity data. Distributed computing frameworks such as Apache Kafka and Apache Spark provide parallel processing and horizontal scalability.

- **Data Quality**: Organizations need accurate, thorough, and reliable data to get valuable insights. Real-time data analysis makes judgments based on data trustworthiness, which means that the data being analyzed is up to date, accurately captured, and correctly processed to reflect the current situation. It implies that there's confidence in the data's validity and that it hasn't been corrupted or misinterpreted during collection, transmission, or processing. Data integrity and real-time insights depend on data validation and cleaning. Data profiling, data cleaning, and anomaly detection can assist fix real-time data quality concerns. To maintain data quality, companies should implement data governance and monitoring strategies (*Chapter 13, Data Quality and Data Observability*).

These needs require proper tools, technologies, and architectural patterns such as in-memory databases or stream processing framework, which will be discussed in the next sub-section. By meeting these standards, firms may use real-time data analysis to obtain insights, make educated decisions, and remain ahead in today's fast-paced, data-driven business market.

Challenges in real-time data integration

In the realm of real-time data integration, organizations face critical challenges that must be addressed to effectively process and analyze data. This section explores the key obstacles of data volume and velocity, data format variability, and data consistency, offering insights and strategies to overcome these hurdles and optimize real-time data integration efforts.

Data volume and velocity

The volume and velocity of data in real-time data integration present significant challenges that organizations must overcome to effectively process and analyze data. With the exponential growth of data generated from various sources, including sensors, social media, and IoT devices, handling large volumes of data streaming at high speeds has become a critical concern.

Organizations need to design and implement scalable infrastructure and architectures capable of handling the continuous influx of data. For example, a typical organization may ingest terabytes or petabytes of data on a daily basis from various sources such as web logs, mobile apps, IoT devices, and more. This high volume and velocity of streaming data requires robust platforms. This includes leveraging distributed computing technologies, such as Apache Kafka (`https://kafka.apache.org/`) or Apache Flink (`https://flink.apache.org/`), to handle the high data volumes and process the data in parallel.

Apache Kafka provides high throughput, low latency, and fault-tolerant durable messaging through its distributed publish-subscribe messaging system. Key capabilities include persistence, replication, partitioning, and parallel processing. Apache Flink is a distributed stream processing framework with checkpointing, savepoints, and high throughput. Both Kafka and Flink leverage distributed architecture to ingest and process high-velocity streaming data efficiently.

Additionally, organizations must consider data storage options such as Apache Hadoop (`https://hadoop.apache.org/`) and cloud data lakes that can efficiently handle the data velocity, ensuring that the data is ingested, processed, and stored in near real time. The Hadoop ecosystem, including HDFS and tools such as Apache Spark, allows for scalable and resilient data storage and processing. Cloud data lakes on platforms such as AWS, Azure, and GCP also provide managed services for real-time and batch data processing. The choice of specific tools and technologies will depend on the organization's existing infrastructure, budget, and other requirements. However, the key is to leverage distributed systems and cloud-native platforms designed for high-volume, high-velocity data scenarios.

Data format variability

Data format variability is another challenge in real-time data integration. Data sources often have different formats, structures, and schemas, making it difficult to seamlessly integrate and analyze the data. For example, an organization may have data from sensors in JSON format, log files in plain text, database tables in relational format, and external APIs returning XML. The heterogeneity of data formats requires organizations to develop robust data transformation and mapping techniques. Transforming JSON to relational tables, parsing text logs to extract fields, mapping XML schemas to internal data models, and normalizing different units and representations are common challenges. Organizations struggle to build adaptable pipelines that can handle a variety of formats from diverse sources. The effort and complexity of data wrangling should not be underestimated. Choosing flexible data integration platforms that can handle multiple protocols and provide built-in transformers, or developing custom data parsing and normalization logic, are key to overcoming the variability of formats. With careful planning and the right tools, organizations can build real-time data integration flows that unlock insights from diverse data.

Organizations should implement data integration pipelines that can handle diverse data formats and perform real-time transformations. This involves developing data schema mapping rules and employing technologies, such as Apache Avro or Apache Parquet, to standardize the data format. Additionally, organizations can consider using alternative data serialization systems such as Protocol Buffers from Google, Thrift from Facebook, or MessagePack. These provide similar capabilities to Avro and Parquet for serializing structured data in an efficient binary format. When comparing these platforms, Avro and Parquet have the advantage of being supported natively in many big data frameworks such as Apache Spark and Hadoop. Protocol Buffers and Thrift require additional libraries for integration. MessagePack is useful for simpler use cases and has bindings for many programming languages. Additionally, organizations should consider using data catalogs or metadata management solutions, such as Apache Atlas or Alation, to provide a centralized repository for storing and managing metadata, making it easier to understand and reconcile the different data formats.

Data consistency

Ensuring data consistency is crucial in real-time data integration. Real-time scenarios involve continuous data flows, updates, and changes, which can lead to data inconsistencies if not properly managed. Organizations must establish mechanisms to handle data updates, inserts, and deletes in a manner that maintains data integrity and consistency.

One approach is to implement **change data capture** (CDC) techniques, where only the changes to the data are captured and propagated in real time, reducing the processing overhead. This allows organizations to keep track of data modifications and ensure that the integrated data remains consistent. Implementing CDC can be achieved using tools such as Debezium or AWS DMS. Additionally, organizations should implement data validation mechanisms, such as data quality rules and anomaly detection algorithms, to identify and resolve any inconsistencies or errors in real time.

Real-time data integration requires scalable infrastructure, distributed computing, data transformation, and consistency to address volume, velocity, and variability and unlock insights.

Best practices for implementing real-time data integration

When working on real-time data integration, implementing best practices is essential for ensuring efficient and reliable data processing and analysis. This section explores the key considerations for implementing real-time data integration, covering tools and technologies, architectural patterns, performance optimization, and metadata management. By following these best practices, organizations can unlock the potential of real-time data to drive impactful outcomes and strategic direction in today's fast-paced and data-driven landscape. Rather than just passively gathering insights, leaders can activate real-time data to make decisive actions that create tangible value. With the ability to respond and adapt in real-time, businesses can accelerate growth, deepen customer relationships, mitigate risks, and outmaneuver the competition. However, this competitive advantage hinges on having the right real-time data infrastructure and strategies in place.

Tools and technologies

Implementing real-time data integration requires careful consideration of the tools and technologies that can support efficient and seamless data processing and analysis. Organizations can leverage streaming platforms such as Apache Kafka Streams, Apache Flink, or Apache Storm, that enable the ingestion and processing of high-velocity data streams. These platforms ensure a continuous flow of data and enable real-time analytics. Additionally, technologies such as Apache Spark provide powerful frameworks for near-real-time data processing based on micro-batch architecture, allowing for complex computations and analytics. Choosing the appropriate tools and technologies that align with specific requirements and use cases is crucial for successful real-time data integration.

Architectural patterns

To ensure flexibility and scalability in real-time data integration, organizations should adopt suitable architectural patterns. **Event-driven architectures** and **microservices architectures** are commonly used in real-time data integration scenarios. Event-driven architectures facilitate the decoupling of data producers and consumers, enabling efficient data flow and processing. This approach allows for event-driven processing, where data is processed and reacted upon as events occur.

The following schema illustrates an example of event-driven architecture for real-time data analysis:

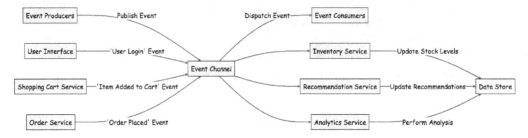

Figure 15.1 – Example of event-driven architecture for real-time data analysis

On the other hand, microservices architectures enable the creation of modular and independent components, providing scalability and agility in handling real-time data. By breaking down the integration process into smaller, manageable services, organizations can scale their infrastructure based on demand and achieve better responsiveness.

The following schema illustrates an example of microservices architecture for real-time data analysis:

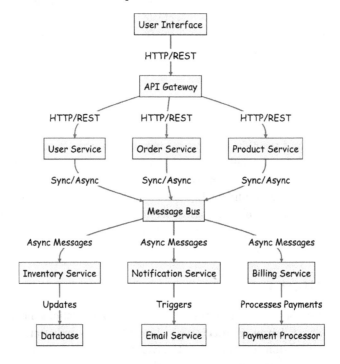

Figure 15.2 – Example of microservices architecture for real-time data analysis

The following table can help you to decide between each architecture and will bring you a comparison of event-driven and microservices architectures:

Criteria	Event-driven architecture	Microservices architecture
Primary focus	Real-time data processing and reaction to events.	Modular development with independent services.
Communication style	Asynchronous, event-based communication.	Synchronous or asynchronous, service-based communication.
Scalability and flexibility	Highly scalable due to decoupled nature.	Independently scalable services.
System coupling	Loose coupling, components interact through events.	Loose coupling, services interact through APIs.
Development complexity	Can be complex due to its asynchronous nature and event management.	Modular but can be complex to manage inter-service interactions.
Technology diversity	Typically consistent within the event ecosystem.	Allows diverse technology stacks for different services.
Real-time processing	Excellent for real-time event processing and reactivity.	Depends on service implementation; generally capable.
Maintenance and updates	Focused on event schema and event handling logic.	Easier to update individual services independently.
Use case suitability	Ideal for reactive systems, IoT, fraud detection, and so on.	Suited for large-scale applications with diverse requirements.
System resilience	Resilient to component failures due to decoupling.	Resilience depends on service isolation and fault tolerance.
Team structure compatibility	Requires expertise in event-driven design and implementation.	Suitable for teams divided by service functionalities.
Integration with existing systems	Easier if existing systems are event-centric.	Easier if existing systems are service-oriented or modular.

Table 15.1 – Comparison between event-driven and microservices architectures

> **Expert advice**
>
> When choosing between event-driven and microservices architectures, the use case plays a pivotal role. However, equally crucial are the context of your company and the skill set of your employees. A mismatch in organizational capabilities or expertise can hamper the effective implementation and maintenance of the chosen architecture. It's essential to align the architecture not only with the project requirements but also with your team's proficiency and the overall company infrastructure.

Performance optimization

Optimizing the performance of real-time data integration is crucial for timely and accurate processing. Organizations can employ various techniques and strategies to enhance performance. Data parallelism and distributed computing frameworks enable the processing of data in parallel, resulting in faster data ingestion and analysis. This approach involves breaking down data processing tasks into smaller units that can be executed concurrently across multiple computing resources. These resources might include on-premises infrastructure, localized cloud services, or even external platforms, providing a flexible and scalable approach to data handling depending on your buying, security, and architecture strategies. Additionally, techniques such as data caching, in-memory computing, and query optimization can significantly improve the speed and efficiency of real-time data integration processes (*Chapter 7, Optimizing Storage Performances*). Continuous monitoring and performance tuning play a vital role in identifying and addressing bottlenecks or latency issues, ensuring smooth and efficient real-time data integration.

Metadata management

Effective metadata management is essential for successful real-time data integration. Metadata provides valuable insights into the data, including its structure, source, quality, and transformations. Implementing a robust metadata management system enables efficient data discovery, lineage tracking, and impact analysis (*Chapter 14, Data Lineage*). Metadata also facilitates data governance, compliance, and data life cycle management. By establishing standardized metadata definitions and implementing metadata-driven processes, organizations can improve the reliability, consistency, and usability of real-time integrated data. This, in turn, enables data consumers to understand and trust the real-time data they are working with, leading to more informed decision-making.

By following these best practices, organizations can ensure the successful implementation of real-time data integration. Carefully selecting the appropriate tools and technologies, adopting suitable architectural patterns, optimizing performance, and implementing effective metadata management practices are key to achieving seamless and reliable real-time data integration. These practices empower organizations to leverage the power of real-time analytics, gain timely insights, and make data-driven decisions that drive business success.

Use case: Real-time data analysis with AWS architecture

To apply these explanations, here is a use case based on the field of retail. We will take the AWS environment as a framework, but we could have taken another cloud, or an on-premises solution.

Example use case: Retail analytics

In the retail industry, real-time data analysis plays a crucial role in monitoring sales, inventory, and customer behavior. Let's explore a use case where a retail company leverages AWS architecture for real-time data integration and analysis:

- *Data sources*: The retail company collects data from various sources, such as **point-of-sale** (**POS**) systems, online transactions, customer interactions, and social media feeds.

- *Data ingestion*: AWS Kinesis is utilized to ingest data from these diverse sources in real time. Kinesis allows the company to capture, process, and store streaming data in scalable and durable data streams.

- *Data processing*: AWS Lambda functions are employed for real-time data processing. These functions enable the company to execute code in response to specific events, ensuring rapid and automated data transformation and enrichment.

- *Data storage*: The processed data is stored in Amazon Simple Storage Service) for its scalability, durability, and cost-effectiveness. S3 provides a reliable data lake where the company can securely store vast amounts of structured and unstructured data.

- *Data analysis*: Amazon Redshift, a fully managed data warehousing service, is employed for real-time data analysis. Redshift allows the retail company to run complex analytical queries on large datasets, providing near-instantaneous insights into sales trends, customer preferences, and inventory management.

- *Visualization and reporting*: Amazon QuickSight, a business intelligence tool, is used to create interactive dashboards and visualizations. These visual representations enable stakeholders to gain actionable insights from real-time data, helping them make informed business decisions.

The following schema illustrates the high-level AWS architecture for real-time data analysis in our retail analytics use case:

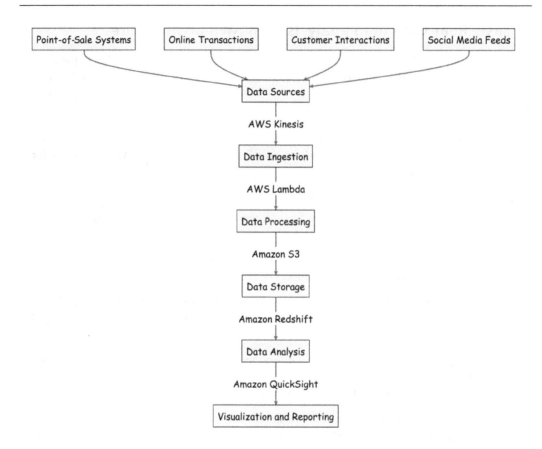

Figure 15.3 – High-level AWS architecture for real-time data analysis in our retail analytics use case

With this AWS architecture in place, the retail company can continuously monitor sales performance, detect trends, optimize inventory levels, and personalize customer experiences in real time. By leveraging real-time data integration and analysis, the company gains a competitive edge in the dynamic retail landscape.

Please note that this is just one example of a use case and AWS architecture for real-time data analysis. The actual implementation may vary based on specific business requirements and data sources.

Next, we'll discuss data integration for cloud-based data analysis.

Data integration for cloud-based data analysis

Cloud-based data analysis has revolutionized the way organizations handle and extract insights from their data. In this section, we will explore the fundamentals of cloud-based data analysis and its significance in today's digital landscape.

Cloud-based data analysis refers to the process of leveraging cloud computing resources and services to analyze large volumes of data in a cost-effective and scalable manner. The cloud offers a flexible and on-demand infrastructure that enables organizations to store, process, and analyze data without the need for extensive on-premises infrastructure.

By adopting cloud-based data analysis, organizations can benefit from various advantages such as scalability, flexibility, and cost optimization.

As with any technology, cloud-based data analysis comes with its own set of challenges, such as security, latency, or compliance and regulatory challenges.

Advantages of cloud-based data integration

Cloud-based data analysis offers immense potential for organizations to unlock insights from their data. Its scalability, flexibility, and cost optimization benefits make it a compelling choice for modern data analysis needs.

Scalability

Scalability is a key advantage as cloud platforms provide the ability to dynamically scale computing resources up or down based on demand. This elasticity ensures that organizations can handle data analysis workloads of any size without experiencing performance bottlenecks. Traditional on-premises solutions often face limitations in terms of hardware capacity, processing power, and storage, which can hinder the integration of large volumes of data or accommodate sudden spikes in demand.

In contrast, cloud-based data integration offers elastic resources that can be dynamically allocated based on the organization's needs. Cloud service providers can seamlessly scale up or down to handle varying workloads, ensuring that data integration processes remain efficient and responsive. This scalability allows organizations to easily accommodate growing data volumes, accommodate seasonal variations, or handle peak demand periods without compromising performance.

Flexibility

Flexibility is another significant advantage of cloud-based data integration. Cloud platforms offer a wide range of tools, services, and integration techniques that cater to different data integration requirements. Organizations can leverage a variety of approaches, such as **extract, transform, load (ETL)**, **change data capture** (**CDC**), or real-time streaming, based on their specific use cases and data sources. Whether it's data warehousing, machine learning, or real-time analytics, the cloud provides a comprehensive ecosystem of services that can be tailored to specific needs.

Cloud-based data integration allows organizations to seamlessly integrate data from diverse sources, including on-premises systems, cloud-based applications, databases, and third-party APIs. It enables the consolidation and harmonization of data, ensuring consistency and accuracy across different datasets. The flexibility provided by the cloud empowers organizations to choose the most suitable integration approach and adapt it as their data integration needs evolve.

Moreover, cloud platforms often offer pre-built connectors and integration services for popular data sources and applications, simplifying the integration process. This flexibility allows organizations to quickly integrate new data sources or adopt new technologies without significant disruptions, enabling agility and responsiveness in data integration initiatives.

Cost optimization

Cost optimization is also a significant advantage of cloud-based data analysis. With the pay-as-you-go pricing model, organizations only pay for the resources they use, eliminating the need for upfront investments in hardware and infrastructure, software licenses, and ongoing maintenance costs. These costs can be prohibitive, especially for small and medium-sized organizations with limited resources. Additionally, the cloud's ability to automate resource provisioning and management further optimizes costs by eliminating idle resources.

In contrast, cloud-based data integration follows a pay-as-you-go model, where organizations only pay for the resources and services they consume. Cloud service providers offer flexible pricing plans, allowing organizations to scale their data integration efforts according to their needs and budgets. This eliminates the need for upfront capital expenditures and enables cost optimization by aligning costs with actual usage.

Cloud-based data integration also eliminates the operational overhead associated with managing and maintaining on-premises infrastructure. The cloud service provider handles the infrastructure provisioning, maintenance, and updates, freeing up IT resources and reducing administrative costs. Additionally, organizations can leverage the cloud's economies of scale, benefiting from shared infrastructure and services, which further drives down costs compared to maintaining dedicated on-premises infrastructure.

> **Expert advice**
>
> However, while the pay-as-you-go model is favorable in many situations, it is not always the most cost-effective pricing model for all scenarios. For example, organizations with consistent workloads may find that a fixed pricing model is more economical over the long term. With use cases where usage is constantly at peak levels especially, the incremental costs of pay-as-you-go could add up quickly, making a traditional bulk purchase or licensing arrangement more financially viable.

Furthermore, cloud-based data integration enables cost savings through improved efficiency and productivity. With cloud platforms, organizations can automate and streamline data integration processes, reducing manual effort and minimizing the risk of errors. This efficiency translates into time savings and increased productivity for data integration teams, ultimately leading to cost savings for the organization.

Challenges in cloud-based data integration

Cloud-based data integration brings forth a set of unique challenges that organizations must overcome to achieve seamless and efficient operations. These challenges primarily revolve around data security and privacy, data transfer and latency, and compliance and regulations, which demand careful attention and strategic solutions:

Data security and privacy

Ensuring robust data security and privacy is paramount in cloud-based data integration. The cloud environment introduces additional risks due to shared infrastructure and potential vulnerabilities. Organizations must implement comprehensive security measures to protect sensitive data from unauthorized access, breaches, and data leaks.

The following screenshot lists the security assets and strategy that must at least be defined on a cloud-based data integration platform:

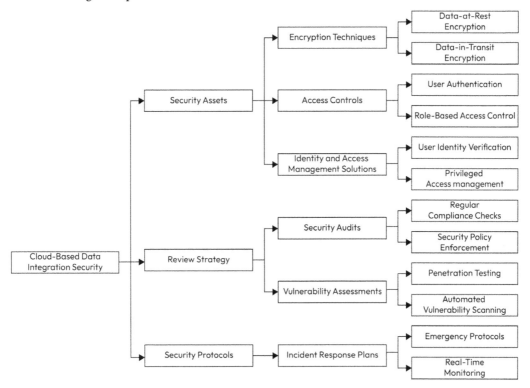

Figure 15.4 – Various security assets and strategy for cloud-based architecture

Security Assets form the core of cloud-based data security. In this category are the following crucial components:

- **Encryption techniques**: These are vital in safeguarding data both at rest and in transit. Data-at-rest encryption ensures that static data stored in databases, filesystems, and other storage mediums is secured, whereas data-in-transit encryption protects data as it travels across networks.

- **Access controls**: These play a pivotal role in regulating who can view or use the data. User authentication mechanisms verify a user's identity before granting access, and role-based access control ensures that access permissions are aligned with the user's role within the organization.

- **Identity and access management solutions**: These solutions are instrumental in managing user identities and their permissions. They include user identity verification systems that confirm the legitimacy of user identities, and privileged access management, which controls and monitors access for users with elevated permissions.

Review strategy is an ongoing process consisting of the following:

- **Security audits**: Regular audits are conducted to ensure compliance with security policies and standards. This includes regular compliance checks and security policy enforcement.

- **Vulnerability assessments**: This includes penetration testing to actively test security vulnerabilities and automated vulnerability scanning to identify potential security weaknesses in the system.

Lastly, security protocols encompass the following:

- **Incident response plans**: These plans prepare the organization to effectively respond to security incidents. This involves emergency protocols for immediate response and real-time monitoring for continuous observation of the system's security posture.

Each of these categories and subcategories plays a crucial role in fortifying cloud-based data integration against a spectrum of security threats. From proactive encryption measures to robust access control and vigilant monitoring, the orchestration of these elements is essential for maintaining a secure and resilient cloud data environment.

> **Tips**
>
> The ultimate layer of security assets, integrated directly within data storage systems, offers meticulous control over data protection at detailed levels, such as tables, rows, or even individual cells. This strategy sharpens the accuracy of data safeguarding, enabling customized security measures that are perfectly attuned to the specific sensitivities and access needs of the data. It encompasses techniques such as data masking or restricting access, ensuring a robust defense against unauthorized data exposure or manipulation.

Data transfer and latency

Efficient data transfer and low latency are critical for successful cloud-based data integration. As data traverses between on-premises systems and the cloud, or among cloud environments, organizations must address challenges such as limited network bandwidth, latency, data transmission reliability, and data movement cost. Optimizing data transfer protocols, employing compression and caching techniques, and strategically planning network architecture can significantly enhance data transfer efficiency and minimize latency. Furthermore, organizations should consider leveraging **content delivery networks** (**CDNs**) and edge computing to bring data closer to end-users and reduce latency.

Compliance and regulations

Compliance with industry regulations and standards is a complex challenge in cloud-based data integration. Organizations operating in sectors such as healthcare, finance, banking, or government face stringent compliance requirements regarding data handling, storage, and processing. Cloud providers must demonstrate compliance with relevant certifications and offer robust security controls to support organizations in meeting their regulatory obligations. To navigate this challenge, organizations must carefully assess the compliance capabilities of cloud providers, establish proper data governance frameworks, and implement auditing mechanisms to ensure regulatory compliance. Organizations can fully leverage cloud-based data integration by prioritizing data security, optimizing data transfer, and keeping pace with evolving compliance standards. A comprehensive strategy encompassing robust security frameworks, network optimization, and diligent compliance management is essential to innovate while protecting sensitive information.

Considerations for implementing data integration in a cloud environment

Implementing data integration in a cloud environment requires careful consideration to ensure optimal performance, scalability, and data management. Organizations must evaluate various aspects, including cloud-native tools and services, data storage and management, and monitoring and maintenance, to effectively leverage the benefits of cloud-based data integration:

- **Cloud-native tools and services**: When integrating data in a cloud environment, organizations should assess and select suitable cloud-native tools and services that align with their integration requirements. Cloud providers such as **Amazon Web Services** (**AWS**), Microsoft Azure, and Google Cloud Platform offer a range of services for data integration, such as AWS Glue, Azure Data Factory, and Google Cloud Dataflow. These tools provide capabilities for data ingestion, transformation, and orchestration, enabling organizations to build robust data integration pipelines. It is essential to evaluate the features, scalability, security, and compatibility of these tools to ensure seamless integration with existing systems and the ability to handle real-time data processing.

- **Data storage and management**: Efficient data storage and management are critical for successful data integration in the cloud. Organizations need to determine the appropriate data storage solutions based on their data volume, velocity, schema, and accessibility requirements. Cloud-based storage options such as object storage (e.g., Amazon S3, Azure Blob Storage), file storage (e.g., Amazon EFS, Azure Files), or database services (e.g., Amazon RDS, Azure Cosmos DB) should be evaluated for their schema requirement, scalability, availability, durability, and performance. Additionally, consideration should be given to data partitioning, indexing strategies, and data life cycle management to optimize storage costs and ensure data availability (*Chapter 7, Data Ingestion and Storage Strategies*).

- **Data security and privacy**: Ensuring data security and privacy is paramount when integrating data in a cloud environment. Organizations should implement robust security measures, such as encryption at rest and in transit, access controls, and data anonymization techniques, to protect sensitive information. Compliance with data protection regulations (e.g., GDPR, HIPAA) and industry-specific security standards should also be considered. Cloud providers offer a range of security services and certifications that can assist organizations in meeting their security and compliance requirements.

- **Data transfer and latency**: Efficient data transfer and low latency are crucial for real-time data integration in the cloud. Organizations should evaluate the available network connectivity options, such as direct private links or **virtual private networks** (**VPNs**), to establish secure and high-bandwidth connections between on-premises systems and cloud environments. Additionally, leveraging **content delivery networks** (**CDNs**) or edge computing technologies can help minimize data transfer latency by bringing data processing closer to the data sources or end-users.

- **Compliance and regulations**: Compliance with industry regulations and data governance practices is essential for data integration in a cloud environment. Organizations should assess the regulatory requirements applicable to their industry and geographic location, ensuring that the chosen cloud provider adheres to the necessary certifications and compliance frameworks. Implementing proper data governance policies, data lineage tracking, and audit trails can help maintain data integrity and demonstrate compliance with regulatory obligations.

- **Monitoring and maintenance**: Continuous monitoring and proactive maintenance are vital to maintain the integrity, performance, and security of data integration in a cloud environment. Organizations should implement robust monitoring tools and practices to track data ingestion rates, data quality, system health, and overall performance. Monitoring should encompass real-time alerts, log analysis, and system metrics to identify potential bottlenecks, performance degradation, or security vulnerabilities (*Chapter 13, Workflow Management, Monitoring, and Data Quality*). Regular maintenance activities, including software updates, security patches, and system optimizations, should be performed to ensure the reliability and efficiency of the integration infrastructure.

By carefully considering these factors during the implementation of data integration in a cloud environment, organizations can achieve efficient and reliable data workflows, seamless connectivity between systems, and scalable data processing capabilities. They can leverage cloud-native tools and services to streamline integration processes, adopt appropriate data storage and management strategies, address data security and compliance requirements, and establish robust monitoring and maintenance practices. These considerations pave the way for successful data integration and enable organizations to harness the full potential of cloud-based data analysis.

Use case: Data integration for banking analysis

In the context of data integration for banking analysis, let's consider a use case involving a multinational bank with multiple branches and a wide range of financial products and services. The bank aims to enhance its decision-making capabilities by integrating data from various sources and analyzing it in real time.

Scenario

The bank collects data from multiple sources, including transactional data, customer data, market data, and external data feeds. These sources generate a vast volume of data that needs to be efficiently integrated and analyzed to gain valuable insights and make informed business decisions.

Data integration requirements

In addressing the complex data integration requirements of a bank, it is necessary to grapple with high transaction volumes and real-time data processing, ensure consistency across varied systems, and adeptly integrate data spanning a spectrum of formats, from structured databases to unstructured customer interactions. We can consider an average amount of 10,000 to 50,000 transactions per hour; this includes a mix of ATM withdrawals, credit and debit card purchases, online banking transfers, direct deposits, bill payments, and other types of transactions. The requirements are as follows:

- **Data volume and velocity**: The bank deals with high transaction volumes and needs to process real-time data to provide up-to-date insights for risk management, fraud detection, and customer engagement.

- **Data format variability**: Data comes in various formats, such as structured data from databases, semi-structured data from logs and files, and unstructured data from customer communications. Integrating and harmonizing these diverse data formats is crucial for accurate analysis.

- **Data consistency**: Ensuring data consistency across different systems and databases is vital to avoid discrepancies and maintain data integrity throughout the integration process.

Tools and techniques for banking data integration

Various tools and techniques play a crucial role in seamlessly consolidating and leveraging diverse data sources.

The following schema illustrates the steps of our example of banking architecture:

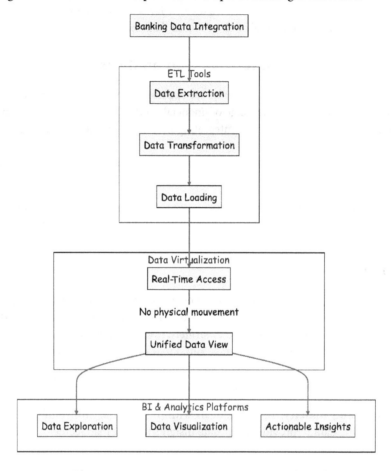

Figure 15.5 – Steps of our example of banking architecture

These tools empower banks to efficiently manage and analyze their data, enabling informed decision-making and enhancing customer experiences.

- **ETL tools**: The bank utilizes ETL tools to extract data from disparate sources, transform it into a consistent format, and load it into a central data repository or data warehouse for analysis (*Chapter 9, Data Transformation and Processing*).

- **Data virtualization**: Data virtualization enables the bank to access and integrate data from multiple sources in real time without physically moving or replicating the data. This approach provides a unified view of the data without the need for extensive data movement.

- **Business intelligence and analytics platforms**: The bank leverages business intelligence and analytics platforms that offer advanced data integration capabilities, allowing analysts and decision-makers to explore and visualize integrated data to gain actionable insights (*Chapter 12*, *Data Preparation and Analysis*).

Benefits and outcomes of the use case

By effectively integrating data from various sources, the bank achieves several benefits and outcomes:

- **Real-time risk management**: The bank can detect and mitigate potential risks promptly, such as compliance or reputational risks, by analyzing real-time transactional and market data, ensuring regulatory compliance, and reducing financial exposure

- **Improved customer experience**: Integration of customer data enables personalized offerings, targeted marketing campaigns, and enhanced customer service, leading to increased customer satisfaction and loyalty

- **Fraud detection and prevention**: By integrating transactional data and leveraging advanced analytics techniques, the bank can identify suspicious activities and detect fraudulent behavior in real time, protecting both the institution and its customers

- **Data-driven decision-making**: With integrated data, the bank's decision-makers gain a holistic view of the organization's performance, enabling strategic planning, optimizing operations, and driving business growth

Overall, data integration plays a pivotal role in the banking sector, enabling financial institutions to harness the power of data and transform it into actionable insights for improved risk management, customer experience, fraud detection, and data-driven decision-making.

Use case: Cloud-based solution for business intelligence solution banking

In the context of banking data management, let's consider a use case involving a leading retail banking company operating across Europe with international subsidiaries. The challenge is to optimize and reshape the accessibility and utility of an immense volume of transaction data for **business intelligence (BI)** teams in different countries.

Scenario

The bank faces the daunting task of managing nearly 700 TB of transaction data, updated daily, and sprawling across multiple countries. The objective is to make this data easily accessible for localized BI operations, thereby enabling efficient and targeted analytics.

Data integration requirements

To streamline the complex datasets, the project has to overcome several hurdles:

- **Data volume and diversity**: Handling the colossal aggregation of transaction records requires a strategy that can accommodate the vast volume and variety of data

- **Localized access**: Ensuring that BI teams in each country can access relevant and high-quality data for analytics and reporting

- **Performance optimization**: Improving data retrieval performance for localized dashboards and reports, facilitating quicker, more efficient queries and real-time insights

- **Integration with an existing platform**: Ensuring that the solution integrates with the existing data platform based on AWS

Architecture, techniques, and patterns

The project adopts a medallion architecture (*Chapter 6, Data Storage Technologies, and Architectures*), concentrating on the gold layer for refined and consolidated data. Initially, transaction data and its metadata are ingested into the bronze layer using a homemade solution. This bronze layer mirrors data just like in the source database, serving various purposes, such as audit and replay scenarios. Subsequently, this data is processed into a cleaner version stored in the silver layer. The processing involves technical operations such as deduplication and format standardization (*Chapter 10, Transformation Patterns, Cleansing, and Normalization*) as well as business-related operations. Finally, data is moved from silver to gold, orienting it toward the use case using modeling concepts such as design by query and split techniques such as partitioning. The preparation of data up to the gold layer was pivotal in ensuring that BI teams across different countries had access to high-quality, reliable data for their analytics and reporting needs.

The partitioning (*Chapter 7, Data Ingestion and Storage Strategies*) is based on a multi-level partitioning strategy. It is pivotal in streamlining data access and improving performance:

- **Country-level partitioning**: Allowing each country's BI team independent access to their local data, aligning with regional data governance policies

- **Yearly segmentation**: Further segmenting data by year within each country partition to manage volumes effectively and facilitate trend analysis

- **Monthly breakdown**: The most granular tier, partitioning by month within each year, optimized for monthly dashboards and performance

It is a choice to stop partitioning by month and not move to partitioning by day, as the consumer patterns and user needs (reports) were reporting by month.

The following schema illustrates the technical architecture of the use case:

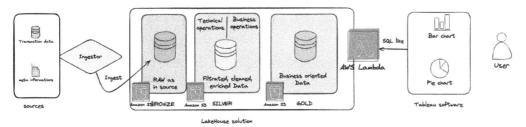

Figure 15.6 – Technical architecture of the use case

To optimize data storage and processing efficiency, the data within each partition is compressed into files up to 512 MB. This approach minimizes I/O overhead and enhances processing speed by reducing the time spent on reading and writing operations compared to scenarios with higher processing demands.

Technical stack

Implementation involves automated scripts and ELT processes to manage the multi-tier partitioning, ensuring data integrity and consistency. Additionally, it is important to incorporate quality checks using the SODA framework.

Advanced technologies supported the strategy:

- **Parquet format**: Parquet serves as the pivotal file format (*Chapter 5, Columnar Data Formats and Comparison*) due to its efficient data storage and retrieval. The choice of the Parquet file format was a strategic one, given its advantages in compression and partition pruning. This was particularly effective in our **online analytical processing** (**OLAP**) use case, enhancing the compute engine's performance. Delta wasn't a choice in this layer as we don't deal with ACID operations or concurrent writing access.

- **Tableau software**: Tableau is the chosen dashboarding tool, providing the BI teams with an easy-to-use interface for visualizing and engaging with data. In this use case, the reports generated in Tableau are configured to send queries directly to Athena. We chose Tableau over Quicksight for the required features that Quicksight does not have as well as the team's skills, which will reduce the learning curve.

- **Amazon Athena & Glue**: This service utilizes a modern MPP engine (*Chapter 9, Data Transformation and Processing*) for serverless querying, allowing efficient and cost-effective data access. Its serverless architecture enables efficient querying of data stored in S3 at approximately $5 per Terabyte scanned, chosen for its affordability when latency is not critical. Athena, configured with Presto and connected to a Glue table based on the gold layer, consolidates data within each partition up to 512 MB per file, optimizing I/O operations against processing overhead.

- **Apache Spark on Amazon EMR**: This is used for cleaning, preparing, and writing the results in the gold layer, handling the processing demands of our large data volumes. We used Apache Spark on Amazon EMR for heavy lifting in data preparation. Its robust processing capabilities were essential for handling large volumes of transaction data.

- **Local ingestion solution (data ingestor)**: A homemade ingestion solution, again leveraging Spark on EMR, was developed. This solution efficiently handled the initial loading and processing of the transaction data from various sources.

- **SODA framework**: This was integrated as a critical component of our data quality management strategy. It provided an open source, highly flexible platform for conducting comprehensive data quality checks across the entire data pipeline. Using SODA, we defined, executed, and monitored data quality rules that ensured the integrity, accuracy, and consistency of data at each stage of the medallion architecture. This included validations for the completeness, uniqueness, conformity, and timeliness of the data. The SODA framework facilitates automated alerts and reporting on data quality issues, enabling the prompt identification and resolution of any anomalies before they impact downstream processes or analytics. By embedding SODA's capabilities into our workflow, we significantly enhanced our ability to maintain high-quality data standards.

Benefits and outcomes of the use case

The project significantly improves data retrieval and system efficiency, empowering BI teams with faster, more reliable access to data tailored to their specific regional needs. The multi-level partitioning strategy, coupled with technological choices, transformed the business's BI operations, setting a new benchmark in efficient, scalable, and accessible data solutions.

Overall, this use case exemplifies a milestone in strategic data management for the banking sector, demonstrating how a well-conceived data integration strategy can revolutionize data accessibility and analytics in a multinational banking environment. Next, we'll explore data integration for geospatial data analysis.

Data integration for geospatial data analysis

Geospatial data analysis refers to the process of examining and interpreting data that is associated with a specific location or geographic coordinates. It involves analyzing various types of spatially referenced data, such as maps, satellite imagery, GPS data, and geospatial databases, to uncover patterns, relationships, and insights related to the Earth's surface and its features.

Geospatial data analysis plays a crucial role in multiple domains, including urban planning, environmental monitoring, disaster management, logistics, and navigation systems. By leveraging geospatial analysis techniques, organizations can gain a deeper understanding of spatial patterns, make informed decisions, and solve complex problems that involve location-based information.

Geospatial data analysis encompasses a wide range of analytical methods and tools. It involves processing and analyzing geospatial data using **geographic information systems (GIS)**, spatial databases, and geospatial data processing frameworks. These tools enable users to store, manipulate, query, and visualize spatial data, allowing them to extract meaningful insights from the vast amounts of geospatial information available.

Geospatial data analysis faces key challenges, including its complexity and diverse formats such as raster (satellite images) and vector (points, lines, polygons). Understanding spatial relationships, such as proximity, is crucial. Quality and consistency issues, such as data errors, necessitate validation and preprocessing for accurate results. Additionally, the large volume and complexity of geospatial data require scalable processing solutions and advanced computing techniques to manage the data effectively.

In summary, geospatial data analysis is a vital discipline that leverages spatially referenced data to gain insights and make informed decisions. It involves using various tools, techniques, and frameworks to analyze and interpret geospatial data, addressing challenges related to data complexity, quality, and scalability. By harnessing the power of geospatial analysis, organizations can unlock valuable information about our physical world and drive informed decision-making processes.

Unique challenges of integrating geospatial data

Integrating geospatial data presents unique challenges due to the inherent characteristics of spatial information. These challenges arise from data complexity and heterogeneity, spatial relationships, and coordinate systems and projections:

- **Data complexity and heterogeneity**: Geospatial data is inherently complex and heterogeneous, often consisting of various data types, such as raster data (e.g., satellite images) and vector data (e.g., points, lines, polygons). Each data type has its own structures and representations, requiring specialized processing techniques to handle the complexity and ensure accurate integration. Additionally, geospatial data may come from multiple sources, each with its own data formats and standards, further increasing the complexity of integration.

- **Spatial relationships**: Geospatial data analysis heavily relies on spatial relationships, such as proximity, containment, and adjacency. Integrating geospatial data requires understanding and capturing these spatial relationships accurately. This involves analyzing the topological relationships between different spatial objects, identifying neighboring features, and determining spatial interactions. Failure to consider spatial relationships can lead to inaccurate analysis and interpretation of geospatial data.

- **Coordinate systems and projections**: Geospatial data is referenced to specific coordinate systems and projections that define how locations on the Earth's surface are represented and measured. When integrating geospatial data from multiple sources, it is essential to account for coordinate system differences and perform appropriate coordinate transformations to ensure spatial alignment. Inconsistent coordinate systems and projections can introduce errors and distortions, affecting the accuracy of the integrated data.

Addressing these challenges requires careful consideration and specialized approaches in geospatial data integration. Techniques such as data standardization, schema mapping, and spatial indexing can help manage data complexity and heterogeneity. Spatial analysis tools and algorithms enable the exploration of spatial relationships and support accurate integration. Additionally, employing coordinate transformation methods and utilizing standardized reference systems ensure the proper alignment of geospatial data during integration processes.

By overcoming these challenges, organizations can effectively integrate geospatial data, unlocking valuable insights and enabling informed decision-making in various fields, such as urban planning, environmental monitoring, and emergency management. The ability to integrate and analyze geospatial data accurately enhances our understanding of the physical world and supports evidence-based decision-making for sustainable and efficient development.

Requirements for geospatial data integration

Geospatial data integration entails specific requirements to ensure successful and effective integration processes. These requirements primarily focus on data quality and consistency, scalability, and performance:

- **Data quality and consistency**: Geospatial data integration necessitates a strong emphasis on data quality and consistency. This involves assessing the accuracy, completeness, and reliability of geospatial datasets. It requires data validation and cleansing processes to identify and rectify errors, anomalies, and inconsistencies within the data. Additionally, standardization of data formats, coordinate systems, and attribute values ensures uniformity and compatibility during integration. By ensuring high-quality and consistent geospatial data, organizations can enhance the reliability and accuracy of analytical insights derived from the integrated datasets.

- **Scalability**: The scalability of geospatial data integration refers to its ability to handle increasing volumes of data, accommodate growth, and maintain performance levels as the dataset size expands. Scalability becomes crucial when dealing with large-scale geospatial datasets, such as high-resolution imagery, global positioning data, and sensor data. Implementing scalable integration solutions enables organizations to process and integrate vast amounts of geospatial data efficiently. It involves adopting scalable storage systems, distributed computing architectures, and parallel processing techniques to handle the data growth and provide timely access to integrated information.

- **Performance**: Geospatial data integration should prioritize performance to ensure efficient processing and analysis of integrated datasets. Performance considerations include data ingestion speed, query response time, and analytical processing capabilities. Optimizing integration workflows and employing efficient indexing structures facilitate faster data access and retrieval. Parallel processing techniques, such as data partitioning and distributed computing, enhance the computational performance of geospatial data integration tasks. By achieving optimal performance, organizations can derive actionable insights from geospatial data in a timely manner, supporting real-time decision-making and analysis.

- **Interoperability**: Geospatial data integration requires interoperability with different systems, tools, and formats. It involves harmonizing geospatial data with other data sources, such as relational databases, web services, and external APIs. Standardization of data schemas, metadata, and interfaces enables seamless integration and exchange of geospatial information across various applications. Interoperability allows organizations to leverage the capabilities of multiple systems and tools, enabling comprehensive analysis and decision-making.

Addressing these requirements enables organizations to leverage the full potential of geospatial data integration. High-quality and consistent data, coupled with scalable and performant integration processes, enhances the accuracy, reliability, and efficiency of geospatial data analysis.

It is essential to establish robust data quality assurance mechanisms, including automated validation and cleansing routines, to ensure the integrity of the integrated geospatial datasets. Scalability can be achieved by adopting cloud-based infrastructure, leveraging distributed storage systems, and implementing parallel processing techniques. Performance optimization requires the selection of appropriate indexing structures, query optimization strategies, and the utilization of advanced computing technologies such as in-memory processing. By addressing these requirements, organizations can unlock the value of geospatial data integration, enabling comprehensive spatial analysis, decision-making, and insights in various domains, including urban planning, environmental management, and transportation logistics.

Tools and techniques for geospatial data integration

Geospatial data integration requires the utilization of specialized tools and techniques to effectively integrate, process, and analyze geospatial datasets. These tools include GIS software and libraries, spatial databases, and geospatial data processing frameworks that provide the necessary functionalities to handle the unique characteristics of geospatial data and enable seamless integration into data analysis workflows. By leveraging these tools and techniques, organizations can harness the power of geospatial data and unlock valuable insights for informed decision-making.

GIS software and libraries

GIS software and libraries play a crucial role in geospatial data integration for effective analysis and visualization. These tools provide a comprehensive set of functionalities to manage, manipulate, and analyze geospatial data, enabling users to extract meaningful insights from spatial datasets.

One popular GIS software is **ArcGIS** (`https://www.arcgis.com/`), developed by **Esri**, which offers a robust suite of tools for geospatial data integration. With ArcGIS, users can perform spatial data processing tasks such as data conversion, georeferencing, and spatial analysis. It provides advanced capabilities for working with various geospatial data formats, including shapefiles, geodatabases, and raster datasets. Moreover, ArcGIS offers a wide range of geoprocessing tools and spatial analysis functions, empowering users to perform complex spatial operations such as proximity analysis, network analysis, and terrain analysis.

Another widely used GIS software is **Quantum GIS (QGIS**; `https://www.qgis.org/`), an open source platform that provides a user-friendly interface and extensive geospatial functionality. QGIS supports various data formats and offers tools for data management, spatial analysis, and cartography. It allows users to perform tasks such as spatial queries, spatial joins, and geoprocessing operations. QGIS also supports plugins, enabling users to extend its capabilities and integrate additional functionalities.

In addition to GIS software, geospatial data integration can be facilitated through libraries such as the **Geospatial Data Abstraction Library (GDAL**; `https://gdal.org/`) and GeoTools. GDAL is a powerful library that supports reading, writing, and manipulating geospatial data in different formats. It provides a unified **application programming interface (API)** for accessing raster and vector datasets, allowing developers to integrate geospatial functionality into their applications easily. GeoTools, on the other hand, is a Java-based library that offers geospatial data processing and visualization capabilities. It provides a wide range of tools for working with geospatial data, including data readers, data writers, spatial analysis functions, and rendering engines.

For example, in a railway analysis use case, GIS software and libraries can be employed to integrate various geospatial data sources, such as railway tracks, station locations, and demographic information. The software can help visualize the railway network, identify bottlenecks or areas of congestion, and optimize train schedules. GIS libraries enable developers to create custom applications that analyze the impact of railway operations on the surrounding areas, assess the accessibility of railway services, and plan infrastructure improvements.

By leveraging GIS software and libraries, organizations can enhance their geospatial data integration capabilities, enabling them to make informed decisions, optimize operations, and gain valuable insights from spatial data in diverse domains such as transportation, urban planning, environmental management, and disaster response.

Spatial databases

Spatial databases play a crucial role in geospatial data integration by providing efficient storage, indexing, and querying capabilities for spatial data. These specialized databases are designed to handle spatial information, such as points, lines, polygons, and spatial relationships, enabling the effective management and analysis of geospatial datasets.

One widely used spatial database is **PostGIS** (`https://postgis.net/`), which serves as an extension to the PostgreSQL relational database management system. PostGIS allows for the storage and retrieval of spatial data using advanced spatial indexing techniques such as R-tree and quadtree, enabling efficient spatial queries. It supports a comprehensive range of spatial functions and operators, facilitating spatial analysis and processing tasks. PostGIS also integrates seamlessly with GIS software and libraries, making it a powerful tool for geospatial data integration.

Oracle Spatial (`https://www.oracle.com/fr/database/spatial/`) is another popular spatial database, which is part of the Oracle Database system. It offers robust capabilities for managing and analyzing geospatial data at scale. Oracle Spatial provides spatial indexing mechanisms, spatial data types, and a wide array of spatial functions and operators. With Oracle Spatial, organizations can store and query large volumes of spatial data, perform spatial analysis operations, and seamlessly integrate geospatial data with other enterprise data sources.

In addition to these databases, modern data processing frameworks such as **PrestoDB** (`https://prestodb.io/`) and **Amazon Athena** (`https://aws.amazon.com/fr/athena/`) also offer spatial functions that can be utilized in geospatial data integration. These frameworks allow users to process and analyze data stored in formats such as Parquet, leveraging the power of spatial operations. For example, with PrestoDB and Athena, users can perform spatial queries, calculate distances between coordinates, and apply spatial filters to extract specific geospatial information from Parquet files.

By incorporating spatial databases, such as PostGIS and Oracle Spatial, and utilizing data processing frameworks, such as PrestoDB and Athena, with their geo functions, organizations can efficiently handle the challenges posed by geospatial data complexity. These technologies enable the seamless integration of spatial data into data analysis workflows, empowering businesses to derive valuable insights and make data-driven decisions based on their geospatial datasets.

Geospatial data processing frameworks

Geospatial data processing frameworks are essential tools for integrating and analyzing geospatial data in a scalable and efficient manner. These frameworks provide a comprehensive set of functionalities for processing, manipulating, and deriving insights from geospatial datasets. By leveraging these frameworks, organizations can effectively handle the unique challenges associated with geospatial data integration.

One popular geospatial data processing framework is **Apache Sedona** (formerly GeoSpark; `https://sedona.apache.org/`), which is built upon Apache Spark, a widely adopted big data processing framework. Apache Sedona enhances Spark's capabilities by incorporating spatial data types, indexing structures, and spatial operations. This allows for the efficient execution of spatial queries, spatial joins, and spatial analytics at scale. Utilizing Apache Sedona, organizations are equipped to process large volumes of geospatial data in distributed computing environments, making it an ideal choice for handling the computational requirements of geospatial data integration.

Another widely used framework is **GeoMesa** (`https://www.geomesa.org/`), which is designed to handle large-scale geospatial data stored in distributed data stores such as Apache HBase, Apache Accumulo, and Google Bigtable. GeoMesa provides spatial and temporal indexing, query optimization, and geospatial analytics capabilities. It allows users to ingest, index, and query massive amounts of geospatial data efficiently. With GeoMesa, organizations can perform real-time geospatial analytics, support spatial queries, and conduct historical analyses on large-scale geospatial datasets.

These geospatial data processing frameworks provide the necessary tools and functionalities to address the complexities of integrating and analyzing geospatial data. They enable organizations to leverage the power of distributed computing, spatial indexing, and advanced analytics to extract meaningful insights from their geospatial datasets. By utilizing these frameworks, businesses can unlock the potential of their geospatial data and make informed decisions based on spatial patterns, relationships, and trends.

Use case: Railway analysis

Railway companies often face the challenge of optimizing their operations and ensuring the smooth functioning of train services. By leveraging data integration and geospatial analysis, they can gain valuable insights to improve efficiency, enhance safety, and deliver a better passenger experience. Let's explore a specific use case of railway analysis involving optimizing train schedules and minimizing delays.

Example of optimizing train schedules

In this use case, a railway company wants to optimize the schedules of their trains to minimize delays and improve overall service efficiency. They collect a variety of data sources, including train operation data with geographic coordinates (latitude and longitude), passenger information, terrain data along the routes, and real-time updates from signaling systems equipped with GPS tracking. By integrating this geospatial data, the company can track the precise location and movement of all trains in real time, identify bottlenecks in specific geographic regions, anticipate potential issues due to terrain or traffic density, and optimize train schedules for better route management and punctuality. Such analysis not only ensures smoother operations but also helps in strategic planning for infrastructure development.

The following schema illustrates an example of the railway analysis architecture:

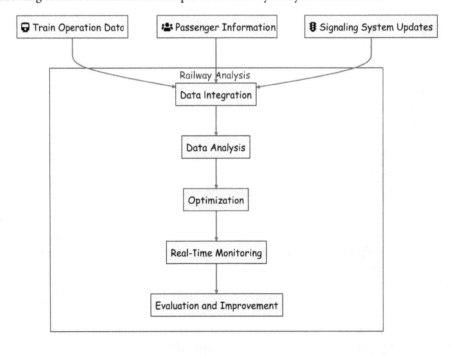

Figure 15.7 – Example of the railway analysis architecture

In the preceding figure, the following information is used as input data for the railway analysis:

- **Train operation data**: This dataset includes information about train routes, stops, departure and arrival times, as well as historical performance data

- **Passenger information**: This dataset contains details about passenger demand, ticket sales, and preferences, such as popular routes and peak travel times

- **Signaling system updates**: Real-time data from the signaling system provides information on train positions, speed, and potential delays

The details of the various steps of the preceding figure are as follows:

1. **Data integration**: The railway company integrates the train operation data, passenger information, and signaling system updates into a centralized data repository. It ensures data compatibility, performs data cleansing, and resolves any inconsistencies.

2. **Data analysis**: The integrated data is then analyzed using geospatial analysis techniques. The company applies algorithms to identify patterns and correlations between train schedules, passenger demand, and real-time signaling updates.

3. **Optimization**: Based on the analysis, the company identifies areas where delays frequently occur or where demand exceeds capacity. They use optimization algorithms to adjust train schedules, allocate resources more efficiently, and minimize delays.

4. **Real-time monitoring**: The integrated data is continuously monitored in real time to track train movements, identify potential issues, and make on-the-spot adjustments to schedules, if necessary. Real-time updates from the signaling system help in proactive decision-making.

5. **Evaluation and improvement**: The company evaluates the impact of the optimized schedules on overall performance metrics, such as on-time performance, passenger satisfaction, and resource utilization. They make iterative improvements based on feedback and data-driven insights.

By implementing this use case, the railway company can achieve several benefits:

- **Improved efficiency**: Optimized train schedules reduce delays, minimize idle times, and improve overall efficiency in resource allocation

- **Enhanced passenger experience**: Timely trains and better coordination of schedules lead to improved passenger satisfaction and reduced waiting times

- **Proactive issue resolution**: Real-time monitoring and analysis enable the company to identify and address potential issues before they escalate, ensuring smoother operations

- **Resource optimization**: By analyzing passenger demand and train schedules, the company can allocate resources more effectively, leading to cost savings and improved resource utilization

In conclusion, the use case of optimizing train schedules through data integration and geospatial analysis demonstrates how railway companies can leverage data to improve operational efficiency, enhance passenger experience, and achieve better resource management. By integrating various data sources and applying advanced analytical techniques, railway companies can make data-driven decisions and drive continuous improvement in the railway industry.

Next, we'll discuss data integration for IoT data analysis.

Data integration for IoT data analysis

The field of **internet of things** (**IoT**) has emerged as a transformative force, generating vast amounts of data from interconnected devices and sensors. This data holds immense potential for businesses across various industries to gain valuable insights and drive informed decision-making. In this section, we will provide an introduction to IoT data analysis, exploring its significance and the key concepts involved.

The rapid proliferation of IoT devices has led to the generation of massive volumes of data, capturing real-time information from sensors, machines, and other connected devices. This data encompasses diverse dimensions such as temperature, humidity, location, motion, and more. By analyzing this data, businesses can uncover patterns, correlations, and anomalies that enable them to optimize processes, enhance efficiency, and deliver innovative services.

IoT data analysis involves the application of advanced analytical techniques to extract meaningful insights from the vast and complex data generated by IoT devices. This process requires a combination of data integration, data processing, and data analytics to derive actionable intelligence. By leveraging IoT data analysis, organizations can unlock valuable insights that can drive operational efficiency, improve customer experiences, and enable data-driven decision-making.

In terms of requirements, IoT data analysis necessitates scalable and flexible infrastructure capable of handling the high volume, velocity, and variety of data. It requires robust IoT data platforms that can ingest, store, process, and analyze IoT data efficiently. Additionally, edge computing plays a crucial role in IoT data analysis by enabling real-time processing and analysis at the network edge, reducing latency and bandwidth requirements.

With the foundational understanding of IoT data analysis established, detailing its potential to revolutionize business intelligence, we now turn our focus to the challenges ahead, including the technical intricacies and infrastructural demands pivotal in harnessing the full spectrum of opportunities presented by IoT's rich data landscape.

Specific challenges and requirements for IoT data integration

IoT data integration presents unique challenges and requirements due to the distinct characteristics of IoT data. In this section, we will explore the specific challenges and requirements that organizations face when integrating IoT data into their data analysis processes.

The variety of formats and the volume of data pose significant challenges for IoT data integration. A scalable and fast architecture capable of processing data streams in real time or near real time is essential in managing this diversity and abundance and enabling proactive decision-making.

To perform effective IoT data analysis, businesses must overcome several challenges. One significant challenge is the sheer volume of data generated by IoT devices, often referred to as the *data deluge*. Managing and processing such large volumes of data requires scalable infrastructure and advanced data processing capabilities.

Furthermore, the velocity at which IoT data is generated presents a challenge. Real-time and near real-time analysis is often necessary to derive timely insights and enable proactive decision-making. This requires efficient data ingestion, processing, and analytics capabilities that can handle the high velocity of incoming data streams.

Another challenge in IoT data analysis is the variety of data formats and structures. IoT devices may generate data in lightweight formats such as JSON or XML, utilize different communication protocols such as MQTT or CoAP, and adhere to various industry standards, including OPC-UA for industrial systems or HL7 for healthcare devices. This diversity turns data integration and normalization into a complex task. Data cleansing and transformation processes are often required to ensure data consistency and compatibility for analysis.

Device heterogeneity is another challenge that organizations face when integrating IoT data. IoT ecosystems often consist of devices from various manufacturers, each with its own unique characteristics, data formats, and communication protocols. Integrating data from heterogeneous devices requires standardized data models, interoperability protocols, and flexible integration approaches to ensure seamless data flow and compatibility.

Data security and privacy are paramount concerns in IoT data integration. The interconnected nature of IoT devices increases the risk of data breaches, unauthorized access, and privacy violations. Organizations must implement robust security measures, including encryption, access controls, and data anonymization techniques, to protect IoT data throughout the integration process.

Last but not least is handling low-power IoT devices, which introduces another layer of complexity, especially in data integration. Most IoT devices, especially those deployed in remote or inaccessible locations, operate on limited power sources such as batteries or solar panels. These devices generally need to perform data collection, processing, and transmission activities within strict power budgets. This power constraint impacts the frequency and volume of data transmission. To conserve energy, devices may use low-power communication protocols, such as **MQTT** (RFC; `https://datatracker.ietf.org/doc/rfc9431/`), and employ strategies such as sending summarized or aggregated data instead of raw data or reducing the frequency of transmissions. Such strategies can affect the granularity and timeliness of the data received for integration, requiring special handling and consideration during the integration process.

Considering the specific challenges of IoT data integration, certain requirements must be met to ensure successful integration and analysis:

- **Data volume, velocity, and variety**: Organizations must have scalable infrastructure and data processing capabilities to handle the large volume, high velocity, and diverse formats of IoT data.

- **Device heterogeneity**: Integration solutions should support interoperability between different IoT devices and facilitate seamless data exchange, regardless of the device manufacturer or communication protocol.

- **Data security and privacy**: Robust security measures should be implemented at every stage of data integration to safeguard IoT data from unauthorized access, data breaches, and privacy violations.

- **Devices energy consumption**: Organizations should consider the power limits of IoT devices. IoT device data integration should balance energy use with data accuracy. Since many devices run on limited energy, integration methods must adjust for changes in data transmission, ensuring data quality while extending device life.

In conclusion, IoT data integration poses specific challenges and requires tailored solutions to address the volume, velocity, variety, device heterogeneity, and security concerns associated with IoT data. By meeting these challenges and requirements, organizations can unlock the full potential of IoT data and leverage it for valuable insights and informed decision-making.

Tools and techniques for IoT data integration

IoT data integration requires specialized tools and techniques to effectively handle the unique characteristics and challenges of IoT data. In this section, we will explore some of the key tools and techniques used for IoT data integration:

- **IoT data platforms**: IoT data platforms provide a comprehensive infrastructure and set of services for managing, processing, and analyzing IoT data. These platforms offer tools for data ingestion, storage, device management, and real-time analytics with respect to the nature of IoT devices. They enable organizations to streamline the integration of diverse IoT data sources, manage data flows, and extract meaningful insights from the data with respect to devices' limited energy.

- **Edge computing**: Edge computing is a distributed computing paradigm that brings data processing and analytics closer to the edge of the network where IoT devices are located. By processing data locally on edge devices or in nearby edge servers, edge computing reduces latency, minimizes bandwidth usage, and enables real-time analysis. Edge computing is particularly beneficial in scenarios where real-time insights and immediate actions are required. This technique also reduces device energy consumption as high energy processes are done on the edge and returns the results to the IoT device.

- **Data processing and analysis frameworks**: Various data processing and analysis frameworks are used for IoT data integration. These frameworks provide a programming model and tools for processing and analyzing large volumes of IoT data. Examples of popular frameworks include Apache Spark and Apache Kafka over the MQTT protocol. **Message queuing telemetry transport (MQTT)** is a lightweight messaging protocol designed for low-bandwidth, high-latency, or unreliable networks. MQTT enables devices to send (publish) messages to a central server (broker), for instance, Kafka. It's efficient, requires minimal resources, and supports quality-of-service levels to ensure message delivery.

In addition to the above tools and techniques, other supporting technologies play a crucial role in IoT data integration:

- **Data storage and management**: IoT data integration requires robust data storage and management solutions capable of handling the scale and diversity of IoT data. Technologies such as distributed filesystems, object storage, NoSQL, and time-series databases are commonly used for storing and managing IoT data.

- **Scalability and flexibility**: Scalability and flexibility are critical considerations in IoT data integration. Organizations must choose tools and technologies that can scale seamlessly to accommodate growing data volumes and evolving IoT ecosystems. Flexibility is also important to adapt to changing data formats, device protocols, and integration requirements.

In conclusion, IoT data integration relies on a combination of tools and techniques tailored to address the specific challenges of IoT data. IoT data platforms, edge computing, and data processing frameworks are the key components in building effective IoT data integration pipelines. By leveraging these tools and techniques, organizations can unlock the full potential of their IoT data and drive valuable insights for improved decision-making and operational efficiency.

Best practices for implementing IoT data integration

When integrating IoT data, it's imperative to implement best practices specifically designed for the intricacies of IoT datasets. IoT integration necessitates a unique approach due to real-time, dynamic data streams and the diverse range of devices involved. The following sets out the key practices refined for IoT data integration, highlighting their application in the IoT landscape:

- **Data ingestion and preprocessing**: In the realm of IoT, data ingestion needs to accommodate real-time data flows and devices with intermittent connectivity or energy constraints. For example, an efficient approach for a network of environmental sensors would involve lightweight communication protocols for transmitting sensor data to a central system, where edge computing processes perform initial data cleaning and noise reduction before further centralized analysis.

- **Data storage and management**: IoT data storage must be adept at handling not just the volume but also the variety of data. Consider vehicle telematics in IoT: appropriate storage solutions would involve databases optimized for a series of data events that are also capable of handling geospatial information. Data management strategies should include robust data partitioning and retention policies to manage the life cycle of data efficiently, optimizing both costs and access performance.

- **Scalability and flexibility**: Addressing scalability in IoT means preparing for an increase in data volume and a growing array of devices. Adapting quickly to new data formats and communication protocols is essential. A smart building management system, for instance, might integrate a microservices architecture to facilitate the addition of new sensor types or IoT devices, leveraging integration platforms that can manage variable and mixed data flows efficiently.

- **Security and privacy**: Given the often sensitive nature of IoT data and the potential vulnerabilities within a vast network of devices, implementing stringent security and privacy measures is critical. IoT systems are particularly susceptible to attacks given their distributed nature and the variety of endpoints:

  - **End-to-end encryption**: Data transmitted from IoT devices should be encrypted to protect it from interception. This means securing data at rest, in transit, and during processing.

  - **Regular firmware updates and patch management**: IoT devices should be managed to ensure they are always running the most secure and up-to-date firmware, which protects against known vulnerabilities.

  - **Access control and authentication**: It's essential to have robust access controls in place to ensure that only authorized devices and users can access and transmit IoT data. Multi-factor authentication can provide an additional layer of security.

  - **Data anonymization and minimization**: When handling **personally identifiable information (PII)** or other sensitive data, it's important to anonymize and minimize the data to protect user privacy and comply with regulations, such as the GDPR or CCPA.

By incorporating these IoT-centric best practices, organizations can confront the challenges posed by the diverse and dynamic nature of IoT data. Responsive data ingestion and preprocessing, versatile storage and management, and the capability to scale with the IoT ecosystem are all critical. These practices ensure that enterprises are able to manage and extract actionable insights from IoT data, leading to greater operational efficiency and the drive toward innovative advancements.

Use case: Sports object platform

In this use case, let's consider a sports object platform that aims to integrate and analyze data from various IoT devices used in sports activities, such as bikes, fitness trackers, and heart rate monitors. The goal is to gather valuable insights to enhance athletes' performance, monitor their health, and optimize training programs.

The sports object platform integrates data from different IoT devices, including smart bikes equipped with sensors, fitness trackers worn by athletes, and heart rate monitors. These devices capture real-time data during sports activities such as cycling. The collected data includes metrics such as speed, distance, cadence, heart rate, and calories burned.

The following schema illustrates the components and data flow within the sport object platform:

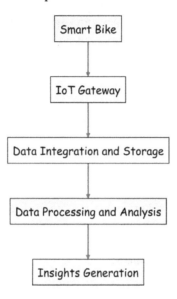

Figure 15.8 – Components and data flow within the sport object platform

The sport object platform consists of the following key components:

1. **Smart bike**: The smart bike is equipped with various sensors that capture data related to speed, distance, cadence, and other performance metrics. These sensors generate real-time data during cycling sessions.

2. **IoT gateway**: The IoT gateway acts as a bridge between the smart bike and the platform's data integration layer. It collects data from the smart bike and ensures secure transmission to the subsequent stages of data processing. This gateway uses low-power protocols such as MQTT to ensure the low consumption of energy by the sensors.

3. **Data integration and storage**: This component is responsible for integrating data from various IoT devices, including smart bikes, fitness trackers, and heart rate monitors. It ensures that the collected data is cleansed, validated, and stored in a centralized repository for further analysis. This operation can be done on the edge or the cloud platform using the platform-provided tools.

4.   **Data processing and analysis**: The integrated data is processed and analyzed using advanced analytics tools and techniques. Algorithms and models are applied to derive meaningful insights related to athletes' performance, health status, training patterns, and potential areas for improvement. This analysis can be achieved by technologies such as AWS IoT Analytics.

5.   **Insight generation**: The final stage involves generating actionable insights based on the analyzed data. These insights can be visualized through dashboards, reports, or mobile applications, providing athletes, coaches, and trainers with valuable information to optimize training programs, track progress, and make informed decisions.

In this use case, the sport object platform enables athletes and sports enthusiasts to gain a deeper understanding of their performance, track their progress over time, and make data-driven decisions to enhance their training routines. By integrating data from different IoT devices and applying advanced analytics, the platform empowers athletes to improve their performance and achieve their fitness goals more effectively.

Summary

In this chapter, we explored various architecture use cases for data integration, focusing on real-time data analysis, cloud-based data analysis, geospatial data analysis, and IoT data analysis. We discussed the requirements, challenges, tools, and best practices for each use case, providing insights into the key aspects of data integration in these domains.

Real-time data analysis highlighted the importance of low latency, scalability, and data quality in integrating real-time data sources. Cloud-based data analysis emphasized the advantages of scalability, flexibility, and cost optimization, along with challenges related to data security, transfer, and compliance. Geospatial data analysis shed light on the unique challenges of integrating complex and heterogeneous data, spatial relationships, and coordinate systems. IoT data analysis focused on the challenges posed by data volume, velocity, variety, device heterogeneity, and data security and privacy.

The use cases presented practical scenarios and demonstrated the potential of data integration to drive insights and improve decision-making in various domains. The integration of different tools, technologies, and architectural patterns played a crucial role in enabling effective data integration for analysis.

The next chapter will equip you with valuable insights into the future direction of data integration and offer guidance on continuing your learning journey in this rapidly evolving field.

16

Prospects and Challenges

As we draw near the conclusion of this book, it's pivotal to take an introspective look at the journey we've embarked upon together. From the very first chapter, we've delved deep into the intricacies and nuances of data integration in the modern world. We've tackled its challenges, opportunities, methodologies, and the tools that have shaped and continued to define this ever-evolving landscape.

However, like any rapidly changing domain, data integration is rife with uncharted prospects and unanswered queries. As we wrap up, it's just as crucial to gaze forward. This chapter doesn't merely summarize what we've learned but also aims to open the door to the unknown. We'll explore upcoming evolutions, looming challenges, and topics that, although not elaborated in detail in the preceding chapters, promise to wield significant influence on the realm of data integration.

In turning this final page, we seek not just to conclude but also to inspire ongoing reflection, encourage curiosity, and kindle the desire to explore the uncovered horizons of this vast universe of data integration.

The following topics will be covered in this chapter:

- Prospects of data integration in the current data stack
- Future challenges and opportunities of data integration
- Advancing your understanding of data integration in the modern stack

Prospects of data integration in the current data stack

The horizon of data integration is in constant flux, shifting and reshaping as organizations embrace novel architectures, infrastructures, and methodologies in their quest for enhanced data accessibility. This transformative journey is punctuated by the emergence of a myriad of technologies, spanning realms such as the cloud, on-premises infrastructures, hybrid configurations, multi-cloud setups, and edge environments. These advancements, while promising, also introduce layers of complexity to the task of integration. This challenge is further amplified by the exponential growth in data volumes, velocities, and varieties, and the ever-expanding roster of use cases, all of which place escalating demands on data integration capabilities.

In this dynamic milieu, the call of the hour is for integration platforms to evolve. They must not only become more adaptable, scalable, and astute but also broaden their scope. The journey of data integration is not solely a technical one; it's equally about navigating the intricate web of organizational dynamics, imbibing the right cultural ethos, and honing the skills of the teams at the helm.

This chapter embarks on a deep dive into the forefront of the data integration realm. We'll traverse the landscape of emerging trends, spotlighting new architectures, paradigms, and technologies tailored to meet the contemporary challenges of integration. The narrative will then shift to the specialized domain of edge computing and IoT, elucidating the unique requirements and innovative solutions for integrating the vast networks of connected devices and the data they generate.

As we delve deeper, the complexities of hybrid and multi-cloud environments will come into focus, revealing the intricacies of orchestrating integration across a diverse spectrum of cloud configurations. Yet, our exploration doesn't stop here. This chapter also casts its gaze into the future, unearthing cutting-edge innovations that stand on the cusp of revolutionizing how data is assimilated and disseminated.

But technology is just one facet of the story. The chapter also underscores the organizational imperatives in this journey. It advocates for a malleable mindset, stresses the importance of skill evolution, and champions the cause of open, collaborative endeavors.

> **Expert advice**
> Data integration is a fast-moving field that requires constant learning and adaptation. To stay ahead of the curve, you should keep an eye on the latest trends, technologies, and challenges that are shaping the future of data integration.

In essence, this chapter equips visionary data leaders with a holistic perspective. With insights spanning technology, processes, and culture, they are empowered to steer their organizations toward a future where data integration is not just a function but a symphony of coordinated efforts, all harmonizing to the tune of a data-centric future.

Emerging trends in data integration

As the data environments we encounter become more complex, the traditional tools and methodologies of yesteryears often fall short. Yet, in the face of these complexities, innovative techniques are rising to the occasion, heralding a new era of data integration solutions tailored for the challenges of today and tomorrow.

Central to this evolution are the transformative trends reshaping the very fabric of data integration. We're witnessing a decisive shift toward more decentralized architectures, epitomized by the emergence of the data mesh. This novel approach redistributes responsibilities, fostering a collaborative ecosystem where each domain takes ownership of its data. Simultaneously, the boundaries of automation are being pushed further, with machine learning and **robotic process automation** (**RPA**) at the forefront, driving efficiency and precision.

Yet, the innovations don't end here. The advent of containerization and microservices heralds a paradigm shift. By encapsulating logic within portable containers, organizations can seamlessly transition across diverse environments, ensuring consistency and compatibility. Complementing this is the rise of streaming integration and event-driven architectures, which pivot toward facilitating uninterrupted, real-time data flows, ensuring that data is as current as it is accurate.

In this dynamic environment, the democratization of data integration stands out as a pivotal trend. Low-code and no-code tools are democratizing the realm of integration, empowering business users to take the helm. However, to truly harness the potential of these tools, integrating a metadata layer is paramount as it adds an indispensable layer of intelligence across hybrid landscapes.

But the horizon of innovation extends even further. As the capabilities of AI mature, we stand on the cusp of AI-driven integration. These systems, with their ability to adapt and cater to contextual needs, represent the next frontier in data integration.

These avant-garde trends collectively address the pressing challenges of agility, scalability, and democratization – areas where conventional approaches often falter. The future belongs to organizations that proactively embrace these innovations as they stand to unlock unparalleled value and capabilities from their data.

ML and AI in data integration

The infusion of ML and AI into data integration is nothing short of a renaissance. What once required meticulous human intervention is now being gracefully handled by algorithms, freeing engineers to grapple with more intricate challenges.

Imagine the tedious task of mapping datasets. Traditionally, this involved laborious pinpointing and labeling of data attributes. Now, this onerous task is streamlined as supervised learning techniques train on labeled examples, automatically mapping new datasets to existing schemas. The result? A significant reduction in manual labor was replaced by precise and logical mappings delivered by machine learning models.

But the prowess of these algorithms extends beyond mere mapping. Anomaly detection models, trained on instances of flawed or malformed data, act as vigilant watchguards. Their keen senses recognize and flag any incoming record that deviates from the expected format. This proactive approach ensures that data remains pristine, catching potential discrepancies early in the integration flow.

The power of natural language processing further embellishes this landscape. It dives deep into documentation and unstructured metadata, deciphering context and meaning. Such insights don't just aid in automated mappings but also serve as invaluable recommendations for engineers navigating the integration journey.

As we delve further into this AI-enhanced realm, we encounter virtual companions in the form of AI assistants and chatbots. Far from passive tools, they actively engage with engineers, offering real-time integration recommendations. By continuously learning from past integration jobs and observing engineer behavior, these assistants suggest specific components, transformations, or parameters. Their input is invaluable, providing context-aware recommendations that guide engineers in designing flows and jobs.

> **Tip**
>
> ML and AI can automate many tedious and time-consuming tasks in data integration, but they are not magic solutions. You still need to understand the data sources, business requirements, and integration logic to ensure quality and correctness. Use ML and AI as augmentations, not replacements, for human expertise.

In this new era, data integration has evolved from a labor-intensive endeavor into a harmonious dance between humans and machines. ML and AI elevate the process, automating repetitive tasks and allowing engineers to focus on the nuances of architecture, performance, and the ever-evolving use cases. The culmination is a realm where data integration becomes a collaborative effort, seamlessly blending human intuition with machine precision.

Data integration for edge computing and IoT

The digital frontier is expanding, pushed outwards by the meteoric rise of edge devices and IoT sensors. As these remote entities multiply, ensuring their integrated data delivery becomes paramount. Innovations such as 5G networks, intelligent gateways, and on-device integration are redefining this space, allowing real-time data analysis to occur right at the source.

A prime example of this transformation is the smart gateway. These aren't just traditional gateways; they're imbued with intelligence. Stationed at the edge environment, they act as vigilant custodians, gathering and integrating streams of IoT sensor data. Their prowess lies in their ability to aggregate, filter, and transform these high-velocity streams, even before they are transmitted to the cloud, ushering in the age of real-time edge analytics. The incorporation of lightweight ETL engines in these gateways ensures they can process thousands of events every second, forwarding only the most pertinent data. This judicious approach not only conserves bandwidth but also curtails cloud storage expenses. Companies such as FogHorn and Tibco are at the vanguard of this movement, offering gateway solutions replete with embedded rules engines, machine learning models, and advanced ETL capabilities for the edge. For instance, imagine an offshore oil rig that leverages these smart gateways, integrating real-time equipment sensor data to preemptively maintain its machinery.

But the challenges of data integration don't stop at singular locales. Enterprises often grapple with data spread across geographically dispersed settings – be it retail chains, vast transportation networks, or manufacturing hubs. Fortunately, specialized integration tools have emerged to bridge these geographic divides. They offer a centralized command center, controlling integration jobs across myriad remote sites, and funneling data from each locale's on-site systems into overarching cloud data lakes. Each data pipeline can be intricately tailored to a site's unique integration prerequisites. Solutions such as Striim and SQLStream exemplify this approach, orchestrating and overseeing integration processes across far-flung locations, from storefronts to vehicles. Consider the retail giant Walmart, which orchestrates data integration across its vast expanse of over 11,000 stores, weaving together data strands to craft optimal customer experiences.

> **Warning**
>
> Edge integration poses unique challenges, such as intermittent connectivity, limited bandwidth, and device heterogeneity. Smart gateways can help overcome these challenges by processing and filtering data locally before transmission. However, they also introduce additional complexity and security risks. Make sure you have a robust governance framework and monitoring system for your edge devices and gateways.

Yet not all integration needs are sprawling in scale. For more rudimentary requirements, edge devices themselves can serve as integration hubs, courtesy of lightweight ETL tools. These tools are marvels of optimization, designed to operate within the memory and storage constraints of devices. Their intuitive drag-and-drop interfaces empower users to craft ETL workflows without delving into code, and they come armed with a repertoire of connectors and transformations tailored for typical device data sources. Furthermore, these tools are equipped to handle the intermittent connectivity of the edge, caching data and syncing it back to core systems when the connection is re-established. EdgeIQ and Waylay are pioneering this domain, embedding rudimentary data collection and integration logic straight into devices, ranging from drones to autonomous vehicles. Picture an energy conglomerate that employs lightweight ETL to weave together data from micro-weather stations stationed on wind turbines, fine-tuning turbine performance in real time.

Hybrid and multi-cloud data integration

In today's dynamic IT landscape, organizations are increasingly embracing a mix of public and private cloud solutions. This mosaic of on-premises, multi-cloud, SaaS, and legacy systems brings with it the complex challenge of data integration. There's a compelling need for architectures that can seamlessly share and synchronize data across this array of platforms.

But why stop at mere synchronization? By processing and integrating data closer to its origin, the true potential of edge analytics is revealed. This approach not only provides real-time insights but also offers the dual benefits of cost control and reduced latency. To truly tap into these advantages, the adoption of specialized integration architectures and tools becomes paramount.

But what's driving this push toward hybrid and multi-cloud integration strategies? A few key factors stand out:

- The looming threat of data silos as cloud data lakes, warehouses, and SaaS applications become more commonplace

- The allure of multi-cloud analytics, which allows organizations to cherry-pick workloads based on specific needs

- The stringent demands of regulatory compliance, which often necessitate data to be kept within regional confines

- The increasing concern over vendor lock-in, where organizations don't want to be heavily dependent on a single cloud provider

- The inevitable IT amalgamations that follow mergers and acquisitions

The ideal hybrid data integration platform should be a veritable Swiss Army knife, equipped with a range of capabilities. It should offer portable integration logic, unified monitoring, consistent metadata management, and bidirectional data replication. Moreover, it should ensure data quality and governance, and provide access to real-time data streams from various applications.

Delving deeper into the mechanics, certain tools and methodologies rise to prominence. Containers, coupled with orchestrators such as Kubernetes, ensure integration logic remains portable. REST APIs and web services serve as bridges to SaaS applications while messaging systems such as Kafka enable seamless data streaming. The microservices architecture stands out as a beacon of portability and scalability.

Yet, the journey isn't without its challenges. The maze of security, access, and governance across various environments can be daunting. The lack of consistent data definitions only adds to the complexity. The task of synchronizing ever-evolving datasets in real time, coupled with cost management across cloud services, makes for a challenging integration landscape.

Industry good practice

Hybrid and multi-cloud integration strategies are becoming more common as organizations seek to leverage the best of both worlds: the flexibility, scalability, and innovation of public cloud services, and the security, control, and compliance of private cloud or on-premises infrastructure. However, hybrid and multi-cloud integration also brings more complexity and cost. To succeed, you need to carefully evaluate your business needs, data workloads, and cloud capabilities, and choose the optimal mix for your use cases.

In conclusion, as the winds of hybrid and multi-cloud adoption gather pace, the onus is on organizations to invest in integration technologies that not only bridge the chasm between diverse data environments but also ensure consistency, governance, and optimal performance. The market already witnesses vendors racing to evolve their solutions, aiming to cater to these intricate needs, heralding a promising future for data integration.

The rise of user-friendly platform solutions in data engineering

In the realm of data engineering, the focus has traditionally been on the intricate art of crafting and maintaining data pipelines. Such a discipline often demanded deep technical prowess. Yet, the modern digital landscape is witnessing the emergence of platforms designed to throw open the gates of data engineering to a broader audience. These platforms, armed with intuitive interfaces and automation, are making core capabilities accessible even to those who don't speak the language of code.

So, what's fueling this shift toward democratized data engineering? A series of factors converge to paint a compelling picture.

First, the sheer volume and diversity of data sources have grown to such a scale that the old ways of manual engineering are being stretched thin. In such a world, self-service tools stand as a beacon, reducing over-reliance on a handful of experts. Moreover, in a fast-paced business environment, agility is the name of the game. Data pipelines that are cumbersome and slow to adapt stifle innovation and experimentation. Enter user-friendly platforms, bringing with them the promise of rapid, iterative analysis.

But the benefits don't stop there. These platforms, with their intuitive designs, act as bridges, spanning the chasm between technical experts and their non-technical peers. This fosters a collaborative atmosphere, breaking down the walls of data silos and facilitating organization-wide insights. Furthermore, with traditional tools being so heavily centered around programming, they inadvertently narrow the talent pool. By lowering entry barriers, these new platforms are addressing the scarcity of skills, opening the doors to a larger cohort of data enthusiasts.

A slew of tools is now entering the market, each aiming to simplify various facets of data engineering. Whether it's ELT automation offerings such as Fivetran and Stitch, visual workflow builders such as Matillion and Keboola, or augmented data discovery tools such as Atlan and Sisu, the focus is clear: balance user-friendliness with enterprise-grade reliability and scalability.

But as with all shifts, this trend carries its own set of implications. While the allure of simplicity is undeniable, it's crucial to recognize potential pitfalls. Over-simplification can sometimes come at the cost of deeper understanding, and there's a danger of being too removed from the technical nitty-gritty. It's also worth noting that, despite the advancements, core programming skills will always have their place, especially when grappling with the challenges that arise as data scales. Furthermore, while automation is a boon, over-reliance on it can lead to inflexible "hidden factories." And amidst all this, the pillars of quality, governance, and responsible data practices must remain unshaken.

Expert advice

User-friendly platform solutions aim to simplify data engineering by providing intuitive interfaces and automation for data integration tasks. These solutions can empower business users to access and analyze data without relying on IT experts. However, they also have limitations and tradeoffs, such as abstraction from technical details, over-automation risks, and quality compromises. User-friendly platforms should complement – not replace – professional data engineering skills and practices.

In conclusion, these accessible data engineering platforms symbolize the industry's endeavor to broaden data literacy. When wielded with thought and care, they have the potential to empower a larger user base to extract insights, foster collaboration, and drive innovation. It's an exciting prospect, promising to unlock the vast potential housed within our ever-expanding data reservoirs.

The democratization of data integration – the self-service revolution

In today's data-driven world, swift and easy access to data integration is no longer a luxury – it's a necessity. Enter self-service data integration, a paradigm shift designed to empower business users to weave together data from diverse systems and applications, sidestepping the traditional gatekeepers: the IT experts. This isn't about sidelining IT; it's about broadening the playing field, and ensuring that the insights and agility offered by data are available to a wider audience.

At its core, the self-service model repositions data integration tasks. Instead of being confined to the IT department, these tasks are disseminated across business teams. The beauty of this approach is twofold. Firstly, business users, with their intimate knowledge of data requirements, can fast-track integration projects tailored to specific use cases. Secondly, it allows organizations to supercharge their data integration endeavors, transcending the boundaries of the IT department and weaving in a more extensive network of stakeholders.

But what does this democratization of data integration bring to the table? Let's take a look:

- Productivity is supercharged as users are liberated from the wait times traditionally associated with IT-led integration
- Agility becomes the order of the day, with organizations nimbly adjusting their integration efforts in response to evolving needs
- Collaboration reaches new heights as business and IT unite, sharing a panoramic view of the data landscape
- The financial angle is not to be overlooked, with a reduction in reliance on specialist integration experts translating to tangible cost savings
- Scalability takes center stage as integration tasks permeate the organization
- And, of course, the overarching theme of democratization ensures a more inclusive approach to data integration capabilities

Powering this revolution are cutting-edge, user-centric integration platforms brimming with features such as intuitive drag-and-drop interfaces, a suite of pre-built connectors, tools for data discovery and mapping, and robust monitoring capabilities. These platforms aren't just about technical prowess – they also prioritize collaboration, ensuring that the process of managing integrations is a collective endeavor.

However, diving into the self-service waters requires preparation. Teams must be equipped with the requisite skills, supplemented with training where gaps exist. Starting small – with clear documentation and straightforward use cases – can ease users into the self-service universe. Moreover, IT doesn't fade into the background. Instead, it pivots to a governance role, ensuring that the principles of data security, compliance, and quality aren't lost in the shuffle.

To gauge the success of a self-service approach, metrics are vital. Tracking usage patterns, performance benchmarks, and overall business adoption can highlight areas for improvement and ensure user engagement remains robust. And, as with any transformative initiative, celebrating milestones and championing success stories can amplify adoption rates.

In essence, the rise of self-service data integration marks a pivotal moment in the data narrative. By equipping organizations with the tools and ethos to distribute integration responsibilities more broadly, it promises not just enhanced productivity and agility but also positions integration as a strategic lever – a competitive edge in a data-saturated world.

Metadata management – illuminating data's context and value

As we navigate the sprawling expanse of the data universe, with its ever-growing volumes and diverse sources, one beacon shines brighter than ever: metadata. Think of metadata as the descriptive backdrop of data, offering a lens through which we can understand the context, attributes, and relationships of the vast arrays of data points we deal with. This understanding, in turn, holds the key to truly unlocking the latent potential of data integration.

So, what exactly is metadata, and why does it matter?

Metadata is, in essence, data about data. It's the underlying story that brings raw data to life, offering insights into its origins, structure, and purpose. Let's delve into the different facets of metadata:

- **Technical metadata**, which encompasses the nuts and bolts of data, such as its schema, structure, and the algorithms it's linked to, serves as the foundation for integrating data with precision

- **Business metadata**, on the other hand, offers a narrative on data's relevance to the enterprise, shedding light on ownership, definitions, and related business parameters

- **Operational metadata** provides a snapshot of data's journey, highlighting its lineage, usage statistics, and other functional metrics that steer governance and compliance

- Lastly, **domain metadata** offers a layer of standardization, weaving in industry-specific concepts and frameworks to ensure a cohesive data narrative

Yet, in the vast sea of data, merely having metadata isn't enough. It's the breadth and depth of metadata coverage that ensures data integration is accurate, compliant, and truly insightful. A lapse in technical metadata can send data flows into disarray, while a void in business metadata can render data almost meaningless to its end users.

Enter the concept of metadata lakes – a reservoir of rich, curated metadata that spans the entire data landscape. Imagine having a consolidated repository that seamlessly amalgamates technical, business, operational, and domain metadata. This unified view empowers organizations to do the following:

- Automate the discovery, assimilation, and organization of metadata from varied sources
- Store diverse metadata types with agility and flexibility
- Facilitate seamless metadata integrations through APIs and other systems
- Drive insights through robust search capabilities, lineage tracking, and impact analyses
- Uphold stringent governance standards, ensuring metadata's integrity, security, and life cycle management
- Provide a visual narrative on metadata, aiding in interpretation and decision-making

Such metadata lakes are emerging as the bedrock of contemporary, metadata-centric architectures. They promise a holistic, unified understanding of metadata, which is indispensable for insightful, accurate, and compliant data integration. However, the true power of these lakes hinges on meticulous curation and governance, which ensure that metadata remains relevant, accurate, and truly reflective of the data it represents.

In a world awash with data, metadata stands as the compass, guiding organizations to derive value, insights, and innovation from their data assets.

Technologies shaping the future of data integration

In the intricate tapestry of modern enterprise, data threads weave patterns of enormous complexity. How we integrate, interpret, and interact with this data has profound implications for businesses and their digital transformation journeys. As we stand on the cusp of a new decade, several groundbreaking technologies are poised to redefine the boundaries of data integration. This chapter delves into these innovations, exploring their potential and the transformative impact they hold for the future.

The rise of serverless architectures in data integration

In the ever-evolving world of data integration, serverless architectures are making waves. At its core, serverless is a paradigm shift, liberating engineers from the traditional constraints of server provisioning. Instead, they can dynamically activate functions that scale effortlessly based on demand, like a well-oiled machine responding to the ebbs and flows of its operations.

Why is serverless capturing the imagination of data engineers and architects?

- First, it introduces a newfound agility to ETL processes. Gone are the days when integrating a new data source meant navigating a maze of infrastructure roadblocks. Serverless lets engineers deftly adapt to changing data landscapes, ensuring that data transformation is as fluid as the business it supports.

- Secondly, real-time data is no longer a luxury but a necessity. Serverless is primed for this era of instantaneous data processing. Whether it's a sudden influx of user activity logs or a surge in IoT sensor data, serverless architectures gracefully handle these unpredictable volumes, ensuring consistent performance.

- Lastly, the economic allure of serverless is undeniable. In the traditional model, you'd provision (and pay for) resources based on peak predictions, often leading to overprovisioning. Serverless, with its pay-per-use model, aligns costs with actual usage, optimizing expenses.

However, every advantage has its disadvantages. Although powerful, the serverless model presents varying challenges.

First, latency can creep in due to "cold starts." Imagine a serverless function as a performer waiting in the wings. The first time it's called on stage, some preparation might be involved, causing a delay. This is especially concerning for applications that demand real-time responsiveness.

Second, debugging, an essential aspect of any development, gets trickier with serverless. The ephemeral nature of serverless functions, coupled with restricted access to the underlying infrastructure, can make issue resolution a more complex puzzle.

Also, going serverless often means hitching your wagon to a particular cloud provider. This can be a double-edged sword, making migrations or transitions to alternative architectures a herculean effort.

However, the tech world isn't one to rest on its laurels. Solutions are emerging to counter these challenges. From optimized containers that combat cold start latency to advanced monitoring tools that offer deeper insights into serverless operations, the ecosystem is evolving.

Tip

Serverless architectures offer a new way of building data integration pipelines that eliminate the need for provisioning servers and allow engineers to dynamically spin up functions that auto-scale on demand. This brings several benefits, such as agile ETL processes, real-time stream processing, and cloud economics. However, serverless architectures also have some drawbacks, such as cold starts, limited debugging, and vendor lock-in risks. To make the most of serverless architectures, you should carefully weigh the pros and cons for your specific use cases and choose the right tools and frameworks to support your development.

In essence, serverless is not just another buzzword. It's an evolution – a response to the growing complexity and dynamism of modern data environments. While it's not a universal solution, it fills a significant gap, offering agility and efficiency in data integration like never before.

As the tools and practices around serverless mature, we can anticipate its deeper entrenchment in the foundations of future-forward data integration architectures. Serverless promises a world where data integration can seamlessly dance to the rhythm of ever-changing business needs.

Graph databases and graph processing

Graph databases represent a fundamental shift in how data relationships can be architected for integration compared to traditional relational models. At their core, graphs store data as networks of interconnected nodes and edges, with each node representing an entity and each edge depicting a relationship. This topology provides native support for capturing complex many-to-many relationships and hierarchical or lateral connections within large datasets.

For example, companies such as Amazon use graph structures to model billions of purchase connections between customers, products, orders, and recommendations. Graph processing frameworks such as **Neo4j** allow high-performance analysis of these rich datasets using parallelized algorithms that traverse links and surface insights.

Specifically for data integration, graph databases excel at mapping heterogeneous, constantly evolving datasets while maintaining context. They can flexibly ingest varied data schemas and data types into an integrated property graph model. Graph traversals make it straightforward to connect related data elements across siloed sources, overcoming key challenges around many-to-many mappings. This relationship-first thinking also simplifies capturing the full context and complexity of real-world entities.

However, graphs come with tradeoffs such as skill gaps among SQL-trained data engineers and complexity in balancing performance with scale. Current research on optimizations such as compact graph representations, approximated graph neural networks, and hardware-accelerated querying aims to improve the scalability and accessibility of graph technologies.

> **Industry good practice**
>
> Graph databases, which alter traditional data integration models, store interconnected data and aptly capture complex relationships, prove advantageous in modeling heterogeneous, evolving datasets. They ease the process of linking related data across varied sources, simplifying the depiction of real-world entities' full context and complexity. While they present challenges such as skill gaps and scalability issues, ongoing optimizations aim to overcome these. Forecasts show significant growth in this technology, potentially becoming a standard tool for advanced analytics, driven by its application in fields such as fraud detection and recommendation engines.

Looking ahead, early adopters in fields such as fraud detection, master data management, and recommendation engines will continue driving graph database growth up to $5 billion by 2025, as per Tractica. As innovations make graph data layers easier to implement and operationalize, they will become a standard tool for modeling interconnected data landscapes, enabling analytics that is not possible with legacy integration systems.

Data virtualization

Data virtualization is set to transform data integration through its innovative approach. Rather than complex ETL processes, this technology creates a semantic abstraction layer to virtually consolidate diverse data sources – from databases and data lakes to cloud platforms and APIs – into a unified data service. This enables simplified access to petabyte-scale data without physical replication. Users can query data on-demand across systems without IT bottlenecks.

Data virtualization provides the agility to effortlessly adapt to new sources and formats. By abstracting underlying complexity, it future-proofs data infrastructure for self-service analytics. This paradigm shift promises improved business insights, governance, and actionability by eliminating friction in data access and delivery. With proper implementation, data virtualization can overcome potential performance and security challenges. It is primed to drive the next wave of innovation as the modern data stack requires flexible, scalable data integration.

Data virtualization's ability to democratize real-time data services will catalyze analytics and power data-driven organizations. This versatile technology will rapidly become essential for businesses to empower users and unlock the full value of their data assets.

Automated data quality and governance tools

As organizations increasingly accumulate diverse datasets with mushrooming volume, velocity, variety, and complexity, ensuring high quality and governance across this modern data landscape poses a formidable challenge. The emergence of automated data quality and governance tools from leading vendors provides a potential solution. Powered by industrial-grade knowledge bases, advanced rules engines, and machine learning algorithms, these tools enable continuous data profiling to detect errors and anomalies, automated data cleansing and standardization, comprehensive metadata management, and end-to-end data lineage mapping.

Leading financial institutions and insurance providers have already implemented these solutions in their data platforms to significant effect – one global bank improved data accuracy by over 30% while a prominent insurer shortened compliance reporting timelines by 50%. By encoding organizational DQ and governance policies into software that can be applied at scale, these tools alleviate the burden of manual governance workflows.

Looking ahead, integrating AI capabilities and managing organizational change will be imperative to fully actualize the potential of automated data curation. While these tools are still evolving, the 10-15% projected annual growth for the data quality software market underscores their expanding value in tackling modern data integration challenges. As automation accelerates, augmented with human oversight, automated DQ and governance will serve as the critical bulwark empowering organizations to harness the full value of their data assets.

Real-time streaming and integration technologies

Real-time data integration is becoming increasingly important for businesses that want to gain insights from data in motion. Several emerging streaming and integration technologies enable organizations to respond quickly to changing data landscapes. Apache Kafka is a popular choice for building real-time data pipelines and streaming applications due to its high throughput and low latency messaging system. However, it is not considered a true real-time technology.

Integration technologies such as Apache Nifi can ingest streaming data from different sources into Kafka topics for downstream consumption. Cloud-native platforms, such as Confluent and AWS Kinesis, simplify messaging infrastructure and operations. Apache Pulsar is another distributed messaging system that is gaining popularity for its flexibility and elastic scalability.

Several lightweight integration frameworks, such as Apache Camel, natively support Kafka integration to simplify messaging routing and mediation logic. iPaaS solutions from MuleSoft, Boomi, and others help seamlessly integrate Kafka streams into enterprise architectures through easy-to-use, low-code interfaces.

As IoT, edge devices, and 5G networks proliferate, near-real-time data integration will become the norm. Future trends include greater adoption of serverless architectures, AI-driven smart data routing, and integration of event-driven design paradigms across organizations. With further advancements, real-time data will enable quicker insights and actions across industries.

Next, we'll discuss future challenges and opportunities of data integration.

Future challenges and opportunities of data integration

As we navigate the current landscape of data integration, it's imperative to cast our gaze forward. The future holds both unprecedented challenges and unique opportunities in this domain. Grasping these nuances will enable us to adapt and innovate, ensuring that we remain at the forefront of data integration advancements.

The evolving landscape of data integration

The data integration ecosystem continues to rapidly evolve as new technologies emerge and architectures shift, such as cloud-native integration, data mesh, and data virtualization. To thrive amidst ongoing change, cross-functional collaboration is crucial to align technical teams and business stakeholders.

Mature data governance and stewardship also grow more critical to ensure quality outcomes as methods change. Forward-looking organizations that build organizational partnerships along with technical capacity will successfully adapt integration approaches to drive value from growing data assets.

Increasing data volume, variety, and velocity

Surging quantities of structured, unstructured, and streaming data put tremendous strain on traditional integration techniques. Organizations struggle to efficiently integrate information at scale to enable real-time data services.

Cloud-native and distributed architectures built on technologies such as Spark and Kafka provide pathways to overcoming volume, variety, and velocity challenges. Lambda architectures that combine batch and streaming processes enable flexible and dynamic pipelines. Metadata layers and knowledge catalogs such as Collibra add critical intelligence. Companies such as Netflix highlight success in leveraging these modern architectures to manage data complexity.

Growing demand for real-time data analysis

Demand for tactical insights based on live data is rising across industries. However, shifting to real-time analytics depends heavily on data integration capabilities. Streaming integration and lightweight APIs allow you to capture data in motion for reduced latency. Cache technologies maintain real-time views while **change data capture** (**CDC**) propagates updates incrementally.

However, technological changes have deep cultural and organizational implications. Change management and alignment are critical when adopting real-time practices. Thoughtful planning and collaboration will increasingly determine which firms successfully transition to live data analysis.

Data security, privacy, and compliance

With proliferating regulations such as GDPR and CCPA, along with rising security threats and privacy expectations, managing sensitive data is profoundly challenging. Modern data integration must prevent unauthorized exposure across systems and workflows.

Encryption, granular access controls, data masking, and context-based policies help safeguard integrity and compliance. However, poor data quality leads to downstream issues, regardless of security protocols. Holistic governance encompassing quality, security, and compliance is imperative for reliable, trustworthy data integration.

The need for adaptable and scalable solutions

In the dynamic world of data integration, the constant influx of new data sources and evolving business needs demands solutions that can adjust and grow with ease. The ever-increasing complexities and volumes make it clear: having adaptable and scalable solutions isn't just a luxury – it's a necessity. Let's delve into why this flexibility is paramount and how it can shape the future of data endeavors.

The importance of flexibility and scalability

As the dimensions of data – volume, variety, and velocity – continue to expand at an unprecedented rate, traditional integration architectures find themselves at a crossroads. The once tried-and-true methods, characterized by hardcoded point-to-point pipelines, monolithic systems, and tightly woven designs, now stand as barriers to agility and scalability.

The path forward requires a paradigm shift. It's not just about embracing new technologies, but also about fostering a cultural transformation. Modular architectures are at the heart of this change. By leveraging containerized microservices and serverless functions, as well as establishing loose coupling through APIs and events, organizations can achieve independent scaling of their integration components, allowing for enhanced on-demand capacity and redundancy.

In tandem with these architectural shifts, distributed computing frameworks such as Spark and Flink have emerged as pillars of scalability, especially when it comes to processing and transport. The elasticity of cloud infrastructure further complements these frameworks, addressing both storage and bandwidth needs.

Yet, technology alone is not the panacea. The delivery approach also demands reimagining. Incremental delivery, characterized by smaller, iterative changes facilitated by DevOps toolchains and robust version control, allows for a more fluid integration process. This approach, coupled with automated testing and the safety net of rollback mechanisms, ensures that rapid updates do not compromise system stability.

In designing these systems, an emphasis on adaptability is paramount. Integration architectures should prioritize loosely coupled interfaces and platform-agnostic components, ensuring they remain resilient to underlying technological shifts. By maintaining abstraction layers, contract tests, and diversifying technology stacks, organizations can ensure sustained flexibility.

However, even the most robust architectures can falter without the right cultural mindset. Cultivating a culture of experimentation is vital. Organizations must foster an environment where trying out new techniques, learning from failures, and swiftly incorporating feedback becomes the norm. Leadership plays a pivotal role here, emphasizing the value of measured risk-taking and continuous learning over strict adherence to the "right way."

For many organizations entrenched in legacy systems, an immediate overhaul may seem daunting, if not entirely unfeasible. But the key lies in starting small. Pilots showcasing the value of new architecture can lay the groundwork for a more extensive transformation. In the intricate and ever-evolving landscapes of today's data integration challenges, the guiding principle should be clear: integrations must prioritize strategic adaptability over rigid optimization.

Addressing the skills gap in data integration

As the landscape of data integration methods continues to evolve and advance, there's an accompanying challenge that organizations must grapple with the widening skills gap. This is not just a matter of grappling with the steep learning curves associated with new technologies. The challenge is further amplified by the inevitable loss of accumulated experience and expertise as workforce turnover rates increase.

To address these challenges, a comprehensive strategy becomes imperative. Cross-training programs emerge as a vital tool in this endeavor. By amalgamating internal training boot camps, fostering a culture of peer mentoring, and offering hands-on project experiences, organizations can accelerate the development of capabilities. Rotation programs further amplify this effect, churning out multifunctional workers capable of bridging different silos of expertise.

Yet, as expertise grows, it's equally as crucial to capture and document it. Process documentation, through standardized templates, codebooks, and internal wikis, becomes the vessel that holds institutional knowledge, ensuring that critical information remains accessible and consistent, even as teams evolve. Such documentation proves invaluable, especially during onboarding and coordination processes.

In parallel, organizations need to rethink their hiring strategies. Instead of seeking the perfect candidate match, there's merit in searching for adjacent skills and inherent aptitudes. Apprenticeships and residency programs offer avenues to nurture and mold talent in line with specific organizational needs. Moreover, a commitment to prioritizing diversity in hiring not only enriches the team dynamics but also amplifies problem-solving capabilities.

Change management, however, remains a linchpin in this transformation. Adapting to new processes, such as DevOps, demands more than just technological proficiency. It requires cohesive engagement across various organizational strata, from management and executives to ground-level staff. This ensures that workflow adaptations are not just effective but also ingrained in the organizational culture.

As teams evolve, a hybrid structure becomes pivotal. Instead of a sweeping turnover, a phased integration of both existing roles and emerging ones ensures continuity. This gradual transformation approach, in turn, cushions the impact of rapid technological changes. Simultaneously, automation and abstraction tools, such as auto-documentation and testing frameworks, become instrumental in streamlining processes. These tools not only reduce specialized backlogs but also mask underlying complexities, making them more accessible.

In the end, the journey of addressing the evolving needs of data integration skills is not a sprint but a marathon. There's no magic wand or overnight solution. However, by intertwining strategies that mitigate knowledge loss, nurture capacity, facilitate smooth transitions, and promote automation, organizations can foster an environment ripe for continuous learning and sustainable innovation.

The role of open source and collaboration

Open source data integration tools such as Airflow, dbt, and Mage have become significant catalysts in the realm of innovation. The transparency and openness of their communities not only enable rapid knowledge dissemination but also present an economic advantage by distributing maintenance costs. Yet, merely adopting these tools is just scratching the surface. The true essence and potential of open source come alive when organizations immerse themselves in active collaboration.

Organizations that limit their engagement with open source tools to passive consumption risk missing out on the opportunity to shape the direction and evolution of these tools. It's essential to contribute to these projects actively, be it through sharing unique use cases, developing extensions and connectors, or enhancing documentation. Such contributions don't just benefit the contributing organization; they accelerate collective progress, ensuring the entire community moves forward in unison.

But collaboration isn't solely about code contributions. Financial support plays an equally critical role. While the spirit of volunteerism fuels a significant portion of open source endeavors, the sustainability, reliability, and security of these tools hinge on consistent funding. It's imperative for companies, especially those that derive substantial value from open source, to reinvest monetarily, ensuring these projects remain vibrant and robust.

Beyond individual projects, there's a larger ecosystem at play. Consortiums, dedicated to crafting shared standards such as CDAP and MISP, hold the promise of broader data interoperability. Engaging with such consortiums is more than just participation – it's a collective investment. The network effects stemming from such collective endeavors often surpass the capabilities of custom, isolated solutions.

While open source thrives on collaboration and community, it's equally essential to ensure these communities are diverse and inclusive. Barriers, which are often subtle, can hinder underrepresented groups from participating, thereby limiting the range of innovative perspectives. An intentional effort to foster inclusivity and break down these barriers can amplify the capabilities of the open source community, benefiting everyone involved.

Lastly, as with any powerful tool, there's an ethical dimension to consider. Open source licenses, particularly the more permissive ones, can be misused by entities with malicious intentions. Developers and contributors bear a responsibility to understand the downstream implications of their licensing decisions, ensuring their work serves the greater good and isn't co-opted for harmful purposes.

In summary, the future of open source data integration is bright and filled with promise and potential. Yet, realizing this future demands more than passive adoption. Active, ethical engagement, both at the individual project level and within the broader community, is the linchpin. When collaboration amplifies investment, the outcome is a robust public data infrastructure benefiting not just individual organizations but society at large.

The intersection of data integration and data ethics

In the rapidly evolving world of integration technologies, the march of progress brings with it a host of ethical dilemmas. The newfound power to seamlessly combine datasets from a plethora of sources can be a double-edged sword presenting opportunities for misuse, especially in the absence of robust governance.

Central to these ethical concerns is the matter of privacy and consent. The amalgamation of data from various systems can inadvertently compromise privacy, especially if the linkage of personal information isn't meticulously managed. It's crucial to maintain vigilant oversight of where data originates from and who has access to it. This ensures that the boundaries of consent aren't unintentionally breached when datasets converge.

Yet, the challenges don't stop at privacy: there's the looming specter of bias and representation. Merging demographic, behavioral, and other types of data can inadvertently perpetuate biases, especially if past exclusions or discriminatory practices aren't addressed. To ensure a fair representation, it's imperative to adopt inclusive data collection and integration techniques.

With the increasing intricacy of data, transparency and explainability become paramount. Stakeholders, be they individuals or organizations, need to trace the logic and pathways through which data is integrated. Without this transparency, trust wanes, and accountability becomes elusive. Moreover, the importance of security and reliability can't be overstated. Faulty data integration practices might introduce errors with far-reaching consequences, especially for vulnerable communities that heavily rely on certain services. Such flaws underscore the need for rigorous testing and continuous monitoring, especially when the ramifications can be felt on a large scale.

In today's data-driven society, surveillance concerns are more pertinent than ever. The blending of data from our everyday activities could inadvertently pave the way for unchecked surveillance. It's essential to impose boundaries on data retention and aggregation to ensure that the reasonable expectations of monitoring aren't breached.

However, even the most stringent technical controls can't replace the significance of informed consent. The expanding horizons of data integration accentuate the need to keep individuals in the loop. Clear, comprehensible explanations about how their data will be merged, and the potential implications thereof, should be the cornerstone of any integration initiative.

While cross-disciplinary reviews in the planning phase can preemptively identify and address many concerns, ethical oversight in the realm of data integration isn't a mere checkbox to be ticked off – it demands continuous vigilance. By recognizing and respecting areas of persistent ambiguity and uncertainty, we can ensure that ethics remain at the forefront of data integration practices. This approach not only safeguards individual rights but also paves the way for innovations that are in sync with human values.

The need for a native semantic layer and unified governance in multi-cloud and hybrid architectures

This section explores the critical need for native semantic layers and unified governance in multi-cloud environments, essential for coherent, secure, and efficient data integration.

The native semantic layer makes data speak the same language

Imagine trying to solve a puzzle where each piece comes from a different set. Frustrating, right? Now, replace those puzzle pieces with data from different sources. The semantic layer acts as a translator, ensuring that all these diverse data sources "speak the same language." It's the bridge that interprets data for business users so that they don't have to be fluent in "data-ese;" otherwise, business users don't need to understand what's happening behind the scenes.

When data platforms integrate this layer natively, you're not just bolting on a patch; you're creating a foundation. This makes everything smoother – data retrieval, interpretation, and decision-making. And in a world where businesses are shifting toward multi-cloud or hybrid cloud setups, this integrated understanding is crucial. Otherwise, you're dealing with an incoherent mess of data.

Unified governance, security, and catalog solutions – the library of your data universe

If the semantic layer is about translation, unified governance and cataloging are about organization. It's like having a library where every book (or in this case, data) has its designated place, and you've got a clear system to know who borrowed which book, for how long, and for what purpose. Why is this so crucial? With data spread across multiple clouds, there's a heightened risk of mismanagement, redundancy, and security lapses. A unified governance system ensures everyone adheres to the same set of rules, making data access secure and compliant. The catalog solution, on the other hand, ensures you can find the right data without the need to rummage through the vast digital universe.

Let's look at an example of a unified central repository (let's say a data lake) that uses both Databricks and AWS to handle its data. Managing data governance, security, and rights access using both "AWS LakeFormation" and "Databricks Unity Catalog" technologies can be very hard to achieve. These platforms, though robust individually, present challenges when operated in tandem. Permissions and policies need double configurations, possibly leading to misalignments and potential security risks. Metadata definitions across the two can overlap, causing redundancy and inconsistencies that can muddle dataset interpretations. Furthermore, the task of maintaining audit trails and data lineage becomes complex due to separate logs from both systems, complicating compliance checks and troubleshooting. Lastly, the operational overhead of synchronizing and managing two platforms increases the resource burden and widens the margin for error.

In a perfect world, our tools would seamlessly integrate and play well together. But as we know, the world of technology isn't always smooth sailing. Recognizing these challenges is the first step. The next? Crafting a cohesive strategy that either bridges these systems more seamlessly – or better, builds a solution or defines a standard to unify data governance, rights management, and security.

Next, we'll discuss advancing your understanding of data integration in the modern stack.

Advancing your understanding of data integration in the modern stack

As you close this book, your journey into the intricate world of data integration is just beginning. The horizon of this domain is vast and ever-expanding. To navigate it effectively and make the most of your acquired knowledge, you must continue to seek opportunities for further growth. This chapter aims to guide you on these next steps, illuminating paths that can deepen your understanding and refine your skills.

Continuous learning resources

The dynamic world of data integration demands continuous learning. To stay ahead, consider diving deep into modern methodologies such as data mesh, progressive delivery, and real-time architectures through books and eBooks from reputed publishers. Engage with articles, blogs, and whitepapers from platforms such as Fivetran, Stitch, and Matillion for practical insights. Online courses on platforms such as Udemy and Coursera offer structured learning paths in both fundamental and specialized areas of data integration. Vendor documentation can also be a treasure trove of information, detailing the capabilities and best practices of commercial integration tools. Websites such as Medium.com house diverse perspectives that can enrich your understanding.

Conferences, meetups, and digital events

Conferences, both virtual and in-person, offer immersive experiences packed with training workshops, presentations, and hands-on labs. The Strata Data Conference, by O'Reilly, DataEngConf, and events by Data Council are notable platforms that offer a comprehensive view of the current data integration landscape. For localized experiences, platforms such as Meetup.com host data and analytics groups globally, with events ranging from talks to hands-on workshops. The hybrid event format, which blends in-person with virtual, is becoming increasingly prevalent, providing flexible learning opportunities.

Delving deeper into knowledge

To truly excel in data integration, you must venture beyond foundational knowledge. Pursue advanced certifications from organizations such as DAMA International or explore certifications from cloud giants such as AWS, Azure, and GCP. Collaborations with universities can provide access to cutting-edge research and methodologies in the domain. For those aspiring to be in leadership roles, executive education programs can help bridge technical expertise with strategic leadership capabilities.

Engaging with open source communities

The open source realm offers a unique opportunity to learn through active participation. Newcomers can start by contributing to issue trackers, creating integrations, or even evangelizing projects through various content forms. As familiarity grows, you can delve deeper, contributing more significantly to core project code bases.

Venturing into emerging technologies

The data integration landscape is continually being reshaped by emerging technologies. Hands-on experimentation with innovations such as serverless ETL workflows, real-time data streaming platforms, or low-code/no-code solutions can cement your understanding. Starting with sandbox environments that model real-world scenarios allows the safe piloting of new approaches.

Building a personal learning network

A rich professional network can amplify your learning journey, opening doors to diverse perspectives and shared knowledge. Seek mentorships, both within and outside your organization, and attend events to meet new contacts. Engage with thought leaders on social platforms and dive into niche communities that resonate with your areas of interest in data integration. Being proactive in sharing resources and developments with peers can also strengthen your network, fostering collaborative growth.

Summary

Throughout this book, we have charted a course through the intricacies of data integration, a domain at the crossroads of technology, strategy, and innovation. From our initial steps, where we demystified foundational concepts, to our deeper dives into current challenges and solutions, each chapter added a layer to our understanding.

But, as with any quest for knowledge, every answer often finds its counterpart in new questions. The proliferation of data, the ceaseless evolution of technologies, and the emergence of new enterprise paradigms mean that the realm of data integration will remain in flux. And it's precisely this dynamism that makes this field so exhilarating and pertinent.

As we wrap up this book, I urge you to view this not as an endpoint but as a launching pad. The preceding chapters have laid the groundwork, but the real journey – of application, continued exploration, and innovation – is just beginning. The future challenges of data integration and the opportunities they present will require a fresh generation of thinkers, practitioners, and innovators. And with the insights you now hold, you are perfectly poised to be at the forefront of this vanguard.

So, as we turn this final page together, remember that the vast and ever-evolving world of data integration awaits you. May your curiosity and passion for learning continue to guide you, for the future of data integration lies in your hands.

Index

www.packtpub.com

Subscribe to our online digital library for full access to over 7,000 books and videos, as well as industry leading tools to help you plan your personal development and advance your career. For more information, please visit our website.

Why subscribe?

- Spend less time learning and more time coding with practical eBooks and Videos from over 4,000 industry professionals

- Improve your learning with Skill Plans built especially for you

- Get a free eBook or video every month

- Fully searchable for easy access to vital information

- Copy and paste, print, and bookmark content

Did you know that Packt offers eBook versions of every book published, with PDF and ePub files available? You can upgrade to the eBook version at www.packtpub.com and as a print book customer, you are entitled to a discount on the eBook copy. Get in touch with us at customercare@packtpub.com for more details.

At www.packtpub.com, you can also read a collection of free technical articles, sign up for a range of free newsletters, and receive exclusive discounts and offers on Packt books and eBooks.

Other Books You May Enjoy

If you enjoyed this book, you may be interested in these other books by Packt:

Driving Data Quality with Data Contracts

Andrew Jones

ISBN: 978-1-83763-500-9

- Gain insights into the intricacies and shortcomings of today's data architectures
- Understand exactly how data contracts can solve prevalent data challenges
- Drive a fundamental transformation of your data culture by implementing data contracts
- Discover what goes into a data contract and why it's important
- Design a modern data architecture that leverages the power of data contracts
- Explore sample implementations to get practical knowledge of using data contracts
- Embrace best practices for the successful deployment of data contracts

Data Modeling with Snowflake

Serge Gershkovich

ISBN: 978-1-83763-445-3

- Discover the time-saving benefits and applications of data modeling
- Learn about Snowflake's cloud-native architecture and its features
- Understand and apply modeling techniques using Snowflake objects
- Universal modeling concepts and language through Snowflake objects
- Get comfortable reading and transforming semistructured data
- Learn directly with pre-built recipes and examples
- Learn to apply modeling frameworks from Star to Data Vault

Packt is searching for authors like you

If you're interested in becoming an author for Packt, please visit `authors.packtpub.com` and apply today. We have worked with thousands of developers and tech professionals, just like you, to help them share their insight with the global tech community. You can make a general application, apply for a specific hot topic that we are recruiting an author for, or submit your own idea.

Share Your Thoughts

Now you've finished *The Definitive Guide to Data Integration*, we'd love to hear your thoughts! Scan the QR code below to go straight to the Amazon review page for this book and share your feedback or leave a review on the site that you purchased it from.

`https://packt.link/r/1-837-63191-3`

Your review is important to us and the tech community and will help us make sure we're delivering excellent quality content.

Download a free PDF copy of this book

Thanks for purchasing this book!

Do you like to read on the go but are unable to carry your print books everywhere?

Is your eBook purchase not compatible with the device of your choice?

Don't worry, now with every Packt book you get a DRM-free PDF version of that book at no cost.

Read anywhere, any place, on any device. Search, copy, and paste code from your favorite technical books directly into your application.

The perks don't stop there, you can get exclusive access to discounts, newsletters, and great free content in your inbox daily

Follow these simple steps to get the benefits:

1. Scan the QR code or visit the link below

https://packt.link/free-ebook/9781837631919

2. Submit your proof of purchase
3. That's it! We'll send your free PDF and other benefits to your email directly

www.ingramcontent.com/pod-product-compliance
Lightning Source LLC
Chambersburg PA
CBHW060642060326
40690CB00020B/4493